Starting & Running a Small Business For Canadians

ALL-IN-ONE

for
dummies®
A Wiley Brand

Starting & Running a Small Business For Canadians

ALL-IN-ONE

2nd Edition

by John Buchaca; Henri Charmasson;
Andrew Dagys, CPA, CMA; Lita Epstein, MBA;
Margaret Kerr; JoAnn Kurtz; Cécile Laurin, CPA, CA;
Jeanette Maw McMurtry, MBA; Max Messmer;
Steven D. Peterson, PhD; Paul Tiffany, PhD;
John A. Tracy, CPA; Nada Wagner, MBA

for
dümmies®
A Wiley Brand

**Starting & Running a Small Business For Canadians
All-in-One For Dummies®, 2nd Edition**

Published by: **John Wiley & Sons, Inc.,** 111 River Street, Hoboken, NJ 07030-5774, www.wiley.com

Copyright © 2020 by John Wiley & Sons, Inc., Hoboken, New Jersey

Published simultaneously in Canada

For general information on our other products and services, please contact our Customer Care Department within the U.S. at 877-762-2974, outside the U.S. at 317-572-3993, or fax 317-572-4002. For technical support, please visit https://hub.wiley.com/community/support/dummies.

Wiley publishes in a variety of print and electronic formats and by print-on-demand. Some material included with standard print versions of this book may not be included in e-books or in print-on-demand. If this book refers to media such as a CD or DVD that is not included in the version you purchased, you may download this material at http://booksupport.wiley.com. For more information about Wiley products, visit www.wiley.com.

Library of Congress Control Number: 2019920283

ISBN 978-1-119-64839-0 (pbk); ISBN 978-1-119-64840-6 (ebk); ISBN 978-1-119-64841-3 (ebk)

Manufactured in the United States of America

V10016634_122719

Contents at a Glance

Table of Contents

Introduction

Businesspeople have to tackle (or get tackled by) any number of issues and overcome any number of obstacles to get started, keep going, and, with a little luck, grow and thrive.

What you need is a guide to some of the important dimensions of a business that haven't changed much at all: getting started; protecting your intellectual property; planning and acting strategically; keeping the books; recruiting and managing employees; and marketing the enterprise. *Starting & Running a Small Business for Canadians For Dummies All-in-One,* 2nd Edition is a mouthful — but it is the point of reference that every businessperson starting or sustaining a business needs.

About This Book

This book is really six minibooks, each covering a topic related to starting and running a small business. Each minibook provides an overview of the subject and more in-depth coverage of specific areas at the core of the subject matter.

The content of each minibook and each chapter stands alone, so you don't have to read all the minibooks — or even all the chapters — in order. You can use this book like an entire series of books on the subject of small business. Scan through the table of contents to find a single topic to refresh your memory or to get a few ideas before beginning a task, or you can read an entire chapter or a series of chapters to gain understanding and gather ideas.

This guide even leads you to the more complete *For Dummies* titles on the issues discussed briefly in this compendium. It can also help you decide where you need more help and more information — so you can find it by doing further research and reading, hiring consultants, or adding expertise in-house by hiring employees with the skills, interests, and experience you lack.

The breadth of topics covered in this book, combined with easy-to-follow tips, make this book perfect for your business, organization, or association. Keep this book on a nearby bookshelf or on your desk so you can reference it often.

One last note: Within this book, you may note that some web addresses (URLs) break across two lines of text. If you're reading this book in print and want to visit one of these web pages, simply key in the web address exactly as it's noted in the text, pretending as though the line break doesn't exist. If you're reading this as an e-book, you've got it easy — just tap the web address to be taken directly to the web page.

Foolish Assumptions

This book is for people who want to go into business for themselves. You have aspirations of being an entrepreneur, but that's all we know about you. We don't assume that you know where your business will be located, or even what it will be. We don't assume that you have any background knowledge about law or income tax or insurance or marketing or anything else for that matter. We do assume that you have a computer with Internet access, although we don't assume that you're a techno-nerd. We assume that you are intelligent and self-motivated. And we assume that you're aware that this book is just the start of a long journey that will entail a lot of work, but will hopefully confer great rewards, too.

Icons Used in This Book

Icons are handy little graphic images that are meant to point out particularly important information about starting your own business. Throughout this book, you find the following icons, conveniently located along the left margins.

The Tip icon marks shortcuts that you can use to make your business life easier.

Remember icons mark the information that's especially important to know. To siphon off the most important information in each chapter, just skim through the paragraphs marked with these icons.

The Warning icon tells you to watch out! It marks important information that may save you headaches.

Beyond the Book

In addition to the material in the print or e-book you're reading right now, this product also comes with some access-anywhere goodies on the web. No matter how hard you work at creating your business, you'll likely come up with a few questions where you don't have a clue. For answers and helpful tips, simply go to www.dummies.com and search for **Starting & Running a Small Business for Canadians For Dummies All-in-One Cheat Sheet** in the Search box.

Where to Go from Here

You don't have to read this book in order. Each minibook and each chapter are self-contained, so you can pick up some information here and some information there about a topic that's of particular interest to you.

The *For Dummies* series also includes dozens of reference books that are pertinent for the small-business owner and that go into many of the topics covered in this All-in-One guide. They can take you into the level of detail you require.

If you're really thinking of starting a business and you haven't been in business before, you really should read all the minibooks before you commit to the perilous, but rewarding, journey that running your own business can be.

1

The Beginning of Your Business and Beyond

Contents at a Glance

Chapter **1**

Small Business Essentials

So you're thinking of starting your own business! Every year, lots of Canadians of all ages and backgrounds get the entrepreneurial urge and take the leap to start businesses. Some of those businesses become very successful, and some of them fail.

Business success or failure isn't the result of fate, or random chance. A business does well for good reasons — like providing a great product or service, having a solid marketing plan, and having an owner with good management skills.

Likewise, when a business goes under, you can often identify the reasons — lack of money to get properly started, poor timing or location for entering the market, or a wipeout on the customer service front. Whatever the reason for a business failure, it usually boils down to this: The business owner didn't look carefully before leaping into a new business frontier.

This chapter helps you think about going into business before you hit the ignition button and blast off. Think of this chapter as "countdown."

Weighing the Pros and the Cons

People start up their own businesses for different reasons. One of the best reasons is that they've found a business opportunity and idea that are just too attractive to pass up. A good reason is that they want to work for themselves rather than for someone else. A discouraging — but still valid — reason is that their other job options are poor (the number of small business start-ups always rises when the economy sinks or stinks).

Whatever your reason is for wanting to become an entrepreneur, you should know that life as an entrepreneur is a bit of a mixed bag. Running your own business has some great advantages, but it also has its share of disadvantages.

The pros

REMEMBER

Here are some of the good things about going into business for yourself:

» **You're free!** You'll have the freedom to

- Make your own decisions — you're in charge now. Only investors, customers and clients (see Chapter 3), government regulators, and so on will tell you what to do.

- Choose your own work hours — in theory, anyway. You may not be able to get away with sleeping in until noon or concentrating your productive hours around 3 a.m. But you're more likely to be able to pick up the kids from school at 3 p.m., or exercise from 10 a.m. to 11 a.m., or grocery shop during normal office hours.

- Create your own work environment (see Chapter 2) — surround yourself with dirty coffee cups and empty candy wrappers if you feel like it.

» **You can be creative!** You can build your business from scratch following your own ideas rather than following someone else's master plan.

» **You'll face new challenges!** Every day. And twice as many on days that end in a *y*. You'll never be able to say that work is always the same old boring routine.

» **Your job will be secure . . . as long as you have a business!** Your business may fail — but no one can fire you. You can ask yourself to resign, though. (See Chapter 4 for information about the depressing prospect of running out of money.)

» **You'll have increased financial opportunities!** If your business is successful, you have the potential to make more than you could as an employee.

>> **You'll have tax advantages!** This is true whether your business is incorporated or not incorporated (a sole proprietorship or a partnership; see Chapter 2).

The cons

WARNING

Do you think the exuberant section just before this one used enough exclamation marks? Bet it got you all enthused and excited about entrepreneurship. But calm down for a minute — being an entrepreneur has plenty of disadvantages, too. For some people, they outweigh the advantages. For example:

>> **You may not make a lot of money.** You may make enough money to live on, but it may not come in regularly like an employment paycheque, so you'll have cash flow predictability and budgeting problems. Or you may not make enough money to live on. You may not even make any money at all. You may go bankrupt, and if you're not incorporated or have not mitigated your risk by removing your assets before you started your business you could risk losing not only your business but also your personal possessions.

>> **You lose easy and inexpensive access to employment benefits if you don't hang on to employment elsewhere.** These may be benefits that you have come to count on — extended health and dental benefits, disability insurance, life insurance, a pension plan, and so on.

>> **You'll have to work really hard.** That is, if you want to succeed — and you won't just be working at the business your business is about. You'll also have to do stuff you may not be trained to do, such as accounting, sales, and collection work.

>> **You may not have a lot of free time.** You may see less of your friends, family, and pets (even if you're working at home) and have less time for your favourite activities. Getting a business up and running takes more than hard work; it also takes your time and commitment. Don't scoff that you won't let that happen to you, at least not until you've put in hours filling out government paperwork (GST/HST for example) on a beautiful sunny day that would be perfect for, well, almost anything else. By the way, you don't get paid for your sacrificed time, either.

>> **You may have to put a lot of your own money into starting up the business.** And even if you can borrow the money, unless the lender is The Bank of Mom and Dad, you'll have to give personal guarantees that the money will be repaid (with interest) within a certain time. The pressure is building! By the way, not to add to the pressure or anything, but you should know that you might lose your own money or not be able to repay borrowed money because of factors beyond your control. You could get sick (and now you probably

don't have disability insurance), be flattened by a competitor, squashed by a nose-diving economy, or whacked by a partner who pulls out on you. (See Chapter 4 for advice on how to deal with some of these problems.)

» **You are the bottom line.** No excuses — success is up to you, and failure is your fault. You'll have to keep on top of changes in your field, the impact of new technology, economic fluctuations. . . .

» **Your personal life can stick its nose into your business life in a major way.** If you and your spouse split up, your spouse may be able to claim a share of your business under equalization provisions in the family law of some provinces. You might have to sell your home, your business, or your business assets (business property) to pay off your spouse.

Choosing Your Business

After you're aware of the upside and the downside to running your own business, start considering how people choose a business to go into. Five main kinds of businesses exist:

» **Service:** Doing things for others, including the professions (doctors, engineers, lawyers, dentists, architects, accountants, pilots); skilled trades (plumbers, electricians, carpet installers, bookkeepers, renovators, truckers, carpenters, landscapers); and a huge range of other things for which you might need a lot of training and skill, or at least some talent and willingness. We're talking about teachers, data scientists, financial planners, real estate agents, painters, insurance brokers, management consultants, taxi and Uber drivers, travel agents, dry cleaners, caterers, event planners, hairdressers, equipment repairers, commercial printers, photographers, gardeners, snow removers . . . this list could go on.

» **Retail:** Selling things to the general public, such as jewellery, groceries, clothing, appliances, books, furniture, antiques and collectibles, toys, hardware, cards and knick-knacks, garden accessories, plants, cars . . . this list could also go on.

» **Wholesale:** Buying large quantities of goods from manufacturers at a discount and selling in smaller quantities to others — usually retailers — for a higher price. For example, you could buy nails in bulk from a manufacturer and resell them to hardware stores. Wholesalers sometimes also sell to the general public, usually without the frills of a retail establishment (for example, bulk food, carpets, and clothing).

>> **Manufacturing:** Making things from scratch — from designing and sewing baby clothes for sale through a local children's clothing store to making furniture in a workshop to manufacturing steel ingots in a mammoth industrial plant.

>> **Extraction:** Harvesting natural resources, including agriculture, fishing, logging, and mining.

TIP

Note that e-commerce is not a new and separate kind of business. E-commerce is simply a tool and channel to help transact business in a more efficient, effective, and economical way.

REMEMBER

Small businesses are most likely to concentrate in service and retail. Service, in particular, is usually the cheapest business to start up, because it requires less financial, human, and physical capital, so it attracts a lot of entrepreneurs.

Now, most people don't look at a short list of the five kinds of businesses or industries and wonder, "Service or extraction? Retail or manufacturing? Electronics or sporting goods? What best expresses my personality?" Instead, they have an idea that happens to fit into one of the five categories. At least, having an idea helps. And most people do, but others don't.

What to look for in a business start-up

To begin with, try to aim toward something you'll enjoy doing. Starting a business is hard enough without choosing a business that you're pretty sure you'll loathe, even if you think it could make a lot of money.

Next, look for something people want . . . as opposed to something they don't want, or that they'll have to be carefully educated to want. It should also be something they'll want tomorrow and next week as well as today — in other words, don't base your business on a product or service that's going out of use or out of style. Ideally, your product or service is something that people want often, rather than occasionally or only once.

Especially in Canada, consider offering a product or service that isn't completely seasonal like skate sharpening or outdoor ice cream stands. Choose something with a good distribution and advertising system in place: For example, a product you manufacture should be one that established retailers will be happy to carry; a product you sell should be one that already benefits from a national marketing campaign by the manufacturer; a service you offer should be positioned within a network that will bring you lots of referrals.

Look for a business with a high profit margin. You'd like your direct cost of performing the work or supplying the product to be a small percentage of what you charge the client or customer. (The service industry lends itself to robust profit margins; manufacturing and corner grocery stores do not.)

What to avoid in a business start-up

While you're searching for a business with lots of advantages, you also have to avoid a business with too many disadvantages.

You'll probably be happier if you stay away from a business that will be immediately overwhelmed by the existing competition. If the field is competitive (as are most fields worth going into), look for a niche where you have a competitive advantage (say, because you have a lot of natural talent or you've acquired great skills and experience; or because you have exclusive manufacturing or distribution rights). Don't go head-to-head with the established players and imagine you'll knock them down! They already enjoy first-mover advantage.

You also don't want a business that will be overwhelmed by regulation — by the federal, provincial, or municipal government — or by the governing body of a professional or skilled trade. You'll find regulation in any type of business, but it's worse in some than in others. For example, food and drug manufacturing are heavily regulated by the federal government, as are telecommunications and commercial aviation. Medical, dental, and many other professional services industries are likewise heavily regulated by provincial and federal bodies. Canada's growing cannabis industry has also joined the ranks of the strongly regulated, and rightly so. Alternately, if you open a restaurant or bar, municipal food inspectors and provincial liquor inspectors will visit you regularly. Look into the extent of regulation when you research the area of business in which you are interested. We tell you about getting information geared to your specific business later in this chapter.

You might prefer to avoid a business that will require expensive insurance from the start (this describes most of the professions, and the manufacture of products that are potentially harmful). See Chapter 3 for more about insurance.

Unless you've got guaranteed access to a big wad of cash, you'll certainly also want to avoid a business with high start-up costs. You may think you can build a better steel mill, but you can't do it on a $25,000 loan. Consider how much money you have to invest in starting up a business, or how much you can raise by borrowing. If you have almost nothing to invest and realistically don't expect anyone else will want to invest a lot in you and your business, choose a business that requires almost no initial investment (that's usually service).

You'll probably also want to steer clear of a business with immediate high labour needs. Paying employees isn't just a matter of cash flow (although that's pretty important). As an employer, you'll also have to deal with a lot of regulations and paperwork — such as income tax, Employment Insurance, Canada or Quebec Pension Plan, provincial workers' compensation, and occupational health and safety rules — and you may already have enough on your plate.

Determining Whether You Have the Small Business Personality

Whatever your reason for wanting to go into business for yourself, and whatever the business you decide to go into, stop and check whether you have the right personality for the adventure before you start. This is true whether you really want to go into business for yourself or whether you think you have no choice but to do so. And it will give you an excuse to put off figuring out your finances.

REMEMBER

Realizing that you don't have the right stuff to run your own business is better done before you sink a lot of time and effort, and maybe even money, into a business. You can always pursue other options.

And if you find you're not going to be the perfect entrepreneur, but you're determined to go ahead anyway, then a self-assessment will tell you where your weaknesses lie and show you where you need to improve or get outside help.

An entrepreneur needs most of the following qualities — whether you were born with them, or developed them, or are about to get working on them now:

>> **Self-confidence:** You have to believe in yourself and your abilities . . . no matter what other people might think. You have to believe that your success depends on the good work you know you can do and not on matters beyond your control. However, your self-confidence should be realistic and not induced by whatever weird thing they put in the coffee at your current workplace.

>> **Goal-orientation:** You have to know what you want, whether it's to revolutionize a particular industry or to be home when your children return from school. However, if your main goals are money, power, and prestige, you probably need to reorient yourself toward something a little more attainable in the small business sector.

- >> **Drive to be your own boss:** The burning desire and the ability to be your own boss — if you need or even want direction about what to do next, you won't make it in your own business. You have to be able to make your own plans and carry them out.

- >> **Independence:** The ability to work independently rather than as part of a team. You've probably had propaganda pounded into your head since you were a kid that teamwork is really important, and maybe even better than working on your own. It isn't if you're an entrepreneur.

- >> **Survival skills:** The ability to survive without a social group is handy. When you start up your own business, you'll probably be working by yourself for some time. If you need people around you to chat with, or else you start to go crazy . . . then you may go crazy.

- >> **People skills:** Even though you have to be able to get along without being surrounded by people all the time, you still have to get along with people. You'll be dealing directly with customers and clients (see Chapter 3), investors, suppliers (see Chapter 3), associates, and employees (see Book 5), and you need their willing cooperation.

- >> **Determination and persistence:** You have to want to succeed, and you have to plan to succeed and keep working at succeeding. It's that "fire in the belly" stuff you hear about from people who look like they haven't slept in the past eight months.

- >> **Self-discipline:** You can't let yourself be distracted from your work by nice weather, phone calls from family and friends, earthquakes, or wrestling matches on TV.

- >> **Reliability:** You'll build most of your important business relationships by always meaning what you say and doing what you promise.

- >> **Versatility:** You have to be prepared to do many different things in short periods of time, probably constantly switching from task to task.

- >> **Creativity:** You have to want to do something new or something old in a new way. If copying what someone else is already doing is the best you can manage, you may not go far.

- >> **Resourcefulness:** Creativity's country cousin, resourcefulness, means being prepared to try different ways of doing things if the first way doesn't work.

- >> **Organizational talents:** You'll be plunged into chaos if you can't organize your goals, your time, or your accounts, to name just a few things.

- >> **Risk-management instincts:** You have to be able to spot risks, weigh them, and come up with a plan to steer around them or soften their impact in case of a collision. (See Chapter 3 for some help in managing risk.)

- » **Nerves of steel in a crisis:** Nerves of granite, titanium, oak, and so on are acceptable. Nerves of rubber, talc, or pasta al dente are not. Crises won't necessarily be frequent, but they will occur. Don't count on gin or prescription drugs to stiffen your spine during a crisis. And you can't collapse until the crisis is over.

- » **Pick-yourself-up-itiveness — a combination of optimism and grit:** You're going to have failures, some of them caused by your own mistakes, and you have to see failures as valuable experiences rather than as signs that you and your business are doomed.

- » **Opportunism:** You need to not only recognize opportunities when they come along, but you also need to seek them out — and even create them yourself.

- » **Success-management instincts:** You can't let yourself be bowled over or lulled by success. You have to be able to see each success as a platform on which you can build your next success.

- » **Objectivity:** For a business owner, it's always reality-check time. You have to have the courage to stare down reality's throat and acknowledge your own mistakes. You also have to corner reality by getting feedback about your business and how you run it from customers and clients, suppliers, professional advisors, competitors, employees, and even your mother-in-law. Then you have to have the strength to make necessary changes.

That's a long list! And you'll also need a Zen-like calm about not having a regular paycheque. Not only will you not get a bank deposit once a month, but you won't get paid for sick days, personal days off, or days when you show up at the office but are too zonked to work.

In addition, it helps if your parents (or close relatives or close friends) are or were in business for themselves. You may have absorbed some business know-how from them, plus you may have easy access to advice. If that's not the case, consider hiring a business coach to help you gain or refine these necessary skills. And to finish you off, good health and physical stamina can do an entrepreneur no harm.

TIP

A great free resource is the online entrepreneurial assessment provided by the Business Development Bank of Canada. Go to www.bdc.ca, hover your mouse over Articles and Tools, and click Entrepreneur's Toolkit. From there, click the Entrepreneurial Potential Self-Assessment link. This robust questionnaire includes 50 statements that will take you about 15 minutes to thoughtfully complete. The questions are not binary — there is no right or wrong answer. All the tool requires is your honest response. When you finish the questionnaire, your answers are summarized in a way that helps you to self-assess your entrepreneurial traits, motivations, aptitudes, and attitudes.

Knowing If and When to Give Up Your Day Job

Should you start a business and keep your day job (if you've got one)?

Conventional wisdom says that you shouldn't give up your day job until absolutely necessary (that's the point when you have to devote the time to your business or give it up) or until you don't need a day job (that's the point when you're making a living from your business). Conventional wisdom also urges entrepreneurs not to go it alone until they've saved up about six months' salary. That's a good joke! It would take most of us years to save six months' salary, unless we were offered a fantastic buyout package.

REMEMBER

Even if you're dying to tell your current employer "I quit!" think about the following questions:

>> **Do you have to have the money from employment?** Even if your business turns out to be a success, you may not have much, or even any, income when you first start your business.

>> **Do you want to keep your employment contacts?** The business you're starting might be something your employer or fellow employees could assist or patronize.

>> **Do you have the time to hold down a job and start a business (and still have time to eat and sleep)?**

>> **Would starting your own business and keeping your day job be problematic because of**

- Your employer's requirement (in your employment contract) that you not carry on any kind of a competing business while you're an employee?

- Your employer's requirement (in your employment contract) that you put your full effort toward your employment work?

- Suspicious superiors and co-workers who would assume you were goofing off by focusing on your own business instead of doing what you were paid to do?

>> **Do you want to be able to fall back on your day job if your business venture doesn't work out?** Remember, if you quit to start a business, you might not get hired back.

Seeking Out General Business Information

How do you find the information you need to start your business? The amount of information about business can appear to be infinite. How do you zero in on the information that's useful to you?

The first step is to get general information about starting and carrying on a business. You can find a fairly comprehensive and self-contained start-to-finish source, such as a book — hey, this book is a great choice! — or a business resource centre, or a website. You've already got the book, so here are some suggestions for resource centres and websites.

The Government of Canada

The Government of Canada maintains an online portal, referred to as Canada Business (www.canadabusiness.ca), that provides access to both government and general business information, relevant to both start-up entrepreneurs and established, small to medium-size businesses in any field. This section shows you what you can expect to find there.

Taking a look at the services offered

The Canada Business website provides information on government services, programmes, and regulations pertaining to business. It has an extensive and up-to-date reference collection of general business information from government and non-government sources — topics include starting a business, writing a business plan, finding financing, marketing, exporting, and being an employer. Service centres located across Canada have information officers to help you navigate your way through everything they offer.

In addition, you can get products, services, publications, and referrals to experts. Here are some examples of the products and services the service centres provide:

>> **Info guides:** These free guides on different topics provide brief overviews of services and programmes.

>> **How-to guides:** These guides provide information about the potential licence, permit, and registration requirements for specific types of businesses.

>> **Fact sheets:** These fact sheets contain information about starting and running a business and are available online.

>> **BizPaL online business permits and licences service:** This online service provides information about business permits and licence requirements from all levels of government.

>> **Specialized Research Service:** This limited business research service is free and provides access to information on topics such as business associations, Canadian demographics, company data, consumer spending, and sample business plans.

Some of the service centres also offer low-cost seminars and workshops on a variety of business topics.

Getting access to the resources you need

TIP

You can obtain resources in three ways:

>> **Website:** The government's website (www.canadabusiness.ca) contains information about business-related programmes and services of federal and provincial agencies. The site allows you to input your province, industry and/or demographic group and receive information tailored to the location and nature of your business, and provides links to the individual websites maintained by some provinces. The main site contains information on such topics as

- Starting a business
- Looking at growth and innovation in your business
- Getting financial assistance through grants, loans, and financing
- Managing federal and provincial taxes
- Complying with business regulations
- Obtaining licences and permits
- Exporting and importing
- Hiring and managing staff
- Creating a business plan
- Managing and operating a business
- Conducting market research and getting access to statistics
- Doing marketing and sales
- Managing intellectual property
- Exiting your business

Some of the provincial sites also provide information about and let you register for business workshops and seminars, as well as links to other useful websites.

>> **E-mail:** Send questions by e-mail from the main website under Contact Us.

>> **In person:** At the offices of your provincial/territorial service centre, you can use the resource materials on your own or with the help of a business information officer. These provincial service centres also have arrangements with existing business service organizations in communities across Canada to provide relevant information. Contact your Canada Business network service centre for the location nearest you. You can find information for your region at http://canadabusiness.ca/about/contact.

Provincial/territorial government websites

Each provincial and territorial government maintains a website. Some of the provincial sites contain good general business information that you can use to get started.

TIP

Here are the websites:

>> **Alberta:** www.gov.ab.ca

>> **British Columbia:** www.gov.bc.ca

>> **Manitoba:** www.gov.mb.ca

>> **New Brunswick:** www.gov.nb.ca

>> **Newfoundland and Labrador:** www.gov.nl.ca

>> **Northwest Territories:** www.gov.nt.ca

>> **Nova Scotia:** www.gov.ns.ca

>> **Nunavut:** www.gov.nu.ca

>> **Ontario:** www.gov.on.ca

>> **Prince Edward Island:** www.gov.pe.ca

>> **Quebec:** www.quebec.ca

>> **Saskatchewan:** www.gov.sk.ca

>> **Yukon:** www.gov.yk.ca

Bank and trust company websites

The major banks' and trust companies' websites have information about the products and services they provide to small businesses. Some have information about general business topics, as well. For example, the Bank of Montreal site (www.bmo.com) contains links to a number of small business resources such as podcasts, planning guides, articles, tips, Internet resources, and business FAQs.

A particularly good example is the Royal Bank of Canada (RBC) website (www.rbc.com). It contains information about many general business topics such as starting a business, expanding a business, and business succession. It also has several web pages promoting entrepreneurship for women. The RBC website has its own "Resource Centre" for businesses to guide you through the steps of developing a business plan. It even provides sample business plans for several different types of businesses. Other bank websites include TD Canada Trust (www.td.com), CIBC (www.cibc.com), HSBC (www.hsbc.com), and Bank of Nova Scotia, or Scotiabank as it is better known (www.scotiabank.com).

Small business or entrepreneurship centres

TIP

A number of small business or entrepreneurship centres provide support and training to start-up and small businesses: For example:

>> **Canadian Federation of Independent Businesses (CFIB):** This group not only offers resources but can also be a big advocate for your business when you need help with legal or HR concerns. Visit www.cfib-fcei.ca/en.

>> **Centennial College Centre of Entrepreneurship:** This Toronto-based centre provides entrepreneurial training, business plan development, analysis of proposed acquisitions, as-needed business advice and consulting, and international business training. It also offers a New Business Start-up Programme, designed to provide entrepreneurs with the basic principles and practices of business, along with the skills to market, operate, and control a business. Visit www.centennialcollege.ca/pdf/new-website/coe/be-your-own-boss.pdf to find out more.

>> **Centre for Entrepreneurship Education & Development Incorporated (CEED):** This Nova Scotia not-for-profit society is devoted to helping people discover and use entrepreneurship as a vehicle to become self-reliant. Its services include technical assistance, entrepreneurship consulting, and entrepreneurship courses. CEED's website (www.ceed.ca) has more information.

» **Chamber of Commerce:** If you're a member, they offer resources and often help you deal with new policies that could impact your business. Most towns, cities, and provinces have a Chamber of Commerce organization. They also provide advertising for local businesses. Check out www.chamber.ca (Canada-wide) or www.bcchamber.org (BC Chamber of Commerce).

» **Ontario Small Business Enterprise Centres:** These Ontario government centres are located throughout the province and provide entrepreneurs with support to start and grow their businesses. They offer a wide variety of support resources, including consultations with qualified business consultants, workshops and seminars, and mentoring and networking opportunities. Visit www.ontario.ca/page/small-business-enterprise-centre-and-community-based-provider-locations for more information.

» **The Stu Clark Centre for Entrepreneurship:** The University of Manitoba's Asper School of Business (www.umanitoba.ca/asper) operates this centre. It aims to encourage the development of new businesses and entrepreneurial thinking among Canadians. The centre supports a variety of programmes aimed at youth, as well as undergraduate students and adults. Its Manitoba Venture Challenge (MVC) is a province-wide competition open to new and established businesses in Manitoba whose owners are seeking outside investment or need advice to start or grow their businesses. The specific web page is www.umanitoba.ca/faculties/management/academic_depts_centres/centres_institutes/entrepreneurship/index.html.

Business incubators

A *business incubator* is a business-mentoring facility that nurtures small- and medium-sized businesses during the start-up period. Business incubators provide management assistance, education, technical and business support services, and financial advice. They may also provide flexible rental space and flexible leases.

Over 1,300 business incubators exist in North America, with about 170 located throughout Canada. Most Canadian business incubators are nonprofit and sponsored by government, economic development organizations, and academic institutions. Some examples of business incubators are

» **CDEM Business Incubator:** Run by the Economic Development Council for Manitoba Bilingual Municipalities and located in St. Boniface, Manitoba. Visit www.cdem.com/en for more information.

» **The Genesis Centre:** Located at the Memorial University of Newfoundland in St. John's. Their website is www.genesiscentre.ca.

>> **Launch Academy:** This organization in Vancouver provides mentorship, resources, networking, and a comprehensive list of training programmes aimed at varying levels of start-up needs. Check out www.launchacademy.ca.

>> **Northern Alberta Business Incubator:** Created by and located in the city of St. Albert, Alberta. Their website is http://nabi.ca/.

>> **Toronto Business Development Centre (TBDC):** Started by the City of Toronto, TBDC's Business Incubation Programme supports the growth of new businesses by providing useful resources, including business advisory support, dedicated office space, and participation in a robust community of successful entrepreneurs from around the world. Their website is www.tbdc.com.

Getting Information Geared to Your Specific Business

After you find out about starting and carrying on a business in general, you can find out more about your field of business in particular. For example, you might want to know these facts:

>> What skills you need for this business

>> What government regulations apply to this business

>> How much it will cost to run this kind of business

>> What the demand is for the goods or services you'll be supplying

>> Who the likely customers are for the goods and services you'll be providing

>> What the competition is like for this type of business

>> What supplies and equipment you require for this type of business

You need a good gateway into the sector you're interested in. Here are some recommendations.

Innovation, Science, and Economic Development Canada

The Innovation, Science, and Economic Development Canada website (www.ic.gc.ca) is particularly useful at the preliminary stage of starting a business because, in addition to general business information, it also contains information on a wide variety of businesses, organized by sector. Each type of business has its own page, with additional pages on a number of subtopics. The subtopics vary for each business category but cover areas such as the following:

- » **Company directories:** Links to lists of Canadian companies carrying on business in the field
- » **Contacts:** Links to major trade associations in the field
- » **Electronic business:** Links to a variety of information about e-business and e-commerce
- » **Events:** Links to major trade shows in a particular business field
- » **Grants:** Links to information about ways to fund your business with government assistance
- » **Industry news:** Links to Canada and U.S. trade periodicals
- » **Regulations and standards:** Links to relevant government regulations and standards organizations
- » **Statistics, analysis, and industry profiles:** Links to North American Industry Classification definitions and to selected Canadian statistics on topics such as the Canadian market, imports, and exports
- » **Trade and exporting:** Links to relevant international trade agreements and export information

Trade and professional associations

Trade and professional associations are another great source of information about particular fields of business. Thousands of associations exist in North America, many of them based in the United States. Whatever your field of business, a related association probably exists. A good association will give you access to industry-specific information. Most associations maintain a website, setting out the services the association provides and membership information.

Simon Fraser University has a web page with a repository of trade and professional associations that can be found at www.lib.sfu.ca/help/research-assistance/subject/business/associations. More general resources can be accessed at www.cpmdq.com/htm/org.canada2.htm and www.canadiancareers.com/sector.html.

The Internet is the best way to track down the trade or professional associations in your field. Use a search engine such as Google (www.google.com) or Bing (www.bing.com) by typing in the name of the specific field you're interested in plus the word **association** — for example, **giftware association**. You can also get information about associations on the Industry Canada website by following the Contact link for your business field.

Many trade and professional associations publish journals or newsletters with current information about the field. They also contain ads for equipment and supplies that the business uses, and some list business opportunities (businesses for sale, partners wanted, premises for lease, equipment for sale, and so on). You may be able to get information about trade and professional journals on the Innovation, Science, and Economic Development Canada website by following the Industry News link offered for some industry sectors.

Many trade and professional associations hold seminars and workshops on topics of specific interest to members. Some offer courses leading to a designation or certification in the field.

Most trade associations hold an industry-wide trade show at least once a year. Trade shows are good places to make contacts in the industry and learn about the latest trends in the field.

Obtaining Essential Business Skills

After you research your chosen business field, you may realize that you need some training before you can start your business. You may need skills specific to your chosen business field (such as how to frame a picture if you're going into the framing business, or how to mediate if you're going into family counselling), or you may want to pick up some general business skills and knowledge such as simple bookkeeping, basic computer skills, or how to prepare a business plan.

When people think of education, they usually think of universities, community colleges, career colleges, vocational schools, and boards of education. But in fact, many different places offer business education and skills training. You may be able to pick up the skills you need from a trade association, a partnering Canada Business network service centre, or the little place in your local mall that teaches keyboarding. In fact, you may want to avoid many of the educational institutions, because they often offer certificate or diploma programmes more suited to people looking for a job, rather than individual courses focused on the specific skills an entrepreneur needs.

Where you go to get your training will depend on the kind of skill you're trying to acquire.

Skills for your particular business

You may be able to pick up the special skills required for your particular business in a day, a weekend, or a week. Or you may need a certificate or diploma in the field that will take months or years to get.

You may be able to find out not only what skills you need, but also where to get them, from Innovation, Science, and Economic Development Canada or from the relevant trade or professional association. Or you can use a search engine by typing in the name of the specific field you're interested in and the word **education** or **training**.

WARNING

If you're not required to have a degree, diploma, or certificate offered by a university or community college, you may want to consider programmes offered by privately run career colleges or vocational schools. These programmes tend to be shorter than university and community college programmes, but be warned — these courses are usually more expensive, sometimes much more expensive!

The trade or professional association in your field may offer short workshops or seminars on individual topics of interest to you as well as complete training programmes designed specifically for your field.

General business skills

To acquire in-depth business skills, you can enroll in degree, diploma, or certificate programmes offered by colleges and universities. These programmes run over the course of a year, or from two to three years. You probably won't be able to take one course of interest to you without taking another course as a prerequisite or without signing on for the entire programme.

TIP

If you want to acquire some business skills as quickly as possible, look for *continuing education* courses offered by your local university or community college. For example, the University of Toronto (http://learn.utoronto.ca) and most other Canadian post-secondary institutions offer courses (usually with classes held once a week for about three months) in a wide variety of business-related areas, including Accounting Fundamentals, Business Law, Business Management, Business Strategy, Taxation for Canadian Business, and Understanding and Managing Conflict. The University of Calgary (http://conted.ucalgary.ca) has seminars on numerous topics, including Time Management, Accounting for Non-Financial Managers, Building Great Customer Relationships, Business Writing Basics, and Creative Negotiating.

Your local board of education may offer courses in business skills as part of its continuing education programmes, and you should have no problem enrolling in individual courses rather than in programmes. Classes will probably be scheduled once a week over several months.

You may also be able to find weekend workshops or evening seminars offered by your trade or professional association, or through your provincial Canada Business network service centre.

Finding Professional and Other Help

Planning a business start-up takes a lot of work. But you don't have to do it all alone. You can and should get professional help with many of the tasks involved. This section helps you determine who you need on your team, and how to find the best candidates.

Determining who you need to help you

At the very least, you'll need a lawyer, a Chartered Professional Accountant (CPA), and a licensed insurance agent or broker. This section also offers suggestions for other professionals you might find useful.

Lawyer

Almost everything that happens in the business world has legal implications. A lawyer can help you navigate through every stage of your business odyssey.

When you're setting up your business, a lawyer can

>> Help you decide whether or not to incorporate (see Chapter 2)

>> Help you form a corporation or partnership (see Chapter 2)

>> Review start-up documents such as loan agreements, leases (see Chapter 2), and franchise agreements (see Chapter 2)

>> Draft standard forms for contracts to use in your business (see Chapter 3)

When you're in business, a lawyer can be of further assistance by

>> Helping you negotiate contracts (see Chapter 3)

>> Giving you advice about hiring and firing employees (see Book 5)

>> Helping you collect your unpaid accounts (see Chapter 3)

>> Acting for you in a lawsuit if you sue or are sued (see Chapter 4)

Even if you decide to get out of the business, you'll still need a lawyer to help you sell it, or give it to your children, or wind it up.

Accountant

In Canada, anyone can call himself or herself an accountant. What you want is a professional accountant — a chartered professional accountant, or CPA. Professional accountants are licensed and regulated by CPA Canada (www.cpacanada.ca).

You'll probably need an accountant to help you

>> Buy an existing business (see Chapter 2)

>> Set up a bookkeeping system (see Chapter 3 in Book 4)

>> Prepare budgets and cash-flow statements (see Chapters 2 and 4 in Book 4)

>> Prepare financial statements (see Chapters 2 and 4 in Book 4)

>> Prepare your income tax returns

>> Deal with the Canada Revenue Agency (CRA) from time to time

Insurance agent or broker

You'll need insurance for your business, including

>> Property insurance to cover loss or damage to your business property

>> Business interruption insurance to cover your loss of earnings if your business premises are damaged

>> General liability insurance to cover claims made if you cause injury to a customer, supplier, or innocent bystander

>> Key person insurance to tide over your business in case you, a partner, or an important employee dies or becomes disabled

>> Cyber insurance in case your personal data or intellectual property is hacked by some kid in his mother's basement

Find out more about insurance in Chapter 3 of Book 1.

An *insurance agent* (a person who deals with and sells the policies of only one insurance company) or *insurance broker* (a person who deals with and sells the policies of several insurance companies) can give you advice about what kind of insurance you need and how much. Both agents and brokers are regulated and licensed by provincial governments.

Other assistance

TIP

Depending on the nature of your business, you may also want help from any of the following professionals (in no particular order):

>> **Advertising firm and/or media relations firm:** To help you get the word out about your business (see Book 6 for more about marketing)

>> **Business coach:** To help you do various things such as acquire presentation skills, get pointers on power dressing, pick up business etiquette, and even improve your table manners (for those four-fork lunches with potential investors and customers)

>> **Business valuation expert:** To help you decide on the value of a business you are thinking of buying

>> **Computer systems consultant:** To help you choose and set up your computer equipment and choose and install your software

>> **Graphic designer:** To help you design a business logo, your business cards, and letterhead

>> **Human resources specialist (also known as a head-hunter):** To help you hire staff (see Book 5 for details on human resources)

>> **Interior designer:** To help you set up your business premises attractively

>> **Management consultant:** To help you polish your management skills

>> **Marketing consultant:** To help you identify the market for your product or service and determine how best to reach that market

>> **Website designer:** To help you create a great website for your business (see Chapter 5 in Book 6)

Finding peer support

Even though you're going it alone in the business universe, you may want to seek out the companionship of fellow travellers with whom you can share your experiences and from whom you can get advice. Whatever demographic group you fall into, you'll likely find a business organization for you. These organizations provide opportunities to network and get advice geared to your demographic.

Here's a sampling:

>> **Canadian Association of Women Executives & Entrepreneurs:** An organization that provides networking, support, mentoring, and professional development to businesswomen at all stages of their careers (www.cawee.net).

>> **Canadian Council for Aboriginal Business:** A national, nonprofit organization that promotes the full participation of Aboriginal individuals in the Canadian economy (www.ccab.com).

>> **Canadian Gay & Lesbian Chamber of Commerce:** An organization designed to improve opportunities for gay, lesbian, bisexual, transgender, transsexual, two-spirited, and intersex owned/operated/friendly businesses (www.cglcc.ca).

>> **Futurpreneur Canada:** A national, nonprofit organization that provides financing, mentoring, and support tools to aspiring business owners ages 18 to 39. A mentoring programme exists to match young entrepreneurs with a business expert from a network of almost 3,000 volunteer mentors (www.futurpreneur.ca/en).

your product or service

» **Looking at off-the-shelf businesses and franchises**

» **Selecting the best place for your business**

» **Thinking about ownership and incorporation issues**

Chapter **2**

Getting Started

Your business will be in big trouble if you offer a product or service that not a soul wants, or that your chosen customer group is not interested in. This chapter helps you avoid those problems and give you hints on how to develop a product or service tailored for your target customers or clients. You also find out about taking on an off-the-shelf business or a franchise, selecting a place of business, and handling ownership incorporation issues.

Developing Your Product or Service with a Market in Mind

To start a business, you need a product or service to sell. And it needs to be something that customers or clients want to buy. Developing a product or service requires quite a chunk of your time and energy. You'll need to take on some tasks that may seem kind of challenging, such as researching potential customers and existing competition.

TIP

If your idea is new and innovative, you may be able to get assistance with the evaluation, for example from The Canadian Innovation Centre (CIC) (www. innovationcentre.ca) in Waterloo, Ontario, an organization that grew out of the invention commercialization activities of the University of Waterloo. Their website has information for inventors as well as links to other useful organizations such as the U.S. National Inventor Fraud Center (www.inventor-fraud.com), which offers advice on how to steer away from invention marketing companies that are set up only to scam inventors.

WARNING

Don't get mixed up with a company that combines high-pressure sales tactics with a low success rate.

Is this idea right for you?

Or is this a good idea at all, when you get right down to it? For example, is it legal? (And if it's legal now, will it become illegal once it takes off? Remember radar detectors for the travelling public?) Is it hands-off? The reverse is also true. Consider the whole area of cannabusiness, a business sphere that was generally illegal just a while ago, but is now legal. The idea may already be patented (see Book 2 on intellectual property) and the patent owner doesn't want to license to you.

Are you legal? Some products and services can be provided only by a licensed individual or business. Is the product or service safe — or will you cause harm to someone and end up getting sued? And if everything's legal, hands-on, and safe, do you have the reputation or expertise needed to develop the idea into a business and reel in customers or clients?

Does anyone want the product or service?

Your idea may seem wonderful to you, but you're going to need a slightly larger market than yourself to prosper. So you have to do some *customer research* — identify a target market for the product or service and estimate the size of the market.

First, think generally about who your customers or clients might be (keep in mind that you could be wrong about this, though). For example, are they

>> **Other businesses?** A whole bunch of them or just one or two? Are the businesses service providers or retailers or manufacturers?

>> **Individuals?** Do the individuals live in a particular neighbourhood or geographic area, or do they live all over the country or around the world? Are they men only? Women only? The young? Older people? The well-to-do, or just anyone with a buck to spend?

After you've identified a starting point, you can proceed with your customer/client research to find out if anybody would want your product or service. Different research methods exist, so try a combination of them. From the least expensive to most expensive, here they are:

>> **Review of publicly available information:** This includes websites (including blogs), TV programs, newspapers, trade journals, newsletters, and market analysis materials from the business reference section of a public or university library.

>> **Direct observation of potential customers or clients:** You can use your own personal knowledge of a business you're in or have followed, you can visit stores and trade shows, or you can attend presentations and conferences.

>> **Interviews with experts in the field or with potential customers or clients:** This isn't as hard to do as you think. If you start with people you know and ask for names of other people who wouldn't mind talking to you, if you just ask for an opinion or advice and don't try to sell anything, and if you keep the interview polite and brief, you will very likely meet people who will agree to give you 20 minutes or half an hour of their time. It's really amazing how many people are open and amenable to sharing their thoughts and insights, especially if you compliment them by referring to them as experts or thought leaders in their field.

TIP

Try to meet face-to-face if you can — the interviewee will remember you better if it later turns out that she needs the product or service you want to provide.

>> **Focus groups:** See if you can lure groups of potential customers or clients together to talk about the product or service. The lure should be something significant, like a free meal or a chance to win a prize.

TIP

Unless you can find friends and acquaintances who'll participate in a focus group, you may be better off hiring a market analysis firm to run focus groups than trying to corner strangers on your own.

>> **Surveys and questionnaires:** These are short written, telephone or online questionnaires distributed or conducted on a large scale. You'll have to come up with the right questions to ask, and pay for printing and distribution of written materials, find your nerve to make calls or hire trained interviewers to phone people at dinnertime, and then you'll have to analyze the results . . . if anyone answers the questions (a lot of paper surveys will be considered garbage and thrown out, and a lot of people won't answer telephone interviewers).

Doing door-to-door surveys in a neighbourhood, or approaching people on the street in a business or shopping area, will probably earn you a lot of suspicion and brush-offs. As with focus groups, you may prefer to have a professional market analysis firm handle a survey. (Surveys and questionnaires are easier to handle yourself if you've already got an established customer base.)

At the conclusion of your market research, ideally you should have an idea about whether the product or service is attractive to some target group or groups, and you should also be able to estimate roughly the size of your market. Your market is the number of customers you'll win times the number of sales per customer.

TIP

There could be lots of statistics and market analysis already done on your business. Statistics Canada (www.statcan.gc.ca) is a great resource, as is the Canadian Marketing Association (www.the-cma.org).

Who's the competition?

Who is your competition? And what are they up to? This information is known as "competitive intelligence." Your competitors may already have claimed all of the customers or clients you identified by doing your market research. Or they may not. You can find out by assessing your potential market share.

Your competition is made up of the following:

>> **Direct competitors** — who offer exactly the same product or service

>> **Indirect competitors** — who offer an alternative product that more or less meets the same need as your product

>> **Who-was-that-masked-man competitors** — who offer something completely different that potential customers will spend their money on instead of on your product or a similar product, much to your regret and amazement

>> **Inertia** — the tendency of customers and clients to do nothing at all when brought face-to-face with your wonderful product or service

As an example, if you want to offer a service tutoring children in math or reading, your direct competition is other private tutoring services, your indirect competition is the public and private schools in the area (they may be doing a fine job of teaching, in which case your services won't be required); your who-was-that-masked-man competition is social media and video games; and inertia is parents letting their kids sink or swim through school on their own.

Look carefully at your direct and indirect competitors and see if you can find out whether

>> They've cornered the market and are doing such a good job at such a good price that you haven't much hope of taking market share away from them. Or whether you should be able to relieve them of market share because you can offer better value — for example, a lower price, a higher-quality product or service, a more convenient location, greater expertise, friendlier service, and so on. Sometimes the first competitor into the market may just have collected and educated your potential clients for you!

>> Their business is profitable — are they growing or shrinking?

>> They're big enough and mean enough to run you out of town if you show your face on the street (have you noticed how small airlines regularly get eaten?).

How much money can you put behind this idea?

You likely can't get your idea off the ground for free. So the last sober second thought involves figuring out

>> **Approximately how much it will cost to launch your business.** This involves adding up your start-up costs plus bridge financing for your operating expenses until your business is generating income.

>> **Approximately how much money is available to you for a business start-up.** The cash you have on hand or can raise through family contributions may be enough to get your particular business up and running; or you may need a bank loan for a larger amount; or you may need a significant investment from an angel investor or venture capital firm or from a crowd-funding campaign, such as Kickstarter (www.kickstarter.com).

How much you'll be able to raise (especially from outsiders) is linked to the likely return on investment for your idea. So just because it will take $1 million to build a plant to produce your product doesn't mean you should scrap the idea. It could be full steam ahead if an investor believes that your business could generate profits of $2 million annually after a couple of years or that the business might be worth $50 million in five years.

Finding the Best Route to Your Target Market

REMEMBER

Okay, so you think you've got a product or service that can go the distance. Now you have to figure out how to get it from you to the person who will actually use it — so you have to decide on one or more distribution channels. You have two basic choices:

>> **Distribute directly:** The product or service goes from your business to your buyer (most services and products take this route).

>> **Distribute indirectly:** The product or service goes from your business to another business to the buyer. Although your target market is the buyer, your customer is the "middleman" business.

If you choose direct distribution, you can deal with customers or clients in two ways:

>> **Face-to-face:** In your retail store or your office.

>> **Facelessly:** Through an order system that uses a website, e-mail, mail, phone, or even fax. If you choose this option, remember that you'll need a place to keep your inventory, such as a room in a warehouse, and you'll need a delivery system, such as mail or courier. (Certain kinds of services provided this way may be deliverable electronically.)

If your customer is a middleman, you'll probably need fewer customers to make a go of your business. However, a middleman may be more demanding about low prices, so your profit margin may be lower. Middlemen include

>> **Retailers**

>> **Wholesalers or distributors** — who in turn sell to retailers, and sometimes to the general public

>> **Re-packagers** — who also sell to retailers after — you guessed it — repackaging the products they buy from you

You may be able to or may want to sell directly to the middleman yourself, or you may want to employ a manufacturer's agent or representative to do the selling for you (on commission). First you'll have to choose an agent who sells to the kind of middleman you want in the regions you want. Then you'll have to persuade the agent to carry your line and talk it up to customers.

Pricing Your Product or Service

You can make a profit in different ways — for example, by combining a small profit on each item or service provided with high sales volume, or by combining a low sales volume with a big profit on each transaction. (Best, of course, is high profit on each unit and high sales volume, but not many businesses are that lucky.) But if you underprice, you'll lose money on every sale even if you sell a gazillion units; if you overprice, no one will buy at all. How do you figure this whole thing out? This section talks about how to settle on the right price to charge.

Deciding on the minimum price you can charge

REMEMBER

Minimum price is not all that difficult to figure out. As a rule, you don't want to charge less for your product or service than it costs to produce. (An exception to the rule is offering the product or service as a loss leader, to lure customers in — but you can't keep that up for long, and certainly not on an important part of your line.) The formula that tells you, as the owner of a start-up business, your cost to produce (your *break-even cost*) is

> Total direct and indirect costs over a given period (say, one to three months) ÷ Total number of products or services that it would be reasonable for you to provide over the given period = Your break-even cost for that period

Your break-even cost for the period is the amount you need to charge for each unit of your product or service to pay your direct and indirect costs. (See the next section for more information.)

Direct costs, also known as variable costs, include

>> Materials required to manufacture the product, and cost of shipping the materials to your site

>> Lease payments for factory space or storage space

>> Energy (or other utility) costs of production (for example, electricity, water)

>> Wages paid to subcontractors or employees to produce the product or service

>> Cost of delivering the product or service to your customer

Indirect costs, also known as fixed costs or overhead, include administrative expenses such as the following:

>> Wages for office staff

>> Electricity, telephone, and other office utilities

>> Office supplies

>> Advertising expenses

>> Rent on your office space

If your business involves supplying a service rather than manufacturing a product, you'll probably have higher indirect costs than direct costs.

Deciding on the maximum price you can charge

Now over to the other end of the price scale. Here, the ceiling for your price is the value of your product or service to the customer or client. Value is what the customer perceives that he or she is getting in exchange for the cost of the product, and includes things such as quality and reliability of the product or service, image or prestige associated with the product or service, uniqueness of the product or service, backup from your business such as support and guarantees, convenience of dealing with your business (such things as good location or inexpensive delivery or the helpfulness of your staff), and incentives such as rebates (money back following a purchase), discounts (money off the purchase price), and other freebies.

If customers believe that your price (their cost) is greater than the value of your product or service (the benefit to them), customers won't buy from you. Ouch!

Setting your price

Setting a price comes down to supply and demand. If a product is essential or useful and it's hard to find, the price can be higher and the product will still sell (until people run out of money). If a product is not a must-have or is readily available, the price has to be lower if you want to sell. Higher or lower than what? The competition's price.

So see what your competition is charging. Once you know that, then you can implement one of the following three strategies:

>> **Charge more than the competition.** This will work only if your product is seen as more valuable than the competition's. You can increase the value of the same product or service offered by the competition by (for example) creating a higher-end image for your business or by trading on your reputation as an expert.

>> **Charge the same as the competition.** But you still need to increase the value of your product over the competition's to drive actual sales. You could do this, for example, by offering a more convenient location to your target customers.

>> **Charge less than the competition.** Just be careful not to undercut your own cost of production, and keep in mind that you'll acquire a "reputation." Whether it's true or not, customers and clients will tend to associate lower prices with lower value. Only in rare cases will people think they've made a marvellous discovery of a business that carries exactly the same product as the competition, but at a lower price. It's also a good idea to keep prices fluid. Flexibility never hurts.

Considering an Off-the-Shelf Business

TIP

If you don't already have your eye on a particular business, where do you look for one that's for sale?

>> Read the ads.

>> Search the Internet. (You can start with https://canada.businesses forsale.com.)

>> Place an ad.

>> Visit trade shows and conventions.

>> Tell business professionals that you're interested in buying.

>> Ask a business owner if he or she wants to sell.

>> Use a business broker.

REMEMBER

Before the owner agrees to answer your questions, show you around the business premises, and let you see documents, he or she may ask you to sign a *confidential disclosure agreement* (often also referred to as a *nondisclosure agreement* [NDA]). By signing the agreement, you agree not to tell anyone else what you find out about the business, and usually you also agree not to use the information for any purpose but assessing the business for a possible purchase. The information and the business are protected if you decide you don't want to buy, because the owner can sue you if you don't honour the agreement.

Take a very careful, even cynical, look at any business before deciding to buy. The upcoming sections set out some questions to guide your examination of a business that's up for sale.

Why is the owner selling the business?

This may be the most important and fundamental question to ask. Many reasons exist for selling a business, but from the buyer's point of view, some are better than others.

These reasons shouldn't set off alarm bells for you:

>> The owner is retiring because he or she no longer needs to work, or because of age or ill-health (. . . as long as the business didn't cause the ill-health).

>> The owner wants to pursue a different career or business opportunity (unless a problem with this business triggered that desire).

>> The owner is having marital problems.

These reasons may signal trouble:

>> The business is not profitable.

>> The owner cannot raise enough money to finance the business.

>> Competition for the business is heating up.

>> Markets for the business's product or service are drying up.

>> The work hours are too long and/or the work is unpleasant.

The owner may be very forthcoming about her reasons for selling, or she may be reluctant to talk. Even if she does talk, don't just believe what she tells you. Seek internally consistent information from others in the same industry — business owners, employees, suppliers, and customers.

What is the reputation of the business?

A major reason for buying an established business is to get the benefit of its reputation. You hope that it has a base of loyal customers and suppliers who will continue to deal with you. Speak to the business's customers and suppliers to find out what they think of the business. Contact the Better Business Bureau (www.bbb. org), industry associations, and any federal or provincial licensing bodies to see if any complaints have been made against the business. Search on Google, Bing, Yahoo!, and social media for reviews of the business.

What is the reason for the success of the business?

You want to make sure that the business has been successful because of a lasting reason. So here are some areas to check out:

>> Does the business have a great product or service — or was it built on a passing fad?

>> If the business was built on a small number of enthusiastic clients or customers, are they likely to stay on with you?

>> If the business was built on exports, what's the economic and political outlook for the countries where the exports go?

>> If the business has done well because it had little competition, is competition likely to increase in the future?

How's the neighbourhood?

Perhaps your main reason for buying the business is that it has a wonderful location that draws customers like a magnet, or it's perfectly placed for receiving supply deliveries and shipping out products. If so, be sure to check the terms of the lease for the location:

>> Is the rent reasonable? (And is it locked in, or what percentage increase could happen each year?)

>> How much time is left on the lease — and does the lease contain any rights to renew?

>> If the business is located in a mall, does the lease protect you from competition by other tenants?

>> Does the lease affect the hours you can or have to work? Some retail mall leases require storeowners to operate whenever the mall is open, and that may include evening and weekend hours you do not wish to work. Access to office, industrial, or warehouse space may be restricted to certain hours, and even if you can get in, the power, light, heat, air-conditioning, and elevators may not be operational.

If the location of the business is not the main reason you want the business, then make sure that the location is not a reason you'll come to regret your purchase:

>> If this business has been at its location for only a short while, what happened to the business that was there before? Does this location have a history of failed businesses? You want to be sure that the past success of the business wasn't tied to its previous location.

>> Does the municipality or landlord have any plans for the property that will affect traffic, parking, or access to the property? A major renovation of the building or major road construction or anything else that limits customer or supplier access could be bad news for you.

What do the financial statements tell you?

REMEMBER

When you're looking over a business, you should ask to see its audited and otherwise vetted financial statements for the preceding three to five years. The financial statements of a business contain information that will be very useful to you in deciding whether the business is worth buying at all, and, if it is, in deciding on the price you should pay. But you have to be able to understand the financial statements. Financial statements are introduced in Chapter 2 of Book 4, and if you don't know very much — or anything — about financial statements, flip to Chapter 2 of Book 4 now and read about them before continuing. For a more detailed look at these statements, check out the latest edition of *Bookkeeping For Canadians For Dummies* by Lita Epstein, MBA, and Cécile Laurin, CA (Wiley).

Have a professional accountant (Chartered Professional Accountant) or business valuation expert (Chartered Business Valuator) review the financial statements before you make a final decision to buy — even if you think you've got the business's financials all figured out yourself.

What is the "corporate culture"?

The employees of every business develop attitudes that govern the way they deal with management, customers, suppliers, and each other. In some businesses, management, staff, suppliers, and customers may treat each other like family. (We mean like family who like each other.) In others, they may treat each other very formally and follow a rigid structure. In a few, they may be engaged in guerrilla, or even open, warfare. Do you like what you see of the corporate culture? If you don't, do you think you will be able to change the culture — and still keep the business's staff, customers, and suppliers?

Culture is a set of values, beliefs, and attitudes shared by members of an organization. They are seen, heard, and believed (unconscious assumptions and beliefs). If you're buying a new business and wish to change the culture, focus on the first two levels (practices that are seen and/or heard) because unconsciously held assumptions and beliefs about a company are difficult to change.

Deciding on a Price for a Business

If you've checked out the business and are pleased with it, don't just say, "I'll take it!" You must first decide what the business is worth and what price you're willing to pay. Buying a good business for the wrong price can be as big a mistake as buying a bad business. This section tells you about different approaches to valuing businesses and where to find information on the value of a business.

Don't make a final decision to buy a business without getting professional help — from a Chartered Professional Accountant (CPA) and/or a Chartered Business Valuator (CBV) and/or a lawyer — perhaps from all three.

What's a business worth?

When you buy a business as a going concern, you're buying more than the physical assets of the business. You're also buying the business's *goodwill* — the likelihood that the business will be successful in the future. So in arriving at a price for a business, you have to find a price that includes both.

Valuing assets

You can value physical (or "tangible") assets in different ways, including the following:

>> **Fair market value** — the price you would have to pay on the open market for equipment or inventory of the same age and condition. This is usually the best way to determine what the assets are "worth," but the owner may expect you to pay more than the fair market value of the assets in order to get the business as a going concern.

>> **Replacement value** — the price you would have to pay for new inventory and equipment to replace what the business currently has. Generally, you would not pay replacement value when purchasing used assets. However, if the assets of the business are difficult to replace, that drives their value up.

>> **Book value** — the value at which the assets are shown in the business's balance sheet. It may be higher or lower than the fair market value of the assets.

Another is *liquidation value* — the price for which the equipment and inventory could be sold if the business were liquidated (turned into cash) — for example, in a bankruptcy. However, liquidation value is not normally used when the business is a going concern, because it's lower than fair market value.

Note that if you will be taking over the debts of the company (and that's the usual scenario if you buy a going concern), to arrive at a value for the assets you have to deduct the amount of debts from the value of the assets.

Valuing goodwill

If you're buying a business as a going concern, you're not just shopping for some equipment and inventory. You also want the business's goodwill, which is an "intangible" (untouchable) asset of the business. Goodwill is valuable because it affects the business's continuing success. Theoretically, goodwill is often defined as the likelihood that customers will keep coming back if you ceased advertising and promotion. From an accounting perspective, goodwill is the amount of money you pay to buy the business minus the fair market value of the tangible assets, the intangible assets that can be identified and valued, and the liabilities obtained in the purchase.

All of the following affect a business's goodwill:

» The customer base it has established

» The business's age and reputation, including its name and any trademarks or intellectual property that it possesses

» The location

» The exclusive rights the business might hold

» The talent of its employees

» The reliability of its suppliers

» The amount of competition the business faces

How do you place a value on the business, including goodwill? Most valuation methods involve examining the past earnings of the business as the best indicator of what future earnings are likely to be.

One valuation method that's often used is the *multiple of earnings* method. With this method, the business's earnings (its revenues less its expenses) over the past three to five years are averaged, and then that average is multiplied by a given number to arrive at a value for the business as a whole, not just for goodwill. The given number (known as a "multiple") varies from industry to industry. The best way to figure out the multiple for the business you're thinking of buying is to get information about recent sales of comparable businesses. (You get some suggestions for finding that information in the next section.) Divide the price for which a business sold by its average annual earnings. That will give you a multiple to use for this particular type of business. Other business valuation methods include discounted cash flow and capitalized cash flow, both outside the scope of this book but well within the scope of the work of a CBV or even a CPA.

TIP

After you come up with a proposed purchase price, check how reasonable it is by calculating the return you would likely get on your investment if you bought the business for that price. Take the average annual earnings of the company over the past three to five years and divide them by the proposed purchase price. That will give you the rate of return you may reasonably expect from your investment. (For example, if you're thinking about paying $250,000 for a business that has had average earnings of $15,000, the rate of return is 6 percent.) How does the rate of return compare to what you might earn on the same sum put into a different investment? Is the rate of return worth it when you take into account the work and risk involved in this particular business?

Sources of information for valuing a business

The best way to figure out what a business is worth is to find out how much comparable businesses have sold for. Unfortunately, getting sales information about businesses is harder than getting it about homes. Here are some possible sources of information about sale prices, and also about valuing businesses generally.

» Trade publications

» Businesses that you've looked at

» Accountants, lawyers, and consultants

» Business brokers

TIP

Using a Chartered Business Valuator (CBV) is probably your best bet. If you've reached the point where you're ready to make an offer, you should seriously consider hiring a CBV who will, for a fee, estimate the value of the business you're interested in. The amount of the fee varies with the size and complexity of the business, but may well be several thousand dollars. Your lawyer, accountant, or business consultant may be able to refer you to an appraiser or valuator. Or you can contact the Canadian Institute of Chartered Business Valuators (https://cbvinstitute.com) for a list of members in your province.

Considering a Franchise

A *franchise* isn't exactly an off-the-shelf business. It's more like a pre-packaged business — you add water and stir. The *franchisor* (the company that created and developed the original business) owns the business name and trademarks and practices and procedures; the *franchisee* (the "buyer" of the franchise that is essentially granted the rights to the franchise) gets a licence to use them. The franchisee pays an up-front franchise fee and then also makes continuing payments (royalties) based on the franchise's earnings. The franchisee sets up his or her own business, but sets it up as if it were part of a chain with one name and with standardized products, design, service, and operations.

Checking out the advantages of a franchise

Being granted the rights to an established franchise provides the benefits of belonging to a large organization, while still being your own boss, including

>> A business concept that has been thought out, and a product or service that has been researched and developed

>> A recognized business name, centralized advertising, and sophisticated marketing

>> Assistance, training, and support in management and production

>> Economies of scale in buying supplies and services, because purchasing is centralized

>> Assistance in choosing a business location (reputable franchises check out the strength of the local market before selling a new franchise in an area)

Investigating the disadvantages of a franchise

WARNING

Buying a franchise can sometimes lead to trouble for the franchisee because

>> Franchises like Harvey's are standardized operations, and standardization can be stifling to a business owner who has his or her own ideas.

>> Successful franchises like McDonald's are very expensive — and new franchises are a gamble because costs may be higher than expected and/or profits lower than expected.

>> Franchise agreements are always drafted by the franchisor and they favour the franchisor over the franchisee.

>> The franchisor may promise training and support, but they may not be as good or thorough as promised.

>> Franchisees may be charged more than the going market rate for supplies if they have to be purchased through the franchisor or specified suppliers.

>> Franchisees are often required to pay substantial amounts for advertising and they may not see that they're getting anything in return.

>> Sometimes the franchisor leases premises for a franchise location and subleases them to the franchisee. Then the franchisor can use its rights as a landlord to lock the franchisee out of the premises without notice if the franchisee doesn't make all the payments required under the franchise agreement.

» If the franchisor opens too many coffee shops in one area, for example, or starts distributing products through eBay or Shopify, it can drastically reduce the profits of franchisees.

» Franchisees often don't have special legislation to protect them against franchisors, because only about half of the provinces to date have passed franchise statutes.

Finding a franchise

Franchises are available in just about any business area, from accounting and tax services to pet care to lawn services to senior care services. So the first step in finding a franchise is to decide on the kind of business you want to be in. You find out about choosing your business in Chapter 1 of Book 1.

After you decide on the kind of business you want to be in, find out whether any franchises exist in that kind of business, and if so, whether any franchises are being offered in the location you're interested in.

You can look for franchises that are available in Canada in a number of ways:

» **Read franchise magazines:** A number of magazines are geared to people interested in buying a franchise, such as *Canadian Business Franchise Magazine* (www.franchiseinfo.ca), and *Franchise Canada Magazine* (http://franchise canada.cfa.ca), the official publication of the Canadian Franchise Association (CFA). These magazines and resources contain general information and advice about franchising and contain ads for franchises for sale.

» **Check a franchise directory:** The *Franchise Canada Directory*, published by the Canadian Franchise Association, lists available franchises.

» **Search the Internet:** Many websites contain information about franchises for sale. The Canadian Franchise Association's website (www.cfa.ca) contains a "Find a Franchise" feature that allows you to browse franchises either by name or by category. Only CFA members in good standing are listed. You can also check BeTheBoss.ca (www.betheboss.ca) or Franchise Solutions (www.franchisesolutions.com).

» **Visit franchise shows:** A number of franchise shows are held across Canada throughout the year, such as the National Franchise and Business Opportunities Show (www.franchiseshowinfo.com); and the Franchise Show, which is organized by the Canadian Franchise Association.

» **Use a franchise advisor:** Some accounting firms, such as BDO Dunwoody or Grant Thornton, provide help in finding and evaluating potential franchises. You can also find business brokers who deal in the resale of existing franchises.

Evaluating the franchises you find

A franchise is a very expensive purchase. Many require an investment of at least $100,000. And when you buy a franchise, you're not just purchasing a product and walking away; you're entering into an ongoing relationship, somewhat like a partnership. So you should be confident that you want to go into business with the franchisor. Make a list of the franchises you find, and then investigate each of them thoroughly and carefully.

What information are you looking for?

You should know a number of things about a franchise opportunity before you buy.

>> How does the franchisor make most if its money?

>> What is the franchisor's business record?

>> How much will the franchise cost, and does the franchisor offer any financing?

>> How much can you expect to earn?

>> What is the term of the franchise agreement?

>> Where will your franchise be located?

>> Will the franchisor train you?

>> What rights do you have to sell the franchise?

Where can you find it?

TIP

You can get your franchise information from several sources:

>> **The franchisor:** Alberta, New Brunswick, Ontario, Manitoba, British Columbia, and Prince Edward Island have franchise legislation or regulations that require a franchisor to give prospective franchisees a franchise disclosure document containing, among other things, the business backgrounds of the franchise and its directors, audited financial statements and credit reports, and copies of all franchise agreements. If you live in another province, but the franchise operates in Alberta, Manitoba, British Columbia, New Brunswick, Ontario, or Prince Edward Island, ask to see the disclosure document required in those provinces.

Canadian Franchise Association member franchises agree to abide by a code of ethics that requires full and accurate written disclosure to prospective franchisees. Ask the franchisor to provide you with the names and contact information of existing franchisees, and of financial institutions and suppliers willing to act as references. This is an important part of the franchise disclosure process. Be very suspicious if the franchisor is less than forthcoming about any of the information you request.

- » **Other franchisees:** Talk to several current and former franchisees either by phone or in person. How much did they have to invest? What were the hidden costs? How long have they been in business? How long did it take for the business to make a profit? Did they receive adequate training and ongoing support? Has the franchisor lived up to its side of the agreement? Would they advise you to purchase a franchise? Ask them if they would want to gain the rights to this franchise again if given the opportunity.

- » **The Internet:** Search the franchise on Google, Bing, and Yahoo!, and see what turns up.

- » **The Better Business Bureau and trade associations:** Check to see if any complaints have been filed against the company or its products with the Better Business Bureau in your area and the area where the franchisor's head office is located. Find out the franchisor's reputation within any industry trade association and within the Canadian Franchise Association and/or the International Franchise Association.

Doing due diligence before you sign

REMEMBER

Get advice from your accountant and your lawyer:

- » Have your accountant review the franchisor's financial statements to see if they disclose any problems, and to tell you whether the financial projections are based on reasonable assumptions.

- » Have your lawyer, one experienced in franchise law, review the franchise agreement. At the very least, your lawyer should make sure that you understand the agreement fully. If appropriate, your lawyer should try to negotiate necessary changes to the agreement.

Deciding on a Place of Business

You need to know the cost of your location to determine the financing you'll need for your business, and you may have to hold off on your final decision until you see how much financing you can get.

REMEMBER

When choosing your business premises, aim to spend as little as possible while making sure that your place of business satisfies the needs of your newly launched enterprise.

Working from home

There's no doubt about it — working from home is the cheapest way to go. With computers, high-quality multifunction printers, e-mail, and voice mail, a home-based business doesn't have to look like an amateur operation. And the Internet allows even the smallest company to have worldwide exposure. You can project a big business image even if your head office is the kitchen table.

In addition to cost, working from home has other advantages, too:

>> You'll be able to claim an income tax deduction (percentages vary by province) for a portion of the expenses of running your home, even though you would have to pay these expenses anyway.

>> You won't have the cost, irritation, and wasted time involved in commuting to and from work.

>> You'll have more flexibility to deal with your children, aging parents, or pets.

WARNING

Working from home does have some disadvantages as well, though:

>> You may have little, if any, room for expansion as your business grows.

>> You may find it hard to accommodate employees.

>> You may find that you need facilities and services that you can't have at home.

>> You may feel isolated from business associates.

>> You may find yourself not isolated enough from family and friends!

But you can overcome most of these disadvantages, and so you should operate your business from home if at all possible, at least in the beginning.

Space-sharing arrangements

If you can't work from home, it doesn't mean that you have to rent and equip your own retail store, suite of offices, or industrial space. You have other options for premises that may be of modest size, and cheap to rent and equip, and that may be available on a short-term basis. One of these arrangements may be right for you:

>> If you need office space, you may be able to sublet a single office from another business, or rent an office in a business centre or executive suite — the landlord provides reception services and use of a boardroom and office equipment (as part of your monthly rent) and access to secretarial and other support services (usually for an additional fee).

>> If you need retail space, you may be able to operate from a booth or cart in a shopping mall or in a pedestrian area. If your goods are seasonal, this may allow you to operate on a seasonal basis. A booth is also a good way to test your product before investing in a traditional store.

>> If you need industrial space, you may be able to use a self-storage unit for your warehousing needs and maybe even for some light manufacturing or assembly of merchandise.

TIP

If you need space for your business, you should see if a business incubator is right for you. These mentoring facilities usually provide flexible rental space and flexible leases for start-up businesses accepted into their programs. See Chapter 1 in Book 1 for more information about business incubators.

You can also rent space from a coworking space without being part of their start-up or incubator programs. Most coworking spaces allow you to pay a fee for the membership, and depending on your level you can choose a dedicated work spot, and so on. Meeting rooms are also available for rent. Coworking spaces often have cool vibes, and you could choose one based on who you might want to network with to grow your business. In Toronto, for example, Make Lemonade (www.makelemonade.ca) has created a vibrant coworking space for women entrepreneurs.

REMEMBER

After you finalize arrangements for the space, you will be entering into a contract. Make sure that the contract is in writing, that you understand it, and that it sets out all the terms that are important to you.

Renting business premises

If you can't work from your home or share a space, you'll have to look for business premises elsewhere. Different types of premises are available, and the type you choose will primarily depend on the nature of your business and where your customers typically work and live:

>> **Retail:** If your business involves selling directly to the public, you need retail space. You can find retail space in a variety of locations, such as indoor shopping centres, outdoor strip malls, free-standing buildings, airports, train stations, hotel lobbies, office buildings, university campuses, and theatres. You may also be able to set up a retail operation in an industrial plaza.

>> **Office:** You can find office space in downtown or local office buildings, business parks, above stores on streets with retail character, or in suburban shopping malls.

>> **Industrial:** If your business involves manufacturing or large-scale distributing, you'll need industrial space for your manufacturing plant or warehouse facility. Industrial parks or plazas are zoned by municipalities to offer space designed for light manufacturing operations and for businesses that need showroom as well as manufacturing facilities.

Most small businesses that need permanent retail, office, or industrial space rent the space (rather than buy). You should consider a number of factors before you rent space.

REMEMBER

When you rent business space, you enter into a contractual relationship with the landlord called a commercial tenancy, and you'll sign a contract called a commercial lease. Commercial tenancies are very different from residential tenancies. Commercial tenants don't have the legal protection from their landlords that residential tenants have.

Knowing what you're looking for

Before you start to look for rental premises, stop and think about your business needs:

>> What kind of space are you looking for — retail, office, or industrial?

>> What kind of image are you trying to project for your business — upscale, middle of the road, economy, grunge?

>> What location is most accessible to your potential clients or customers and employees?

>> What kind of parking do you need for yourself, your employees, and your clients or customers?

>> Is it best to locate near competing businesses or away from them?

>> How much space do you need now? How much are you likely to need in the future?

>> What kind of layout or floor plan do you need?

>> What are your electrical and plumbing requirements?

>> Will your suppliers need special access to make deliveries to you?

>> Are you willing to pay for improvements to the property you rent?

>> How long do you want to rent these premises for?

>> How much rent are you willing and able to pay?

Finding what you're looking for

TIP

To find commercial rental space, you can look at classified ads in the newspaper or on online classified websites such as Craigslist (www.craigslist.org) or Kijiji (www.kijiji.ca) under headings such as Commercial, Industrial Space, Office Space, or Stores for Rent. You can also search for those terms on the web, or you can drive around areas that seem suitable and look for For Rent signs. But your best bet is probably to use a real estate or leasing agent who specializes in industrial, commercial, and investment properties.

An agent will know what space is available and can save you time by weeding out properties that don't suit your needs or meet your budget, and by taking you to see only those properties that might be appropriate. If you find a property you're interested in, the agent can help you negotiate the deal.

Usually the real estate or leasing agent is paid a commission by the landlord if you enter into a lease. If the landlord's agent shows you a property, the agent is legally the landlord's agent, not yours. A landlord's agent still has a legal and ethical duty to answer your questions accurately and honestly, and can

>> Help you decide how much you can afford to spend

>> Help you screen and look at properties

>> Identify and estimate the costs involved in the transaction

>> Prepare offers or counteroffers on your instructions and present them to the landlord

However, a landlord's agent cannot

>> Recommend a price to you other than that set by the landlord

>> Negotiate on your behalf

>> Tell you the landlord's bottom-line price

>> Disclose any confidential information about the landlord

If you're working with the landlord's agent, you shouldn't tell him or her anything that you would not say directly to the landlord. If you'd rather work with an agent who represents only your interests, you can hire and pay for your own agent.

TIP

Look around before you choose your space, even if you think you know just the location you want or you've had your eye on some particular building for years. It may turn out that other premises actually suit your needs better or come at a better price.

Determining the cost of your space

The rent charged for business space varies widely based on the economy, the area of the country, the type of space, and the specific location, so looking around before choosing your space is important. A real estate or leasing agent can give you information about the costs of comparable space.

REMEMBER

If you're looking for office space, the cost will depend not only on the location of the building, but also on the "class" of the building. A new, tall, luxurious Class A skyscraper can cost quite a lot more than the perfectly respectable but older and smaller Class C building just across the street. Be sure to look at a range of buildings in several locations.

TIP

You may be able to find space in a building you're interested in at a lower rent than that offered by the landlord if you can find an existing tenant who wants to sublet the premises or assign the lease. You'll deal with the tenant rather than the landlord, and the tenant may have had a much better deal from the landlord than what the landlord would offer you as a new tenant.

If you're looking for retail space, the rent will vary by shopping area — so be sure to look at stores in a number of locations. You may be able to get the same type and volume of clientele in several different areas in town. When you find an area you like, be sure to compare the price of similar space in the same location.

Ownership Issues: Should You Go It Alone or Take on a Co-Pilot?

Before you can start your business, you need a vehicle for carrying on your business — a "form of business" or a "business organization." Only a few forms of business exist. After you've looked at all of them and thought about your own business circumstances, you can decide which form of business is right for you.

You'll often get asked, "What's your business?" But right now, the question is "Who's your business?" Is your business you and only you? Is it you and a pal? You and a group? If your new business is a team effort, you can skip ahead to

"Should You Incorporate?" now. If your new business is a one-person show, stick around and read this section.

Certainly, being the only owner of a business has its advantages. Here are just a few of them:

>> The profits of the business will be yours alone.

>> You have the only say in what the business does and you don't need anyone else's agreement to do what you want to do. So there.

>> Setting up a business with just one owner is usually easier, faster, and cheaper.

But here are reasons that you might want to, or have to, have a co-owner:

>> You may want someone else to share the financial risks of the business with you.

>> You may want company — being in business all by yourself can be lonely.

>> You may need someone else to provide skills or knowledge that you don't have.

>> You may want someone to share the workload.

REMEMBER

Ultimately, the reason you decide to go on alone or take a co-pilot with you should be that it will give your business a better chance of success.

Should You Incorporate?

"Should I incorporate?" is a very common first question that entrepreneurs ask, whether they're working alone or in a team. But it's not the right first question. It can't be answered in a vacuum. And before you even ask the question, you need to know about the alternatives to incorporation.

What are your options?

When you ask whether or not you should incorporate, what you're really asking is "What form of business organization should I choose?" You have choices, and the choices available to you depend on whether your business will have only one owner, or two or more owners.

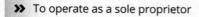

If you will be the only owner of the business, your choices are

>> To operate as a sole proprietor

>> To operate as a corporation that is owned by you

If two or more people will own the business, your choices are

>> To operate as a partnership

>> To operate as a corporation that is owned by you and your co-owner(s)

What's the difference?

The main distinction between a business that's incorporated and one that's not is that an incorporated business is a legal being separate from the owner of the business. So if you incorporate your business, your personal assets (property owned by you personally) and the assets of the corporation (property owned by the business) are separate. Your personal debts (money owed by you personally) and the debts of the corporation (money owed by the business) are also separate. In theory, then, your personal assets can't be seized to pay the debts of the business.

What many people don't realize is that, in practice, keeping the business debts of your corporation away from your personal assets is not always possible. Many people are also unaware that you can protect your personal assets without incorporating your business. (For more about this, see the later section "Protecting Your Assets without Incorporating.")

Here are two other main differences between an incorporated and an unincorporated business:

>> The profits of a corporation are taxed differently by the Canada Revenue Agency (CRA) than the profits of a business operated as a sole proprietorship or partnership.

>> The amount of paperwork increases greatly when you're setting up and running a corporation.

REMEMBER

Incorporation should not be an automatic step, because it may or may not make sense for you and your business.

The Corporation: A Form of Business with a Life All Its Own

A corporation is probably as close as most people will get to an alien life form, barring abduction by extraterrestrial beings for bizarre medical experiments. And it's not a joke when people call a corporation a "life form."

Understanding corporations

A *corporation* is a legal being that is created by the process of incorporation, and that has a separate legal identity from that of the individuals who create it and own it as shareholders. Even though a corporation is not human, it has many of the legal powers, rights, and duties of a Canadian resident. But because it is not human, it must act through its human directors and officers.

Corporations can be public or private. A public corporation, or offering corporation, can sell its shares to the public. A private, or non-offering, corporation is very limited in its rights to sell its shares. Whether you know it or not, if you're thinking about incorporating a new business, you're thinking about a private corporation. This section is talking about private corporations. Very few private corporations ever become public.

Who owns a corporation?

The shareholders of a corporation own the corporation through their ownership of shares in the corporation. The shareholders acquire their shares for a set price and they pay for them by giving money, goods, or services to the corporation. (The money and goods become the property of the corporation. Shareholders are not the legal owners of the corporation's property.) If the corporation is a failure, the shares will go down in value — maybe even down to zero — and the shareholders' investment will diminish and disappear. But the shareholders will not usually lose more than what they already gave in exchange for the shares, because they are not ordinarily responsible for paying any debts the corporation has.

Who runs a corporation?

Every private corporation must have at least one director, whose role it is to manage the corporation's affairs. No upper limit exists on the number of directors a corporation can have, but even big public corporations don't usually have more than 10 or 20. A director has a duty to be reasonably careful in running the corporation's affairs, to act in the corporation's best interests, and to carry out his or her duties honestly and in good faith. If a director doesn't fulfil these duties, the shareholders can take the director to court.

A director must be at least 18 years old, of sound mind, and not bankrupt. In federal corporations and in most provincial corporations, a majority of the directors must be Canadian citizens who reside in Canada; and in some provinces, at least one director must also be a resident of the province.

In many corporations, the director(s) and shareholder(s) will be the same people, so the people who own the corporation also run the corporation.

Setting up a corporation

You incorporate a business by filling out and filing incorporating documents with the government and paying government fees. You can incorporate your business as a federal corporation (in which case you file with the federal government) or as a provincial corporation (in which case you file with your provincial government).

TIP

In most provinces the incorporation forms are available on the government website, and the forms themselves look relatively simple to fill out. You don't legally need a lawyer to incorporate your business, but if you do it yourself you may make mistakes that will be difficult to correct later. We strongly suggest that you use a lawyer or at the very least a qualified paralegal.

After the documents are filed and the fees paid, the government will issue a certificate of incorporation or, in Prince Edward Island and Quebec, a charter by letters patent. This is the moment when your corporation is "born." Before it can actually start to carry on business, though, it has to have a first directors' meeting. At this meeting, the first directors pass the corporation's by-laws — the rules about how the corporation will be run — and make resolutions appointing officers of the corporation (such as the president, treasurer, and secretary, who will run the corporation day-to-day according to the directors' orders), among other things. You can buy standard printed by-laws and standard forms for the first directors' resolutions if you don't have a lawyer help you with the incorporation and this initial organization.

Running a corporation

You can't be freewheeling when you're running a corporation. You need to follow certain procedures and protocols for making decisions, keeping records, and telling the government what you've been up to. For example, you must

>> Hold directors' meetings as necessary to make decisions, in the form of resolutions passed by a simple majority of the directors, about the affairs of the corporation — although meetings can be bypassed if all the directors agree in writing to a resolution. (A "simple majority" means 51 percent.)

» Hold annual shareholders' meetings to elect directors, appoint (or dispense with) an auditor to examine the corporation's finances, and review the corporation's financial statements. Most shareholders' decisions are made by a simple majority vote. (Again, meetings can be bypassed if all the shareholders agree in writing to resolutions making the decisions.)

» Keep complete corporate records, including the incorporating documents, corporate by-laws, minutes of (a written report about what happened at) directors' and shareholders' meetings, and resolutions in writing.

» File required documents with the government, such as notices about changes that have occurred in the corporation. And if you don't file as required, the government can dissolve the corporation.

Protecting Your Assets without Incorporating

Most people incorporate to protect their personal assets in case their business has debts that it can't pay — but that strategy doesn't always work. And incorporating may not be right for you in any event (see the previous section for more). But all is not lost, because you can protect your assets without incorporating.

The classic method for protecting personal assets from business debts is to put those assets in the name of a spouse or other family member who is not an owner of the business. That means

» Legally registering the title to your home, cottage, or other real estate in the other person's name.

» Legally registering the ownership of your car, boat, or other vehicles in the other person's name.

» Changing your personal bank accounts or investment accounts so that they are in the other person's name only.

TIP

For this method to work, you must change ownership *before* your business runs into trouble. If you wait until your business starts to encounter financial problems, transferring your property to another person is considered a form of fraud, and anyone trying to collect money from you is entitled to have the property transfer set aside.

WARNING

After you put property into someone else's name, the property belongs to that person. So this approach involves risk. If your marriage or relationship with your family member falls apart, your property may disappear with the relationship. You have to decide what you're more worried about financially — the failure of your business or the failure of your relationship.

You can also protect yourself from certain financial liabilities through business insurance. See Chapter 3 in Book 1 for more on that subject.

Chapter **3**

Operating Your Business

ny business can be a risky business. Although you may have a risk-taking personality and an instinct to seize a small business opportunity (you wouldn't be going into business for yourself if you didn't), you don't want your business to run any risks that aren't identified, evaluated, and managed well. You do want to run your small business in a risk-aware way. This chapter shows you how.

This chapter also talks about managing your relationship with your customers or clients so that you'll both be satisfied. Customers and clients need special handling. On the one hand, you have to satisfy them — by providing good quality products or services and by treating them well. On the other hand, you have to get them to satisfy you — principally by paying you in full and in good time.

Your own business needs goods and services too. So finally in this chapter, you find out how to be a customer, and get the most out of your relationship with your suppliers.

Insuring against Your Risks

You would be correct to think that steering clear of risks seems to be counterintuitive to the fact that you're considering seizing an opportunity, which essentially means you're a risk taker. But the reason the two are *not* mutually exclusive; if you do seize the opportunity, you should do so in a risk-aware way. This means being aware of the brand-new set of risks you'll face when you start a small business and, therefore, seize an opportunity. So don't ignore risks. This chapter is dedicated to showing you how not to ignore them.

Risk awareness, to be clear, means actively managing risks you identified as being inherent in and pertinent to your business, assessing their likelihood and impact, finding ways to *mitigate* (reduce, eliminate, or transfer) those risks, and seeing if the *residual risk* left over (risk after mitigations are considered) is acceptable to your personal tolerance or appetite for risk. To be sure, this is extra work, just as many aspects of running your own business, involves extra effort. But rest assured that most businesses that fail do so because of significant risks that were not identified and managed, and this oversight resulted in severe or catastrophic outcomes like bankruptcy and insolvency. Ouch. So if you want to stay out of trouble's way, engage in and take very seriously this discipline that almost all successful businesses perform: *risk management.*

TIP

A useful acronym is RIM, short for "risk, impact, and mitigation," which answers the questions: "What can go wrong?" "How bad can it get?" "What are we doing about it?"

You can't eliminate every possible risk, even if you try. So you also need to pass at least some of your risks off to somebody else. Who's going to be stupid enough to take over your risks? In case you hadn't already guessed — an insurance company.

Do you already have insurance?

WARNING

You may think you've already got enough insurance to cover your business, but you probably don't. For example, if you're going to run your business out of your home, your home insurance probably doesn't cover your business. Most home insurance policies exclude or limit coverage for business activities. If you're going to use your car as a business delivery vehicle, your existing car insurance probably doesn't cover that kind of business use. Key people in your business may already have life insurance — but the beneficiary is unlikely to be your business: It's probably their family members or their estate.

Do you really need insurance?

Some businesses need certain kinds of insurance, whether they want it or not, because they're required to be insured under legislation governing their field, or under a contract they've entered into. (Commercial leases typically require the tenant to have insurance.)

But if you don't have to have insurance, do you need to have insurance? You don't need insurance against every risk. But insuring against certain risks makes a lot of sense.

Having insurance protects you from going out of business if you're sued and the court rules against you. And it also ensures that anyone you injure receives compensation for the damage you've caused.

TIP

For risks that are unlikely to materialize or that won't cause big losses, you can consider self-insuring. That means bearing the risk yourself. Sometimes a risk is so remote, or the loss is so small, that you're throwing away money taking out insurance against it. You're also self-insuring in a way if you choose a high insurance deductible. Until your loss is higher than the deductible amount of your policy, you can't make a claim. (A higher deductible means a lower premium.)

REMEMBER

You need to talk to an insurance agent or broker (agents work for just one company, brokers deal with several companies) about your business's needs. An agent or broker will help you evaluate the risks in your business and suggest what insurance coverage you need and in what amount. It is critical that you begin by knowing what perils (risks) you and your business face and, after that, which ones are insurable and to what extent.

Choose someone who is knowledgeable about your kind of business. Ask business associates for recommendations, and then make an appointment to talk to two or three of the agents or brokers recommended, before choosing one who seems best able to give you advice and find the coverage you need. Make sure the one you choose has errors and omissions insurance, as well as directors and officers insurance if you have a duly constituted board of directors. (Chapter 2 of Book 1 discusses incorporation issues.) Errors and omissions insurance protects you if you make a costly mistake and damages result. Directors and officers insurance provides coverage for defence costs and damages (awards and settlements) stemming from wrongful act allegations and lawsuits against a board of directors and/or its officers. Then, if the agent or broker makes a mistake in getting the right coverage, you'll be able to recover compensation for any damage you suffer as a result.

REMEMBER

You may need different insurance from year to year, so you should review your coverage annually with your agent or broker.

Examining different insurance policies

Various kinds of insurance policies are available. You can often get a package policy geared to your particular kind of business. For a home-based business you may be able to get a home business insurance package that provides coverage for things such as your business property (inventory, samples, supplies, filing cabinets, computers and software, tools, customers' goods) on and off the premises, loss of cash, business interruption if your home is uninhabitable, and legal liability (for products or services, or business-related accidents on the premises). Alternatively, you may be able to get an extension of your existing home insurance policy to cover your business. You may also be able to find packages for retail businesses, skilled trades, manufacturing, day care, or office-based businesses.

Separate kinds of coverage can come in packages or can be purchased on their own:

>> Insurance in case your business causes damage

>> Insurance against damage to your business, staff, and data

>> Insurance to protect the people working in your business

Making the Sale

Don't make the mistake of thinking that if a customer is interested in you and your product or service, you've already made the sale. You've still got some work to do. Briefly, here's what you or your staff should do:

>> Know your product or service thoroughly so that you're prepared to answer all questions about it and not have to give lame answers like "That's a good question" or "I can look that up for you." You may also want to include a list of FAQ's on your website if appropriate.

>> Listen to the customer or client so you know what he or she really wants, and gear your sales pitch to the customer's needs.

>> Propose a deal that you think will meet the customer's needs (and yours too, of course), and close the deal if the customer is willing to accept the offered terms and you're able to deliver on your commitment. (And try again if the customer isn't willing.)

When your customer agrees to buy the product or service you're offering, you have entered into a contract. After you have a contract, you have a legal obligation to deliver your product or service, and your customer has a legal obligation to pay you for it. (Find out more about contracts later in this chapter.)

TIP

Customer service is an important part of any business and of every stage of contact with your customers or clients. Your customers will get the first taste of your customer service when they make contact with your business and while you're making your pitch. Treat them properly. Don't keep them waiting. Greet them politely and then pay attention to them. They do not want to be ignored in favour of other customers or, even worse, your personal business. Listen to their concerns and show that you're interested in solving their problems rather than in simply making a sale. If customers or clients come to your place of business, make sure your premises are always clean, organized, and well maintained.

WARNING

Customer service doesn't end after the customer agrees to buy your product or service. You may still lose the sale if you take your customer for granted while processing the sale — for example, by taking too long to complete the paperwork or by failing to be attentive to the customer while he or she is waiting.

Documenting Your Agreement

One of the keys to good customer relations is to make sure that both you and your customer or client have a clear understanding of exactly what each of you is expected to do. What goods or services must you provide and when? What is the customer to pay? Does the customer have to do anything to enable you to do your work and/or deliver your product (for example, remove the old kitchen cabinets so that you can install the new ones, or provide certain documents for you to review), or does he just sit back until it's time to pay you?

The way to ensure clear expectations on both sides is to have a contract that both of you understand and are reasonably happy with. A contract doesn't have to be a pages-long document filled with small print and incomprehensible language. Contract documents and their contents vary from business to business. (In fact, a contract doesn't have to be in writing at all.) This section tells you about the things you should be aware of, no matter what form your contracts take.

Contracts for the sale of goods

You may be a manufacturer who sells your goods to wholesale or retail businesses, or you may have a retail business in which you sell goods to other businesses or directly to consumers. Every time you make a sale, you and your customer are entering into a contract for the sale of goods.

When you and your customer enter into a contract, you come to terms on many matters. All contracts for the sale of goods involve agreement about the following points, whether or not the contract is put in writing:

>> **The parties to the contract:** One party (you) agrees to provide the goods; the other party (your customer) agrees to pay for the goods. Your customer may be an individual, a partnership, or a corporation.

If it's a partnership or a corporation, make sure you're dealing with a person who has the legal authority to contract on behalf of the partnership or corporation. Be suspicious of someone who wants to sign but is not an officer of the corporation (for example, vice-president is a much more comforting title than administrative assistant), and ask for confirmation from a corporate officer that the person has delegated authority to bind the corporation.

>> **The goods being sold:** Include quantity, brand name, and model number, or any other important details.

>> **The price the buyer is to pay for the goods:** Any amounts for GST and PST, or HST, should also be identified, but separately from the basic purchase price. (**Note:** The buyer pays from the province it is being sold in not what province they might reside in.)

>> **The date(s) payment(s) is to be made:** If your contract doesn't address this question, provincial sale of goods legislation says that the buyer must pay at the time of delivery. If you agree to accept payment after delivery of the goods, your contract should set out the amount and date of each payment, and the interest rate being charged.

>> **The quality of the goods:** If your contract says nothing about the quality of the goods, provincial sale of goods legislation implies a promise on your part that the goods are of reasonable quality. If the goods turn out not to be of reasonable quality, the customer can return them and get his money back. If you want to limit your responsibility and the customer's right to return the goods, your contract needs to say so. For example, the contract might say that you will replace or repair the goods free of charge within 90 days after the sale if a defect in materials or workmanship exists. Or (if you are not the manufacturer) the contract might state that the buyer must deal with the manufacturer rather than you if anything is wrong with the goods.

Note that if you are selling goods to a consumer (rather than to another business), provincial consumer protection legislation will not allow you to limit your responsibility for the quality of your goods.

>> **The place and date that the goods are to be delivered:** If your contract doesn't address the place, provincial sale of goods legislation says that your customer must pick up the goods at your place of business. If your contract addresses the place but not the date, the legislation says that the goods must be delivered within a reasonable period of time.

>> **The right of the buyer to return the goods:** In the absence of a problem with the quality of the goods, a buyer has no right to return the goods unless the seller agrees to give that right. Your business should have a returns policy set out clearly in the contract — for example, no returns; or returns for exchange or credit only; or full returns, no questions asked.

If your goods will be shipped to your customer, your agreement must also deal with

>> How the goods are shipped

>> Who pays for shipping

>> Who bears the risk of damage or loss to the goods during shipping

TIP

Consider the customer relations aspects of your contracts:

>> Think about how your customers will feel about your contract terms before you finally decide on them. (For example, having a strict no-returns policy may cost you business.)

>> Make sure that your customers are aware of your contract terms (whatever they are) when they enter into the contract. (You may lose repeat business from a customer who doesn't notice that you don't take returns until the customer is standing in your store asking for his or her money back.)

Contracts for services

If your business is providing services to other businesses or consumers, you will be entering into a contract every time you agree to do work for your client.

REMEMBER

All of your contracts should be in writing, and the more complicated the deal, the more detail you will want in the contract. By putting the contract in writing, you and your client are forced to define the details of your agreement — and that's how you'll be sure that you really are in agreement. As you perform your services, your agreement will serve as a checklist of the work you are supposed to do. And, if a dispute occurs later on, a detailed written contract serves as evidence of what was in fact agreed to.

WARNING

Make sure each party has an original signed contract. Especially make sure that *you* have an original signed contract and that you keep it in a safe place. A client may lose his or her copy and then come up with all kinds of wild fantasies about what was in the contract in the first place.

Whatever kind of services you are providing, your contracts with your clients should always deal with the following terms:

>> **Who the parties to the contract are:** One party (you) agrees to provide the services; the other party (your client) agrees to pay for the services. Your client may be an individual, a partnership, or a corporation. If it's a partnership or a corporation, make sure you're dealing with a person who has the legal authority to contract on behalf of the partnership or corporation.

>> **What services are to be performed:** The contract should state in detail the nature of the services and (if appropriate) the standard of quality they must meet.

>> **What the services will cost:** The cost could be fixed, or based on the amount of time you spend doing the work. Have the contract show any amounts for GST and PST, or HST, but separately from the basic price for the services.

>> **How payment is to be made:** Will you be paid in full at the beginning, or paid in full at the end, or paid in instalments as you do your work or after you complete the work? If you will be paid in instalments as you provide the services, try to schedule the payments so that your costs are covered as you incur them and you are paid some of your profit as you go. If you agree to accept payment over time after you've finished providing the services, the contract should set out the amount and date of the payments, and the interest rate being charged.

>> **When the services are to be performed:** The contract should give a starting date, and perhaps an end date — especially if the customer needs you to finish by a certain date.

>> **What rights the parties have to change or end the contract:** You may want to give yourself the right to end the contract for certain reasons, and you may want to limit the customer's right to end the contract due to some sort of wrongdoing on your part. You may also want to give yourself the right to change the contract in certain circumstances — for example, the right to raise the agreed price if the cost of materials rises.

>> **What happens if you don't perform the services properly:** You may want to offer a *warranty*, under which you agree to remedy problems for a fixed period of time after your service has been performed. And/or you may want to limit what you have to do if a problem occurs — for example, reduce the agreed payment by a fixed maximum amount.

>> **What happens if you cause injury to someone or cause damage to property:** You may want to include in your contract an exemption or *exculpatory clause* that limits your liability if you cause damage or injury. (With or without an exemption clause, you should make sure that you have proper insurance in place, as covered earlier in this chapter.)

TIP

Lawdepot.ca is a great resource for sample contracts.

Speaking to your lawyer about contracts

Before you open for business, have your lawyer prepare your standard documents, such as sales order forms and invoices, and standard form contracts.

TIP

If a customer presents you with a purchase order form or standard form contract that you don't understand clearly and agree with fully, have your lawyer review it before you fill the order. Ditto if a customer wants to make a change to your standard sales order form or standard form contract. If the terms of the customer or client are unfavourable to you, you may be able to negotiate changes. You may also want to consult your lawyer if you are negotiating a contract that involves a lot of money or a long-term commitment.

Doing the Work

After you enter into a contract with a customer, you have to do what the contract says you will do. If you don't carry out your promises, even if you don't get sued, you won't stay in business very long.

Keeping customers happy

TIP

The first step in keeping your customers happy is to do what you agreed to do. However, just doing the work isn't enough if you want to be paid promptly and get repeat business and referrals from your customers. You must also keep an eye on customer service:

>> Don't make promises you can't keep.

>> Keep the promises you make.

>> Document all changes.

>> Communicate well.

>> If you make a mistake or miss a deadline, deal with it.

WARNING

Especially don't admit in writing that you did something wrong. Your words could come back to haunt you if you get taken to court over the mistake.

Dealing with unhappy customers

Even if you do everything right, you're still going to encounter unhappy customers. Sometimes things go wrong, and sometimes it's not even your fault. Sometimes you'll have a customer who is simply impossible to please. But you must be able to deal with complaints, whether or not they're justified.

TIP

Here are the keys to dealing with a difficult customer:

>> **Listen to what the customer has to say:** That's the only way that you'll learn what the problem is. Also, your customer may not be able to think about any kind of solution to his problem until he's had a chance to let off some steam.

>> **Show that you understand the customer's problem:** Say things like

- I understand.
- This must be very upsetting.
- I can see how frustrating this must be.
- I can sympathize with the way you feel.
- I'm sorry.

>> **Try to solve the customer's problem:** Before you come up with a solution, ask the customer what solution he or she would propose. See if you can reasonably do what the customer wants, or if necessary, politely ask the customer for a different solution.

In this type of scenario, where customers are unhappy, it's helpful to remember the three As: acknowledge, apologize, and assure. As mentioned earlier, make sure that you listen well to their concern and that you acknowledge what they said and understand their frustration. This extra step lets them know you empathize with them. Then apologize for what happened. When you show that you're truly sorry, acknowledge the concern, and apologize, the situation tends to defuse itself. Then you can proceed to solve the problem and protect your reputation.

WARNING

Customers will now often complain and leave negative reviews on social media before even addressing the company. It is important to monitor social media or set up automatic alerts to be notified when potentially damaging reviews appear. And when they do appear, be sure to respond. If they are false, you can usually also get them removed or dealt with.

TIP

Even if you decide that you never want to have anything to do with a particular customer again, and you doubt that the customer will ever refer any business to you, try not to send the customer away angry. You don't want him or her bad-mouthing you to potential customers.

Getting repeat business and referrals

If you want your customer to use your business again and refer other customers to you, first of all you've got to do your work right. But your relationship with your customers isn't over just because you've done your work and you've been paid. You have to go on paying attention to your customers.

Your customers may have questions or problems that come up days or weeks after you've provided the product or service, and even at that point it's still important to give them good service. If your customers think that you don't care about them once you've got their money, they're less likely to deal with you again or refer other customers to you.

TIP

And if your customer doesn't contact you, you should contact him or her. After delivering a product or performing a service, call to say thank you for the business and to ask whether he or she is happy with your work or product. As time goes by, contact your customers about new products or developments in your field that may be of interest to them. (Of course, you can do all of this only if you have permission to use a customer's contact information for these purposes.) Send holiday greeting cards, and, depending on how personal your relationship with your customers or clients is, perhaps birthday and anniversary cards as well (but only if you have collected birth dates and anniversary dates with consent, naturally).

Getting Paid

Often you won't get paid until after you do your work or deliver your goods, but that doesn't mean that you should put off thinking about payment until then. In fact, it's essential to lay the groundwork at the time you and your customer make your deal.

Planning to get paid

TIP

The best way to make sure that you get paid is to avoid situations in which you risk not getting paid. Here are some tips:

>> Turn some customers away if you don't have the time ability to do a job well, or if a customer can't really afford to pay for your services.

>> Make sure your agreements are fair to your customers.

>> Get paid up front if you can.

>> Don't be sneaky when you bill customers.

>> Don't extend credit.

>> Protect yourself if you do extend credit.

>> Do what you promised to do.

Collecting your accounts receivable

Your accounts receivable are money owed to you by your customers. It's often necessary to make a concerted effort to collect them. Nobody's keen on paying bills.

TIP

You (or your bookkeeper) have to establish a method for keeping track of and collecting what your business is owed. That includes the following:

>> Your outstanding receivables should be *aged* at least once a month. Calculate the number of days that every unpaid invoice has been outstanding (typically 30, 60, 90, or 120 days).

>> Have a policy about what to do with unpaid accounts when they have been outstanding for periods of time — for example: Add interest after 30 days (if your contract doesn't prevent that); send a reminder invoice requesting immediate payment (with interest) after 30 and 60 days; write a polite letter and make a follow-up phone call after 90 days; threaten legal proceedings after 120 days.

>> Cut off customers who don't pay within a certain time. Do not continue to ship goods or provide services to a customer who has not paid a bill already owing, or else insist on payment before delivery.

REMEMBER

If you are assertive in collecting an account, you may lose the customer. But keep in mind that a customer who doesn't pay is not the kind of customer you want.

Getting paid online

If you'll be selling goods through your website, you should have a way to get paid before you process your customer's order. You can either set up a credit card merchant account with a credit card company, or you can use a third-party credit card processing company.

Merchant account

Setting up a merchant account valid for accepting online credit card payments can be very expensive, because the risk of fraud is higher when you process credit card payments without seeing either the credit card or the purchaser. The application fee alone can be several hundred dollars. In addition, you'll have to pay a monthly charge *and* a percentage commission on each transaction. You can get information about setting up a merchant account with Visa at `www.visa.ca/en_CA/run-your-business/accept-visa-payments.html`, and with MasterCard at `www.mastercard.ca/en-ca/merchants.html`.

Stripe (stripe.com/en-ca) is also a very common way to accept credit card payments online.

Third party processor

When you use a *third-party processor,* your customer is directed to the processor's website to complete his or her payment. In return, you pay a transaction fee plus a commission to the processor for each payment processed.

PayPal (www.paypal.com) is one of the most popular third-party processors for small businesses. You might also want to investigate Canadian-based third-party processors such as PSiGate (www.psigate.com) based in Toronto, Ontario; and Bambora (www.bambora.com/en/ca) based in Victoria, British Columbia.

REMEMBER

If you use a third-party processor, you are not responsible for the security of your customers' credit card information, but you must still comply with the privacy provisions of PIPEDA by making sure via a written contract that the third-party processor complies with PIPEDA. For more information about PIPEDA, see the later section "Addressing Customer Privacy."

Apple Pay

Customers who use Apple products like iPhones can pay you in a really cool way. They can use their fingerprint or passcode or even face ID to confirm payment within the Wallet app on their iPhone 6 or above (and iPhone 10 and above for face ID), iPad Air 2, iPad mini 4, and iPad Pro to complete purchases protected by robust technology. In Canada, Apple Pay works with Visa, Mastercard, American Express, Interac, and other card providers.

Accepting Apple Pay is faster than traditional credit and debit card payment methods. Your customers can check out with a single touch or glance. Accepting Apple Pay is also more secure for your small business than accepting traditional cards because every transaction requires your customer's face ID, touch ID, or a passcode. In addition, you don't receive your customer's actual card numbers, so you aren't handling actual credit or debit card numbers in your systems, which protects you (and your customers) in the unlikely event that you get hacked.

TIP

If your small business is a store, you need to have a contactless payment–capable point-of-sale terminal to enable and accept Apple Pay. The full technical, financial, and other details are found at http://support.apple.com/en-ca/HT204274.

Addressing Customer Privacy

In the good old days, you could keep extensive files about your customers' birthdays, wedding anniversaries, and tastes in scotch. You could harass your customers by cold-calling their homes at dinner time, sell your customer lists to another business so *it* could harass your customers at dinner time, and much more — all without asking your customers' permission or risking more than a telephone receiver being slammed down. Alas, the good old days ended on January 1, 2004, which was the date that the federal *Personal Information Protection and Electronic Documents Act (PIPEDA)* came into force across Canada for all commercial activities. What with all the weekly news about data breaches by hackers, it's no wonder that this important piece of legislation is gaining in prominence, and in enforcement. This is another important section with yet another important message.

If you want to collect, and keep and use or disclose any personal (factual or subjective) information about an identifiable individual, you have to get that individual's consent beforehand, and even then you can use the information only for the purpose for which consent was given. And *even then* you can collect, use, or disclose the information only for purposes that a reasonable person would consider appropriate in the circumstances. The customer can call the Privacy Commissioner of Canada on you if you violate PIPEDA. (However, the Commish isn't necessarily a heavy by nature; he or she will work toward finding a solution to privacy problems and complaints, rather than immediately throwing you in jail . . . even if you probably should be thrown in jail. Having said that, the Commish is beginning to lose patience with the growing number of scofflaws, so beware.)

Personal information includes

>> Name, address, phone numbers, identification numbers (like a social insurance number or a driver's licence number)

>> Age, social status, ethnic origin, medical information and records

>> Income, or credit or loan records

>> Existence of a dispute between a customer and a business

>> Opinions, intentions, and comments (even the printable ones)

Personal information does not include the name, title, business address, or business telephone number of an employee of an organization.

Individuals have a right to look at the personal information that your business holds about them, and to correct any inaccuracies.

Note that if PIPEDA doesn't apply in your province — don't jump for joy yet. There's a stinger in the tail here: If the province has enacted legislation that the federal government has deemed "substantially similar" to PIPEDA. (In other words, this means that you may not have to comply with PIPEDA itself . . . just with PIPEDA under another name.)

A whole pile of responsibilities goes with PIPEDA. For quite a lot of useful information about privacy in the commercial sector, and how a business goes about complying with PIPEDA, go to the Privacy Commissioner of Canada's website at www.priv.gc.ca. Or you can call 1-800-282-1376.

Dealing with Suppliers

Unfortunately, when you're in business, being a customer doesn't automatically give you a licence to be demanding, snarky, and unreasonable (even if you see these as the defining characteristics of your own customers). Although you can indulge yourself occasionally, for the most part you're going to want to concentrate on building good relationships with your suppliers. Most businesses need suppliers as much as they need customers.

This section eases you into the supplier universe. You find out how to decide what products or services you need from providers, how to make up a list of providers of those products or services, and how to choose a suitable provider from your list.

Determining what goods and services you need

Some of the purchases you make for your business simply support your business — for example, furniture for your office, computer peripheral devices, or office supplies or courier services. When you buy these goods and services you're essentially a consumer, and you'll make your purchases the way you'd make any consumer purchase — such as groceries or an oil change — by looking for a supplier with the best combination of price, selection, quality, service, and convenience. If you're not happy with the supplier, just go to someone else the next time you need to make a similar purchase.

But your business may (also) need specialized products, and their providers may be choosy about the businesses they deal with or the terms on which they deal with them. They may also not be easy to find.

Goods and services that don't just support your business but almost are your business are

>> The things you sell, called *inventory*, such as shoes for a shoe store, greeting cards and wrapping paper for a card store, ready-made desserts for a food shop

>> Parts and materials you use to make your product, such as the leather for making shoes if you're a shoe manufacturer, the paper for printing cards if you run a printing shop, fresh fruit and baking supplies if you have a dessert bakery

>> Ongoing services you need for your business operations, such as an Internet service provider for a web-based business, a pest-control service for a restaurant, or a window display service for an upscale clothing store

TIP

Before you decide on what your particular business needs, do some research to find out what businesses in your field generally need. You can get help from the following sources:

>> **Trade associations:** Find the trade association for your industry using Innovation, Science, and Economic Development Canada (www.ic.gc.ca) or use a search engine such as Google (www.google.com), Yahoo! (www.yahoo.com), or Bing (www.bing.com) to locate the association's website. The website may have useful information or contact information if you want to speak directly to someone at the association. Many trade associations hold seminars and workshops. Contact the association to find out if they have seminars on necessary supplies and services.

>> **Trade publications:** Many trade associations publish journals and/or newsletters with current information about the industry. These publications contain advertisements for equipment and supplies used by businesses in the field, and may contain articles from time to time about useful products and services.

>> **Trade shows:** Most trade associations hold an industry-wide trade show at least once a year. They are a good place to make contacts in the industry and learn about the latest trends in the field.

See Chapter 1 in Book 1 for more about researching your business online.

Finding suppliers

TIP

After you have an idea of what goods and services you need, you have to find a business that offers them. You can locate suppliers in a number of ways:

>> Speak to colleagues in your field.

>> Contact your trade association.

>> Read trade publications.

>> Go to trade shows and conventions.

>> Use a searchable Internet database like Thomas (www.thomasnet.com).

>> Search the Internet.

>> Search on www.yellowpages.ca to find the locations and phone numbers of suppliers in your local area.

Gather the names of a number of suppliers and make a list.

Choosing a supplier

After you figure out what you need and see who's selling it, you have to narrow your list of suppliers down to the supplier who's right for you. Take care, because this is a supplier with whom you'll be dealing on a regular basis and on whom you'll depend to keep your business in business.

WARNING

If you rely on a single supplier for any of your important needs, you can run into serious problems if deliveries are interrupted for any reason. Sometimes you may have no choice about whom you deal with because only one supplier has what you need. Other times, you may be seduced into committing to a supplier because you're offered very good terms if you agree to deal with that supplier exclusively.

TIP

If you do deal with just one supplier, try to stay informed about other available suppliers, just in case you need them.

Inventory and parts suppliers

When you're deciding on a supplier of inventory or parts for your business, be sure to consider all of the following:

>> Does the supplier have the full range and selection of products that you need?

>> How competitive are the supplier's prices? Does the supplier ever offer any specials? Do large or standing orders receive discounts?

>> How reliable is the supplier? What is the supplier's track record for filling orders completely and on time?

>> Does the supplier have a robust and modern online e-commerce platform with electronic payment capabilities, and a decent web presence that includes multiple contact and communication channels? Does the supplier have an online catalogue you can conveniently browse? Does it take protection of your digital payment and personal information seriously?

>> What is the supplier's delivery time from the date an order is received until the date it's shipped? How are goods shipped? Who pays for shipping?

>> Will you be able to return or exchange defective, damaged, non-selling, or overstocked merchandise? If so, who pays for shipping, and will you have to pay a restocking charge?

>> Does the supplier provide good customer service? Will the supplier give reliable advice about what you should purchase? If you're buying complicated equipment, either for your own use or for resale to your own customers, does the supplier offer training in the operation of the equipment to you and your employees or to the customer? Does the supplier have a good reputation for responding to customer complaints?

>> Does the supplier extend credit? What do you have to do to establish credit? When you're granted credit, can you get a discount for cash payments on delivery or for early payment?

>> If you're buying goods for resale, does the supplier offer any advertising support?

Ask potential suppliers for names of customers you can contact for references.

Service suppliers

With some service suppliers you may have a close working relationship — that might be the case with a pest control company or a security firm or a window dresser. But some of your service suppliers may almost end up living in your back pocket — they'll be more like employees of your business than independent businesses themselves. If you hire a business that provides secretarial or bookkeeping services or provides support for your hardware and software, you may be dealing with your supplier almost every day.

Take special care in choosing a supplier who will become an integral part of your business. To avoid unpleasantness, when you're deciding on a supplier of services for your business, consider the following:

>> Does the supplier offer the services that you need?

>> How competitive are the supplier's prices?

>> How reliable is the supplier?

>> Does the supplier stand behind his or her work?

>> Will it always be the same individuals performing the work?

>> Does the supplier extend credit?

Ask for names of customers you can contact for references.

Establishing credit with your suppliers

Most businesses like to have some flexibility when it comes to paying their bills. When you're the supplier, cash on delivery is very nice. But when you're the customer, you'd much rather have time to make your payments. You may need the time to collect your own accounts receivable so that you'll have money in the bank when the supplier cashes your cheque.

As a new customer, you may not be able to get credit from a supplier immediately. You may have to put up with being a COD (cash on delivery) customer until the supplier has had a chance to look you over and decide that you won't take the goods or services and then skip town without paying. After the supplier stops being suspicious of you, you may be granted a line of credit so you no longer have to pay on delivery. The supplier may first ask for financial statements and credit references. (If your business is just starting, you'll show your supplier your projected statements and you'll offer personal credit references instead of references for your business.)

After you've got credit, the supplier will still invoice you for the product when it's delivered or for the services when they are provided. But you'll be allowed a grace period (usually 30 days) in which to pay the bill without interest being charged. If you pay the bill before the 30 days are up, you may be given a discount. Suppliers commonly give a discount of 2 percent if a customer pays within ten days.

TIP

When you first get your credit, make sure that you pay your bills on time. Then you'll be able to use the supplier as a credit reference for new suppliers. Over time, you'll acquire a good credit rating and suppliers will be able to get credit information about you from credit rating agencies instead of from your suppliers.

Establishing a good relationship with your suppliers

TIP

When you find suppliers you're happy with, you want to make sure that you do what you can to establish a good working relationship. Here are some tips:

>> Be clear about what you need and when you need it every time you place an order. Confirm that the supplier has or can get what you're ordering and can deliver on your schedule.

>> Communicate with your supplier. If you have a minor problem, let your supplier know. Don't wait until you accumulate many minor problems or until a minor problem becomes a major problem. Let your supplier know sooner rather than later, because doing so gives the supplier a better chance to correct the problem.

>> Don't squabble over every invoice, or try to get price reductions on everything you buy. Your supplier will quickly get tired of you, and call you unpleasant names behind your back, and won't be in a big hurry to offer you discounts or other freebies that come along. The supplier may even fire you!

>> Pay your bills promptly. If you know that you're going to have a problem paying on time, let your supplier know, especially if it's a temporary problem that you'll be able to fix.

>> Treat the supplier's sales and service representatives courteously, even if you have a complaint.

>> Ask for special service only when you need it. Don't ask for last-minute deliveries or extra goods or services unless you're in an unusual situation.

In return, you expect quality goods or services, reliably delivered. Over time, as a valued customer you should expect some extra service. You would like your supplier to

>> Tell you about new products that become available

>> Tell you about discounts, rebates, or special deals on products you often buy, or that might be of interest to you

>> Advise you of any possible delays in delivery before they happen

>> Help you out if you occasionally need extra inventory or immediate delivery

>> Be flexible if you have an occasional problem paying a bill on time

As a new, and perhaps small and rather insignificant, customer, you can't immediately expect the same kind of service a long-standing customer would get. Building that kind of relationship takes time, so be patient.

TIP

If a supplier does not meet your expectations of quality, price, service, and reliability, don't fume, don't fight . . . just find another supplier. It's important from a business continuity perspective to keep your bases covered — even if things are going well with your suppliers, try to stay informed about other suppliers in case you need them one day. It just makes good business sense to do so.

TIP

If you ditch a supplier with whom you've had a long-term or important relationship, show good business etiquette and inform the supplier that you're moving on.

Chapter **4**

Looking to the Future of Your Business

N
o matter how careful you to try to be with your business affairs, problems can — and do — arise from time to time. This chapter discusses some of the trouble that a business can encounter.

In this chapter, you also briefly stop with the doom and gloom and get to the exciting possibility of growing your business.

No Money, More Problems

So your creditors are after you. They want their money and you haven't got it at the moment. What's going to happen and what can you do?

TIP

Even though you may be broke, consider talking to your lawyer. Borrowing and lending are subject to legal rules and you may be in a better position than your creditor thinks (and your creditor may be in a worse position). Your lawyer may be able to help you negotiate an extension of the deadline for repayment, or more favourable repayment terms.

REMEMBER

Don't fight your creditors out of sheer pig-headedness. If you lose the fight, you'll owe even more money — because creditors are usually allowed to pass on the cost of collecting their debts to you, the debtor. (And you'll still have to pay your own legal fees.)

Your business can't make a payment that's due

If you borrow money, you're expected to repay it. If you don't repay, the lender is liable to get a little exercised. But what the lender can do depends on the nature of the lender and the loan. If you end up getting sued, see the later section "Litigation." And, because you can try to work out a deal with your creditor, check out the later section "Negotiation of a settlement."

A payment on a loan from a non-commercial source

You got *love money* from a family member or friend to set up your business but the lender doesn't feel so loving now — maybe he needs the cash desperately, or maybe you've ticked her off by not taking her canny business advice.

Besides giving you the cold shoulder, the lender can sue for return of the money. This is true whether or not you have a written contract. An *oral contract* (a contract made through conversation) is as valid as a contract in writing. Although proving the terms of an oral contract is more difficult because no one wrote them down, your lender is legally able to tell the court about the conversations you had when the loan was made (the terms of the loan agreement will be the lender's word against yours). Your lender can require other people who have heard you talk about the loan to repeat in court what they heard. Also, your lender can show to the court documents such as a note or letter you wrote to the lender acknowledging the loan or saying that you would pay the money back.

So don't ignore the lender or tell him to buzz off. If you have no money to pay now, try to reach an agreement:

>> See if the lender will agree to wait a few weeks or months until you do have the money.

>> See if the lender will agree to accept smaller payments over a longer term, or smaller payments now and "balloon" payments later to make up for the smaller payments now.

>> Offer something other than money in full or part payment of the loan — something you own or the business owns, or your services for free.

>> Offer security for the loan, such as a mortgage on property you own; or offer a share in your business (although doing these things could create more problems for you in the long run).

Then put into writing the agreement you've reached, and sign it and have the lender sign it. Each of you should get and keep an original of the signed agreement.

A payment on a loan from a commercial source

If you have a commercial loan, you probably agreed to pay it off in instalments, so you may think that not being able to pay one instalment is not such a big deal. You're wrong. Most commercial term loans have an *acceleration clause*. That means that the lender can demand that you repay the entire loan as soon as you miss one payment by more than a few days. And if you have a line of credit, it's probably repayable on demand — so you don't even have to miss one payment before the lender has the right to tell you to repay the full amount.

If a lender demands repayment and you can't repay, the lender has the right to sue you for the outstanding amount of the loan, plus interest owing, plus the lender's costs of collecting the debt from you. If you've given security for the loan (a *right against property*), your agreement with the lender probably allows the lender to realize on the security after you miss a payment. That means that the lender, after demanding repayment of the loan and waiting a few days for payment:

>> Can take property you offered as security and either keep it or sell it (or start a lawsuit for possession of the secured property if you won't let the lender have it)

>> Can demand that a person who guaranteed the loan pay back the loan (plus interest)

>> May be able to appoint a receiver/manager to take possession of the secured property and sell it, depending on the terms of the loan agreement

If a lender seizes secured property, you may have the right for a short period (a couple of weeks) to get the property back by paying what you owe plus interest and costs. If the lender sells the property, it has to make sure that it gets a fair price, and afterward has to account to you for the property. The lender is not allowed to keep more than it's owed (don't forget that this includes interest and the costs of taking and selling the property), and it has to pay you any surplus from a sale.

If you know that you don't have the money to make a payment, but you think that you'll have money soon to get back on track:

>> First, try to find the money for the payment from another source, if you can.

>> Then, if you can't get money from another source, talk to your lender before the due date of the payment that you're going to miss. The lender may agree to overlook your default for a short time, especially if you offer some additional security.

Be careful about borrowing more money and offering more security for a loan that you're already having trouble repaying. You may be digging yourself deeper into a hole and you may lose more in the long run.

If you're in a really bad financial position and you don't think that a little extra money or a little extra time is going to do anything but delay bigger trouble, you should think about making a proposal to all of your creditors or even going bankrupt (see the later section "Your business is insolvent").

A payment for an asset bought on credit

If you've bought assets (such as equipment or vehicles or furniture) for your business and are paying for them over time, you've almost certainly entered into a financing agreement such as a *chattel mortgage, conditional sales agreement, purchase money security interest,* or a *lease with an option to purchase.* If you stop making your payments, the other party to the financing agreement can

>> Sue you for the full amount still left to pay (plus interest)

>> Seize the asset and sell it (and account to you after the sale)

The best you can do is see if the financer is willing to give you more time to pay (and then try to find some money).

A payment under an equipment lease

If your business leased assets instead of buying them outright or on time, you're not in any better position if you stop making your regular payments. The terms of a commercial asset lease normally don't allow you to stop making your lease payments for any reason — including the fact that the asset is broken or defective and the fact that you have no money. You have to make all the payments for the full term of the lease. If you miss a payment, the lessor can

>> Sue you for the full amount owed under the lease

>> Seize the asset (and, if you have an option to purchase, sell it and attribute it to you)

Again, the most you can do is try to negotiate more time to pay, and look for some money to pay with.

You've personally guaranteed a debt for your business and your business can't pay

If you've given a personal guarantee for a business loan and your business can't make a payment, the lender can demand payment from you. If you don't pay, the lender can sue you for the full outstanding amount of the loan, plus interest. If you gave security (such as a mortgage on your home) as well as guaranteeing the debt, the lender can realize on the security you provided.

WARNING

If you've co-signed a loan with your business, the lender doesn't even have to wait for your business to miss a payment — it can demand that you make the payment instead, because you're equally responsible for the loan from the get-go.

Note that if you're a member of a partnership, in most provinces the partners are individually responsible for paying debts of the partnership if the partnership itself can't pay.

Your business can't pay its rent

If you can't pay the rent owing under your commercial lease, your landlord can do a variety of nasty things to you, including

>> Sue you for *arrears of rent* (rent owing) or for *damages* (money compensation) for breach of the lease, while letting you stay on under the lease.

>> Retake possession of the premises and terminate the lease.

>> Retake possession of the premises and terminate the lease with notice for future loss of rent.

>> Retake possession of the premises without terminating the lease, and re-letting the premises acting as your agent (you remain responsible for the rent, minus whatever the landlord collects from the new tenant).

>> *Distrain* (seize and sell your property on the premises) to satisfy arrears of rent.

TIP

If your landlord terminates your lease, retakes possession of your premises, or distrains, consider seeing a lawyer to find out whether the landlord is within his rights. Landlords sometimes ignore the fine print of the law, and you may have some rights of your own.

Your business can't pay a mortgage on real property

If you took out a mortgage to buy real property for your business and you can't make your payments, the *mortgagee* (the lender) has the right in many provinces to *foreclose* on the mortgage (become the legal owner of the property), or to sell the property — under court supervision in a *judicial sale,* or privately under a *power of sale*.

TIP

If the mortgagee starts a legal action for foreclosure or judicial sale, you can stop it by paying off the entire mortgage, or in some cases by paying the payment(s) you missed plus a penalty. If you can't pay the entire mortgage immediately, you can ask the court for a delay (from about two to six months) to come up with the money. You can also stop foreclosure by asking for judicial sale. If the foreclosure goes through, in most provinces your mortgage debt is cancelled and you don't owe the mortgagee anything, even if the property is worth less than the debt you owe (however, the mortgagee doesn't owe you anything if the property is worth more than the debt you owe). If the property is sold in a judicial sale, any money left over after payment of the mortgage debt plus interest plus legal costs is yours; but if a shortfall remains, the lender can require you to make it up.

Most mortgagees prefer to act under a power of sale, if they can, because they don't have to go to court to sell the property. The lender has to notify you that it's going to exercise its power of sale, and you'll be given a short time (about a month) to stop the sale by paying off the mortgage or, in some cases, by making up the payment(s) you missed. As with a judicial sale, the proceeds from the sale will be used to pay the outstanding amount of the mortgage, as well as interest and costs; the mortgagee can sue you for any shortfall, but if money is left over, the mortgagee has to return it to you.

TIP

If the mortgagee wants to sell the property, see if it will let you try to sell the property yourself first. Buyers may think they can get a good deal and may offer a lower price when they see it's a judicial sale or sale under a power of sale. The more money the property sells for, the less you'll owe the mortgagee or the more you'll get to keep.

Your business can't pay its taxes

The Canada Revenue Agency (CRA) has a *statutory lien* against the personal property (as opposed to real property, or real estate) of a taxpayer who does not pay taxes or remittances that are due. This lien lets the government seize your business's personal property — which is your personal property, if you're a sole proprietor or partner — after giving 30 days' notice (during the notice period you can pay up and avoid the seizure).

If you own real property in a municipality and you don't pay your property taxes, the municipality will almost certainly add interest charges and penalties to your property tax bill. If you still don't pay your taxes, the municipality has the right to sell your real property. (The municipality doesn't get to keep all the money from the sale, only the amount that you owe in taxes.)

Your business is insolvent

Your business is insolvent if it owes at least $1,000 and cannot pay its debts and obligations as they become due. Being insolvent in itself isn't so wrong (apart from the fact that you have no money), but if you're insolvent, you're in danger of being forced into bankruptcy (covered later in this chapter). A creditor to whom you owe more than $1,000 and who has no security from you for the debt can petition your business into bankruptcy if your business commits an act of bankruptcy — such as not paying a debt when it's due or not complying with a court order to pay a creditor who's won a lawsuit against the business, or telling a creditor that you're not going to pay your debts, or hiding or disposing of property to avoid paying a creditor.

If you're dealing with unsecured creditors

If you're insolvent, what can you do before someone petitions you into bankruptcy? You can try to reach some kind of agreement with your creditors — for example, that they'll give you more time to pay, or accept part payment of your debt. Put any agreement into writing. By the way, your creditors won't likely be interested in cutting you any slack unless your business has decent prospects.

TIP

If your business does have prospects, it might be wise to get some advice from a lawyer who specializes in insolvency, or from a *licensed insolvency trustee* who deals with businesses (rather than with consumers). Your advisor might recommend making an informal offer to your creditors, or a formal proposal under the *Bankruptcy and Insolvency Act* (see the next section).

If you're dealing with secured creditors

If you're insolvent and a secured creditor notifies you that it's going to realize on its security, you should consider making a formal proposal under the *Bankruptcy and Insolvency Act*. If you do nothing, your secured creditors are going to make off with the secured property, and you probably need it to keep your business running. You should get a trustee in bankruptcy to advise you and to file in bankruptcy court a *notice of intention to make a proposal*. After the notice is filed, your business has some protection from secured and unsecured creditors for at least a month:

>> Creditors can't seize any property.

>> Companies that supply utilities such as electricity, heat, water, and telephone can't cut off service.

>> Parties to contracts with your business can't terminate the contracts or invoke *acceleration clauses* (an acceleration clause makes a debt you're paying off in instalments come due all at once).

On the downside, you have to pay cash up front for any supplies you buy.

WARNING

After you file your notice of intention, you have to file the actual proposal, and then your creditors meet within about three weeks to vote on it. Here's another downside to the proposal process: If your secured creditors reject the proposal (even if your unsecured creditors don't), they can immediately realize on their security. In addition (as if you needed an addition at this point), your business is deemed to have made an *assignment in bankruptcy* (a transfer of its property to the trustee in bankruptcy) and will be officially declared bankrupt.

You can choose to go bankrupt

You can be forced into bankruptcy, but you can also choose to go into bankruptcy by making an assignment in bankruptcy. Why would you actually want to go bankrupt? Well, when a court declares you bankrupt, your trustee in bankruptcy deals with your creditors. Your trustee will make arrangements to sell the business's property to pay the debts. And you'll be able to start over again.

If you're carrying on business as a sole proprietorship or a partnership, you'll go bankrupt as an individual. If you're carrying on business as a corporation, the corporation will go bankrupt. As an individual you'll probably be discharged from bankruptcy after nine months, and if you receive an absolute discharge, almost all of your debts are cancelled. (If you receive a conditional discharge, you'll still be responsible for repaying certain debts — income taxes, for example.) A corporation can't be discharged until it has paid all its debts, but you can always start up a new corporation (however, you may find that the creditors you stiffed won't be very anxious to deal with your new corporation).

See the next section for more about bankruptcy.

You have (or choose) to file for bankruptcy

After the bankruptcy court has made an order that your business is bankrupt, it appoints a trustee in bankruptcy. The trustee becomes the legal owner of all the unsecured property that formerly belonged to your business (and to you if your business is a sole proprietorship or a partnership — see Chapter 2 in Book 1) and it uses the property to pay off debts. Your secured creditors keep their rights over secured property — it doesn't go to the trustee.

If you're a sole proprietor or partner and you go bankrupt, you'll be allowed to keep some personal property — about $5,000 to $10,000 worth (depending on the province) of clothing, furniture, and other household items, as well as "tools of your trade" and, in many provinces, a car.

WARNING

If your business is a corporation and you're a director, you may not escape having to make some payments personally if your business goes bankrupt. You'll be held responsible for up to six months' worth of unpaid wages for employees, for unpaid amounts owed to the CRA for income tax and GST/HST, Canada Pension Plan and Employment Insurance, and for unpaid provincial sales tax owed to your provincial department or ministry of finance. And that's on top of paying any business loans for which you gave a personal guarantee.

If your business disposed of any property to save it from creditors, you can be personally charged with a criminal offence. And your trustee in bankruptcy can sue to get his hands on property that was improperly transferred away from the business, so that it can be distributed among the creditors.

WARNING

If a person or business is an undischarged bankrupt, he, she, or it can't borrow more than $500 without telling the lender about the state of bankruptcy (and not telling is an offence punishable by a fine or imprisonment). If a person is an undischarged bankrupt, he or she cannot be the director of a corporation.

Handling Disputes

Suppose that somebody doesn't like what you've done (or what you've charged). Or you don't like what somebody else has done (or charged). Maybe you feel like a fight . . . maybe you don't. But you're a businessperson, not a doormat, so you have to do something.

Disputes can escalate and end up in court, but they don't have to. (On the other hand, some disputes belong in court.) This section leads you through the mechanisms available for resolving a dispute. They range from negotiation of a settlement through mediation and arbitration, and all the way to litigation.

REMEMBER

But before you go any further, consider the following two things about any dispute you get into:

>> **Wrap it up in writing.** If you and the other side reach an agreement, write it down. A written document will help keep the resolution from unravelling and will be valuable evidence if the dispute erupts again.

>> **Learn from this experience.** Ask yourself what you can do to prevent a dispute like this from occurring again.

Negotiation of a settlement

When you find yourself in a dispute, before you start shouting "I'll see you in court!" (or before anyone else starts shouting it), consider whether the dispute can be cleared up through negotiation.

The traditional way to negotiate a settlement is for each side to state what it wants and then use whatever power it has at its disposal to persuade or force the other side to agree. The sides sometimes exaggerate what they want so they'll have maneuvering room if they're forced to make a compromise. The purpose of traditional negotiation is to win, not necessarily to solve the problem effectively.

The following sections give you some help to learn how to be a successful negotiator without upsetting the traditional negotiation pattern too much. You discover various negotiation techniques, including how to focus not on what you want (or on what the other side wants) but on interests that you and the other side may have in common.

Preparing for negotiations

TIP

If you want to be successful in your negotiation, you can't just rush in punching as soon as the bell sounds — first, you have to prepare to negotiate. Preparation involves two steps: studying the situation and planning your moves. When you study the situation, you will

>> **Gather information about the matter in dispute.** If you've got the facts at your fingertips you'll be much more effective at arguing for the resolution you want.

>> **Separate your *position* in the dispute from your short-term and long-term business *interests*.** Your position, for example, might be "I want to be paid the full amount for the work I did." Your interests are a lot more various — they might include needing X dollars to keep the business running, or wanting to keep a customer.

>> **Think about what the other party's business interests are.** Just like you, they have lots of different interests, and you can use that fact to help find a solution that gives something to both parties.

>> **Think about your goals in this negotiation.** Again, your goals are different from a position. For example, a position would be "I want to be paid the full amount for the work I did." Your goals might be getting as much of the full amount as possible while keeping the customer.

>> **Gather information about the other party in the dispute.** Get information about the business *and* about the individual you're going to be dealing with. Talk to people who know them or have dealt with them.

>> **Think about the side problems you may encounter in the negotiating process and how you might deal with them.** For example, a history of bad blood exists between you and the person you'll have to negotiate with, or the person you're supposed to negotiate with doesn't have authority to make a deal with you.

>> **Think about the leverage you can use to argue for your interests.** No matter how grim things look for you in the dispute, you've probably got something to use. Leverage includes things like contract wording that supports your position, or law (either legislation or court decisions) that supports your position.

Planning

Next, you plan — but if you did all that preparation, the planning is easy. Here are the steps:

1. Create a list of alternatives to the position the other side is taking or is likely to take.

2. Choose your own opening position.

3. Marshal the arguments you think you can use to persuade the other party of the strength of your position; use the list of leverage you made in the planning stage.

Opening discussions

REMEMBER

Don't let discussions get under way until you're ready. If you haven't finished your planning and preparation when the other side announces that it's ready to negotiate, tell them that you have to look into the matter and will be back in touch as quickly as possible. If they won't go away, encourage them to chat about the problem. If the issue is personal to the other party, he or she can blow off a little steam; and you may be able to get valuable information about the other party's position, interests, and side issues just by listening to the person talk.

But after you're ready to discuss the problem via a meeting, video call, or phone call:

>> See if you can make a connection with the other individual if you don't already know (and hate) each other.

>> Don't be in a hurry to state a position or describe your interests.

>> Be courteous to the individual you're dealing with.

>> Do your best not to get aggressive, angry, or upset.

>> Really listen to the other side.

>> Admit that the other side has reason to be annoyed with you and/or your business, if the reason is legitimate.

>> Focus on your interests and champion them.

>> Look for ways of putting your interests and their interests into the same basket.

>> Deal with solvable issues.

>> Avoid using threats or pressure tactics against the person or organization.

>> Offer the other side ways of moving from its original position toward your position.

Calling it quits

Quit while you're ahead. But how will you *know* when you're ahead?

>> Use the objective criteria you dreamed up in the planning stage.

>> Ask yourself what your best alternative to a negotiated agreement may be if you don't agree to the other side's offer.

>> Ask yourself whether you and/or the other side will be able to or will want to go through with the terms of the deal.

Alternative dispute resolution (ADR)

The "alternative" in alternative dispute resolution means alternative to going to court. Litigation is expensive and usually leads to bad feelings between the parties — and just because you're facing a dispute doesn't mean you want to spend as much money as possible to resolve it or end up never doing business again with the other side.

The two usual forms of ADR are mediation and arbitration.

Mediation

In *mediation*, a neutral third person (a *mediator*) meets with the parties to try to help them reach an agreement. Mediation is negotiation with a kind of coach present. The parties choose the mediator — someone who has experience in the particular area of the dispute and who has good mediation skills. (Ask around for recommendations.) The mediator doesn't take sides and doesn't judge between the parties as to who's right and who's wrong, but merely tries to help the parties find a solution that meets everyone's needs. The solution can be more flexible than one the parties could get by going to court. (Courts are best at awarding money to one side, not at coming up with creative answers to problems.)

Mediation is *useful* if the parties

>> Want to save face by not backing down on their own (a mediator will be able to point out the issues that aren't worth arguing about)

>> Want to save time and money by not going to court

>> Want to maintain a good business relationship

WARNING

Mediation is *not useful* if

>> One of the parties does not want mediation — the parties both have to have some desire to settle the matter and must both be willing to meet with a mediator.

>> One of the parties has a lot more power than the other and is going to use it to impose a solution on the weaker party.

In some provinces, the parties to a lawsuit are required to go to mediation shortly after the lawsuit starts, to see if the matter can be settled without going any further through the court system.

Arbitration

Arbitration gets closer to court proceedings. In *arbitration*, a neutral third person (the *arbitrator*, but sometimes three arbitrators are involved) is chosen by the parties to hear both sides' stories. The parties can design their own process, or they may prefer to conduct proceedings under provincial arbitration legislation. (As part of the design, the parties can agree on rights to appeal the arbitrator's decision to a judge or can agree that the decision cannot be appealed.) After listening to each side's presentation, the arbitrator makes a decision that one side or the other has won, and usually makes the kind of order that a court would make in the same circumstances. The decision can be registered with the court and enforced the same way as a judge's decision.

The advantages of arbitration are that

>> Arbitration can be faster and cheaper than a lawsuit (although the bigger and more complex the dispute, the closer arbitration costs get to litigation costs).

>> Parties can choose an arbitrator who has expertise in the area of the dispute (instead of just hoping that the judge they draw knows something about it). This can be very important in specialized areas of business.

>> Arbitration proceedings are private and confidential — unlike court proceedings, which are public.

>> Arbitration decisions do not set precedents (establish examples that have to be followed in later cases) the way court decisions do.

Litigation

When disputes arise, the parties often think of a lawsuit as the first option. As discussed earlier in this chapter, a lawsuit is just one of several options and may even be the last option. This section talks about deciding whether a lawsuit is your best option.

Should you sue?

REMEMBER

If you're the injured party, you decide whether to take the dispute to court. You need to talk to a lawyer about deciding whether to sue. Your lawyer will help you make the decision, based on the following matters:

>> What are your chances of winning the lawsuit?

>> What will you get if you win?

- » What's this going to cost?

- » Where's the lawsuit going to take place?

- » What are your chances of making the other party carry out the court order if you win?

- » Will you be able to stand the litigation process?

If you do decide to start a lawsuit, you'll be happy to know that most lawsuits do settle. Only a small fraction actually go to trial.

If you decide not to sue, you can still try to settle the matter through negotiation or mediation (possibly with the threat of court proceedings hanging over the head of the other side).

What should you do if you're sued?

If you are sued, your options are narrower than if you're the one deciding whether to sue. You can put in a statement of defence and then defend the action vigorously, or you can put in a statement of defence and then try to negotiate a settlement. In some cases you can put in a statement of defence and a *counterclaim* (a lawsuit against the other side) or a *third-party claim* (a lawsuit against other people who were really responsible for causing the problem in the first place — hey, the more the merrier, right?). Or you can do nothing.

WARNING

Doing nothing is a poor option. If you don't defend, and the other side continues with its lawsuit, the court will quickly enter judgment against you and the other side can start trying to enforce the judgment right away. However, doing nothing is a possibility if your business has nothing to lose or if you have nothing to lose personally.

TIP

In the no man's land between doing absolutely nothing and responding formally to the lawsuit, you could see a lawyer and try to

- » Settle the matter before the deadline for putting in a defence has passed (the defendant usually has several weeks after being notified of the lawsuit to file a statement of defence, but sometimes the allowed reaction time is much shorter).

- » Persuade the other side to call off the lawsuit even if the dispute can't be settled right away.

Getting Bigger

You launched your business some time ago, and now your business is expanding, or you'd like it to be. In any case, you have to have some idea of what you're getting into when your business expands, and how you can finance an expansion and manage a bigger, busier business. And if you aren't expanding but want to, you have to know how to find more business.

What "doing more business" means

If you're thinking that "doing more business" means "making bigger profits," "having access to more opportunities," or "becoming a more important player," you're right. But that's not all. They say that every action has an equal and opposite reaction — well, in this case the reaction can seem bigger than the action! Here are some of the things that go along with doing more business:

>> You'll probably do even more work than you're doing now.

>> You may have to travel more.

>> You may have to create new lines of products or services to entice customers and clients to your business (or to satisfy their demands).

>> You'll probably need new accounting and bookkeeping and/or inventory control systems to handle the increased business (see Book 4 for more on accounting matters).

>> You'll need a more sophisticated (and costly) system of management controls and automated business processes.

>> You'll need employees, or more employees, to help you (see Chapter 1 in Book 5 for more on hiring employees).

>> Your employees will need training, or more training.

>> You'll need more equipment.

>> You'll need more inventory if you're in the retail or wholesale business.

>> You'll need bigger premises to hold the new employees, new equipment and increased production capacity, new product lines and increased inventory, and to provide larger areas for client meetings.

>> And last but not least, you'll need money.

WARNING

Expanding a business will upset its equilibrium. You and your business will probably have trouble coping, at least in the beginning. In fact, you may never be ready to cope. Sometimes expansion is just not the best thing for you, and you and your business will be happier if things stay the way they are.

Finding more business

If you're reading this section, you probably want to expand your business and you believe that expanding won't lead to disaster. So how do you go about increasing the amount of business you do so you can get on with the expansion process?

>> Do more of what you're already doing for the customers you already have.

>> Find new customers for the work you already do.

>> Do new work for the customers you already have.

>> Find new customers for new work.

See if you can do more of the same work for existing customers

You already know your product and your customers. Doing more for the customers you have costs a lot less than going out and finding new customers or hunting down or creating new products. That's because you'll have to spend additional time and money to find new customers and develop new products, as opposed to simply connecting with the customers you already have.

The first place to start in your quest to do more work for your customers is to review your customer turnover rate and, if it's significant, to find out why customers aren't coming back to you. Speak to non-returning customers, if you can. Ask what they like about the business they're dealing with instead of you, and if they'd be interested in doing business with you again if you made some changes. If you can't talk to the lost sheep, chat with the customers who're still with you and try to get a sense of what they like and don't like about your business. Make reasonable changes as required.

Next, go to work on the customers you've got. Try to "generate new demand" by getting them to use more of your products or services, or use the same amount but more frequently. Apart from persuading your customers or clients that they'll benefit from using more of your products or services (for example, be healthier, smell cleaner, save money), here are some moves you can try out on them:

>> Make sure they know everything you can do for them.

>> Reward your customers.

>> Bundle your products or services.

>> Make your product or service more appealing.

>> Come up with new uses for the product or service.

>> Make your product or service more convenient to get.

TIP

Overall, one of the most important things you can do is to develop a good relationship with your customers. Make them your friends. Listen to them — and give them lots of convenient ways of talking to you, such as voice mail, your URL, e-mail, a 1-800 number, and, if possible, regular opportunities to meet face to face. If they have complaints or concerns, respond to them. If they have suggestions, pay attention to them.

Don't waste or lose any information from your clients. Keep a customer information file for each client (or at least for the best ones or up-and-coming ones) that includes notes and records of

>> Which products or services the customer buys, how frequently the customer buys, and how much the customer spends

>> How the customer makes the purchase and payment (and any interesting collection history) and takes delivery

>> Any complaints the customer has made, and what you did in response

>> Which products or services you provide that your customer buys from someone else, and why; and which products or services you provide that your customer doesn't buy at all, and why

>> Any notes about the customer's plans (that might tie in with your goal of providing more to the customer)

>> Any of the customer's special interests and important dates (these may not involve flogging any of your products or services; remembering them may just be good customer relations)

>> Any ideas you have about how you might persuade the customer to buy more of your products or services

Customers and clients will be pleased that you consider them important enough to remember details of past transactions, and they'll be thrilled if you remember something about them that isn't immediately linked to making a sale. This is why data mining and analysis has been one of the hottest business trends in the last decade. Businesses that "know their customers" tend to do well.

Find more customers for the same work

If you're sure that your current customers are satisfied with the work you're doing, then you can go out and look for new customers in similar situations or business sectors. You can also look for them in a new geographic area or in a new target group. When you go into a new area or after a new group, focus on it and make a good job of capturing it before you move on to another area or group. Don't try to expand on too many fronts at once.

Do new and additional work for existing customers

Don't go wild if this is the route you decide to take. Just because your customers love what you're doing with their stock portfolio doesn't mean they'll also be eager to buy pedicures and facials from your business. The best way to proceed is simply to ask your customers what more they'd like from you — or even just listen to what they're saying in your regular contacts with them. You'll probably find that your customers and clients are the best sources of new ideas for you.

TIP

When you bring in new products or services, consider having a testing period with free samples or with an "on approval" arrangement. This will give your customers a chance to try out the new product or service without any financial risk (to them, that is).

Find new customers for new products or services

If you're looking for new customers and new products, it almost means you're starting over again! But steering your business off in a new direction isn't as hard as setting up a new business.

In addition, you may have some money that you've made and set aside that can fund this venture. Or your business may have more capacity than it's using right now — maybe you could produce more, or sell other products through your existing channels.

Alternatively, you may be nervous about keeping your business based on one product or service and you want to branch out as a form of insurance.

Financing Your Expansion

The following list talks about where to get the money for an expansion.

>> **Sale or sale and leaseback of equipment:** If you already own equipment, you can sell it to a leasing company and then lease it back. Or you can sell one thing, and then lease something else. Or you can sell and not buy anything. Whichever way you go, you free up some cash for other purposes.

>> **Retained earnings:** *Retained earnings* are money you've set aside out of the profits of your business. As soon as you can, you should start building a fund from your profits for unforeseen problems and for expansion . . . instead of

blowing every penny that comes in on fancy office furniture or by taking all your profits as salary.

» **Equity investment:** An *equity investment* is capital for your business in exchange for partial ownership of your business. For example:

- **Venture capital and angel capital:** You're no longer a start-up, but you're still eligible for an investment from an angel or from a venture capital firm. In fact, you may be more eligible because you've been in operation for a while and it will be easier for an investor to tell whether your business is going places (or not). Venture capitalists will probably see you as looking for "first stage financing" (to increase production) or "second stage financing" (to increase production and expand your markets). You may even be ready for "mezzanine financing" (to expand prior to an *initial public offering* or a buyout of your business by another business).

- **Investment from within your business:** If you bring in new people who are going to run the business with you, you'll usually ask them to buy a partnership share (if your business isn't incorporated) or to buy shares in the corporation (if it is incorporated). This gives you some fresh capital to play with. The new guy may have to take out a loan to make the purchase; the interest payable on the loan is deductible from his or her income.

WARNING

If your business is incorporated, you can set up a stock plan that allows employees to buy shares in the business. This not only brings in capital, but also gives employees an incentive to work hard to make the business more profitable. However, to get much money via employee investment, you'll probably have to sell a significant percentage of shares, and even though you make sure you keep at least 51 percent of the shares, you can still end up with conflict about control of the corporation.

- **Investment from outside the business:** Under provincial securities laws in Canada, up to 50 people who are not employees of the corporation can own shares in a private corporation. So you can go looking for a few individual investors. But if you want more money than 50 outside investors can provide, you'll have to "go public" or make an *initial public offering* (IPO) — in other words, become a corporation whose shares are traded on a stock exchange such as the Toronto Stock Exchange (TSX) or the Canadian Securities Exchange (CSE).

WARNING

An IPO is complicated and costly to set up, and you aren't guaranteed to get any money out of it. As a result, there aren't many IPOs in Canada. In 2017, there were only about 40 issues from Canadian companies or companies listing on Canadian exchanges. That's a very low figure.

Managing a Bigger Business

The bigger a business grows, the more managing, and the more expert managing, it needs. Poor management is probably the most common reason for a business to fail.

The first thing this section talks about is how to manage yourself. If you can't manage your own time and work efficiently, you're going to have a lot of trouble managing anybody else. And because you're the most important person in the business at this point, you won't have a business to manage if you can't keep it together personally.

Personal management techniques

As your business expands, you're going to have more and more to do and less and less time to do it. So you're going to have to make the time you do have go further. Here's some advice about managing your time and work.

Schedule your time wisely

TIP

Don't rely on your memory! You haven't got one anymore — it drowned in the sea of details that a business floats in. So plan ahead in writing. Plan your year, your month, your week, your day. Keep a calendar or daybook — just one, if possible — or a calendar on your computer or smartphone. If you have more than one calendar, make sure that they're always synchronized. Otherwise, you'll end up with two incompatible schedules. When you plan:

>> Include your personal as well as business commitments and intentions, so you don't end up with conflicts, or miss dental appointments.

>> Schedule more than appointments in your calendar. Also schedule phone calls you intend to make and matters you intend to deal with. Make lists of to-do jobs for the day, week, or month (some calendar systems incorporate to-do lists). At the end of each day, week, or month, cross off the jobs done and carry forward the ones not done or not finished.

Schedule as efficiently as you can:

>> Schedule meetings and work that require your full concentration at the time of day you're at your sharpest; schedule mindless tasks for the time of day when you're mindless.

>> Schedule in the right order. For example, if a client wants to talk to you about the poor quality of a product you provided and what you're going to do about it, don't schedule that appointment before making an appointment to talk to the supplier of the product first.

>> When you're on the road, plan your trips so that they cover a number of tasks. For example, if you have to travel to another city to meet a client, see whether you can also meet with other clients, or a supplier or potential investor you have in that city. Plan even short trips to accomplish several things — on a drive to meet with a local client, work in other destinations that aren't too far off your route, like the gas station, business supply store, or dry cleaner's.

>> Combine some of your down time — lunch, golf, a hockey game — with a low-key meeting with a client, supplier, or investor.

>> Allow yourself some flexibility in your schedule so that you don't end up running late or wasting time. Some meetings take longer than planned; others get cancelled. So don't plan important meetings back to back, and always have a plan B if you unexpectedly have extra time.

TIP

Remind yourself what you're supposed to be doing now or next — have a tickler (reminder) system. Use your calendar or organizer to enter reminders of what you have to do in a day, week, or month, such as following up on a letter you just sent. Get into the habit of glancing frequently at your tasks for the month, week, and day. Every night before you close up shop (or before you go to sleep, whichever comes first), look over your schedule and to-do list for the following day. If you don't, you'll end up missing a morning meeting or phone call.

REMEMBER

Whenever you do something, keep a record of the action taken. Otherwise, a day or two later you won't remember whether or not you've done something, and what you did. And when a matter has been finally disposed of, put documents relating to it in your storage area, not in your active files area, so you won't be wondering if you're *still* supposed to do something.

TIP

Meetings can be terrible time wasters. So always make sure that a meeting is necessary, and that a phone call or an e-mail can't replace it. Then make sure that you're properly prepared for the meeting . . . and that everyone else is too:

>> In preparation, review your files, gather any additional information that's necessary, make notes about what you've done and what you want to talk about.

>> If you're hosting the meeting, send around a detailed agenda, so everyone else knows what the meeting is about and what they should do to prepare for it. If you're not the host, request an agenda.

>> At the end of a meeting, prepare *minutes* (a summary of what was said or what happened at) of the meeting, or request that someone else provide minutes, and send them around to all the participants. The minutes should include an "action agenda," so that everyone knows not only what's been discussed and decided but also what the participants are supposed to do and by when.

Screen and bundle

Don't let your phone and e-mail and faxes and mail and drop-in associates or employees rule your time. Organize your day so that you have blocks of time when you give your full attention to matters that require thought and concentrated effort, and other blocks of time when you read and answer your mail and return phone calls. Let customers or clients and suppliers know that you return phone calls and e-mails within 24 hours, but that they should not necessarily expect an instant response.

>> Don't answer your phone every time it rings (or at least get caller ID if you're afraid of missing important calls). You've got voice mail, let it do its job. Don't check your e-mail every ten minutes (or ten seconds). E-mails will wait quietly until you reply. Don't leap up every time you hear the sound of the e-mail alert.

>> Screen incoming voice messages, e-mails, and mail according to whether they are urgent and should be dealt with immediately, or should be dealt with within your normal 24-hour period, or should be answered within 24 hours but require longer to deal with, or can be delegated to someone else. Some items can probably be filed without a response or even completely ignored (like junk mail).

>> When you check your messages, e-mails, and mail, group them by category and deal with them by category. For example:

- Matters you can deal with by phone.

- Matters you can deal with by e-mail.

- Matters that you can deal with by writing and mailing a letter.

- Bookkeeping matters that require you to enter expenses or write cheques or create bills.

Put off procrastinating

Putting off work that must be done is one of the biggest thieves of your time. So no matter how much you DON'T WANT TO DO IT, start your work right away — and finish it too. Here are some tips for the hard-core procrastinator who's looking to reform:

>> Divide up complex work into smaller segments.

>> Don't avoid starting something just because you won't be able to finish it in one sitting.

>> Set a deadline.

>> Reward yourself.

>> Get an employee or business associate or family member to nag you.

Delegate

Do what you do best, and delegate the rest. If you're not a secretary and you're doing a lot of secretarial work; if you're not a bookkeeper and you're doing a lot of bookkeeping; if you're not a salesperson and you're making a lot of sales calls; if you're not an office manager and you're spending all your time marshalling employees and ordering supplies; if you're not a janitor and you're doing a lot of cleaning — you need to hire someone to do these tasks. Your time is better spent doing what you're expert in. Try outsourcing this work, or hiring a temp or a part-time worker, before you hire a full-time employee.

WARNING

While we're on the subject of delegation, don't let people you've hired delegate to you. "Upward delegation" is a sneak attack. If someone you've delegated to isn't doing the work right, don't do it for him. Provide more training, or give guidelines for correcting the work and have the person try again until he gets it right. Otherwise you'll end up doing the work *and* paying someone else to do it.

Just say no

The word *no* has a lot of power. Sometimes you have to use it to keep other people from hijacking your time and your energy.

>> Whenever someone makes a demand on you, consider what's in it for you.

>> Don't hold or attend useless meetings.

>> Discourage drop-in visits from colleagues and clients.

>> Tell your family and friends not to call you all the time to chat.

TIP

Don't forget to take care of yourself

Finally, make sure you keep yourself in good shape to run your business:

>> Take time off to refresh yourself.

>> Eat properly.

>> Get enough sleep.

>> Get regular exercise.

Business management techniques

As your business expands, it's turning into an enterprise that needs professional management. You may be able to turn yourself into a professional manager, or you may need to bring managers on board. While you wait to discover whether you have what it takes to be a professional manager (management may be something you left your employed life to avoid), you can think about the issues in this section.

Give up control (at least a little)

Giving up control isn't something you want to hear about — unless, of course, someone's buying you out for an obscenely large amount of money. One of the reasons you went into business for yourself was so you could run things the way you wanted to! But the fact is that you can't do everything yourself, so you're going to have to share some of the responsibilities with others or even hand responsibilities over entirely.

Start off slowly, if you like:

>> Have brainstorming sessions to solve problems.

>> Take your time to think about important matters, and gather information and get advice before you make a decision.

>> Find yourself an understudy, or even hand over primary responsibility to someone else (whom you've carefully chosen, of course).

>> Set up formal systems to make business decisions.

Set goals

You've probably had goals all along. But do they still match the direction your business is taking? Are you following the right strategies to reach them? Review your goals, and set new ones if that makes sense. Rethink your strategies if your goals are fine but you're not making headway in reaching them.

Your goals should take into account the underlying values of your business (such as fairness, honesty, reliability) and the purpose of your business. They shouldn't focus purely on making money, or you'll find yourself going astray pretty quickly.

When setting your goals, keep in mind that they should be "SMART":

>> **Specific** — but with enough flexibility built in that you can go off course if the right opportunity arises.

>> **Measurable** — use actual numbers. And build milestones into your plan so that you'll know as you go along whether you're going to meet your target.

>> **Achievable** — so that you can stay motivated to reach a realistic target.

>> **Relevant** — so that your goals align with the nature of your business and its overall strategy.

>> **Time limited** — set a deadline to meet the goals.

As an example, after reviewing your profit and loss statement, you might set a goal to increase sales by 5 percent in one year, or to reduce expenses by 10 percent within six months. Your milestone #1 to increase sales might be to identify a specific number of new customers or identify customers for whom you could do more work. Milestone #1 for reducing expenses might be to perform an audit of your business activities. You'd create a document setting out your goal and the tasks involved in reaching the goal, your deadline, your milestones and milestone dates, and assigning the appropriate people to take charge of the tasks. You'd circulate the document, meet with the people in charge of the tasks, and you might also hold a general staff meeting to explain the plan for reaching the goal.

Focus on your strengths

TIP

Focus on your areas of strength. Have you heard of the "80/20" rule? It says that the most significant areas of your business (whether significant for good or bad reasons) actually make up a small percentage of your business. For example, about 20 percent of your customers give you about 80 percent of your business, about 20 percent of your products bring in about 80 percent of your revenue, and about 20 percent of your employees do about 80 percent of the work. (And about 20 percent of your clients and employees give you about 80 percent of your headaches.)

So concentrate on your best customers, your top-selling products, and your best employees. If you can't move your unproductive customers into your Best Customer category, maybe you should gently try to find them another home. If you've got products that aren't moving and you can't get them moving, maybe you should drop them and free up shelf space. If you can't get more work out of an employee, maybe you should encourage the employee to depart. Don't spend a lot of your time and effort on customers, products, and employees who aren't going to generate a return on your investment.

Learn to live with change

In fact, go beyond living with change and learn to embrace it. Change brings you opportunities as well as challenges.

>> Keep your eyes open for change at all times.

>> Be ready to act on a change.

>> Assume change will happen even when things look pretty stable.

>> Learn from your mistakes.

Make good use of employees

You're the boss. If you hire people to work for you, make sure you help them do a good job.

>> Communicate clearly.

>> Encourage employee input.

>> Don't discourage employee questions.

>> Run a tight ship — but not too tight.

>> In fact, try not to be a control freak in general.

>> Don't let the sun set on employee conflicts.

2

Intellectual Property

Contents at a Glance

Chapter **1**

Doing a Patent Search

Preparing and filing a patent application takes time and a good chunk of change. After all that work, how would you feel, some months down the line, if a patent examiner says that a complete description of your invention can be found in patent number so and so?

In Canada, it is strongly encouraged that you conduct a preliminary search before applying for a patent. The preliminary search results cannot tell you for sure whether your patent application will go through, but it can give you a better idea of whether your invention has been patented. Knowing this before you start can save you time, money, and lots of work applying for a patent.

You can conduct this search on the Canadian Patents Database located on the official website of the Canadian Intellectual Property Office (CIPO). You can search free of charge with a number of search options. Go to www.ic.gc.ca/opic-cipo/cpd/eng/introduction.html. You can also go in person to the CIPO Client Service Centre located in Gatineau, Quebec. Many Information Patent Officers are available to help, as the process can be overwhelming.

Most inventors don't understand what they can gain or lose by conducting a preliminary patent search, or whether one is even indicated. This chapter talks about conduct a search and interpreting what you find. It also provides some tips to the "do-it-yourself" searcher.

Check out www.ic.gc.ca/eic/site/cipointernet-internetopic.nsf/eng/h_wr00001.html for an introduction to the patent process in Canada.

Making a Preliminary Online Search

Before the Internet, people spent lots of time scanning trays and trays of index cards in musty libraries under the judgmental, enforcing eye of the assistant librarian, often getting nowhere. But now, anyone with a mouse, an itchy index finger, and an afternoon to kill can do a pretty decent preliminary anticipation search.

The preliminary online search of the Canadian Patents Database can be overwhelming. It is advised that you seek professional help from a registered patent agent, as preparing and corresponding with the CIPO is a complex task. There are different types of IP professionals, such as patent agents, trademark agents, and IP lawyers, who can help identify and then further file your IP.

The best place to start a preliminary online search is through the Canadian Intellectual Property Office (CIPO) website (http://brevets-patents.ic.gc.ca/opic-cipo/cpd/eng/search/basic.html), which is structured to service both the knowledgeable old hand as well as the greenhorn. Afterwards, you can try a broad-based Internet search by using Google, Yahoo!, or another search engine.

As always, you should be careful when typing information into a field on a web page, even if it's one as presumably trustworthy as that of the CIPO. Although it may be unlikely, there are dozens of ways for your information to get diverted into the wrong hands.

The search at the CIPO website is keyword based, which sounds good at first but more often than not yields spotty results. You see, unfortunately, most patents are not written by normal people. They're written by a bunch of IP professionals who seem to have an odd-word fetish. Instead of describing a spring as . . . well . . . a *spring*, these wacky characters are more likely to call it a *resilient biasing member*. So, a good keyword search includes lots of synonyms. Keep a thesaurus handy. Keep in mind that you're not looking for a prior patent that shows every detail of your invention, but something that comes close to it or might suggest its main features.

On the CIPO website, you can do a basic search, a number search, a Boolean search, or an advanced search. Play around.

If you've already hired a patent lawyer or agent, you may want her to conduct a quick preliminary keyword search for you. Most IP professionals have had some experience doing these types of searches and may find just what you're looking for quickly and inexpensively.

Moving to the Professional Search

So you've pulled an all-nighter, drunk a whole pot of coffee, but you found nothing resembling your invention at the CIPO website or on the rest of the Internet. You're starting to feel a little confident. And, although you don't admit it to yourself, you're starting to think about whether you're going to retire to Hawaii or Florida.

But now is the time to splash some cold water on your face. Most inventions turn out to be unpatentable — even after a favourable result to a preliminary patent search. This means that you should treat the favourable result as just another rung on the ladder to getting a patent, nothing more.

So far your journey to a patent has used up a lot of brain cells, but there hasn't been much out-of-pocket expense. The next step requires you to decide whether or not to turn on the spigot attached to your wallet and hire a professional searcher.

Hiring a professional searcher is a tough decision, but it may be the most important one. A professional search can tell, with much greater confidence than you can, whether your creation is patentable. However, because a professional search delays the filing of your patent application, isn't cheap, and is no guarantee that you'll get a patent, you shouldn't jump into it without weighing the pros and cons. The following sections do that.

Compelling reasons to do a professional search

If your professional search uncovers something very close to your invention, you save yourself the cost and aggravation of filing a patent application only to have it rejected after two or three years of futile pursuit. But don't despair; you can possibly use this information to improve and refine your invention or to help you draft a more focused and convincing patent application — one that forestalls the examiner's rejection of the invention in view of the closest prior art. Avoiding even one sweaty round in the ring duking it out with the examiner can save you more than the money it costs to do the search.

Perhaps the best reason to do a professional search: It gives you some peace of mind and confirms that you and your invention are starting down the right road.

Some valid reasons for skipping the professional search

One potential hazard of doing a thorough patent search is that while you're waiting for the results before filing your application, someone else may file for a similar invention. And he'll end up with the patent — not you.

No one can ever safely rely on a search to positively conclude that your gadget is new and deserves a patent, or that there's absolutely nothing patentable in its design.

The high cost of a professional search and interpretation, which start at $500 and could increase significantly depending on the complexity of the invention, is another reason some people avoid doing one. And extending a search to technical publications may end up costing more than the preparation and filing of the application itself. The Canadian Government provides an estimate of fees here: www. ic.gc.ca/eic/site/cipointernet-internetopic.nsf/eng/wr04547.html.

You could file a patent application right off the bat to nail down an early filing date. Later, after you receive your search results, you can file a second patent application claiming priority over the previously regularly file application.

Deciding whether a professional search is right for you

Why would anyone bother with such a time-consuming and costly procedure instead of just filing the patent application? It's all a matter of balance — weighing the peace of mind that a successful search can give you against the high cost in time and money.

Here's a simple, reliable, cost-effective approach: Do a professional search only if you suspect that your invention may not be new.

A search may be a good idea if your invention meets two or more of these criteria:

>> The invention is relatively simple.

>> The invention belongs to a low-tech field.

>> The invention isn't fully developed.

» The invention is marginally useful or practical.

» The invention uses very old or obsolete technology.

» The invention is just another version of a very common device.

» The invention closely resembles something that already exists.

» The invention is outside your area of expertise.

Getting a second opinion

Like every inventor, you may tend to overestimate the importance and novelty of your creation. Before you get carried away, get a second opinion from an expert in the field. Let your technical expert (or a patent lawyer) review the criteria listed in the preceding section and give you an educated guess as to whether your invention is unique before you do a long and expensive search.

Finding someone who's willing to stick his neck out and give an opinion without the benefit of a search may be hard to do. You may have to agree, in writing, not to hold it against him if he guesses wrong.

Conducting Your Own "Professional" Search

When you perform an anticipation patent search, you're trying to anticipate how the patent examiner will deal with your application. Therefore, your search shouldn't be limited to looking through documents for something resembling your invention. You also need to analyse what you find under the rules of patentability to decide whether your invention qualifies for a patent. To do this, you must step into the shoes of a patent examiner and

» Look for information about the area of your invention, commonly called the *relevant prior art*. Go to www.ic.gc.ca/eic/site/cipointernet-internetopic.nsf/eng/wr04009.html.

» Apply the patentability test (for novelty, utility, and inventiveness) to your invention in view of the relevant prior art to determine whether your invention is patentable. See www.ic.gc.ca/eic/site/cipointernet-internetopic.nsf/eng/h_wr03652.html for more information.

Looking for relevant prior art

When rejecting patent applications, examiners have been known to rely on prior publications as diverse as the writings of Homer, the ninth-century BC Greek poet, scholarly papers of all types and languages, and, of course, domestic and foreign patents.

Prior art's definition, according to the Canadian government's website, is all information and documentation "that has been disclosed with the public about an invention before the filing date of a patent in question." Prior art doesn't apply to abandoned or secret applications, confidential disclosures, or trade secrets.

The Internet makes it much easier for anyone to publish potential prior art. For example, your wife's nephew's best friend's older brother Scooter could have posted on his blog the idea of a Bluetooth fountain pen that automatically inputs chicken scratch handwriting into a computer text file. Without any discussion of accelerometers, wireless data communication protocols, and character-recognition software, Scooter's blog entry may be enough to qualify as prior art and torpedo your broadest claims to the concept.

Here's an example of prior art from the Canadian government's website:

> You are aware of a Canadian application to patent an electric door lock. But, you have evidence of an earlier electric door lock, either yours or another inventor's, which is already known, publicly described or demonstrated. The public disclosure of the door lock constitutes prior art and it does not need to be in existence nor be available on the market to be considered so. You may inform the Canadian Intellectual Property Office (CIPO) that such a door lock was previously known, before the current application was made.

See `www.ic.gc.ca/eic/site/cipointernet-internetopic.nsf/eng/wr04009.html` for more about prior art.

Moving beyond keywords

A patent examiner can use any assortment of documents (including expired, cancelled and abandoned patents, or even published applications) as proof that your doodad is neither new nor non-obvious.

It's almost impossible to contemplate sifting through a mountain of documents without using keywords. However, keyword searches have their limitations. It is often very difficult for the search engine and the searcher to come up with all useful synonyms. Plus, the full text of many earlier patent documents have yet not made it into many searchable databases. The CIPO database only provides laid-open applications and patents granted since August 1978.

According to the Canadian government's website, for patent documents that are either public inspection applications or are patents granted since August 15, 1978, the CIPO Canadian Patent Database contains bibliographic data, textual data (titles, abstracts, and claims) and image data. For patents granted prior to August 15, 1978, the CIPO Canadian Patent Database contains bibliographic data, the text of titles only (no text of abstracts and claims) and image data.

In Canada, patent documents filled prior to October 1, 1989, are classified according to the Patent Classification (CPC) system. Patent documents filed on or after October 1, 1989, are classified according to the International Patent Classification (IPC) System. The latest versions can be found on the World Intellectual Property Organization (WIPO) website.

For more information, visit the WIPO (World Intellectual Property Organization) website at `https://www.wipo.int/classifications/en`. The classifications are listed here: `https://www.wipo.int/classifications/ipc/ipcpub/?notion=sc heme&version=20190101&symbol=none&menulang=en&lang=en&viewmode=f&fip cpc=no&showdeleted=yes&indexes=no&headings=yes&notes=yes&direction=o 2n&initial=A&cwid=none&tree=no&searchmode=smart`.

Analysing your search results

In Canada, there is no guide to help examine current patent documents that might be closely related to your invention, but when you search for them, you will get a patent number and a hyperlink to drill down on the details of the patent.

The bibliographic data includes the following:

>> Canadian Patent Classification (CPC)

>> International Patent Classification (IPC)

>> Inventors

>> Owners

>> Applicants

>> Agent

>> Issued

>> Filed Date

>> Availability of Licence

>> Language of Filing

>> Patent Cooperation Treaty (PCT)

Following this information, there may also be abstracts, claims, descriptions, drawings, admin status, owners records, and other documents to access.

So you have found a stack of patents and documents related to your invention. Now what? It's time to act like a patent examiner and apply the novelty and inventiveness tests to your invention in view of the relevant prior art found during the search. (Visit www.ic.gc.ca/eic/site/cipointernet-internetopic.nsf/eng/h_wr03652.html for more information.)

Would a patent examiner reject your application based on this material? As with all legal concepts, many nuances and exceptions blur the rules about novelty and inventiveness. The prosecution of a patent application is like a court battle. Patent lawyers and patent examiners often fight like cats and dogs and seldom find common ground.

Only in a clear and blatant case of exact duplication can a layman safely conclude that the invention is not patentable. Usually, only a competent patent lawyer, after a careful analysis of the search results, can provide a reliable opinion of non-patentability.

To locate a patent agent in your province, check out the updated CIPO site of who is taking new clients: http://www.ic.gc.ca/cipo/pa-br/agents.nsf/pagents-eng?readform.

Chapter **2**

Preparing and Filing a Patent Application

ere's some advice: Let your patent agent or lawyer prepare your utility patent application for you. But he or she can't do a good job without your supportive participation. You're the one who came up with the invention after all. This chapter gives you a basic understanding of the purpose, structure, and function of the patent application, so that you can efficiently and effectively assist your IP professional.

You probably think that the hardest part is over after the patent application is prepared. It's true that a lot of the detail work is done, but you still have a lot of things to keep in mind when getting ready to file your application, and even more things to keep track of after your application hits the Canadian Intellectual Property Office (CIPO). Your patent lawyer takes care of most of these details, but you need to have a clear view of the filing process, so this chapter describes that here in some detail.

REMEMBER

For lots of helpful information on the entire patent process, check out the CIPO Patents website at www.ic.gc.ca/eic/site/cipointernet-internetopic.nsf/eng/h_wr00001.html. There you'll find guidance on preparing an application, applying for a patent, requesting an examination, and much more.

Understanding the Patent Application

A patent application is a formal request addressed to the Canadian government for the exclusive legal right to a certain area of technology. Your primary goal when preparing your patent application is to make that area of technology as broad as possible within the scope of your invention. Your patent may eventually cover inventions that are inconceivable today but that fall within your exclusive area of technology.

The strength of your patent depends as much on the skills of your lawyer or agent to persuade the patent examiner to grant legal rights to the broadest area of technology as it does on the merits of your invention. However, the patent examiner's duty is to make certain that your patent doesn't carry more rights than your invention deserves.

REMEMBER

Patents aren't granted for the asking. The complex application process often takes unexpected turns into long appellate detours, procedural sidetracks, and disappointing dead ends. The process breaks down into three major phases:

1. **Preparing the application:** For patents, preparation is definitely the key to success, and this chapter covers that.

2. **Filing the application:** It's more than just tossing forms in the mail. The nuts and bolts of filing are covered later in this chapter.

3. **Pushing the application through the CIPO:** Technically, this phase is called the *prosecution*. At this point, your lawyer may have to answer communications from the patent examiner or state your case before one or more appeal boards.

TIP

Check out the CIPO's tutorial on putting together a patent application here: www.ic.gc.ca/eic/site/cipointernet-internetopic.nsf/eng/wr01398.html.

Deconstructing the Patent Application

A well-drafted utility patent application should contain the following:

>> **Abstract of the invention:** A concise description of the invention in one paragraph of 150 words or less. The abstract gives a general overview of the invention. It ends up on the front page of the patent.

If you can, try to use lots of different key words and synonyms in the abstract. Many people search abstracts rather than the entire text of patents. With lots of key words, potential licensees searching for patents may have an easier time finding you.

» **Drawing:** An illustration, in as many sheets and figures as needed to support the disclosure. You don't need to be an artist. But you do need to be able to show the important functional parts of your invention. When in doubt, keep it simple.

» **Reference to any prior application:** A short statement that ties the application to any previously filed application by the same inventor that discloses the whole or part of the invention.

» **General field of the invention:** A one- or two-sentence summary of the area of technology affected by the invention.

» **Background and circumstances of the invention:** Give a good argument for the need for the invention and the problems it resolves.

» **Summary of the invention:** A condensed explanation of the nuts and bolts of the invention, its utility, and, if necessary, its honest, broadly stated advantages.

» **Description of each figure of the drawing:** A short sentence explaining each figure.

» **Description of the preferred embodiment of the invention:** A description of what the inventor considers the best implementation of the invention. It's not necessarily what was built and sold, but what would be built and sold under the best practical circumstances. This part refers to the figures in the drawing.

» **Formal definition of the invention in the form of at least one claim that defines the area of technology over which you want exclusivity.**

It takes a well-rounded IP professional to draft a good patent application. The strength of the eventual patent depends on the completeness of the specification and claims. If you're a tech-savvy good writer, you can write an acceptable description of your invention. But the specification isn't the most important part of a patent application. What legally defines the rights of the patent owner and the area of technology covered by the patent are the *claims* — and your patent lawyer needs to write the claims.

Disclosing Your Invention in the Specification

Writing a good patent specification requires your participation and candid communication with your lawyer or agent. You're the only one who knows all the ins and outs of your invention and can point her in the right direction when its embodiments, applications, functions, and great advantages have to be explained. Primarily, the specification must provide full support for the claims in respect to the substance (technology) and the form (words used in the claims). In addition, the specification must meet two basic requirements:

>> **The enabling rule:** The specification must clearly and concisely disclose enough for a person skilled in the field of the invention to practise the invention without a lot of experimentation.

>> **The best mode rule:** The disclosure must state what you consider to be the best manner of carrying out the invention.

Complying with one rule but missing the other can make your patent invalid. For example, you may clearly explain how to practise your invention, but this may not be your best mode. On the other hand, your description of the best way to apply your invention may be too sketchy to meet the enabling requirement. These guidelines should keep you on the path to compliance:

>> **Select the best mode:** You must reveal what you believe is the most efficient way to practice your invention, which may not necessarily be the manner you build your own prototype. If you've thought of other ways to exploit the invention, you can add them as alternate embodiments. Don't be shy about mentioning various ways to construct a particular structure or perform a specific process step.

>> **Teach enough but no more than required:** When you try to meet the enabling requirement, you're writing for a person skilled in your field, so you can use technical jargon and skip obvious details. Don't waste time explaining how to use every little component or tool. Your skilled readers can figure out which tasks are necessary on their own. Just make sure that they don't need to do a great deal of experimentation before they can use your invention. You can require their time but not their head-scratching. For example, if you're disclosing a computer program, draw a flowchart and briefly describe the step represented by each box on the chart. You don't need to provide a program code listing.

WARNING

Don't treat the specification like a promotion or marketing tool. It's not the place for puffery about your product or for disparaging comments about your competitors. Your lawyer or agent should stick to legal requirements.

Arguing Your Case for Patentability

According to the law, your patent application only has to include a description of the preferred embodiment of the invention and one claim. But you need a lot more to make a case for the patentability of your invention. Convincing the examiner or the appeal board (if you have to appeal a rejection by the examiner) that you deserve a patent usually requires a little extra. You need to provide your IP professional with as much information as he needs to establish the utility, novelty, and inventiveness of your invention.

How do you convince a patent examiner that your invention is the greatest thing since the corkscrew? You must persuasively demonstrate that

» A technological problem has existed for some time.

» Others have tried to resolve this problem with questionable success.

» You have taken a fresh and different approach.

And the places to demonstrate these things are the *Background of the Invention* and *Summary of the Invention* sections of the patent application.

Defining the problem

TIP

Here's a simple approach to the background section:

1. **Define the general application of the invention.**

   Strap-tightening ratchet mechanisms, commonly called strap ratchets, are used in connection with cargo-securing harnesses. . . .

2. **Note the shortcomings of the current devices.**

   The ratchet mechanisms are usually provided with short tightening levers that yield very little torque force. Accordingly, the harness cannot be tightened to the fullest extent possible. . . .

3. **Describe the prior approaches for resolving the problem, including their shortcomings.** You can refer to prior patents, publications, or well-known devices already on the market.

Some mechanisms of the prior art have been provided with extended levers as disclosed in Canadian Patent No. . . .

. . . The length and bulk of these extended levers often interfere with the placement of the ratcheting device near a corner of the cargo. . . .

4. **Close the section by stating that your invention is an attempt to resolve the outlined deficiencies in the prior mechanism.**

Laying out your solution

Provide a very condensed explanation of the primary features of the invention and their utility in addressing the problems described in the background, but don't merely recite advantages. Contemporary practice limits the *Summary of the Invention* to a sober, to-the-point statement of what is recited in the claims without mention of advantageous results. Some practitioners simply restate the abstract and the claims. This has the advantage of guaranteeing that all words used in the claims are also found in the description.

If you anticipate an obviousness fight with the examiner and can't help yourself from describing some of the advantages, at least make them easily attainable and open for interpretation. Also, it's good to refer to the invention as "some embodiments." For example it's better to say, "Some embodiments provide an improved way to trap a mouse" rather than, "The invention can trap more than ten mice in an hour."

REMEMBER

Except in connection with chemical inventions, which usually can be fully described by formulae, a drawing must illustrate the invention with as many figures as might be required to understand the invention. The critical rule is that each element or feature recited in the claims be shown on the drawing.

Giving a good example

This is where you describe in detail the best embodiment of your invention you can think of, including alternate or supplemental embodiments. You must use reference characters to point out where each described element is shown on the drawing. Your description must be sufficient to support both the wording and the substance of the following claims.

Staking Your Claims

REMEMBER

Your patent claims define the area of technology covered by the patent and, in the end, are the only parts of the patent that really count because they legally define your rights to the invention. The specification has only one primary purpose — to support the wording of the claims. Notice that the claims don't *define* your new device or process, which is a tangible or concrete thing, but an area of technology *represented by* it. Your actual invention is an abstract construct that can't be easily or precisely defined; the specific device or process is only one of many possible applications. Your patent lawyer needs to take care of the claims, but here's a crash course on what she'll be doing.

Mastering the mechanics of claims

The wording of a claim is like the description of a piece of real property in a deed. Just as a deed description defines only the limits of the lot and not anything on it, a claim recites only the minimum elements that must be present for a device or process to be covered by the patent. Anything that falls within these limits belongs to the title owner — the landlord or patent owner.

REMEMBER

A claim usually covers a lot more than the limits it spells out. And the shorter the claim, the broader its coverage. For an example of this less-is-more rule, consider the first horseless carriage, invented by Nicolas Cugnot around 1769. If Cugnot had asked us to draft a patent application for his invention, we would have worded the first claim as follows:

A vehicle comprising:

a cargo-carrying member,

at least two wheels supporting said member, and

an engine driving at least one of said wheels.

Cugnot's carriage had a back axle supporting a pair of wheels. The steam engine was coupled to a front wheel. But we could also imagine motored vehicles riding with only two wheels because 80 years earlier, another Frenchman, Mede de Sivrac, had developed a crude bicycle. We therefore listed the minimum components necessary for a workable device. And it's a good thing we did. If the patent were still in effect today, it would cover locomotives, cars, trucks, and motorcycles. But someone could get around this claim by using only one wheel (possibly a long roller) or by detaching the engine from the wheels (by using a jet engine). Plug these loopholes by rewriting the claim as follows:

A vehicle comprising:

a cargo-carrying member,

at least one wheel supporting said member; and

an engine positioned to propel said vehicle.

Because the second claim lists only three elements instead of four like the first, more devices out there are likely to fall within its limits. So the more concise second claim has a broader scope than the first and can catch more infringers.

Checking the various types of claims

Not all inventions can be described by a concise list of components, as in the Cugnot example in the preceding section. That's why the law provides more than one way to describe them.

Listing elements in a claim

The kind of component–listing claims illustrated in the Cugnot example are commonly used with machine, device, and composition of matter inventions. Here are variations on the theme that lend themselves to other inventions:

>> **Using functional limitations:** If you have to list a component that has many equivalents capable of performing the same job, you can describe that component in a *means-plus-function* form. For instance, a wheel can be attached to a vehicle frame by means of an axle or a pin or with a complex articulated structure, like the one used on the front wheel of a car. You can effectively describe the component or limitation like this:

. . . *means for rotatively securing the wheel to the vehicle frame* . . .

Can't find *rotatively* in your dictionary? It doesn't matter. When you write claims, you can create your own vocabulary, as long as you clearly define the new term in the specification section of the application.

In an infringement action, the judge will interpret the scope of a means-plus-function claim to cover the component described in the specification, plus any *equivalent structure* that achieves the same results (with insubstantial differences) as the one described in the specification, so long as that equivalent structure is available when the patent is granted. You may enhance your patent by describing as many equivalent structures as possible in the specification. For example, the means for securing the wheel only recited in a general form in the claim must be specifically described in the specification as an axle, pin, or complex car front wheel mounting structure.

>> **Grouping similarly effective components:** Another way to cover a large gamut of similar components in a single claim is to list a group of applicable elements. This style of claim is narrower than the means-plus-function mode but is often used to define chemical inventions. The only requirement is that the group of alternate components must be introduced by the all-inclusive phrase *consisting essentially of.* Elements not listed as part of the group are excluded from coverage. For example:

. . . a dry lubricant taken from a group consisting essentially of graphite, molybdenum sulphide, and boron nitride . . . excludes talcum powder.

REMEMBER

The specification must mention the utility and effectiveness of all listed components. For example, you may explain that tests were conducted with each type of lubricant with substantially the same effective results.

Claiming a method or process

An invention component can also be defined in a claim by its unique manufacturing method:

. . . spacer made by bending a length of steel wire into a closed loop . . .

If your invention is a method or process, you can describe it as steps:

An online method for confirming receipt of an electronic purchase order contained in an e-mail message, said method comprising the steps of:

assigning to said order an account number and a job number;

clicking a reply button on a toolbar of said e-mail message;

typing said account and job number; and

clicking a send button on said toolbar.

This is just an example. It's doubtful you could get a patent on that method.

Focusing on an improvement

When the invention consists of a refinement to an existing structure, you can first recite the basic structure in the opening phrase. Then follow the opening phrase with a linking term such as *an improvement comprising*. And finally, list the limitations of the invention:

> *In the manufacture of a body armor in which metal plates are piled into a plurality of stacks and each of said stacks is spread in a substantially flat pattern of overlapping plates on the bed of a riveting machine, an improvement for facilitating said spreading, said improvement comprising the steps of:*
>
> *sprinkling a light coat of a dry lubricant over each metal plate before piling into one of said stacks;*
>
> *after riveting, placing said metal plates into a vertical position; and*
>
> *shaking said vertically positioned plates to slough off said coat of dry lubricant.*

Combining structures

A claim can recite a combination of two or more objects — particularly handy when the inventive gadget's utility and novelty are only evident as applied to an existing device. However, the combined structures must have interaction between them. For example, a phone mounted on a washing machine for the convenience of the housekeeper isn't a patentable combination because the two devices don't work together, but are only located together. However, the combination of a cylindrical eraser mounted at the end of a pencil might be patentable because the pencil acts as a handle for the eraser.

Playing a medley

An astute IP professional will cleverly use a cocktail of various claiming styles to obtain the broadest coverage possible. He or she can also claim the same invention in a series of differently phrased claims.

Building a claim pyramid

Your name may not be Ramses or Nefertiti, but you can erect a mighty monument for posterity — by building one claim upon another. A claim may be *dependent* upon one or more earlier *parent* claims that it incorporates. For example, if a Claim 2 begins with *The method of Claim 1 which further comprises . . .* or *The device of Claim 1 wherein . . .*, Claim 2 includes all the limitations recited in Claim 1, plus some.

Claims can be spread in a radial pattern, where all dependent claims directly connect to a single parent claim. This technique allows you to add just one more element to the basic and most concise independent claim.

Claims can also be lined up in a cascading or daisy-chain pattern where a claim can be both parent and child — to avoid continuously repeating the same series element where you keep adding one more element in each additional claim while keeping the elements entered in the previous one.

Finally, claims can be scattered in a mixed pattern of radial and linear single and multiple dependency. This may be the most common way to cover an invention with many complex variations.

Following the grammatical rules

Claim drafting is more than a science — it's an art at which any patent lawyer worth his "whereas" should excel and which requires every semantic and legal trick possible. Don't feel bad if you can't comprehend the full scope of each claim in your application. Rules for interpreting claims are even more complex than those that control drafting them. In a patent infringement proceeding, only the judge can interpret the claims of the patent. It's assumed that jurors can't competently make these types of determinations themselves.

Claims must comply with very peculiar grammatical rules. With apologies to your grade-school English teachers, get used to the following oddities, which are just a few of the crazy grammatical twists and turns you'll run into:

>> A claim must be written in a single sentence, even if that sentence extends over three or more pages. So, run-on sentences are now okay.

>> A claim must begin with a preamble that briefly states the framework of the invention, followed by a linking phrase such as *which comprise(s), including,* or *which essentially consist(s) of,* followed by the limitations (elements) of the invention. If necessary, you can tack on a *whereby* clause after a limitation in order to clear up any potential confusion as to the nature, application, or function of the invention. The whereby clause doesn't define a necessary limitation of the invention and is often discarded by the judge interpreting the claim. See the earlier section "Focusing on an improvement" for an example.

>> You can't use a definite article in front of an element unless you've already introduced that element in the body of the current claim or in a parent claim. For example, you can't start a claim like this:

   A video camera which comprises a shutter behind the lens . . .

The word lens hasn't been defined yet, so you have to write:

   A video camera which comprises a lens and a shutter behind the lens . . .

>> You can use the terms *which comprise(s), comprising, including, having,* and so on, without excluding other elements in the claimed invention. However, the phrase *consisting of* or *which consists of* excludes any other element. So a claim that recites *a table which comprises a flat top and three legs* also covers tables

with four or five legs. However, a claim stating *a table which consists of a flat top and three legs* wouldn't cover a four-legged table. You can use *consisting essentially of* to slightly expand coverage beyond the specific elements to known equivalents.

>> You can reference previously introduced elements with the term *said* without repeating the qualifying terms, for example:

> *A camera comprising a zoom lens;*
>
> *a shutter positioned behind said lens*

>> Don't use the conjunctions *or* and *nor* or the phrase *such as* if they make the definition ambiguous. For example, *a camera having a lens made of a material such as glass or plastic . . .* won't cut the mustard. Instead, use multiple claims, each reciting one type of lens, or better yet use a claim that covers a number of substitutable components: *A camera having a lens made of a material taken from a group consisting essentially of glass, plastic, and silicone.*

>> Words have the meanings that you give them in the specification, even if they are different from the ones found in dictionaries. You can't go so far as calling a cat a *dog*, but you can call a joint an *accouplement*.

>> You can't list voids, holes, and cavities in structures as primary elements, but can use them to qualify an element. For example, *a wooden beam and a transversal hole in a mid-section thereof* is a no-no. Write *a wooden beam having a transversal hole in a mid-section thereof.*

>> Any descriptive words you use in a claim must first be mentioned and if necessary defined in the specification.

Compiling the record

What do you need to help your legal eagle draft your patent application?

REMEMBER

If you kept a good notebook while you were developing your invention, dig it out now — it contains a lot of what your IP professional needs. Otherwise, here's a helpful list:

>> Short definition of general fields of technology to which the invention relates. Include any device or process your invention applies to.

>> Reasons that led you to develop the invention.

>> Explanation of how the invention came about (unexpected discovery, trial-and-error approach, a flash of genius, in a dream . . .).

>> Where you developed the invention (for example, as part of your employment or contracted job, or using someone else's resources or facilities).

>> Outline of the existing problems the invention resolves.

>> Account of how these problems were handled in the past.

>> Your opinion about what the invention does that couldn't be done before, or why it's an improvement over past devices or methods.

>> Depiction of the closest thing to your invention.

>> Documents or references that best describe the most recent advances in the field of the invention.

>> Lists and copies of all patents, publications, treatises, articles, and other written material at your disposal that may be relevant to your invention. You are not required to conduct any particular research. If you've done a search (described in Chapter 1 of Book 2), you'll have this info at your fingertips.

>> Anticipation search results and any professional patentability opinion.

>> All records of your development efforts.

>> Dates of conception of the invention, first sketch or description, first prototype construction, first public showing, first published description, first public use, first offer to sell, first advertisement, and first sale.

>> Explanation of the circumstances if the invention was first implemented in a foreign country.

>> Identification of all persons (including children) who contributed to the conception and a brief description of each co-inventor's contribution. Include full names, addresses, residences, and citizenships.

>> Copies of any prior filings, such as prior patent applications, whether still active or abandoned.

>> Copies of any assignment, licence, or business agreement related to the invention.

>> Copies of identifying documents, such as Articles of Incorporation, Partnership Certificates, and fictitious name registrations, for any business that is (or may become) owner of the patent or the invention.

>> Complete description of the invention, including drawings, photographs, prototypes, test results, newspaper accounts, testimonials, and anything else that could help your IP pro understand and appreciate the invention.

>> Concise description (a single paragraph of 10–15 lines) of the basic structure of your invention that can serve as a model for the *abstract* portion of the application. Don't get into the invention's advantages here. (See the earlier section "Deconstructing the Patent Application.")

>> Brief account of how you plan to exploit your invention, either through your own manufacturing, by licensing others, or by outright sale.

Looking over the pro's shoulder

You just received the first draft of your patent application and are about to review it alone or in a tête-à-tête with your lawyer. Be sure to ask your IP lawyer or agent to clarify anything you don't understand or change anything that doesn't adequately describe your invention.

Scrutinizing the claims

Because the claims are the most important part of the application, you should go over them with a fine-toothed comb. Be sure that you and the claim drafter are on the same wavelength. Verify that the part of the technology that's recited is exactly the one that needs to be protected.

You may discover that the most critical aspect of your invention is recited in a dependent claim. Because you can claim only one invention in a patent, ask your lawyer to reverse the organization of the claims to recite the most important portion of the invention in an independent claim. It can't hurt to include both separate independent claims drawn to each aspect. Although this inclusion will likely provoke a restriction requirement, it will also establish your right to eventually get a patent for each "invention."

REMEMBER

If a claim lists every detail of the structure, down to the kitchen sink, stove, and oven, talk with your lawyer about eliminating or rewriting it. A narrow claim doesn't provide much of a net to catch an infringer, it takes up too much space, and it adds to the filing fee (see the upcoming section "Paying the piper"). Do make sure that every inventive feature is listed in one or more claims. Don't worry too much yet about whether you're claiming more than one invention in a single application. Later, you can answer the patent examiner's objection by reshuffling the claim pyramid or by withdrawing some claims to be resubmitted.

Focusing the abstract

Verify that the abstract describes the gist of your invention in plain language, without using legalistic terms such as *means for* and *whereas*. Typically, the abstract reflects the principal claim (usually Claim 1).

Checking the drawing

The drawing must be done in accordance with CIPO guidelines. Patent lawyer and agents use professional patent draftspersons, who work from sketches prepared by the professional based on your description. The drawing must illustrate every item recited in the claims. It can be as simple as a block diagram or a flowchart. Don't include more figures than absolutely necessary to describe the preferred embodiment of the invention. Don't draw every nut and bolt. A patent drawing is an illustration, not a manufacturing blueprint.

Reviewing the disclosure

When you look at some patents, you may think that the drafter was paid by the page. There's too much information, including verbiage that's not legally required and doesn't advance the case for patentability.

TIP

Brevity gives you a practical advantage. When you file abroad, you're charged by the word or page for translation and filing. You can save hundreds of dollars with a little literary restraint. For example, the *Background of the Invention* section is no place for a lengthy listing and discussion of prior patents and publications. To make your application short and effective, cross out anything that doesn't support the language of the claims or any detailed description of things well known to a person skilled in the field of the invention.

Paying the piper

Now is the time to painfully reach for your wallet. Most IP professionals insist that you pay their fees before they file the application. After an IP professional enters the papers in the CIPO under her Joan Hancock, she is obligated (whether or not she's been paid) to do everything reasonably necessary to advance your case (unless relieved of her duty by petitioning the Commissioner of Patents). You also have to pay the application filing fee, which is based, in part, on the number and types of claims you present.

Sending Your Application

The current mailing address for your patent application is: Commissioner of Patents, Canadian Intellectual Property Office, Place du Portage, 50 Victoria Street, Room C114, Gatineau QC K1A 0C9. But check the CIPO website for any changes.

TIP

If you're familiar with the terms *browser, PDF,* and *upload,* you should consider filing your utility patent application online. Apart from the added peace of mind of getting immediate feedback that your application has been successfully filed, you currently save money on the filing fee. Visit www.ic.gc.ca/eic/site/cipointernet-internetopic.nsf/eng/wr01477.html to access the application form online.

TIP

Make sure you leave yourself plenty of time to navigate your way through the system. While filing your application, keep a browser window open on the filing wizard and another one open on the FAQ for quick reference (check out www.ic.gc.ca/eic/site/cipointernet-internetopic.nsf/eng/h_wr03652.html#faq).

Meeting Your Filing Deadlines

Dates are everything, and we're not talking about what you're doing this weekend. In Canada, a patent application must be filed before all the following time deadlines:

>> A reasonable time from the date of invention. Any unjustified delay may be legally construed as an abandonment of your invention, which can allow a later inventor to get the patent.

>> Within one year from

  ● Your offer to sell the invention.

  ● A public use or showing of the invention.

  ● A description of the invention in a publication.

  ● The filing date of a foreign application upon which you want to claim priority.

>> As soon as possible after you've developed a viable invention. If you know you're going to apply for a patent, why wait?

REMEMBER

Most foreign countries require that you file your first domestic patent application before *any* public disclosure of the invention and that you file your application abroad within one year of the first filing.

Patent applications are automatically published about 18 months after the filing date (or from any earlier priority date you may have claimed based on a prior domestic or foreign application). Until an application is published on the CIPO website, only you and your patent lawyer can access the application file.

Speeding Up Your Application and Other Special Provisions

In general, patent applications are examined in the order of their *effective filing dates*, typically their actual filing dates or their priority dates, whichever came first. This statement is qualified with words such as *in general* and *typically* because this rule is subject to many exceptions. What else is new? Not to get into irritating details, but your application may not rise to the top of the pile for one to two years.

However, if your trigger finger is itchy enough, you may be able to benefit from some special patent provisions:

>> You can ask to fast-track your patent application examination if it's related to clean technology.

>> You may be able to fast-track your patent application examination if you have an application with one of Canada's Patent Prosecution Highway (PPH) partners.

>> You may be able to pay fees at the small entity level for small businesses and universities.

>> You may be able to provide CIPO with relevant information if you think a patent application may create barriers for your business.

And of course, hiring an IP agent can also help speed up the process, and you can also go in person to the Gatineau office.

TIP

Check out `www.ic.gc.ca/eic/site/cipointernet-internetopic.nsf/eng/wr04204.html` for full details on these special provisions.

Doing a Few Wise Things While You Wait

Years may pass before a patent is issued — if it's issued. While you wait, you can exploit your invention in the same ways you'll use to make some cash after you get your patent: manufacturing and selling products embodying the invention, licensing your invention and patent to others for royalties, and selling the invention and patent rights.

WARNING

Do *not* disclose the contents, serial number, or filing date of your patent application to anyone, except under strict conditions of confidentiality, before it is published by the CIPO. Even if the receiving party has signed a confidentiality agreement, don't disclose the wording of the pending claims.

While your patent is pending, someone who's filed an application for the same invention may challenge your application. This process determines which of two inventors claiming the same invention deserves the patent. Someone privy to your patent application can file his own application, copy some of your claims, and trigger an interference proceeding. If the person knows the date of your patent application filing, he can claim an earlier date of invention. Just the expenses and delay associated with the interference are enough to give you nightmares. Further, the usurper might walk away with the patent.

TIP

Don't forget to mark your products "Patent Pending" and make your licensees do the same. Although it can't support an infringement claim, the notice deters potential copycats. They'll hesitate to invest in manufacturing your product, for fear they may be shut down within months. But if you let it be known that you *just* filed your patent application, a copycat may speculate that he has two or three years to compete without consequences — a good reason to keep your filing date secret until your application is published.

Chapter **3**

Making Your Copyright Official

Copyright law casts a very broad net. It's hard to imagine a human endeavour that doesn't have a copyrightable component. Whether you write a book, peddle hotdogs from a street cart, lead an exercise class, teach a knitting course, sell real estate, or design a sophisticated, scientific instrument, copyright issues are all over the place.

While bouncing about your exercise studio, teaching your knitting class, decorating your street cart, programming your computer, or designing a new electronic package, you use recorded music, textbooks, audio-visual teaching aids, graphics, promotional material, mask works or multiple listing compilations — all *original works of authorship* (OWAs) protected by copyrights.

Each of these OWAs raises ownership and protection issues and conceals potential legal pitfalls for the unwary. And as you create your masterpiece or hire someone to do it for you, understanding who created an OWA, and consequently, who has the rights to it, is vitally important. An oversight or mistake in this area can have disastrous consequences.

This chapter talks about how to decide whether you own a copyright (and if not, who does), how to give or sell your copyright to someone else, and how to track down copyright ownership. Often, it's fairly simple and you can figure it out yourself. But if it all seems incredibly confusing, your IP lawyer can help you unravel the tangle of copyright ownership.

You don't have to do anything to get a copyright, except create and own an original work of authorship. However, before you can go to court and stop a copycat, you must first register your copyright with the Canadian Intellectual Property Office (CIPO). Luckily for you, in most cases, the registration is a relatively simple and inexpensive process that you should be able to handle by yourself after you read this chapter.

REMEMBER

If you have an unusual case and you face a complex situation that raises a legal issue, consult a copyright lawyer. CIPO also has a detailed website on copyright at www.ic.gc.ca/eic/site/cipointernet-internetopic.nsf/eng/h_wr00003.html. You can find a simple guide to copyright at www.ic.gc.ca/eic/site/cipointernet-internetopic.nsf/eng/h_wr02281.html?Open&wt_src=cipo-cpyrght-main&wt_cxt=learn.

Making Sure You Own the Copyright

Any original creation is a potentially valuable intellectual property. And when you start throwing the word *valuable* around, you know things won't remain simple for long. If you've been locked away in your home office writing a masterpiece or developing the next world-famous pantomime routine, the question of who owns the original work of authorship (OWA) is probably simple — you do. However, if you developed a script while working for a movie production studio, or wrote the background music as a freelance composer, chances are that the studio owns the copyright in your creation. But if you're reading this chapter, your situation may be a bit more complex.

Many of the difficulties and costly litigations that you can have with copyrights involve questions of ownership. The usual participants in the great ownership debate are you and your associates. Anyone who contributed to an OWA may have a full or partial interest in the work. You need to be aware of how the legalities of ownership affect your role in the creative process.

Under Canadian copyright law, the creator (or author) of the work is the owner of the copyright in it. There are many circumstances where work is created as part of the author's work duties, which may give the employer the copyright ownership. Without getting a clear agreement first, even if something was created for your company such as a graphic, the copyright might not belong to you.

REMEMBER

The Canadian Copyright Act states that the author of the work is the first owner of the copyright in it. There are examples of each: correspondence, images, newspaper or magazine contributions, collective works, co-authored works, music, translation, and so on. A big section of the act deals with work that is made during employment, which is where it can get tricky and there are several factors to consider. Read the act at https://laws-lois.justice.gc.ca/eng/acts/c-42/.

TIP

One of the big differences in Canadian copyright opposed to the United States is that Canada has the copyright duration set as the author's life plus 50 years where in the United States it is the author's life plus 70 years, and the term of protection may also vary in the United States depending on the circumstances. Visit http://www.ic.gc.ca/eic/site/cipointernet-internetopic.nsf/eng/h_wr02281.html?Open&wt_src=cipo-cpyrght-main&wt_cxt=learn.

If you work (on your own and not as someone's employee) with a coauthor, you two jointly own the copyright, unless you have an agreement to the contrary. For example, when two or more authors collaborate in creating a novel or journal article, it is considered joint ownership. The authors jointly own the copyright as well as the ability to exercise their rights. For example, they cannot sell their work without the permission from one another.

Joint ownership of the copyright, just like a business partnership or a marriage, can be messy and quickly turn nasty when a disagreement surfaces. Contrary to patent law, which allows each co-inventor to exploit the invention independently without accounting to the other, joint owners of a copyright must account to each other for any benefit realized from the licensing or sale of the work or the copyright — and share the benefit. However, a joint owner can exploit the copyright or even transfer it to a third party without permission from the other owner — which can lead to very awkward situations.

REMEMBER

The main thing to keep in mind is to get a clear agreement first with whatever you co-author or otherwise joint copyright applies, and if the work is complex with many individuals or could have an impact from your employer, it is best to check with a lawyer for the agreement. Having agreements in business is a smart practise, especially when dealing with ownership and the right to work and how to use it. If you want to use the co-owned work for a different purpose, you must also ensure that you have permission from the original copyright owner, whether it be the original author or someone they have assigned the copyright to.

If you can't avoid joint ownership of a copyright, you and the other joint owner should sign a written comprehensive agreement that spells out all critical and potentially contentious issues, such as the following:

» **Respective percentages of ownership:** The interest of co-owners of a copyright can be apportioned in any percentages the parties decide. If you can't agree, the law presumes that all parties have an equal, undivided interest in the copyright.

» **Joint or separate right to exploit the copyright:** Whether or not you and the other co-owner are equal owners, you can exploit the copyright jointly or allow each other to take advantage of any opportunity separately. You must also decide whether to pool your benefits or let each party keep his or her own receipts.

» **Right to prepare a derivative work:** A derivative work can become more lucrative than the original, even to a point where there's no more market for the original.

For example, John and Rob together devise an asset management computer program, tailored to Rob's tool-rental business. Both are co-authors of the program and co-owners of the copyright. Larry, Rob's friend who operates vending machines, hears about the program and asks Rob to help him write a similar program for his business.

Starting with the tool-rental management program, Rob and Larry develop a more sophisticated program to manage Larry's vending machine operation. The new program adapts easily to other businesses. Rob and Larry, finding more and more applications for the program, embark on a very lucrative licensing venture.

Rob must account to John for all proceeds collected from the exploitation of the initial program. However, knowing that the new program is far more elaborate than the original program, Rob thinks that John only deserves a very small percentage of the proceeds from the second program (if any).

If John sues Rob and Larry for a reasonable share of those proceeds, a court would most likely award half of the proceeds to Larry (the half owner of the new program) and a quarter of the proceeds to each Rob and John, the owners of equal and undivided shares of the copyright in the original program, upon which the derivative work is based.

Here's why: Although John and Rob created the original program, when the second program was developed, Larry also became a part owner. If John didn't want any more partners, in an initial agreement between Rob and John, he should've specified that each party has veto power over a joint authorship of a derivative work with a third party.

>> **Right to transfer one's interest to a third party:** If you aren't comfortable with joint ownership, you should arrange for each party to have first choice in buying the interest of the other.

>> **Right of succession in case of death or disability of one party:** Succession laws vary from province to province. You can bypass those laws with a well-drafted agreement that guarantees an orderly transfer of the copyright to the surviving co-owner upon paying a stipulated sum to the deceased party's estate. You can fund and guarantee that payment by each taking an insurance policy on the life of the other.

REMEMBER

All these considerations have important legal implications that deserve the attention of a competent lawyer.

Transferring Copyright Ownership

The copyright to an OWA can be sliced like salami into separate ownership portions (legally called interests) that you can then assign (transfer) to different people. You can also assign to different parties all or some of the various exclusive rights of a copyright owner. For example, a movie studio can get the right to make a TV sitcom from your story, while a magazine can serialize it over a number of weeks.

REMEMBER

Transferring copyright ownership is simple essentially unless there are legal issues or disputes among the owners. In Canada either the whole or a part can be transferred to another party, but the transfer must be in writing and signed by the copyright owner. A lawyer should be involved.

The law is very clear that an OWA isn't created until it is *fixed* (in a tangible or reproducible state). Furthermore, when a work is prepared over a period of time, the portion of it that is fixed at any particular point in time constitutes the work as of that time.

WARNING

You can only transfer copyright ownership on what is fixed at the time of the transfer. The transfer doesn't automatically cover any part of the work that will be created and fixed in the future. Accordingly, if you ask a contractor to assign (transfer) a copyright on his contribution to a project before the work is started or fixed, the assignment document will have no legal effect.

REMEMBER

The basic rule of transferring an entire copyright interest is to get it in writing. Any transfer, other than by court order, inheritance, or other automatic manner specified by law, is invalid unless it's in a written conveyance (the transfer of an interest from one person to another) signed by the owner.

Note that the conveyance of a partial interest, such as a nonexclusive licence, need not be in writing to be legally effective. But who would be foolish enough to enter into a license agreement by oral agreement?

A written conveyance assignment effectively transfers copyright ownership. But you need to go one step further. You must have the conveyance notarized (or sworn before an authorized person) to use it in court as *prima facie evidence* (evidence admissible without any further proof) of the transfer.

TIP

If you assign the copyright abroad, have it witnessed by a diplomatic or consular officer or by a foreign official authorized to administer oaths (much as a notary would be here). Make sure that the official certifies his or her authority, for example with a seal or stamp.

TIP

Check out `www.ic.gc.ca/eic/site/cipointernet-internetopic.nsf/eng/wr00054.html?Open&wt_src=cipo-cpyrght-main` for more information on transferring copyright ownership.

Investigating the Status of a Copyright

Imagine yourself in one of these situations:

>> You're writing a coffee-table book about Renaissance gardens. You found an encyclopedia containing beautiful engravings of wild roses, and you'd like to use them to illustrate your own work. You need to find the owner of the copyright covering these engravings and get permission to copy them.

>> You're writing a short skit for a high school performance and want to use the music of a popular song with your own lyrics. You need permission to create your derivative work from the song's copyright owner.

>> You own a small bronze statue of a Tom Sawyer character that you'd like to reproduce as part of a painting or photographic print. You can't do it without permission from the owner of the copyright in the statue.

>> You want to incorporate a number of pre-existing OWAs in your own creation, but don't have the time or resources to obtain necessary licences or permissions from copyright owners. So you decide to select pre-existing works are in the *public domain,* which means they were never or are no longer copyrighted.

Your course of action in any of these four situations isn't easy. In addition, the older the work, the harder identifying the current copyright owner becomes. If you're lucky enough to identify and find the copyright owner, getting a licence or permission can be like pulling teeth, unless you're ready to plunk down a good amount of cash.

REMEMBER

Before you spend time and money searching for a copyright owner, keep in mind that finding the owner is no guarantee that you'll readily get the licence or permission you need. The copyright owner may be unwilling to grant you one or may be under a legal obligation to prohibit anyone from using the work. The price you can pay for the permission or licence isn't worth what the copyright owner's lawyer might charge to prepare the necessary paperwork.

WARNING

If you can't secure the permission, don't even think of using the copyrighted material without it. A copyright owner can get a relatively large damage award for a single infringement act — without having to prove any loss resulting from the infringement. Not good news for you.

Here are some general guidelines for your quest to find a copyright owner and secure permission. First, find your best good luck charm — you're gonna need it.

>> If you're certain that a work has been on the market or that the copyright has been registered for more than 95 years, you can safely assume the work is in the public domain. However, make sure you're not copying a more recent edition or adaptation that may still have a copyright.

>> For a book, first contact the publisher. You may get lucky and talk with a very understanding lawyer or licensing agent who can answer all your questions and give you the licence or permission you're after. Based on our own experience, even if you find him, he's unlikely to be that cooperative. Unless you get a final refusal by the copyright owner, you need to keep digging. To find the copyright owner, first check the copyright notice on the work.

>> If you're interested in a musical work, start with the record company. If you have no luck there, try to contact a mechanical licensing agency — a clearing house that a songwriter or a music publishing company uses to license record companies.

>> When dealing with a statue or other sculptural work, consult an art dealer if you can't decipher a recognizable name on the work. She may be able to identify the author and the approximate date of distribution.

>> Search the Canadian Copyrights Database. Visit `www.ic.gc.ca/app/opic-cipo/cpyrghts/dsplySrch.do?lang=eng&wt_src=cipo-cpyrght-main&wt_cxt=toptask` for details.

>> Some companies offer copyright clearance and licensing services over the Internet. For a start you can try `www.copyright.com`.

>> As a last resort, consult a copyright lawyer.

Registering Your Copyright

REMEMBER

Registering a copyright consists essentially of filling out an official application form provided by CIPO, filing it along with a nominal fee ($50 for online filing and $65 for mailing at the time of this writing), and submitting some material that identifies your creation. When the good people at CIPO get to your application, they'll either stamp it and return it to you as a proof of registration, send you a request for more info, or heaven forbid, flatly reject it because you didn't follow our directions.

Seems pretty straightforward, doesn't it? Hold your horses. As with all legal formalities, a few tricky twists and turns await you along the way that require careful consideration about when to apply for registration. Don't worry. You find out all about that, but as an incentive to register your copyright, you discover all the good things the registration will accomplish for you.

REMEMBER

Registration isn't mandatory. That's what they say, but don't believe it. If there is a chance someone might copy or unlawfully use your work, you'll want it to be registered. Because discretion is the better part of valor (or of a savvy business mind), and the bad guys really are out there, you should always register the copyright in your creations.

Getting to court

REMEMBER

The main reason for registering your copyright is to give you the right to file an action for infringement in court. Basically, *infringement* is the unauthorized use of a copyrighted work. Unless you're a foreign resident, you can't file a complaint against a copycat if you didn't register your copyright.

CIPO may take some time to process your application and confirm the registration, but don't fret — it's supposed to be effective from the day it reaches them. You can send your application today, and file an infringement complaint tomorrow. If the judge finds your application in good order and upholds your complaint, she may direct authorities to seize infringing goods and issue a restraining order to suspend all infringing activities. If the validity or your application is iffy, she may wait to see what CIPO does with it before issuing her orders.

Making it legal

A registration made within five years of the publication of your work becomes *prima facie* (legally sufficient) proof that your copyright is valid. After you introduce the registration in evidence, the burden of proof shifts to the infringing defendant, who must then establish the invalidity of your copyright or use another persuasive defense like "The devil made me do it."

Giving public notice

Registration puts potential infringers on notice that your work is copyrighted, preventing copycats from pleading ignorance. Imagine that some deceitful character named Zook convinces The Bamboozle Company that he's the author of your song or the owner of the copyright. For a fee, Zook feloniously grants Bamboozle a licence to record your ballad. In an action brought against Zook and Bamboozle, the latter can't plead ignorance and innocent infringement. The law presumes that the company checked the ownership of the copyright in the CIPO records.

Making the most of your day in court

Hopefully you never have to bring a legal action to stop an infringement of your copyright, but if you do, it's good to go into court as soon as you can, armed with all the evidence you need to win your case.

» **Collecting more at court:** If you registered before the infringement, you can ask for statutory rather than actual damages. *Statutory damages,* contrary to actual damages, don't require proof and accounting of your losses. Instead, the judge looks at the conduct of the defendant to determine how much to give you, much like with punitive damages in a personal injury action. If you haven't yet exploited your work, you may be unable to show actual loss that you can attribute to the defendant's conduct. That's when statutory damages are a better deal. Even better, the law specifies minimum statutory damage amounts — which may top the amount of losses you could document and prove in court.

Having your registration on file before your copyright is infringed also allows you to receive an award of lawyer's fees when you win the infringement action. Considering what lawyers charge these days, that award may far exceed any actual or statutory damages.

» **Getting a second chance:** Your registration may be refused for a number of reasons, such as lack of substantiality, lack of original creativity, or mere functionality of the work. Of course, the refusal is the opinion of an application examiner and is never final. Talk to your copyright lawyer. If, in his opinion, your application for registration has some merit, he'll suggest an appeal. An appeal takes time. (That's why it's always advisable to file your application for registration as early as possible and get the matter settled before you need to sue someone.)

Timing is everything: When to register

REMEMBER

To get the maximum protection, you should register your copyright within three months from first sale, distribution, or other disposition of your work. Any of these acts constitutes a *publication* of your work. That way you're covered for any infringement that took place right after the publication and before registration. But you don't have to wait that long. You may gain the following advantages by doing a pre-publication registration:

>> Your pre-publication application allows you to confront and resolve any eventual registration problems very early in the game.

>> The pre-publication registration acts as an early notice of your claim. It allows you to ask for statutory damages and lawyer's fees from an early copycat or other infringer.

>> You don't have to file a post-publication registration unless you have added copyrightable material to your work.

>> In a pre-publication application, you may group a number of related works, such as a series of posters or postcards in a single application. After publication, you can only bundle works that were published together, forcing you to file multiple applications.

Finding and Filling Out Forms

TIP

Filling out a copyright registration form couldn't be easier. You have two choices:

>> You can file online at the CIPO website here (you need an account to get started): www.ic.gc.ca/app/scr/opic-cipo/da-cpr/depot-filing/connexion-login_eng.htm.

>> You find links to the copyright registration PDF here, along with other helpful forms: www.ic.gc.ca/eic/site/cipointernet-internetopic.nsf/eng/h_wr00021.html. The PDF itself is at www.ic.gc.ca/eic/site/cipointernet-internetopic.nsf/vwapj/DA-CR-form1-eng.pdf/$file/DA-CR-form1-eng.pdf.

Note: There's a different form to use if you're registering a copyright in a performance, sound recording, or communication signal. Check it out here: www.ic.gc.ca/eic/site/cipointernet-internetopic.nsf/vwapj/DA-CR-form2-eng.pdf/$file/DA-CR-form2-eng.pdf.

Although copyright registration forms come with guidelines on how to fill them out, applications may be rejected or delayed because of errors. Most errors are because the applicants (and even their lawyers) misunderstand the terminology used on the forms or the basic concepts behind copyright law.

The following sections address the most common mistakes people make when filling out these forms and give you some additional guidelines.

Title

Just like every file in your computer needs a name, the CIPO needs a handle to process your application. So make sure you enter a title, any title, for the work in Section 1 of the application form. "My Creation: Volume 1" will do if you can't think of something more specific (but being a creative person, you'll surely do better than that).

Category

Verify the category (or categories) to which your work belongs. Then pick the appropriate form from the list in Section 2 of the application form. "That's so simple," Simple Simon says. Yet misclassifying your work is one of the most common mistakes found in copyright registration applications. The consequences can be costly.

REMEMBER

Do your homework. Read the instructions on the forms, brush up your expertise by rereading this chapter, and carefully review all the forms before you send in your registration application. If you use a lawyer, make sure he's expert in the field.

Publication

If the work was published, indicate the date, city/town, province/state, and country of first publication in Section 3. Giving a false date, especially one that's later than the actual date, can invalidate your registration. If you don't remember the exact day or month, enter the earliest date you earnestly believe your work may have been published.

Publication occurs when you dispose of *copies* of your work, which means that you temporarily or permanently give up possession and control of at least one copy of the work by sale, rental, lease, or free distribution. For example, temporarily lending your novel to a publisher for consideration isn't publication. But giving copies of your manuscript (even an early draft) to your friends is.

REMEMBER

Publication concerns physical copies that can be passed around. Disposing of the original isn't a publication. Neither is performing or displaying it publicly or transmitting it over the airwaves.

Ownership, authorship, and declaration

Enter the name and address of the current copyright owner as the claimant in Section 4 of the form. A copyright owner isn't necessarily the person in possession of the original work, but the entity holding the copyright. In other words, the owner can different from the author named in Section 5 because the copyright was transferred.

REMEMBER

An assignment or transfer of exclusive rights must be in writing and signed by the transferor. A handshake agreement won't do.

Section 6 contains a declaration that the person applying for the copyright is either the author of the work, the owner of the copyright of the work, an assignee of the copyright, or a licensee of the copyright.

Administrative matters

Section 7 is only for agents working on behalf of the applicant; it asks for the agent's name and address, with the option to include a telephone number, a fax number, and an email address. Section 8 reminds you to pay your filing fee!

REMEMBER

If you're mailing the form (rather than filing online), be sure to sign the application and enclose your check for the filing fee.

Marking Your Copyrighted Work

REMEMBER

Placing a copyright notice on every published copy of your work, in one of the following forms, fulfils some important functions. It

>> Warns people that the work is covered by copyright and deters infringement.

>> Prevents a person charged with infringement from claiming innocence.

>> Increases damage awards for willful infringement.

>> Improves your chance of foiling infringers with procedures such as restraining orders, preliminary injunctions, and seizure of counterfeit goods. A restraining order or a preliminary injunction stops the infringer until a trial on the issue or an amicable settlement of the case.

>> Identifies the copyright owner.

>> Informs the public of the date of publication.

Formatting the copyright notice

A copyright notice consists of three elements:

>> The word *Copyright,* the abbreviation *Copr,* or the symbol ©. Use the *circled P* in the case of a sound recording.

>> The year the work was first published (distributed).

>> The identification of the copyright owner (name, abbreviation, or symbol by which the name can be recognized).

TIP

Always use the © symbol. It's the only one recognized by certain countries under the Universal Copyright Convention.

Placing the notice

Depending on the nature of the work, you need to place the notice in a conspicuous place:

>> **Book:** On the first page, the title page, or the back of the title page.

>> **Magazine or other periodical:** Same as for a book or near the title, volume number, and date. One notice covers all articles in the periodical, except for advertising by someone other than the magazine owner.

>> **Collective work:** On each separate contribution under or near the title or at the end of the contribution.

>> **Work on machine-readable media:** Disks, tapes, or CD-ROMs must display the notice at sign-on, near the title, at the end of the screen-displayed image, on printouts, or on the medium or its container.

>> **Movie or other audio-visual work:** Embodied into the work's medium, so that the notice appears near the title, at the beginning or end of the work, or with the cast of characters or credits. If the work lasts 60 seconds or less, the notice can be on the film or tape leader. The notice must also appear on the permanent housing (cassette body) or container (cardboard pocket).

>> **Pictorial, graphic, or sculptural work:** On any visible part of the work. If the work is too small or doesn't have a front or back surface that can bear the notice, use a label or tag attached to the work.

>> **Phonorecord:** On the label or any visible portion of the phonorecord.

TIP

You don't have to place a copyright notice on the original work, only on copies. If the work is not yet published, you don't need to have a notice, but displaying it on copies anyway is a good idea — just in case they fall into some unscrupulous person's hands. Just write it as ©2003 Jane Deer (unpublished).

Chapter **4**

Naming, Establishing, and Registering Your Trademark

You're very excited — you've just come up with the perfect name for your new business. But is it up for grabs? Probably not. Finding an available trade name or trademark on your first try is like winning the lottery! Count on researching at least three options before you stumble on an available moniker. This chapter fills you in on what an availability search is (and what it isn't) and the purpose of a search. You then discover what an appropriate availability search involves, a search strategy that you can use, and how to analyse your findings. Finally, you read about the many advantages of registering your mark.

REMEMBER

This chapter is restricted to word identifiers. Common graphical elements like "triangles" and "arrows" are too common to narrow search results. Unless your mark uses a fairly uncommon graphical element with a well-known definition (for example, a Gaelic cross), there's no practical way to research prior use of graphic and configuration marks except by thumbing through thousands of pages of trademark registers and electronically searching for keywords in the description of these marks found in some of these registers.

REMEMBER

These few pages can't cover all the complex aspects of applying to register a mark. The bottom line? Don't dispense with the advice and services of a good intellectual property (IP) professional. To find out all about trademarks, check out this site from the Canadian Intellectual Property Office: www.ic.gc.ca/eic/site/cipointernet-internetopic.nsf/eng/h_wr00002. html. You can find out a roadmap of the trademark registration process here: www.ic.gc.ca/eic/site/cipointernet-internetopic.nsf/eng/wr04355. html?Open&wt_src=cipo-tm-main. Plus a guide to trademarks is available here: www.ic.gc.ca/eic/site/cipointernet-internetopic.nsf/eng/h_wr02360. html?Open&wt_src=cipo-tm-main&wt_cxt=learn.

Defining the Scope of Your Search

The extent of your search depends on the identifier that you want to use and register. So before you get ready to search, make sure that you understand your own identifier. You can then set the search boundaries.

Assessing your choice of identifier

The scope of your search and the interpretation of your search results (see "Analysing the Results," later in this chapter) depend upon two factors:

>> The legal strength of the identifier

>> The intended field and territory of use

The *legal strength* of a commercial identifier is its ability to prevent other businesses from using the same or confusingly similar identifiers. So your first order of business in the great name search is to assess where your prospective commercial identifier falls on the *legal strength scale* — generic, descriptive, suggestive, or arbitrary.

After you've taken your legal-strength reading, you need to delineate the anticipated *field and territory of use.* In other words, define the nature and utilization, collectively called the *definition,* of your goods or services and the geographical areas where they'll be marketed. It's a three-step process:

1. **Write a concise definition of the nature, role, or function of the business, product, or service for which you want to use the prospective identifier.**

   Here are some examples:

   - A business manufacturing automotive engine parts
   - An engineering inspection and certification service for dwellings
   - A single retail shop for high-end female fashion apparel
   - A series of medical tomography scanners
   - A nationwide fast-food restaurant chain
   - An adult table game

2. **Compare your product or service definition with those found in the CIPO's Goods and Services Manual** in order to determine which *international class* (IC) or classes you should search.

   The listing of terms is classified according to the Nice Classification — the International Classification of Goods and Services for the Purposes of the Registration of Marks. You can see a list of classes under the Nice Class Search tab here: `https://www.ic.gc.ca/eic/site/cipointernet-internetopic.nsf/eng/wr03980.html`.

3. **Write down the jurisdictions where the commercial identifier will be used.** For example, you may choose a province or a number of provinces.

Setting boundaries

So, you've narrowed your search down to one or more ICs. But that's still a pretty big sea to swim in — you need to narrow it even further. Enter your old friend — the legal-strength scale:

REMEMBER

» **Distinctive:** If your commercial identifier is distinctive because it's either suggestive or arbitrary, you must extend your search to practically all areas of commercial activities. The trademark Kodak, for example, could refer to anything, so you'd need to look wider than the photographic industry and into every IC.

Folks before you already have a ton of legal protection for their distinctive marks. But after you clear your distinctive mark, you're afforded the same protection.

>> **Descriptive:** If your commercial identifier is merely descriptive, you can limit your search to fields related to your industry. If you're searching for the trade name Banff Brewers, for example, limit it to the wine, beer, and liquor classes. The downside is that even if you find no one else using your mark, a descriptive mark offers very little protection against infringers.

>> **Generic:** If your commercial identifier is generic, don't bother searching because anyone is free to use it.

TIP

If your name is a combination of words, try to identify the word or words that are least descriptive of your goods or services. For example, for the name Lonely Loon Lawn Services, focus your assessment on Lonely Loon.

Carrying Out Your Search

You can search a few places to see whether the trademark you have in mind is in use. If you find the name you had in mind already taken on your first go-around, at least you've saved some time that you can devote to coming up with another name.

On the Internet

The Internet, that cornucopia of information, is a bonanza for name searches. You need only type in a word, and the search engine fetches hundreds — sometimes thousands — of references. Sometimes the volume retrieved is so overwhelming that you need to narrow it down by adding words to the search criteria. You can request an advanced search, where you can search on a number of keywords or an exact combination of words. For example, if you search for tornado as a mark for a drain cleaner, you get over three hundred million references with one search engine. But if you enter the combination *tornado* and *drain*, you get only around seven million results. At least it's a start, right?

TIP

If your name uses a "borrowed term" — an already existing word, such as *tornado* — your search will turn up hits where the word is descriptive rather than part of a commercial identifier. To reduce these hits, try subtracting words related to the descriptive use. For example, try "tornado -weather" (many search engines interpret a minus sign immediately in front of a word as *not*). However, keep in mind that this may eliminate some useful hits as well.

If you don't find your moniker on the Internet, you have a pretty good chance that nobody is already using it. But unless you have coined a very unique term like Kodak or Xokkox, you're more likely to hit so many references that you have to sift through and then interpret them, as explained later in this chapter.

In the CIPO database

The CIPO maintains a comprehensive database of trademarks. You can access the Canadian Trademarks Database at www.ic.gc.ca/app/opic-cipo/trdmrks/srch/home?lang=eng.

TIP

Feeling stuck on how to proceed? The CIPO provides a step-by-step tutorial on using the Canadian Trademarks Database at www.ic.gc.ca/eic/site/cipointernet-internetopic.nsf/eng/wr00036.html.

WARNING

If your search results in no hits, don't start celebrating just yet. Double-check to make sure that you haven't misspelled your name or used some overly restrictive criteria.

TIP

Make sure you try different definitions of your goods or services. For example, after *bar*, try synonyms such as *tavern, barroom, saloon,* or *lounge.* After plugging in *washcloth*, also try *towel, sponge, wash rag, bathrobe, bathtub,* or *washbasin.*

Using foreign searches

If you're planning to export your products or services, you may want to verify that your mark doesn't conflict with any mark used in other countries.

TIP

Many foreign trademark registers are accessible online. Each country has its own way of doing things, so be prepared to master a new search syntax for each country of interest. Find these sources by typing in the name of the country of interest followed by "trademark office" into your favorite Internet search engine. Again, use the site that looks most like a government site instead of a commercial site trying to get your business. Stay away from the .com and .co extensions. If you want more confidence in your search result, use a native trademark agent to conduct this type of search. Most domestic intellectual property (IP) lawyers have correspondents in major industrial countries whom they call upon for international inquiries.

The World Intellectual Property Organization (WIPO) in Geneva, Switzerland, maintains databases of international trademark applications and registrations filed under the Madrid system. This system allows you to get a single international trademark registration which gets submitted to the individual country trademark offices you designate. For trademark info, look on the organization's website, www.wipo.org, and work your way from the intellectual property section to the trademarks area. Visit www.wipo.int/madrid/en/ for more about the Madrid system.

TIP

The laws pertaining to commercial identifiers vary from country to country. In most parts of the world, you can only acquire exclusive rights by registration. Consult an IP lawyer before you spend time and resources checking foreign trade names and marks.

Analysing Your Search Results

Keep in mind that finding no reference to your prospective name in all the available sources of commercial identifiers is no guarantee that it's available. Because so many commercial monikers are unregistered and unsearchable, the possibility of inadvertently infringing on some obscure yet protected trade name or trademark is always there. On the other hand, finding out that your baby is already in use doesn't necessarily prevent you from using it as well.

If you do find that your commercial identifier (or something resembling it) is already in use, you have to consider the legal issue of whether using this identifier is likely to cause confusion in the marketplace.

REMEMBER

Only an IP specialist can give you a fairly reliable answer on this complex question, but even that would only be a guesstimate. Because the standards for determining likelihood of confusion are so imprecise and dependent upon the circumstances of the case, many lawyers and law firms plainly refuse to issue a definitive opinion on the subject. Foolish would be the lawyer who cleared a name of all risks of infringement.

Yet you have to make that judgment, unless you decide to drop any candidate name that is identical or vaguely similar to one already in use. Because of the sheer number of names and marks already used in commerce, you may have to change your selected name dozens of times before you stumble on that unblemished pearl nobody has seen before. The following sections lay out the most common criteria that the courts use to decide the issue of infringement of commercial identifiers and give you a few examples.

Determining likelihood of confusion

REMEMBER

Common sense is your best guide in analysing likelihood of confusion between your commercial identifier and those you find during your search.

Likelihood of confusion is hard to define. Courts are still trying, without great success or consistency, to quantify likelihood of confusion. It really boils down to a logical, honest, fair evaluation of all the circumstances.

REMEMBER

First, ask yourself earnestly, "Am I trying to launch my product or business on the coattails of a well-known one?" Many people do just that without admitting it to themselves. For example, the servicemark Toys "R" Us triggered a flurry of imitations. Then there was the Depot craze: Home Depot, Office Depot, Auto Depot, and so on; and the Club vogue: Sam's Club, Price Club, Auto Parts Club, and a few others. Avoid this type of piggybacking if you want to steer clear of legal problems.

Although different courts use slightly different standards to determine the likelihood of confusion between two commercial identifiers, the most used factors are described in the following sections.

Legal strength or weakness of the pre-existing identifier

The protection afforded to a commercial identifier is proportional to its distinctiveness. You can't apply an arbitrary term to any kind of product or service, no matter how your predecessor used it. For example, the Eastman Kodak Company was able to prevent the use of its unique mark on watches and other products totally unrelated to photographic goods.

If the name you want is suggestive of your product or service, you may be able to use it — even if it's already used for a different type of product or service — because a suggestive term doesn't immediately make the customer think of a specific product or service. For instance, in order to make the connection between the servicemark Tour de France and a bike shop, you have to know what the famous competition is about, and then speculate that bicycles or bicycle-related goods or services may be involved. Finding that the mark has already been used in connection with casual wear wouldn't, under normal circumstances, prevent you from using it for your bike shop.

If you settle for a descriptive term like The Hair Palace for your beauty shop, salons in other provinces with the same name are no problem. The controlling issue is whether a customer may frequent both establishments.

WARNING

Watch out for a local service that sells related goods online under the same brand name. If The Hair Palace in Montreal sells hair relaxer under the same name on its website, you may have a problem using the name for your salon in Vancouver, regardless of whether you sell relaxer.

Quality of the prior goods

A mark used on high-quality goods is entitled to more protection than one used on average or low-quality merchandise. For example, if you plan to sell expensive, high-fashion dresses for "full-figured" ladies under the mark Strong & Striking through up-scale fashion shops, you might not be in conflict with the owner of the same mark who sells ready-made women's wear through Wal-Mart stores because there's little chance that your customer would patronize this type of department store.

Similarity of the two identifiers

The similarity in appearance, sound, and meaning of the two identifiers is taken into account. Obviously, the more your commercial identifier resembles the pre-existing one, the more likely the confusion among the customers.

WARNING

The courts tend to give more importance to the sound of a mark than its look, so you can't get away with misspelling an established name. Cauddac won't differentiate your goods from Kodak, and Pleidow won't distinguish your product from Play-Doh. That said, adding a logo may be enough to negate any likelihood of confusion, especially when the marks are descriptively weak.

Similarity of the goods or services

You need to give considerable weight to the similarity of your goods or services to those of your predecessor. Again, a small difference between the marks or the goods may get you off the hook if you're dealing with a descriptively weak mark, but you won't get away with imitating a suggestive or famous mark even if your goods or services aren't similar. For example, a toiletry manufacturer was allowed to use the mark Sport Stick in connection with its deodorants, despite the fact that another party was already using the mark Sport-Stick on a lip balm. However, you can't sell or do anything under the mark Playboy because it's such a famous, and, therefore, strong name.

Likelihood of bridging the gap

You must also anticipate that the person already using your selected identifier for different goods or services may one day bridge the gap by offering the same goods or services as yours. Say you plan to offer a college transcript registering service under the name Curriculum Now knowing that Curriculum.Com already operates a résumé-writing service. What's the likelihood that Curriculum.Com may offer a college transcript processing service in the future? You may be exposing yourself to future infringement problems. Use your best judgment. Don't guess. Err on the side of caution.

Marketing channels

Are your goods likely to appear next to those with the similar mark? Could your loan brokerage services and other services with the same mark be offered by the same bank or financial establishment? If so, that would cause customer confusion, so you must abandon the name. If the identifier is descriptive, a slight difference in marketing channels may be sufficient to preclude likelihood of confusion.

Cost of the goods and sophistication of the buyer

The likelihood of confusion is increased when goods sold under similar marks are inexpensive and subject to impulse buying. Candies and magazines fall into this category. More expensive and complex products, such as automobiles and computers, are less subject to name confusion because they require more customer consideration of their functions and capabilities. Very expensive or customized equipment for discriminating buyers is almost immune to confusion. Better-educated people are less likely to be confused. All things equal, marks used to sell goods to 10-year-olds face a tougher time overcoming a likelihood of confusion than marks used to sell goods to PhDs.

Putting it all together

In the end, the only way to analyse your search results (especially if you found an identical or similar identifier) is to look at *all* the criteria listed previously to determine whether your prospective mark is a good choice.

Say you're about to market a new type of CAT scan machine to be sold for a quarter-million dollars to medical groups, hospitals, and health centres. Your marketing group has coined the mark NovaRad, but an availability search uncovers NovaRay, used for X-ray equipment and also marketed to the healthcare and medical research fields. Take a look at each of the factors outlined in the previous sections and see where you come out:

>> NovaRay is suggestive and deserves a broad scope of protection.

>> The NovaRay X-ray equipment has been sold for many years and maintains a good reputation in the field.

>> *Ray* and *Rad* (short for radiation) are quasi-synonymous words, making the marks NovaRay and NovaRad very similar.

>> The two brands of equipment are used in the same field, by the same people, for the purpose of looking into someone's anatomy.

>> The manufacturer of the NovaRay device may someday expand its product line to CAT scan equipment, as has already been done by companies like General Electric and Siemens.

>> The two machines are sold through the same channels of distribution.

Here you've gone through six criteria and have come up with six good reasons to coin another moniker. However, the "sophistication of the buyers" test will save the day and trump all. Is there any chance that the MDs and PhDs who purchase your equipment will be confused about the source and purpose of such an expensive piece of equipment? No way. Therefore, the first six negatives present no obstacle to using the NovaRad mark.

REMEMBER

There's no foolproof way to analyse the likelihood of confusion between two commercial identifiers. Although some factors, such as the strong legal clout of the senior mark, carry more weight than others, a certain factor may override all the others, as in the NovaRad example. Common sense must be your guide, and you'll have a good chance of avoiding any legal difficulties.

Registering Your Trademark

When you register a trademark, you get the sole right to use it across the country for ten years; after that point, you can renew it every ten years. The CIPO registers your mark on the Register of Trademarks (makes sense!). But before you get a registration certificate, your application must survive a thorough examination and any eventual opposition by some other dude displeased by your mark (covered in the later section "Getting Your Application through the System").

In general, registering your mark gives you a procedural advantage to stop an infringer in a wider geographic area. It does the following:

>> **It arms your lawyer.** It's a really big stick to beat away someone trying to copy or imitate your mark.

>> **It acts like the deed to your house.** It tells the world that the CIPO has investigated your mark, confirmed your ownership, verified its commercial use, and concluded that the mark is valid and enforceable.

>> **Anyone doing an availability search will find your registration.** Anyone as smart and honest as you are will keep clear of your mark.

>> **The burden of proof shifts to the infringing defendant.** In a legal action, introducing your registration certificate shifts the burden of proof away from you. Without a registration, you'd have to prove that you own the mark by introducing evidence that you used the mark first.

>> **You can get temporary restrictions placed on the infringer.** Registration makes it easier to get a restraining order, preliminary injunction, or seizure of counterfeit goods while awaiting trial. These temporary, but very effective and often decisive, remedies usually stop an infringer dead in his tracks.

>> **You get federal protection.** When you register your mark, you're protected by federal laws. And without a federal registration, you can't go before a federal judge without proving that the accused infringer is headquartered in a different province.

>> **You can stop the entry of infringing foreign goods.** The Borders Service Agency can seize imported goods bearing your marks and eventually destroy them if the importer doesn't challenge the seizure.

>> **You can obtain cancellation of domain names that conflict with your mark.**

>> **International registration is easier.** Federal registration makes it easier to register your mark abroad under many international treaties and conventions (in some foreign jurisdictions, it's a requirement).

According to the CIPO, the term *trademark* refers to "a sign or combination of signs used or proposed to be used by a person to distinguish their goods or services from those of others." Specifically, a trademark "may be one or a combination of words, sounds, designs, tastes, colours, textures, scents, moving images, three-dimensional shapes, modes of packaging or holograms, used to distinguish the goods or services of one person or organization from those of others."

Any mark that doesn't breach the Trademarks Acts can be registered. (If you're really interested in reading the act, check out `https://laws-lois.justice.gc.ca/eng/acts/T-13/index.html`.) However, you generally can't register the following (exceptions do apply):

>> A name or surname

>> A clearly descriptive mark (for example, "sweet" can be used to describe all candy and therefore can't be registered as a trademark)

>> A deceptively misleading mark

>> A place of origin

>> Words in other languages

>> A mark that is confusingly similar to a registered or pending trademark

>> A mark that is identical to or likely to be mistaken for a prohibited mark (for example, a graphic that looks like the Canadian flag)

TIP

For an excellent official guide and links to plenty of additional information, visit `www.ic.gc.ca/eic/site/cipointernet-internetopic.nsf/eng/h_wr02360.html?Open&wt_src=cipo-tm-main&wt_cxt=learn`.

Getting Your Application through the System

The process of registering your mark begins with preparing and filing your application. According to the CIPO, a complete trademark application consists of the following items:

» The applicant's name and mailing address

» A representation of the trademark, a description of the trademark, or both

» A statement in specific and ordinary commercial terms of the goods and services associated with the trademark

» The statement of goods and services grouped according to the Nice Classification (discussed earlier in this chapter)

» The application fee (at the time of writing, it's $330 for the first class of goods or services that the trademark relates to, and $100 for each additional class)

» Any other requirements specific to the trademark that the applicant wants to register

TIP

You can log into the Trademark E-Filing system here: https://www.ic.gc.ca/app/scr/opic-cipo/mc-tm/depot-filing/connexion-login_eng.htm. If you don't yet have an account, you can sign up there too.

After you finish filing your application online, you may think you're home free. Think again! The journey of your application through the CIPO has just started. If your online application has met all the filing requirements and you've paid the fee, a filing date and an application number will be assigned; you'll receive acknowledgment and a proof sheet to review within seven business days of receipt of the application. Then, according to the CIPO, here's a rundown of they do next:

1. They search the trademark database to find any registered or pending trademark that may be confused with your trademark. (Don't worry; the CIPO will tell you if they find anything concerning.)

2. They examine your application to make sure it doesn't contravene the Trademarks Act and Regulations. At this point, they can raise objections to your trademark registration, and they will let you know if any pieces of your application are outstanding.

3. They publish your application in the Trademarks Journal, which is a weekly official publication listing all applications approved for advertisement in Canada. At this point, anyone in the public may file an opposition to your application. (In other words, they can challenge it.)

4. If no one challenges your application (or if you win a challenge against your application), your trademark is registered. Congratulations!

TIP

Fun fact: You're not legally required to use a symbol with your trademark. But many people use one of the following anyway: R (registered), TM (trademark), SM (service mark), or MC (marque de commerce).

TIP

You can find an easy-to-understand overview of the application process here: `www.ic.gc.ca/eic/site/cipointernet-internetopic.nsf/eng/wr00035.html?Open&wt_src=cipo-tm-main`. A specific roadmap is available here: `https://www.ic.gc.ca/eic/site/cipointernet-internetopic.nsf/eng/wr04355.html?Open&wt_src=cipo-tm-main`. Finally, more details about trademarks in general appear in the Trademarks Guide at `www.ic.gc.ca/eic/site/cipointernet-internetopic.nsf/eng/h_wr02360.html?Open&wt_src=cipo-tm-main&wt_cxt=learn`.

Losing Your Trademark

The Canadian trademark system is based on use, so a trademark must be used to register an issue with it. A registered trademark must also be used to avoid expungement, which means it could be removed permanently which is typically three years after use according to Section 45 of the Canadian Trademarks Act. See `www.ic.gc.ca/eic/site/cipointernet-internetopic.nsf/eng/h_wr01843.html`.

The Trademarks Act distinguishes between the use of a trademark in association with goods, and the use of a trademark in association of services, and many examples of how to show evidence can be found on the Canadian government's website. See `www.ic.gc.ca/eic/site/cipointernet-internetopic.nsf/eng/h_wr02360.html` to get started.

You can lose your exclusive rights to a trademark under the following circumstances:

>> **Failure to use:** If you don't use your trademark for a while and show no intent to use it in the future, someone else can assume that you abandoned it and begin using it. To keep your trademark, you must show credible evidence that you intend to use it and were prevented from doing so by circumstances beyond your control. Proving these circumstances is difficult, if not impossible. Use it or lose it.

>> **Failure to go after infringers:** If you tolerate infringement, competitors may assume that you deserve a very narrow scope of protection. This clears the way for the copycats to use it. The longer you delay pursuing an infringer, the less likely you'll be able to stop him.

>> **Genericness:** If you're lucky enough to have a successful and profitable product marketed under a strong mark, the public may eventually adopt your mark as the generic term for that kind of product. The court may then declare your mark generic and unenforceable. This has happened before: Aspirin, linoleum, and cellophane were all famous brand names.

3

Business Planning

Contents at a Glance

resources

» **Preparing for each part of a business plan**

» **Identifying your business's values and principles**

» **Declaring your business's vision**

» **Putting together a mission statement**

» **Setting goals and objectives that make good business sense**

Chapter **1**

Knowing Where You Want to Go

For any initiative, from a winter vacation to starting a business or developing a new way to operate some aspect of an existing business, there are lots of good reasons to have a plan and no good reasons not to have one. Plans can take a global view of the business or be very specific. They can be used simply to guide your decision making or they can help others, like lenders, make decisions relating to things such as giving you a line of credit, joining your business as a partner, or otherwise helping you fund growth.

This chapter looks at the fundamental values, the objectives, and the goals of your business to help chart what you stand for and where you want to go.

Preparing to Do a Business Plan

Planning is serious business. For many companies, a solid business plan is the difference between success and failure. Many people going into business for the first time want to rush right in, print business cards, hang up the sign, and start making money — a natural response for anyone excited about a new business idea. But taking a little extra time up front to prepare pays off down the line, especially when it comes to writing a business plan. Face it, after your business is up and running, you won't have much time to write the major pieces of your plan.

Identifying your planning resources

Having the right resources at the right time can make business planning easier and more successful. Fortunately, you can now find more useful and usable business-planning resources than ever before, from books and software to websites and professional experts such as business coaches. Of course, you may also find plenty of stuff that isn't worth looking at — much less paying for. And you can't always judge a book (or software program) by its cover.

As you begin to put together your business plan, you may discover that you need some additional tools — a book devoted to marketing, for example, or business-planning software that can help you create and maintain your written document.

Hitting the corner bookstore

Obviously, you already selected one of the best hands-on, business-planning books around. But okay, you can also find other useful business-planning books — particularly books that concentrate on specific areas, such as marketing or financial planning, and books that focus on particular kinds of businesses, such as nonprofits or sole proprietorships.

You can find out a lot about a book by reading through its table of contents. You should also dip into the first chapter.

TIP

The basic principles of business planning may be timeless, but certain subjects — digital marketing, for example — change rapidly. A book that was published three years ago may already be ancient history. If you want to find timely information, such as details about tax considerations for a small business, be sure to check the book's publication date.

TIP

For the timeliest info, turn to magazines, newspapers, and journals. They are terrific for keeping up with the business world, in general — and your industry, in particular. The business press also provides an efficient way to routinely scan for trends or new developments that may affect your business plan. If you're not sure what periodicals focus on your particular industry or your region, do a quick online search (see the following section for more details).

Surfing the Internet

Today, hundreds of websites offer information on business planning. You can access the information on some of these sites for free; other sites tease you with a sample and then charge you for more details. Some of the freebies can be just as helpful as the subscription sites, so you should check first to see what's free for the asking before you plunk down your hard-earned cash.

In particular, the federal government offers heaps of solid information on planning, starting, and operating your own business through its Canada Business site (www.canadabusiness.ca) and its network of provincial and regional sites. Even the Canada Revenue Agency (CRA) has helpful planning tips, which you can find at www.cra-arc.gc.ca.

Beyond sharing some basic business-planning tools, the Internet is also a great place for the latest information about competitors, markets, business trends, and new technologies — all the things you need to put together a complete picture of your business environment.

WARNING

The Internet may be a gold mine of business information, but you may also find plenty of fool's gold.

Follow three simple rules when you use the web for business research:

REMEMBER

>> Make sure the material is current.

>> Know your sources.

>> Double-check key facts and statistics.

Installing business-planning software

Business-planning software allows you to automatically assemble all the components of a business plan, turning them into a printer-ready, spiffy-looking document. The best programs also make easy work of the financial parts of business planning — creating income statements and cash-flow statements, for example, or making financial projections. Following are a couple popular sites to check out:

» Go Small Biz (https://gosmallbiz.com)

» Live Plan (www.liveplan.com/)

REMEMBER

Business-planning software programs can sometimes make the job of business planning *too* easy. Keep in mind that the best software-planning tools guide you through the important aspects of business planning and then keep track of your words, sentences, and paragraphs. But they don't think for you. You do the serious mental work yourself.

TIP

Investors and bankers who make a living reviewing and funding business plans are all too familiar with the look and feel of the most popular software-generated, business-planning documents. If you use one of these programs, customize your plan to make it unique.

Seeking professional help

No one knows the ins and outs of planning and running a business better than people who have done it. And most business people are happy to share their experience and expertise, as long as you don't plan on becoming a competitor! Many will even mentor first-time entrepreneurs. Don't be afraid to turn to a grizzled veteran for advice if you run into questions that you can't answer or run out of ideas to get your business off the ground.

Finding expert advice is surprisingly easy. The first place to look is in your own address book. Ask your friends and colleagues for suggestions. Other good places to look for help are the Chamber of Commerce, provincial government business centres, a local college or university, or the business section of your newspaper.

REMEMBER

Choose experts with experience in a business similar to the one you're planning. After you identify a person, decide exactly what kind of assistance you need. You can't ask someone to plan your whole business for you, after all. But you can ask them to fine-tune your marketing strategy, for example, or review and critique your financial projections.

Finding friendly advice

Many communities have organizations of business people who convene to share ideas, exchange contacts, help each other out, and socialize. Some organizations focus on helping specific groups, such as women, Aboriginals, immigrants, youths, gay/lesbian/transgendered, or freelancers; other organizations, made up of local people across the business spectrum, are open to the public. Thanks to the Internet, you can find business groups that regularly schedule online support meetings.

TIP

Business networking organizations are an invaluable resource for help in planning and running your business. For information about what's available in your community, check with your local Chamber of Commerce. Ask whether they have a mentoring programme. Because websites change so fast, look for a networking organization online by using a search engine.

Setting steps and schedules

REMEMBER

Putting together a business plan resembles any project that involves teamwork, from building a house to running a relay race. The clearer the ground rules, the smoother the process — and the happier your team. Make sure that your ground rules do three things:

>> **Identify key steps.** Typically, the process of writing a business plan includes five distinct steps: research, first draft, review, revised draft, and final review.

>> **Clearly assign duties.** Everyone involved needs to know exactly what you expect from them. You can use the key steps to create separate sets of tasks, and then you assign each task to members of your team.

>> **Establish a schedule.** Although writing a business plan is a big job, the process doesn't need to be a long and drawn-out affair. After you complete the preliminary research, the rest of the steps are fairly straightforward. To keep your project on track, set due dates for each component of the plan and each step in the process.

Planning Each Part of a Business Plan

When you first set out to create a business plan, the task may seem overwhelming. Right off the bat, you need to answer fundamental and sometimes difficult questions about your business and what you see for the future. You have to decide what targets to aim for when you look ahead and set business goals and objectives. To succeed, you have to take the time to know your

>> Industry

>> Customers

>> Competitors

- » Business resources
- » Business's unique qualities
- » Business's advantages
- » Basic financial condition
- » Financial forecast and budget

You also need to prepare for changes that you make to this list down the road. That means thinking through other options and alternatives and being on the lookout for new ways to make your business prosper.

REMEMBER

You don't want to scare people — yourself included — with a giant written plan. The longer your plan is, in fact, the less likely people are to read it. Ideally, your written plan should be 15 or 20 pages, maximum.

To avoid becoming overwhelmed, and to keep the business-planning process in perspective, break the plan up into the basic sections that every good business plan needs to include. The following sections outline the sections of a business plan.

Executive summary

Your executive summary touches on every important part of your business plan. It's more than just a simple introduction; it's the whole plan, only shorter. In many cases, the people who read your plan don't need to read any further than the executive summary; if they do, however, the summary points them to the right place.

You don't need to make the executive summary much longer than a page or two, and you can wait until you complete the rest of the business plan before you write it; that way, you only have to review the plan to identify the key ideas that you want to cover.

REMEMBER

If you want to make sure that people remember what you tell them, summarize what you're going to say, say it, and then reiterate what you've just said. The executive summary is the place where you summarize what your business plan says.

Business overview

In the overview, you highlight the most important aspects of your industry, your customers, and the products and services that you offer or plan to develop. Although you should touch on your business's history and major activities in the overview, you can leave many of the details for later sections.

To put together a general business overview, you need to draw on several key planning documents, including the following:

>> **Values statement:** The set of beliefs and principles that guide your business's actions and activities

>> **Vision statement:** A phrase that announces where your business wants to go or paints a broad picture of what you want your business to become

>> **Mission statement:** A statement of your business's purpose — what it is and what it does

>> **Goals and objectives:** A list of all the major goals that you set for your business, along with the objectives that you need to meet to achieve those goals

Later in this chapter, you find out how to begin constructing these statements.

Business environment

Your business environment section covers all the major aspects of your business's situation that are beyond your immediate control: the nature of your industry, the direction of the marketplace, and the intensity of your competition. Look at each of these areas in detail to come up with lists of both the opportunities and the threats that your business faces. Based on your observations, you can describe what it takes to be a successful business.

REMEMBER

Pay special attention to how your industry operates. Describe the primary business forces that you see, as well as the key industry relationships that determine how business gets done. Talk about your marketplace and your customers in more detail, perhaps even dividing the market into sections that represent the kinds of customers you plan to serve. Finally, spend some time describing your competition: their characteristics, how they work, and what you think you may see from them in the future.

For more information on how to explore your business circumstances and the overall environment that your business competes in, check out Chapter 2 of Book 3.

Business description

In the business description section, go into much more detail about what your business has to offer. Include information about your management, the organization, new technology, your products and services, operations, and your marketing potential — in short, anything special that you bring to your industry.

In particular, look carefully and objectively at the long list of your business's capabilities and resources. Separate the capabilities that represent strengths from the ones that show weaknesses. In the process, try to point out where you have real advantages over your competitors.

Examining your business through your customers' eyes helps. With a consumer viewpoint, you can sometimes discover something of value to the customer that you didn't know you provide, and find additional long-term ways to compete in the market.

Business strategy

Business strategy brings together everything that you know about your business environment and your business to come up with future projections.

Map out your basic strategies for dealing with the major parts of your business, including the industry, your markets, and competition. Talk about why your strategy is the right one, given your business situation. Describe how you expect the strategy to play out in the future. Finally, point out specifically what your business needs to do to ensure that the strategy succeeds.

You need to talk about the ways your business world may change. List alternative possibilities for action, and in each case, describe what your business is doing to anticipate the changes and take advantage of new opportunities.

Financial review

Your financial review covers both where you stand today and where you expect to be in the future.

Describe your current financial situation by using several standard financial statements. Reference your financial statements in the text so that they support the assumptions and arguments that you make in the other sections of the business plan. The basic financial statements include the following (see Chapter 2 in Book 4 for more information):

>> Income statement

>> Balance sheet

>> Cash-flow statement

Your projections about your future financial situation use exactly the same kind of financial statements. But for projections, you estimate all the numbers in the statements, based on your understanding of what may happen. Make sure to include all the assumptions that you made in other sections of your business plan to come up with your estimates in the first place.

Action plan

Your action plan lays out how you intend to carry out your business plan. It points out proposed changes in management or in the organization, for example, as well as new policies or procedures that you expect to put in place. Also, include any new skills that you, your managers, and your employees may need to make the plan work. Finally, talk about how you plan to generate excitement for your business plan inside your business, creating a culture that supports what you want to accomplish.

Defining Values and Principles

A successful business plan must start with a statement of business values, as well as a vision for the future. Values and a vision give your business a moral compass that guides you if you encounter trouble along the way. The two Vs also keep everybody in your business — even if that means only two of you — on course and heading in the same direction. What if you're a business of one? Taking time to establish your values and vision still guides you as your business grows.

The upcoming sections point out why values are so important in the first place. You identify your business's values by evaluating the beliefs and business principles that you already hold. You find out how to put together a values statement, along with a set of rules to work by. Finally, you create a vision statement for your business.

Understanding why values matter

Your business faces all sorts of options, alternatives, and decisions every day. If you take the time to define your business's values, your principles and beliefs can guide your managers, employees, or just you (if you're in business for yourself) as your business wades through complicated issues that sometimes don't have easy answers. When the unexpected happens, you can react quickly and decisively, based on a clear sense of what's important. Even when your business is sailing along just fine, a strong sense of value helps motivate you and your employees.

Facing tough choices

REMEMBER

Values provide a framework to guide people who confront difficult choices, especially as a business grows and more people have to face tough decisions. Also, research suggests that principled companies with strong values tend to attract and retain better employees, and those companies are often more successful as a result.

Consider one scenario. Frank is an independent consultant working for a large Canada-based petrochemical firm that we'll call Canuck Oil. Frank conducts market analysis for one of the business's largest divisions and is involved in an important project concerning the development of new overseas business.

Frank sketches out several options for the production, distribution, and pricing of petrochemicals in three countries. In one of his most promising scenarios, the numbers for a country that we'll call Friedonia yield substantially higher short-term profits than the other two — primarily because the nation doesn't yet have expensive pollution-control procedures in place. The other two nations have environmental laws similar to those in Canada.

Here's Frank's dilemma: By introducing the Canuck Oil product line into Friedonia, Frank's client could make huge profits. Sure, the resulting pollution may cause ecological damage that environmentalists could possibly trace back to Canuck Oil. But the business would do nothing illegal, according to Friedonia's current laws, and Frank stands to get a lot more business from Canuck Oil if the project goes ahead.

He agonizes over the situation and his report. What should Frank recommend to senior management? His options include

>> Going for the short-term bucks

>> Voluntarily enacting procedures to control pollution, even though the business isn't legally required to do so

>> Forgetting Friedonia until the country has stronger environmental laws

Maybe you can relate to Frank's quandary, having faced similar kinds of ethical questions and trade-offs in your own business. If Frank has taken the time to set out his core values in advance, those values can help him out of his quandary.

Applying ethics and the law

A *values statement* is a set of beliefs and principles that guide the activities and operations of your business, no matter what its size. To make the statement mean anything, the people at the top of your business must exemplify your stated values, and your business's incentive and reward systems should lead all employees to act in ways that support your business's values.

Having a values statement can keep you and your colleagues on the right side of the law. After a spate of stunning financial scandals in the United States, Canada moved to protect and build confidence with investors. The Canadian Security Administrators developed new rules that include stringent standards of disclosure. The rules require senior managers of publicly traded companies to certify the accuracy of their financial statements and take responsibility for internal financial controls. Failing to do so can land you in jail. No longer can top-level executives say they don't really know what's going on in the companies that they run. Now, the executives are responsible for every number on a financial statement.

If your business isn't big enough to be publicly traded, you're still certain to come up against the law every time you file a tax return, whether you run a corporation, a partnership, or a sole proprietorship (refer to Chapter 2 in Book 1 for more about forms of business). Having a clear set of values can keep you from getting too well acquainted with the Canada Revenue Agency (CRA).

Recognizing the value of having values

A clear values statement can be most important when the unexpected happens.

In the late 1980s, the United States experienced what many consider a terrorist attack. Someone in the Chicago area tampered with bottles of Tylenol, the best-selling pain reliever from McNeil Laboratories, a subsidiary of the health-care giant Johnson & Johnson. An unknown number of Tylenol capsules were laced with cyanide, and eight people died. The tragedy created a business crisis for Johnson & Johnson.

Johnson & Johnson reacted quickly and decisively to the threat against its customers. The business pulled every bottle of Tylenol from retail shelves throughout America — a massive undertaking that ultimately cost the business more than $100 million — and it did so immediately upon discovering the problem.

When the crisis was over, Johnson & Johnson became a corporate role model. Its lightning-fast response to the Tylenol incident earned it a reputation as one of the most responsible companies in the world, one that takes its civic duties seriously and puts the public good ahead of its profits. Johnson & Johnson's many businesses benefited accordingly.

Why did Johnson & Johnson behave so well when so many other companies act paralyzed in sticky situations? The reasons are summed up in the business's statement of values, an extraordinary document called the Johnson & Johnson Credo. (You can read this document at `www.jnj.com/connect/about-jnj/jnj-credo`.) For more than half a century, the Credo has successfully guided behaviour and actions across the sprawling Johnson & Johnson empire.

The Johnson & Johnson Credo works so well because each employee takes it seriously. With the active encouragement and involvement of top management, from the chairperson on down, the Credo is invoked, praised, and communicated throughout the company. Old-timers and new hires alike are reminded of the importance of the message. Promotions depend, in part, on how well managers live up to and disseminate the values of the Credo within their areas of responsibility. The Credo is a significant factor in Johnson & Johnson's continued performance near the top of its industry — and an indication of why the company is so well regarded by so many people.

Clarifying your business's values

Values statements often address several audiences. The Johnson & Johnson Credo mentioned in the previous section speaks to doctors, patients, customers, suppliers, distributors, employees, stockholders, and the community and world at large.

You put together a values statement primarily for the benefit of your employees, of course (or just for yourself, if you operate a business alone). But your business's values have an obvious impact on all your stakeholders, including the owners, investors, bankers, customers, suppliers, regulators — and heck, even your mother if she loaned you $10,000 to start your business. When you start to identify your business's most important values, you have to consider different viewpoints, including the following:

>> The demands of your investors (if you have any)

>> The interests and expectations of all your stakeholders

>> The beliefs and principles that you and your business already hold

After you come up with a preliminary list of values that you feel are most important, you're in a good position to create your values statement.

Focusing on existing beliefs and principles

Drawing up a list of beliefs and principles is one thing; putting those beliefs to the test is another. Tough choices are bound to come along, and they force you to examine your beliefs closely. If you run a one-person business, you already know something about what you stand for. In a bigger business, certain beliefs and values are inherent in the ways that the business operates. The best way to get to the heart of your business's beliefs and principles is to imagine how you'd respond to dilemmas.

Think about the situations described in the Beliefs and Principles Questionnaire (see Figure 1-1). Ask other people in your business, or trusted colleagues from outside your business, to do the questionnaire to see how they'd react to each scenario. Include a box on the questionnaire labelled Other or Don't Know. And note that the whole point of situations that put your values to the test is that they're not always easy.

TIP

Keep in mind that answers aren't right or wrong; you don't have to send a note home or give anyone a bad grade. You're simply trying to identify the basic values with which your business already feels comfortable. Completed questionnaires give insights into the general beliefs and principles that your business considers important.

Beliefs and Principles Questionnaire

Situation	Possible Response
A disgruntled customer demands a full sales refund on a product. The product isn't defective but can't be resold. The customer insists that it just doesn't work right. Would you be more inclined to	❏ Send the customer away, keeping the sale on the books ❏ Refund the customer's money, absorbing the loss but betting on repeat business and loyal customers
You're faced with filling a key position in your company. Would you be more inclined to	❏ Hire a person from the outside who has the necessary job skills but little experience in your industry ❏ Promote an experienced and loyal employee, providing job-skills training
You're forced to let one of your employees go. Would you tend to dismiss	❏ The young, recently hired college grad, inexperienced but energetic ❏ The 55-year-old manager with 20 years at the company, solid and hard-working but somewhat set in his or her ways
You find out that a long-term supplier has been routinely under billing you for services, increasing your own profit margins. Would you be inclined to	❏ Let the matter pass, assuming that it's ultimately the supplier's mistake and responsibility ❏ Take the initiative to correct the billing error in the future ❏ Offer to not only correct the mistake, but also pay back the accumulated difference

FIGURE 1-1:
Answers to the questionnaire point to beliefs and principles.

Putting together your values statement

Your business's values statement represents more than a quick to-do list. The description of your values reaches beyond quarterly goals or even yearly targets. Your values should guide you through tough decisions while you build a sustainable business that lasts and grows.

Maybe your business has some sort of values credo in place. If so, you're a step ahead of the game. (You lose points, however, if you have to glance at the dusty plaque on the office wall to remember it.) If you can't dig up a ready-made values statement to start with, begin putting together your own.

You may not have the luxury of spending weeks or months developing a values statement, so this section shows you a quick way to create one that sets your business on the right track. If your business is small, you can follow the steps yourself or with one or two of your colleagues — no need for long meetings and careful review.

REMEMBER

You can't create a values statement quickly, but you *can* quickly begin a process to help capture and articulate the values intrinsic to your business.

Follow these steps to start creating a value statement:

1. **Gather your business's decision-makers (you, your partners, and your trusted advisors) to talk about the general business values that should (and do) guide employee behaviour.**

2. **Prepare a first-draft list of all the values discussed in the meeting and circulate copies for review.**

3. **Schedule one or two follow-up meetings to clarify and confirm a final set of values.**

4. **Create a values statement that captures the agreed-upon values clearly and concisely, and get it approved by the senior managers and chief decision-makers.**

5. **Meet with managers at all levels to make sure that they understand the importance of, and the reasoning behind, the business values statement.**

6. **See that every employee gets a copy of the statement.**

   If you're in business for yourself, place a framed copy of the values statement near your desk at work or in your home office. Don't let it gather dust. For a bigger business, print the values statement on wallet-size cards to hand out, and don't forget to include the statement in the annual report. Post it on the business website and make sure it reaches all the stakeholders. Refer to and rely on the business values and let them be a guiding force in the actions and activities of every person who represents your business.

REMEMBER

Don't forget to include two other important groups — customers and shareholders. Both can help you figure out what values are essential to your business.

Following through with your values

A values statement can sometimes turn out to be a bit too simplistic, using words that sound good on paper but that are difficult to put to practical use. We recently looked through a stack of values statements from some of the biggest companies around. Over half of them included the word "integrity" or something close ("ethical conduct," "doing the right thing"). The next most popular value showing up was "respect for others," followed by "teamwork," "excellence," and "customer service."

To make your values statement really useful, you need to take the next step and link your values to basic, sensible rules. If you have employees, a good place to start is to ask them to fill out a questionnaire similar to the Beliefs and Principles Questionnaire shown in Figure 1-1. And if you have enough employees, you may also want to create an anonymous suggestion box in which employees can express their own ideas about values and about how your business is fulfilling its stated values.

WARNING

The values statement of the infamous Enron Corporation, by the way, boasted four key words: "respect," "integrity," "communication," and "excellence." Nice words. But Enron went from one of the highest-flying businesses in the country to bankruptcy and scandal in months. The lesson of its fall is a simple one: Values must matter. And you must integrate those values into the way your business operates day-to-day and week-to-week.

Creating Your Business's Vision Statement

Your business's *vision statement* should be a precise, well-crafted document announcing where your business wants to go and painting a picture of what your business wants to become. To people on the inside and outside of your business, your vision statement is a compass, showing the whole world the direction in which your business is heading.

A vision statement not only points the way to the future, it also makes you want to get up and go there. It represents your business's best hopes and brightest dreams. The best way to create a meaningful vision statement resembles the best way to create a values statement. Just follow these steps:

1. **Select a small group of partners and trusted advisors.**

2. **Have the group reread your business's values statement and review the list of stakeholders who have an interest in your business.**

3. **Begin a verbal free-for-all where each volunteers opinions and ideas.**

4. **When you feel comfortable with the results, add the finishing touches to the wording and choice of medium to get your vision ready for prime time.**

Although you may end up with only a couple of sentences or even just a phrase, the vision statement is the compass that provides your business's direction into the future. Spend enough time with your statement to make sure that the north on your business compass truly is north — that it does indeed point in the direction in which you want to go.

REMEMBER

Assume that your vision statement could serve the business for the next decade. Does this mean that you can never change the statement? No — but you should change a vision statement only if business conditions truly warrant a new course of action. Keep in mind that no one should cross out or rewrite the ideas that you capture in your business's vision statement on a whim; those ideas represent the lasting themes that guide your business at any time and under any circumstance.

But only diamonds are forever. If a changing environment throws you an unexpected curve, by all means, alter your vision to reflect the new reality. You should craft your statement in such a way that it's flexible enough to respond to a changing environment. If the words on paper no longer have meaning for your business, they become useless. Again, the vision statement is useful only to the extent that it has the power to move your business into the future.

Mapping Out a Mission Statement

You probably have a good idea of what you want your business to become. But how do you make your idea a reality? You start by defining the business activities that your business plans to engage in, the goals that you expect to meet, and the ways in which you're going to measure success.

This section helps you create a basic overview of your business and its activities, and you get guidance as you shape your expectations into a mission statement. It introduces business goals and objectives and shows you how to use them to measure the results that you expect to achieve. It also helps you prepare to set your business's goals and objectives, and you look at how you can use those goals and objectives to improve the overall efficiency and effectiveness of your future business.

Crafting an effective mission statement

Mission statements have become very popular with business types in the last few years. Many people remember the days when you'd find a business's mission statement turning yellow on the cafeteria bulletin board, completely ignored by everyone but the people who wrote it. That's no longer the case.

More and more companies, in fact, post their mission statements for everyone to see. Some put mission statements in their brochures, on letterheads, or feature them prominently on their websites.

Many businesses are finding out that they can use a mission statement as a powerful tool to communicate the purpose of the business to people both inside and outside the organization. It establishes who you are and what you do.

REMEMBER

To be effective, your mission statement must

>> Highlight your business activities, including the markets that you serve, the geographic areas that you cover, and the products and services that you offer.

>> Emphasize what your business does that sets it apart from every other business.

>> Include the major accomplishments that you anticipate achieving over the next few years.

>> Convey what you have to say in a clear, concise, informative, and interesting manner (a little inspiration doesn't hurt, either).

Answering questions

A mission statement doesn't need to be long. In fact, the shorter, the better. Even so, the task of creating one can seem daunting — the Mount Everest of business-planning chores. A mission statement has to sum up some pretty grand ideas in a few sentences. Also, writing a mission statement requires you to ask yourself some fundamental questions — and come up with solid answers. And don't forget, your mission statement should closely reflect the values and vision that you set for your business (both values and vision are covered earlier in this chapter).

A little preparation up front can make the process a bit easier. Ask yourself some background questions when you get ready to work on your business's mission statement. Don't worry if the answers are fairly general at this point because you're only interested in the basics right now. Research your goals and the practices of the competition, and then answer these questions:

>> Which customers or groups of customers do you plan to serve?

>> What needs do you want to satisfy?

>> What products or services do you plan to provide?

>> How will your business's products differ from competitive items?

>> What extra value or benefits will customers receive when they choose your business over the competition?

>> How fast do you expect these answers to change?

In other words, a mission statement answers the basic question:

What is your business?

Need some help? You should enlist managers who are familiar with all the aspects of your business. Follow these steps to begin the process:

1. **Get together with a small group including your partners and trusted advisors.**

2. **Ask them to prepare for the meeting by coming up with their own answers to the background questions listed earlier in this section.**

3. **Review the reasons for having a business mission in the first place and go over what the mission statement should include.**

4. **Meet so group members can present their perspectives, brainstorm, and form a consensus.**

5. **Create, revise, and review the business's mission statement together until you are satisfied with the final product.**

REMEMBER

A well-crafted mission statement is clear, concise, and easily understood. You should also make it distinctive (from the competition) and up-to-date (give the business's current situation).

Capturing your business
(in 50 words or less)

Your business's mission statement has to draw a compelling picture of what your business is all about. You can refer to drawing this picture as creating a *tangible image* of the business. Begin with a first stab at a mission statement:

> *Our gizmos bring unique value to people, wherever they may be.*

Not a bad start. This statement says a little something about geography and a bit about being different. But you're far from done. To work toward communicating the business's activities, accomplishments, and capabilities with more clarity and punch, consider expanding the statement:

> *We provide the highest-quality gizmos with unmatched value to the global widget industry, which allows our customers to be leaders in their own fields.*

This statement conveys what the business does (provides the highest-quality gizmos), who it serves (the global widget industry), and what sets it apart from its competitors (unmatched value, which allows customers to lead their own fields). The energy makes it a far more compelling mission statement than the earlier version.

Zeroing In on Goals and Objectives

Your mission statement is a giant step forward; in it, you articulate the purpose of your business by defining the business that you're in. But the definition is just the beginning. When Canada decided to assist the United States with its space shuttle program, it set its sights on building robotic arms (now known as Canadarm 1 and 2). Stating the nature of the mission was the easy part. Actually figuring out, step by step, how to get there was the trick. It involved carefully formulated goals and objectives.

You don't have to be planning a trip to outer space to know that goals and objectives are important. If you've ever planned a long car trip, you know that choosing the destination is essential (and often painful, especially if the kids want to go to Canada's Wonderland and you want to go to the West Edmonton Mall). But the real work starts when you begin to work out an itinerary, carefully setting up mileage goals and sightseeing objectives so that your three-week getaway doesn't turn into a *National Lampoon* vacation. Goals and objectives are vital to successful business planning.

The following sections introduce some important ideas that you can take advantage of when you begin setting your own goals and objectives.

WARNING

If your business opportunities are so obvious and so overwhelming that you don't need to define a particular course of action to reach your ultimate destination, you've won the business planner's lottery. You're more likely, however, to run into one hazardous crossroad after another, and a lack of careful planning can be dangerous. Just look at the following examples:

>> The manufacturing breakdown of the sports car Bricklin in 1976, which cost taxpayers close to $23 million, resulted from a failure to create sound processes and quality assurance.

>> Monumental planning blunders have been partly blamed for fiascos involving certain infamous product introductions, including the Ford Edsel in the 1950s and New Coke in the 1980s.

Not setting goals and objectives created financial chaos in the situations discussed in the preceding list, and not knowing customers and competitors, and how they play into the business mission resulted in product failure. Setting goals and objectives provides an important insurance policy for your business: the opportunity to plan a successful course of action and keep track of your progress.

Comparing goals and objectives

REMEMBER

After you complete a mission statement, your business goals lay out a basic itinerary for achieving your mission. *Goals* are broad business results that your business absolutely commits to attaining. Goals are typically stated in terms of general business intentions. You may define your business's goals by using phrases such as "becoming the market leader" or "being the low-cost provider of choice." These aims clearly focus the business's activities without being so narrowly defined that they stifle creativity or limit flexibility.

In working toward set goals, your business must be willing to come up with the *resources* — the money and the people — required to attain the intended results. The goals that you set for your business should ultimately dictate your business choices and may take years to achieve. Goals should forge an unbreakable link between your business's actions and its mission.

REMEMBER

Simply setting a general goal for your business isn't the end of the story; you also need to spend time thinking about how to get there. So, your business must follow up its goal with a series of *objectives:* operational statements that specify exactly what you must do to reach the goal. You should attach numbers and dates to objectives, which may involve weeks or months of effort. Those numbers help you realize when you reach a given objective.

Objectives never stand alone. They flow directly from your mission and your values and vision (as discussed earlier in this chapter), and outside the context of their larger goals, they have little meaning. In fact, objectives can be downright confusing.

The goal "Improve employee morale," for example, is much too general without specific objectives to back it up. And you can misinterpret the objective "Reduce employee grievances by 35 percent over the coming year" if you state it by itself. (One way to achieve this objective is to terminate some employees and terrorize the rest of the workforce — effective, but not really the way to run a good business.) When you take the goal and objective together, however, their meanings become clear.

TIP

Want an easy way to keep the difference between goals and objectives straight? Remember the acronym GOWN: G for goals, O for objectives, W for words, and N for numbers. For goals, you use words — sketching in the broad picture. For objectives, you use numbers — filling in the specific details.

If you already use different definitions for goals and objectives, don't worry; you're not going crazy. What you may find crazy is the lack of any standard definition of terms when it comes to business planning. The important task is to settle on the definitions that you want to use and stick with them in a consistent manner. That way, you prevent any unnecessary confusion within your business.

Setting goals and objectives

Your business's goals and objectives reflect your primary business intentions, and they determine both the itinerary and timetable for fulfilling your intentions. In other words, your goals and objectives focus the business on the important work at hand and provide a mechanism for measuring your progress.

Goals and objectives are ultimately meant to make your business more efficient and effective. But how do you ensure that setting them is an efficient and effective process? Here are some guidelines to get you started.

Creating your business goals

Goals are the broad business results that your business commits to achieving. To jump-start the process of setting your business's goals, use this useful list of guidelines:

>> Determine whom to involve in setting your business's goals. Because goals are the core of your business, the group members should include the people who are responsible for all your major business activities. If you're going it alone in business, try to develop a core group of advisers who can meet with you periodically to set goals.

>> Develop a procedure for monitoring your business's goals on a routine basis, revising or reworking those goals as business circumstances change.

>> Create individual goals that clarify your business activities without limiting flexibility and creativity.

>> Confirm that your business's goals, taken together, provide an effective blueprint for achieving your broad intentions.

>> Make sure that your business's stated goals closely tie in to your mission statement (see the earlier section "Mapping Out a Mission Statement").

>> Rely on your goals when you communicate your business intentions to people both inside and outside your business.

Laying out your objectives

Objectives are the statements that fill in the details, specifying exactly how you plan to reach each goal. As much as possible, you should tie your objectives to cold, hard numbers: the number of new customers you want to serve, products you want to sell, or dollars you want to earn.

This list of guidelines provides a useful template when your business starts to develop objectives:

>> Determine who should set business objectives in your business. (If you're on your own, that would be you.)

>> Develop a system for reviewing and managing business objectives throughout your business.

>> Make sure that objectives are achievable and verifiable by including numbers and dates where appropriate.

>> Create business objectives that can clearly advance and achieve larger business goals.

>> Confirm that your business's objectives, taken together, result in an efficient use of *resources* — money and people — in pursuit of broader business intentions.

Matching goals and objectives with your mission

REMEMBER

You see it over and over throughout this book, but this statement is so important that it deserves repeating: Your business's goals and objectives must be closely tied to your mission statement.

Avoiding business-planning pitfalls

Goals and objectives are meant to motivate everyone in your organization. They also help channel every employee's efforts in the same direction, with the same results in mind. When human nature is involved, nothing is certain. But you can improve the odds that your actions will produce the results you expect by avoiding several common pitfalls while your business works toward specific goals and objectives:

>> **Don't set pie-in-the-sky goals for yourself.** If you don't have a prayer of achieving a particular goal, don't bother setting it. The best goals are *stretch goals:* goals large enough to propel your business forward without causing you to stumble along the way.

>> **Don't sell your organization short.** Although trying to reach too far with your goals can be dangerous, you don't want to wimp out, either. Goals often become self-fulfilling prophecies. If anything, try to err a bit on the high side, creating goals that expand your organization's capabilities.

>> **Be careful what you aim for.** Your goals should clearly state what you want to see happen with your venture. If your goals contradict the intentions of the business, you may end up pursuing misguided aims.

>> **Beware of too many words or too many numbers.** Keep in mind that a goal is a broad statement of a business intention that flows directly from your business's mission. Objectives are more narrowly defined and always tie in to a specific goal; they fill in the details, specify time frames, and include ways of verifying success. You define goals in words, and you define objectives in numbers.

» **Don't keep your goals and objectives a secret.** If you want goals and objectives to focus and direct your organization's behaviour, every employee has to know about them. Prominently display your business goals and objectives in your business newsletter or website.

Knowing that timing is everything

What's the proper time frame for you to reach your goals and objectives? How far out should you place your planning horizon — one year, three years, maybe five? The answer is . . . it depends on the pace of your industry.

Certain industries remain tortoise-like in their pace. Many plastics companies in Canada, for example, operate today much the same as they did 30 years ago, with perhaps the addition of a website. The needs of plastics end-users have changed slowly, and the types of materials used and levels of materials required have stayed pretty much the same. But change is definitely on the horizon, with producers overseas adopting leading-edge innovations, investing in research and development, and delivering quality plastics at significantly lower costs.

Change is perhaps the only constant for other industries. Take health care, for example. The world of doctors and hospitals was at one time a predictable universe in which organization goals and objectives could be developed years in advance. In the last decade, the Canadian health-care system has gone through a sea change. Changes in government regulation, new technology, outdated facilities, labour shortages, and increasing demand from an aging population have all conspired to create a very uncertain world. If you're in hospital management today, you don't worry about five-year horizons; you're now pressured to measure your planning cycles and reviews in months.

REMEMBER

When dealing with change, business planners have to maintain a balancing act between moving too fast and not fast enough. You need to set business goals and follow them up with verifiable objectives, basing time frames on your comfort level with what you expect to happen down the road. Build in some flexibility so that you can revisit your goals and objectives and account for the changes you see.

Chapter **2**

Describing Your Marketplace

O ne of the most important questions you can ask yourself as you prepare to create a business plan (refer to Chapter 1 of Book 3 for help with planning) is "What business am I really in?" You also want to know what part of the market you serve and where you stand with the competition. If you can answer these basic questions correctly, you take the first giant step toward creating an effective business plan.

In this chapter, you can find out how to capture your big picture by defining the business that you're really in. You analyse your industry and search for critical success factors, and then you get some pointers on preparing for the opportunities and threats that may appear on your business horizon.

Understanding and Analysing Your Business

Okay, so what business are you *really* in? Don't say that you're in the widget business, if widgets are what you produce; go beyond the easy answer that you base simply on what you do or what you make. You have to dig a bit deeper and ask yourself what makes your marketplace tick:

>> What basic customer needs do you fulfil?

>> What underlying forces are at work?

>> What role does your company play?

No matter what kind of business you're in, you're affected by forces around you that you must recognize, plan for, and deal with to be successful over the long haul. Ivory-tower types often call this process *industry analysis*.

How much do you already know? Take a moment to complete the Industry Analysis Questionnaire (see Figure 2-1). If you're unsure about an answer, check the ? box.

TIP

Your answers to the questionnaire in Figure 2-1 provide a snapshot of what you think you know. The boxes that you check highlight the areas that need a closer look. Now you can roll up your sleeves and make a serious stab at completing your industry analysis.

The good news is that many smart people have already worked hard at analysing all sorts of industries. Although no two businesses are exactly the same, basic forces are at work across many industries (see Figure 2-2).

The following sections describe the most important of these forces — those factors in your industry — and provide some hints on how you can think about these forces in terms of your business planning.

Solidifying the structure

Every industry, from fresh-flower shops to antique stores, has a unique shape and structure. Here are a few tips on how to recognize the particular structure of your industry.

Industry Analysis Questionnaire

Number of competitors in your industry:	❏ Many	❏ Some	❏ Few	❏ ?
Your industry is dominated by several large firms:	❏ Yes	❏ No		❏ ?
The combined market share of the three largest companies in your industry is:	❏ <40%	❏ In between	❏ >80%	❏ ?
New technologies change the way your industry does business every:	❏ 1 year	❏ 5 years	❏ 10 years	❏ ?
The barriers that stop new competitors from entering your industry are:	❏ High	❏ Medium	❏ Low	❏ ?
The barriers that prevent competitors from getting out of your industry are:	❏ High	❏ Medium	❏ Low	❏ ?
Overall market demand in your industry is:	❏ Growing	❏ Stable	❏ Declining	❏ ?
There's a large, untapped market that your industry can take advantage of:	❏ Yes	❏ Maybe	❏ No	❏ ?
Your industry offers a selection of features and options in its product lines that's:	❏ Extensive	❏ Average	❏ Limited	❏ ?
Customers buy products in your industry based almost entirely on price:	❏ Yes	❏ No		❏ ?
Customers can find other alternatives to take the place of your industry's products:	❏ Easily	❏ With difficulty	❏ No	❏ ?
Suppliers to your industry have a lot of influence when it comes to setting terms:	❏ Yes	❏ No		❏ ?
Customers have a lot of bargaining power when buying your industry's products:	❏ Yes	❏ No		❏ ?
Distributors have a lot of power and play a major role in your industry:	❏ Yes	❏ No		❏ ?
Overall costs in your industry have been:	❏ Declining	❏ Stable	❏ Rising	❏ ?
Profit margins in your industry are:	❏ Strong	❏ Average	❏ Weak	❏ ?

FIGURE 2-1: Use the Industry Analysis Questionnaire to test your industry knowledge.

The number of competitors, taken by itself, has a major impact on the shape of an industry. An industry can be a *monopoly* (one monster company with no competitors), an *oligopoly* (a small number of strong competitors), or a *multiopoly* (many viable competitors). Actually, the word *multiopoly* is made up because you need a word to represent the vast majority of industries in this competitive world.

In addition to the number of competitors, check out how many of the companies are big and how many are small, as well as how they carve up the various markets that they compete in.

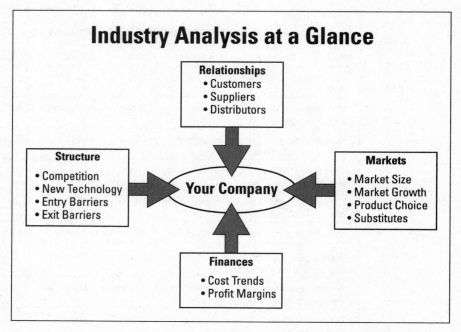

Industry Analysis at a Glance

Relationships
- Customers
- Suppliers
- Distributors

Structure
- Competition
- New Technology
- Entry Barriers
- Exit Barriers

Your Company

Markets
- Market Size
- Market Growth
- Product Choice
- Substitutes

Finances
- Cost Trends
- Profit Margins

FIGURE 2-2:
The four major components of analysing an industry.

© John Wiley & Sons, Inc.

Make a list of all the major competitors in your industry. Find out their sizes, based on revenue, profits, or some other readily available measure, and estimate their relative market shares for the markets that you want to explore. Take advantage of the extraordinary range of information on the Internet to gather as much data as you can find. Use patience and persistence as you sift through all the raw data to find the gems.

Measuring the markets

Competition comes down to customers, and customers make up markets. Ideally, the customers you intend to target represent a market that you feel is ripe for new goods or services. The following sections give you tips to help you judge for yourself.

How big is big?

The size of a market tells you a lot about what's likely to happen to it over time, especially when it comes to competition. Large markets, for example, are always big news and can't help but attract competitors. Smaller markets don't get the same attention, however, and because competitors can easily overlook them, they often represent business opportunities. You hit the real jackpot if you can turn a small market into a bigger market by discovering a *usage gap* — finding a new use for your product or service that no other company has thought of before.

TIP

Try to work out some estimates of the overall size of your market based on current usage patterns. Try your luck at coming up with novel approaches or applications that have the potential to redefine your market. Make some market projections based on the new uses that you're thinking about.

Growing or shrinking?

If large markets are good news, rapidly growing markets are great news, and competitors are going to come crawling out of the woodwork. A growing market offers the best odds for new players to gain a foothold and unseat the existing competition. As for shrinking markets, you can bet that the old competitors get leaner, meaner, and fiercer. So, as markets change size in either direction, the competition is likely to heat up.

TIP

Identify changes in the size of your market over the past five years, in terms of both units sold and revenue generated. If the market is changing rapidly in either direction, look for opportunities and predict the likely effect on both the numbers and the intensity of the competition. Business journals and the Internet are good places to start gathering data. Also, try talking to customers, suppliers, and even other competitors in the market.

What choices do customers have?

A quick survey of the similarities and differences among products or services in a market measures something called *product differentiation.* If each product looks pretty much like every other product (think sugar or drywall), you can bet that price is important to customers in what's known as a *commodities marketplace.* However, if each product is different and offers customers something unique or special — from laptop computers to hot little roadsters — product features are likely to determine long-term success or failure in the market.

TIP

Take a hard look at the products or services that the top three competitors in your market offer. How similar are they? In what ways are they unique? Think about what you can do to differentiate your business — adding special features to products or offering value-added services — so that you can compete in ways beyond simply raising or lowering your price. Your competitors' websites can offer a wealth of inside information.

What about something altogether different?

Sometimes, a completely new type of product or service suddenly makes a debut in a market and crashes the party. The product often comes out of another industry and may even be based on a different technology. The new product becomes an overnight rival for the affections of existing customers — the rise of e-mail to challenge fax machines and snail mail, for example, or the proliferation of digital cameras to overtake film-based cameras. The threat of *product substitution* — new products taking the place of existing ones — is real, especially in fast-changing, highly competitive markets.

Think about what your customers did 5, 10, or even 20 years ago. Did they use your product or a similar one back then, or did a completely different kind of product serve their needs? What about 1, 5, or 10 years from now? What types of products or services may satisfy your customers' needs? Although you can't predict the future, you can envision the possibilities.

Remembering the relationships

Business is all about connections. Connections aren't just a matter of who you know — they involve who supplies your raw materials, distributes your product, and touts your services. Connections are about who your customers are and what kind of relationship you have with them. The tips in the following sections can help you spot the key connections on which your business depends.

Recognizing supply and demand

One obvious way to think about products and services is how a business puts them together. Every business relies on outside suppliers at some stage of the assembly process, whether for basic supplies and raw materials, or for entire finished components of the product itself. When outside suppliers enter the picture, the nature of what they supply — the availability, complexity, and importance of that product or service to the company — often determines how much control they have over the terms of their relationship with a company. That means everything from prices and credit terms to delivery schedules.

Think about your own suppliers. Are any of them in a position to limit your access to critical components or to raise prices on you? Can you form alliances with key suppliers or enter into long-term contracts? Can you turn to alternative sources? Are any of your suppliers capable of doing what you do, transforming themselves into competitors? How can you protect yourself?

Keeping customers happy

You've probably heard the expression "It's a buyers' market." As an industry becomes more competitive, the balance of power naturally tends to shift toward the customer. Because customers have a growing number of products to choose among, they can afford to be finicky. As they shop around, customers make demands that often pressure businesses to lower prices, expand service, and develop new product features. A few large customers have even greater leverage as they negotiate favourable terms.

The last time that you or your competitors adjusted prices, did you raise or lower them? If you lowered prices, competitive pressures no doubt are going to force you to lower them again at some point. So think about other ways in which you can compete. If you raised prices, how much resistance did you encounter? Given higher prices, how easy is it for customers to do for themselves what you do, eliminating the need for your product or service altogether?

Delivering the sale

No matter how excited customers get about a product or service, they can't buy it unless they can find it in a store, through a catalogue, on the Internet, or at their front doors. *Distribution systems* see to it that products get to the customers. A *distribution channel* refers to the particular path that a product takes — including wholesalers and anyone else in the middle — before it arrives in the hands of the final customer. The longer the supply chain, the more power the channel has when it comes to controlling prices and terms, not to mention smart marketers who partner with channel members to create a superior delivery network. The companies at the end of the chain have the greatest control because they have direct access to the customer.

Think about what alternatives you have in distributing your product or service. What distribution channels seem to be most effective? Who has the power in these channels, and how is that power likely to shift? Can you think of ways to get closer to your customers — perhaps through direct-mail campaigns or online marketing?

Figuring out the finances

Successful business planning depends on you making sense of dollars-and-cents issues. What are the costs of doing business? What's the potential for profit? The following sections give you some tips that can help get you started.

The cost side

With a little effort, you can break down the overall cost of doing business into the various stages of producing a product or service, from raw material and fabrication costs to product-assembly, distribution, marketing, and service expenses. This cost profile often is quite similar for companies competing in the same industry. You can get a handle on how one firm gains a cost advantage by identifying where the bulk of the costs occur in the business and then looking at ways to reduce those costs.

Economies of scale usually come into play when major costs are fixed up front (think of large manufacturing plants or expensive machinery, for example); increasing the number of products sold automatically reduces the individual cost of each unit. *Experience curves* refer to lower costs that result from the use of new technologies, methods, or materials somewhere during the production process.

Separate your business into various stages and ask yourself where the bulk of the costs occur. Can you take any obvious actions to reduce these costs immediately or over time? How does the doubling of sales affect your unit costs? How are your competitors toying with new cost-saving ideas?

The profit motive

Businesses typically have their own rules about expected *profit margins* — how much money they expect to end up with after they subtract all the costs, divided by all the money that they expect to take in. In certain industries, these profit margins remain fairly constant year after year. A look at the history of other industries, however, points to cycles of changing profitability. These cycles often reflect changing *capacity levels* — how much of a product or service an industry sells and delivers compared to what it can actually produce.

Knowing where an industry stands along the cycles of profit margin and capacity, as well as the direction in which the industry is heading, tells you a lot about the competitive pressures that may lie ahead. Ideally, you want to be in an industry without much excess capacity — now or in the near future. Try to answer the following questions:

>> Is your industry one that has well-known business cycles?

>> Traditionally, how long are the business cycles?

>> If you've been in business for a while, have your profit margins changed significantly in recent years?

>> In what direction do profits appear to be heading?

>> Do you think that these changes in profitability may affect the number of competitors you face or the intensity of the competition over the next one to five years?

Don't stop with the list here. No doubt it's missed one or two industry forces that may be important and perhaps unique to your business situation. Spend a little extra time and creative effort coming up with other forces while you work on your own industry analysis.

After you give some thought to the many forces at work in your industry, put together a written portrait. If you're stuck, imagine that someone who has no experience in your industry has come to you for advice, asking if you recommend a substantial investment in your industry. How would you respond? If you get your arguments down on paper, you've made real progress in assembling a serious industry analysis.

Recognizing Critical Success Factors

Time spent doing careful industry analysis rewards you with a complete picture of the major forces at work in your business: the basic structure of your industry; your core markets; key relationships with suppliers, customers, and distributors; and costs and changing profit margins. The analysis can also point out trends in your industry and show you where your company is in terms of general industry and business cycles.

This information is all well and good. But how do you interpret your industry landscape and use it to improve your business planning? Take a fresh look at your industry analysis (as described earlier in this chapter). Ask yourself what your company must do to succeed against each powerful force that you identify. Again, what special skills, organization, and resources do you need to survive and conquer? In the business world, such an asset is called a *critical success factor* (CSF) or *key success factor* (KSF). Critical success factors are the fundamental conditions that you absolutely, positively have to satisfy if you want to win in the marketplace. These factors are different for every industry because they depend so directly on the particular forces that work in each industry.

The CSFs (or KSFs) for your company should be rather specific — a one-of-a-kind set of conditions based on your industry analysis and the forces that you see shaping your business. You probably don't want to juggle more than three or four CSFs at any one time. But no matter how many factors you believe are important, your CSFs are likely to fall into several general categories:

» **Adopting new technologies:** When jet engines became available in the late 1950s, commercial airlines knew they had to adopt this technology to remain competitive. When fax machines replaced couriers and mail for many kinds of business correspondence, business had to adapt to the new standards and expectations of the business environment. When the fax machine was replaced by the scanner and e-mail, and when the corporate brochure was displaced by the website, the same thing happened. Most businesses can't afford to lag behind in technology. Other businesses have to always be at the forefront.

» **Getting a handle on operations:** For commodity products, such as steel or oil, large-scale mills or refineries are often the critical factors that lead to low-cost production and the capability to compete on price due to economies of scale. In high-tech industries, however, automation and efficient, clean rooms may be the critical ingredients that allow the production of competitively priced consumer electronics products.

>> **Hiring human resources:** Consulting firms usually recruit only at the top business schools because those firms sell the expertise of their consultants, and clients often equate skill with educational background. In the same way, software companies are nothing more than the sum of the talent, creativity, and expertise of their programmers. In each case, people themselves are the CSFs.

>> **Minding your organization:** The long-term success of movie companies that consistently produce hits and make money often hinges on logistics — the capability to evaluate, organize, and manage independent writers, actors, site scouts, and production companies, as well as the media and distribution outlets. In the health care industry, insurance companies must excel at record-keeping, efficiently steering patients, suppliers, and insurance claims through the system. Even a simple bookstore that sells used books can gain an advantage by offering a quick, easy-to-use inventory of what's available and a system for reserving bestsellers when they appear on the shelves.

>> **Cultivating customer loyalty:** Businesses that offer services sell rather abstract products that customers can't hold or touch, and those services are difficult to copyright or patent. Success often goes to service companies that enter the market first and then work hard to cultivate a following of loyal customers. Chartered Professional Accountants of Canada (CPA) and accounting firms, for example, build impeccable reputations one step at a time.

>> **Looking for a great location:** Profitable mills tend to be located in agricultural areas and brick works crop up near rock quarries; after all, transportation of the raw materials is extremely expensive. But transportation costs aren't the only reason why location matters. At the other end of the spectrum, fast-food restaurants and gas stations also live or die based on their locations.

>> **Benefiting from branding:** Manufacturers of cosmetics, clothing, perfume, and even sneakers all sell hype as much as they do physical products. In these cases, CSFs depend on the capability of companies to create and maintain strong brands. Customers often consider the name, the logo, or the label attached to a product before they buy the lipstick, jeans, or shoes that represent the brand.

>> **Dealing with distribution:** Packaged foods, household products, snacks, and beverages often sink or swim depending on how much shelf space the supermarkets or local grocery stores allot to them. Speed of delivery and logistics can also be critical success factors, especially when freshness matters.

>> **Getting along with government regulation:** Companies that contract directly with public agencies, such as waste-management firms and construction companies, often succeed because of their unique capability to deal directly with bureaucrats and elected officials. Government regulation plays a role in many industries, and the capability to navigate a regulatory sea is often the critical factor in a company's success.

Preparing for Opportunities and Threats

After you have a handle on the major forces that shape your industry and you can point out the critical success factors for coming out on top (discussed earlier in this chapter), you can begin to look ahead.

You can find no end to the number of potential opportunities and threats in an industry. A *situational analysis* is a process of analysis for a company's internal and external environmental factors, successes and failures, as well as past and present resources and abilities. A winning business plan should include a situational analysis that points out both the biggest opportunities and the clearest threats to your company so that you can anticipate ways to deal with both the good and the bad as part of your planning process. Opportunities and threats come from the forces, issues, trends, and events that exist beyond your control as a business planner and owner.

Opportunities don't always knock; sometimes, you have to find the door and know when to open it. Consider the following situations. They can all lead to business opportunities, so see if any of them can generate new possibilities in your industry:

>> Major shifts in technology

>> Availability of new materials

>> New customer categories

>> Sudden spurts in market growth

>> New uses for old products

>> Access to highly skilled people

>> Additional locations

>> Fresh organization models

>> New distribution channels

>> Changing laws or regulations

WARNING

Business is risky. For every big opportunity in an industry, you find an equally powerful threat to challenge the way in which you currently do business. Consider the following examples of how fundamental changes can dramatically alter the business environment and see if any of them apply to your industry:

>> Market slowdowns

>> Costly legislation

- » Changing trends
- » New and aggressive competition
- » Substitute products
- » Exchange-rate volatility
- » Shortages of raw materials
- » Loss of patent protection
- » Labour agreements
- » Laziness and complacency
- » Disasters, natural and otherwise

Slicing and Dicing Markets

As you put together your business plan (refer to Chapter 1 of Book 3), it may seem nice to view each of your customers — the Tom, Dick, and Mary who regularly walk through your doors — as individuals with unique personalities and distinct likes and dislikes. You may also be tempted to make things simple: Lump everyone together and view all your customers in exactly the same way — after all, the whole world should want your products and services, right? Unfortunately, neither of these tactics is very helpful when it comes to creating a business plan that you can use.

Luckily, you have a simple alternative. When you think about who your customers really are, one of the first things you notice is that many of them have a great deal in common. That simple fact gives you a golden opportunity to divide customers into specific groups, based on their similarities. Eureka! By planning your business around these customer groups, you can serve each group's particular needs almost as effectively as if they were individuals. As the saying goes, you get to have your cake and eat it, too.

The upcoming sections show you how to create practical market segments that you can use in your business plan. You explore various ways to identify market segments based on who's buying, what they buy, and why they buy. Finally, you discover things you can do to make sure that your business practices reflect who your customers are and why they come to you in the first place.

Separating customers into groups

Although each individual customer is unique, groups of customers often look a great deal alike. When you make sense of your marketplace by grouping customers together, you create *market segments*.

To be of any real use in your business planning, however, market segments should describe groups of customers that you can easily identify and that respond to your products and services in similar ways — ways that appear distinct from those of other customer groups. A successful market segment allows you to satisfy the particular needs and wants of an entire group of customers.

REMEMBER

Good strategy not only identifies what you are and who you serve, but also what you are *not* trying to do. Similarly, identifying market segments allows you to choose those customers that are *not* a good fit with your business and that you shouldn't spend resources on.

You may remember a time when running shoes (also known as runners or sneakers, depending on where you lived) were simple, rubber-soled canvas shoes that kids played in and maybe used for school sports. Back then, most of the buyers were parents, and most of the wearers were boys. If you wanted to play in the running-shoe market (Keds and Converse, for example, produced black high-tops that parents bought in droves), you kept your eye on what those boys needed and what those parents looked for.

Look at the market for athletic shoes today. The difference is phenomenal. Young males still wear the shoes, of course, but so do girls, toddlers, cool teenagers, serious runners, senior citizens, and everyone else — all demanding athletic shoes in various shapes and colours, with different features and options, and in a wide range of prices. Athletic shoes are designed especially for walking, running, tennis, skateboarding, and even fashion.

Identifying market segments

Despite what the marketing gurus may tell you, you can't find one right way to divvy up your market. You need to view your customers from various angles and describe them based on several factors. The more you can apply your imagination and creativity in this area, the more successful you're likely to be in coming up with unique and effective market segments. One dimension isn't enough.

As Figure 2-3 shows, you can come up with ways to create market segments by asking three basic questions:

>> Who buys your product or service?

>> What do they buy?

>> Why do they buy?

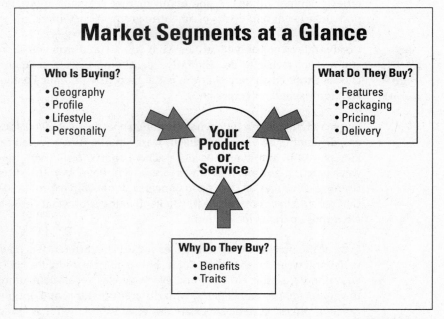

Market Segments at a Glance

Who Is Buying?
- Geography
- Profile
- Lifestyle
- Personality

What Do They Buy?
- Features
- Packaging
- Pricing
- Delivery

Your Product or Service

Why Do They Buy?
- Benefits
- Traits

FIGURE 2-3:
Define market segments by asking three basic questions, and answer those questions from different market viewpoints.

© John Wiley & Sons, Inc.

A good way to begin carving out your market segments is by researching who buys your product or service. If you focus on individual consumers, discover a bit about how they live their lives. If your customers are other companies, find out about their business operations. Think about your customers in these terms:

>> **Geography:** Where do they live?

>> **Profile:** What are they like?

>> **Lifestyle:** What do they do?

>> **Personality:** How do they act?

Where do they live?

Perhaps the simplest and most widely used way to describe your customers is based on where they are, beginning with a simple geographic breakdown by these factors:

>> Country

>> Region

>> Province

>> City

>> Neighbourhood

But geography can also lead to more specialized groups. For example, you may find it useful to describe customers based on factors such as

>> How close their nearest neighbours are

>> How hot or cool their summers are

>> Proximity to the airport and frequency of travel

You can divide customers into groups based on geography to separate them according to regional taste — which often is a significant factor in the distribution and delivery of a product or service. Ethnic foods, for example, tend to sell better in certain regions of Canada. Indian food is hottest in the Toronto area, kosher products are most popular in central Canada, and Asian food is everywhere. Per-capita wine consumption is far higher in Montreal than it is in Edmonton.

Speaking of regions, instead of trying to sell heavy coats throughout the country, you may want to concentrate sales efforts in regions that have cold winters, taking advantage of market differences based on weather patterns. By looking at the geographic characteristics of consumers as they relate to your product or service, you begin to create market segments that you can use.

What are they like?

A profile of your customers includes all the attributes that you may expect to find in a national census. Marketing gurus call these attributes *demographic data,* which include the following:

>> Age

>> Gender

>> Family size

>> Education

>> Occupation

>> Income

>> Ethnicity

>> Nationality

>> Religion

Company profiles, of course, are somewhat different. These profiles can include basic characteristics, such as the following:

>> Industry

>> Size of company

>> Number of employees

>> Years in business

TIP

You can often use customer profiles to spot market trends and take advantage of potential opportunities. Why is the market for health-care products booming today? Because the fabled baby boom generation — those 10 million Canadians who were born between 1946 and 1964 — is coming face to face with its own mortality. And where can you find a growing market for housing and home loans? In regions of the country with plenty of recreation, where people can enjoy their retirement years.

What do they do?

Lifestyle is an awfully tired word these days. People use it to describe anything and everything that you do in the modern world. But when applied to your customers, *lifestyle* has a particular meaning; it captures characteristics that go deeper than what's available in plain old census data. Customer lifestyle factors include the following:

>> Hobbies

>> Television viewing habits

>> Social groups and activities

>> Club memberships

>> Vacation preferences

All this information is sometimes called *psychographic data* because you can use it to map out the psychology of the customer.

When applied to business customers, lifestyle factors include such things as what companies do when it comes to

>> Protecting the environment

>> Donating to charitable causes

>> Investing in employee training

>> Offering employee benefits

>> Promoting people from inside the company

You can use these characteristics to understand how you may better serve a particular segment of your business market.

How do they act?

Your customers are individuals who have their own ways of acting and interacting with the world. But imagine if you could create market segments based on general personality types? Luckily, you don't have to start from scratch. Some behavioural scientists have come up with five basic personality types, which appear in Table 2-1.

TABLE 2-1

Customer Personality Types

Type	Description
Innovators	Risk-takers of the world
	Young and well educated
	Comfortable with new ideas and technologies
	Mobile and networked
	Informed by outside sources
Early adopters	Opinion leaders in their communities
	Careful evaluators
	Open to well-reasoned arguments
	Respected by their peers

(continued)

TABLE 2-1 *(continued)*

Type	Description
Early majority	Risk avoiders whenever possible
	Deliberate in their actions
	Unlikely to try new products until those products catch on
Late majority	Skeptics
	Extremely cautious
	Disappointed by other products
	Reluctant to try new products
	Respond only to pressure from friends
Laggards	Hold out until the bitter end
	Wait until products are old-fashioned
	Still hesitate!

Personality type has a great deal to do with how eager people are to try new products and services. Although some people are adventurous and willing to try new things, others are quite the opposite, never using anything until it has made the rounds. In general, laggards simply take longer to adopt new ideas than innovators do. Experts make all this stuff sound like rocket science by calling it the *diffusion of innovation* (see Figure 2-5 later in this chapter).

TIP

Over the years, marketers have accumulated plenty of data on the typical person in each of the five groups highlighted in Table 2-1. You can use this information in your planning efforts. Identify which personality types are most likely to have a positive response to your product or service. You can begin to assemble a description of your target customers and create a business plan that enables you to reach them efficiently and effectively.

Considering what customers buy

A description of your customers in terms of their geography, profiles, lifestyles, and personalities tells you a lot about them (see the preceding sections for more information on customer research). To begin to understand how customers make choices in the marketplace that you compete in, you need to consider not only who they are but also what they buy.

A description of customers based on what they buy enables you to view them from a perspective that you're very familiar with: your own products and services. After you come up with market segments based on what your customers purchase, you can address the needs of each group by making changes in the following aspects of your product or service:

>> Features

>> Packaging

>> Pricing

>> Delivery options

What can your product do?

Features refer to all the specifications and characteristics of a product or service — things that you often find listed in a product brochure, users' manual, or the company website. When you group customers based on the product features that they look for, the customers themselves turn out to have a great deal in common. Their similarities include the following:

>> **How much they use the product:** Light, moderate, or heavy use

>> **How well they use the product:** Novice, intermediate, or expert

>> **What they do with the product:** Recreation, education, or business

>> **What kind of customers they are:** Adviser, reseller, or user

For example, WestJet Airlines is a major player in the so-called *no-frills* segment of the airline business. The company caters to price-sensitive people who travel relatively short distances and who often have to pay for travel out of their own pockets. You can usually find a cheap ticket to fly WestJet, but don't expect a seat assignment in advance (except do-it-yourself online seating 24 hours before departure) or more than a package or two of munchies after you board. You do get an easygoing, fun airline that respects you, however.

WestJet Airlines customers tend to be different from those of Air Canada, a global, full-service carrier at the opposite end of the airline spectrum. Air Canada offers service to every major airport around the globe. The company targets business customers, frequent flyers, and global travellers who expect a hot meal on a ten-hour flight, help with their international connections, and their luggage to arrive when they do, no matter where they are in the world.

However, more recently WestJet has added more global destinations, and prices are now similar to Air Canada. Flair Airlines has become Canada's low-cost carrier, based out of Edmonton and including direct flights from Vancouver to Toronto. With baggage fees, including for carry-on items, it is a no-frills airline but very cost-competitive.

How do you sell the product?

When marketing types talk about *packaging*, they refer to much more than cardboard, shrink wrapping, and plastic. Packaging means everything that surrounds a product offering, including the following:

>> **Advertising:** Radio and TV, magazines, billboards, T-shirts, and the Internet

>> **Promotions:** In-store sales, coupons, and sweepstakes

>> **Publicity:** Book reviews, telethons, and celebrity endorsements

>> **Product service:** Warranties, help lines, and service centres

The market segments that you identify based on packaging criteria often reflect customer attributes similar to the ones based on product features: frequency of use, level of sophistication, product application, and the type of user.

What does your product cost?

The pricing of a particular kind of product or service creates different groups of customers. Price-sensitive customers make up one camp; financially free customers who are willing to pay for a certain level of quality make up the other. If you've ever had to endure a course in microeconomics (yuck), you might remember two facts: Price is a major market variable, and the price/quality trade-off is a fundamental force in every marketplace. People who buy Timex watches at their local drugstore tend to be price sensitive, whereas shoppers acquiring a Rolex timepiece at a classy downtown jewellery store want luxury, craftsmanship, elegance — and the chance to make a personal statement.

In general, the *mass market* tends to be price sensitive, and the so-called *class market* buys more on the basis of quality, high-end features, and status. But price isn't the only financial factor that can lead to different market segments. Here are other criteria:

>> **Available financing:** Offered by home-furnishings companies

>> **Leasing options:** Offered to airlines that buy airplanes

>> **Money-back guarantees:** Offered regularly on TV

>> **Trade-in arrangements:** Offered by automobile dealerships

Where can consumers find your product?

Distribution and delivery determine how customers actually receive your product or service. In this case, market segments are often based on where your customers shop:

- Factory outlet stores
- Discount centres
- Department stores
- Boutiques
- Catalogues
- On the Internet

For example, Mary Kay Cosmetics reaches its customers directly at home through independent sales consultants, and its products aren't available in any store. The company believes that beauty aids are personal in nature and require highly personalized selling for its lines to be successful. With the same aim in mind, other cosmetic companies strategically place consultants (you can easily spot them by their white coats, perfect faces, and expensive aromas) in department stores.

Market segments based on delivery also may rely on additional criteria:

- Anytime availability (convenience stores)
- Anywhere availability (gas stations)
- Guaranteed availability (car rental)
- Time sensitivity (florists)

Understanding why customers buy

REMEMBER

When it comes to satisfying customers' needs over the long haul, you can't forget the basics. Perhaps the most difficult — and useful — questions that you can ask yourself about customers deal with *why* they buy in the first place. These include questions such as the following:

- What do customers look for?
- What's important to them?
- What motivates them?
- How do they perceive the world?
- How do they make choices?

When you group customers by using the answers to these questions, you create market segments based on the benefits that customers look for. Because these market segments describe your customers from *their* point of view, rather than your own, these segments provide the best opportunity for you to satisfy the particular needs of an entire customer group.

What do they get?

REMEMBER

When you try to figure out exactly why customers buy products and services in your marketplace, start a list of the benefits that you think they look for. Product benefits may sound an awful lot like product features, but in subtle, yet crucial ways, product benefits and product features are really quite different:

>> *Features* are defined in terms of products or services. A car, for example, may have a manual transmission (as opposed to an automatic) and may come with power windows, anti-theft locks, or a dashboard GPS.

>> *Benefits,* on the other hand, are defined by the customer. Depending on the customer, the benefits of a manual transmission may be in handling and responsiveness, or in improved gas mileage. A dashboard GPS may represent an added luxury for the weekend driver or may be an absolute necessity for the travelling sales representative. Again, the benefits are in the eyes of the customer.

Perceived benefits can change over time. Consider the newest generation of cars equipped with hybrid engines, which combine gas and electric power. A customer may buy a hybrid because it pollutes less than a regular engine, satisfying a customer's sense of social conscience. But when gasoline prices soar — like they almost always do — savings at the gas pump may begin to seem like the more important benefit.

You must understand the difference between benefits and features if you plan to use the market segments that you come up with to create an effective business plan. Take a moment to think about the business situations sketched out in Figure 2-4.

Which of the benefits listed represent genuine benefits to the customers of each company? A trick question, of course: *You* don't define benefits — the *customers* do.

TIP

To identify the benefits that your products offer, choose one of your products or services, and follow these steps:

1. Draw a mental image of the product or service, based on its features, attributes, and options.

2. Put that picture completely aside for a moment.

Choose the Customer Benefits

Situation	Potential Customer Benefits
A boutique offers upscale bath and beauty products imported from Europe, tasteful gift wrapping, and hassle-free delivery anywhere in the world.	❑ A nice place to go after lunch when you've extra time to kill ❑ The opportunity to impress relatives back in Sweden ❑ An alternative to divorce after discovering that today's your anniversary ❑ Aromatherapy after an ugly day at the office
A franchised quick-printing outlet provides self-service copy machines; sells custom stationery and business cards; and offers two-hour rush jobs on flyers, posters, and newsletters.	❑ The ability to look like a big company—at least on paper ❑ A money-saving alternative to buying a copier ❑ A threat used to keep the printing and graphics supplier in line ❑ A job-saver when the printed brochures don't arrive at the trade show
A semiconductor manufacturer sells customized chips to high-tech companies for use in brand-name consumer products, including home-electronics gadgets, computers, and games.	❑ An extension of the in-house research and development department ❑ An easy way to expand the product line ❑ A weapon in the cost/price wars ❑ A way to reduce a new product's time to market

© John Wiley & Sons, Inc.

FIGURE 2-4: Consider these business situations.

3. **Place yourself in your customers' shoes.**

4. **Now create a new description of the product or service from your customers' viewpoint that focuses on the benefits that they want.**

Grouping customers based on the particular benefits that they look for when they select a product or service is the key to satisfying individual customers and keeping them happy over the long run.

How do they decide?

Different customers approach your market in different ways, and you can often identify market segments based on certain customer traits as they relate to your product or service category. Some of the conditions that guide customer buying decisions include the following:

» **Speed of the purchase decision:** The *decision-making process* (DMP) that customers go through before they purchase a product or service varies, depending on the product or service's complexity and price tag. People may buy chewing gum at a drugstore without much thought. But car dealerships and real estate agents face a completely different DMP.

- **The actual decision-maker:** Families represent a common *decision-making unit* (DMU) that buys various consumer goods. But who in the family has the final word?

- **Customer loyalty:** The way that companies relate to their customers can easily define a set of market segments. Service industries, for example, go out of their way to identify and encourage customers based on their loyalty. You've probably been asked to join more than one frequent-flyer programme or to keep track of frequent-caller, frequent-diner, or frequent-you-name-it points.

- **Level of product use:** In many industries, a small percentage of consumers account for a large percentage of sales. If you want to sell beer, for example, you may not want to ignore the heavy-beer-drinking population — an estimated 10 million Canadians. Keeping this high-consumption group of customers satisfied can be profitable indeed.

Finding Useful Market Segments

A market segment is useful only if it allows you to deliver something of value to the customers you identify — and to do so profitably. Not all the market segments that you come up with are going to be practical ones. What should you look for if you want to find a really useful market segment? In general, you want to make sure that it has the following characteristics:

- A size that you can manage
- Customers that you can identify
- Customers that you can reach

Sizing up the segment

Identifying useful market segments requires a delicate balance between defining your markets so broadly that they don't offer you any guidance, and planning and defining them so narrowly that you make them impractical and unprofitable. A useful market segment has to be manageable. The right size depends on your particular business situation, including your resources, the competition, and your customers' requirements.

REMEMBER

You can bet that your customers are going to become more demanding over time and that your competitors are bound to become more adept at serving smaller markets. When you choose the manageable market segments in which you want to compete, make sure that you factor in ways to use information technology in your business.

Identifying the customers

While you piece together a complete picture of your customers, take advantage of the many different ways to categorize them (see the earlier section "Identifying market segments" for details). In particular, market segments based on why customers buy are often the best because they define groups of customers who have similar needs. Whenever possible, come up with market segments that take into account your customers' viewpoints — the benefits that they look for, as well as their buying behaviour.

Suppose that while searching for a hot new business opportunity, you discover a group of people who have the same general attitude about their jobs and work. Members of this group want to be more productive on the job, yet they feel neglected and frustrated with their working conditions and office environment. You may have come up with a potential market segment. But what next? How do you identify these potential customers? Well, maybe you go on to discover that many of these workers are left-handed and would feel more comfortable with their numeric keypads on the left side of the computer keyboard and with their handsets on the right side of the telephone. Now, you've taken a major step toward defining a useful market segment because the segment is based on customer wants and needs and is made up of customers who you can describe, observe, and identify.

Given this situation, you may have the urge to take a planning shortcut and base your new market segment entirely on what you observe: left-handers, who, after all, constitute about 10 percent of the population. Bingo! You decide to design and produce office equipment exclusively for left-handed customers. But wait; control that urge. Before you identify a really useful market segment, you need to satisfy one more requirement, which is covered in the following section.

Reaching the market

After you define a promising market segment based on customer wants and needs, and including customers that you can describe, you have to develop ways of communicating with those customers. You must be able to set up affordable ways to contact them through advertising, promotions, and the delivery of your product or service. The next section goes into more detail on reaching the market.

Becoming Market Driven

Remember back in school when you were told to check your homework before handing it in — especially if the teacher was going to grade it? Well, the marketplace is a difficult class to tackle (as difficult as, say, calculus or physics), and the stakes are high. Before you commit to a particular market segment scheme, look back over your homework. Pose these review questions to yourself:

>> What benefits are customers in the market segment looking for?

>> Will product features, options, and packaging satisfy customers' needs?

>> Is the size of the segment manageable?

>> Can you describe, observe, and identify your customers?

>> Can you reach your customers efficiently through advertising and promotion?

>> Will distribution and product service be effective?

Researching your market

At some point, you may want to use a more sophisticated approach to answer some of the questions in the preceding list. *Test marketing* tests your ideas on a carefully selected sample of potential customers in your market segment. Using a test market, you can often gauge how well your product plan is likely to work before you spend *beaucoup* bucks going forward. The bad news is that, like all market research, test marketing can be expensive and time-consuming, especially if you bring in big guns from the outside. So, you may want to start by conducting some preliminary customer interviews on your own.

Customer interviews produce a snapshot of who buys your product, as well as what they think they're buying. You can conduct interviews on an informal basis. Just follow these steps:

1. **Select customers in your market segment.**

2. **Arrange to meet with them individually or in small groups.**

3. **Get them to talk a bit about themselves.**

4. **Have them tell you what they like and don't like about your product.**

5. **Ask them why they buy your product and what they would do without it.**

WARNING

One word of caution: Use common sense. These interviews aren't meant to be rigorous pieces of market research, so be careful to confirm what you see when you start drawing conclusions about customer behaviour from them.

Defining personality types

After you come up with a market segmentation scheme and a useful description of your customers (refer to the earlier section "Identifying market segments" for more info), you're in a good position to say something more about their buying behaviour toward the products and services that you plan to offer. So, look back over your notes and review what you know about your customers and their likely personality types. (If you need help, flip to the section "How do they act?" earlier in this chapter.)

Why are personality types so important? They have a great deal to do with how eager people are to try out new products and services. Although some people are adventurous and willing to try anything new, others are quite the opposite, never using anything until it's been around for quite a while. In general, laggards simply take longer to adopt new ideas than innovators do (refer to Table 2-1).

In Figure 2-5, the percentage of people who represent each personality type is just an estimate, of course. But you get a rough idea of the relative size of each personality group in your own marketplace.

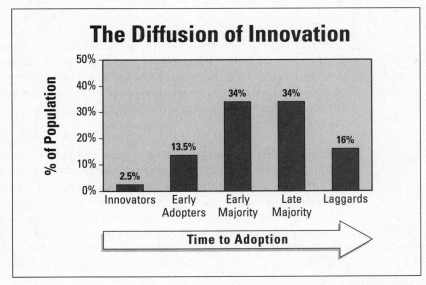

FIGURE 2-5: Product adoption occurs at different times for different personality types.

© John Wiley & Sons, Inc.

REMEMBER

The important thing to note is that if you bring a brand-new kind of business, product, or service to the marketplace, the innovators and early adopters are going to be easier to capture than most consumers. The longer your kind of product or service has been on the market, the more effort you must spend focusing on your customers and understanding their wants, needs, and motives.

Checking Out Your Competition

Spending time with the competition isn't anyone's idea of fun. Think they're out to get you? You bet they are. But the more you know about the competition, the more easily you can figure out their next move — and set a strategy to stay one step ahead.

When the Japanese decided to become global players in the automobile industry in the late 1960s, their car manufacturers planned very carefully. They knew what they had to do because the Western business experts had taught them. First, they needed to understand the consumer markets in Canada, the United States, and Europe; second, they needed to know everything about the worldwide competition.

So, Japanese car-makers came to Canada and the United States to analyse and learn from their competitors-to-be. They visited General Motors, Ford, and Chrysler. They asked questions, taped meetings, took pictures, measured, sketched, and studied. While they did all their research, the Japanese were amazed by the Canadian and American hospitality. When they got back home, of course, they hatched their plans. By finding out as much as possible about their marketplace and the competition in advance, Japanese auto firms were able to successfully penetrate the North American market and other world markets.

North American car companies never knew what hit them, even though the blow was a decade or more in coming. They simply failed to track their competition and take their competitors seriously. Over the last few decades, the automobile industry has dealt with waves of competition, not only from the Japanese, but also from European and Korean car makers. And who knows, your next sedan may just be made in China or India.

The following sections show you why you need to have competitors in the first place. They help you identify your current competitors and your potential competitors. They look at competition from the viewpoint of customers and the choices they make in the marketplace. And they examine your competitors in relation to their strategies and company structure, introducing the idea of strategic groups. After identifying your competitors, the following sections also help you understand them better by looking at what they do; by forecasting their future plans; and by checking out their capabilities, strategies, goals, and assumptions.

Understanding the value of competitors

Competitors are almost always portrayed as the bad guys. At best, they annoy. At worst, they steal customers away and bank the cash — your cash. In short, they make your business life miserable. Is this picture unfair? You bet.

Look up from the fray, and you can discover another way to look at your competitors: They invent new technologies, expand market opportunities, and sometimes create entire industries . . . and believe it or not, they also bring out the best in you. Competitors force you to sharpen your strategies, hone your business plans, and go that extra mile to satisfy customers. After all, your real goal is satisfying customers and developing long-term, rewarding relationships with them.

REMEMBER

Competition is a force to be reckoned with because of the power of customers. Customers are always making market choices, deciding what to buy and where to spend money based on their needs and willingness to pay. How do they do it? The process is based on the *value equation*, which looks like this:

Customer value = Benefits ÷ Price

Figure 2-6 illustrates this equation.

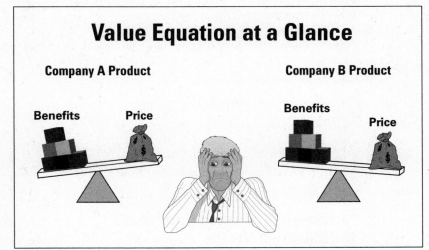

FIGURE 2-6: Customers make choices in the marketplace using the value equation to weigh the value of competing products.

© John Wiley & Sons, Inc.

The equation points to a simple truth: Today's consumers are awfully good at making complex choices. Think about the last time you ran errands. You probably stopped by the grocery store, where you used the value equation to make all sorts of trade-offs. Maybe you chose a certain cut of meat, weighing what you were in the mood for and what looked fresh against the price per kilogram. Maybe you decided that you didn't have time to drive to the warehouse store, so you bought cereal in the more expensive 375-gram box. On your way out, you picked up organic tomatoes for your salad at three times the conventional price. Driving home, you put fuel in the car. You opted for the most conveniently located station, even though its fuel prices were a little higher.

REMEMBER

Competition encourages each player in your industry to figure out how to provide customers with the best value possible. Competition can often create a win-win situation, so don't try to avoid it by ignoring your competitors. Don't ever think that you're immune to it, either. Instead, take advantage of competition and what it can do for your company.

Identifying your real competitors

Two boys go hiking in the woods. They suddenly come across a bear. One of the boys immediately sits down and tightens his shoelaces. The other kid looks down at him and says, "There's no way we can outrun that bear." The first kid replies, "I'm not interested in outrunning the bear. I just want to outrun you!" Like the boy in the story, you need to know who you're really competing against.

You can come up with a list of possible competitors based on any number of factors. The problem is finding the method that most successfully identifies the competitors who impact your business.

To really understand your competition, you need to know the following things:

>> How customers make choices

>> How customers use products

>> The capabilities of your competitors

>> Your competitors' strategies

>> Where future competition may come from

Considering competition based on customer choice

Customers choose to buy certain products based on a value equation, weighing the benefits of several products against their relative prices (refer to Figure 2-6 for more equation info). But which products do customers actually compare? If you want to know who your real competitors are, you need to know how many products — and which products — your customers typically look at before they decide to buy.

If you identify your customers and their *selection criteria* — that is, what they look for in a product or service — you can divide a list of competitors into groups based on how intensely they compete with you.

>> **Head-to-head competitors:** Together, these businesses represent your most intense competition. Their products always seem to be on customers' *short lists* (those three or four competing products that they plan to compare very carefully).

>> **First-tier competitors:** These businesses are direct competitors, but perhaps not quite as fierce as the head-to-head kind.

>> **Indirect competitors:** These competitors are the ones that you don't often think about. Their products surface as alternatives to yours only occasionally. But this group deserves a periodic review because indirect competitors always have the potential to surprise you with competing products out of the blue. Many health-related magazines, for example, find themselves competing indirectly with sites on the Internet that can provide much of the same updated medical information.

TIP

You should be able to count your head-to-head competitors on one hand. You may have twice as many first-tier competitors to track and an equal number of indirect competitors. Be careful to keep the number of competitors that you track manageable. Your head-to-head competition deserves much more attention than your indirect competitors, obviously, but do set up a schedule for reviewing companies in each of the three competitor groups.

Paying attention to product usage and competition

Looking at products and services in the context of how customers use them gives you another viewpoint from which to eye the competition. In this case, follow these steps:

1. **Ask customers to think about situations, applications, or occasions in which they may use your product.**

2. **Ask customers to come up with other kinds of products or services they think are appropriate and may be just as satisfying in the same situations.**

3. **Ask customers to identify two things they would change about the product that they use.**

Spotting strategic groups

If you step back and look at the competitors around you, their differing appearances may amaze you. In certain industries, for example, companies that have a full product line compete with companies that offer a single product. In other industries, companies that gain recognition for their innovative R&D (research and development) compete with companies that don't develop anything on their own.

How can competitors in the same industry be so different? Over time, doesn't every business figure out the best strategies, as well as the most efficient and effective ways to do business? Shouldn't all businesses end up looking pretty much alike? These good questions have two possible answers:

>> Businesses don't always discover a best way to do things. Markets and industries are complex, and different ways of doing business can exist side by side and be equally successful.

>> Businesses that do things one way can't always easily change and start doing things another way.

A *strategic group* is a set of businesses in a particular industry that look alike and tend to behave in similar ways. In particular, firms in the same strategic group have the following traits:

>> They display similar characteristics (size, geography, rate of growth).

>> They operate in similar ways (degree of risk-taking, level of aggressiveness).

>> They demonstrate similar capabilities (people, skills, image, money in the bank).

>> They pursue related strategies (customer segments, distribution, marketing, and product-line decisions).

You can apply all sorts of business criteria to identify the most useful strategic groups. Although every industry is different, you need to consider these general variables:

>> Businesses that manufacture most of their product components versus those that assemble or resell products

>> Businesses that produce name-brand products versus those that produce generic or private-label brands

>> Businesses that rely on their own R&D versus those that license or buy technology

>> Businesses that have a full product line versus those that have limited or specialized products

>> Businesses that emphasize marketing versus those that focus on production

>> Businesses with diverse endeavours versus those that thrive in only one industry

Strategic groups fall somewhere between an individual company and the entire industry. Lumping your competition into groups is helpful because all the businesses in a strategic group tend to be affected by, and react to, changes in the marketplace in the same ways. But grouping works only if those businesses stay put in their assigned groups long enough to be analysed. Fortunately, they usually do.

As part of your industry analysis, you may have already discovered a few *entry barriers* — factors that make getting into your business tough, such as high capital costs, expensive distribution systems, new technology, and regulation. You also may have come up with some *exit barriers* — factors that keep competitors from getting out of the business, such as expensive factories, specialized equipment, and long-term agreements. Strategic groups can have the same kind of *mobility barriers*, which tend to keep competitors where they are, in one group or another.

Strategic groups can be a great time-saver in business planning because, when you put all your competitors in strategic groups, you know where to focus your energies. You can spend most of your time analysing the businesses in your strategic group and deal with the rest of the companies in clusters instead of tracking each business separately.

To divide your list of competitors into strategic groups, follow these steps:

1. **Put your competitors in a small number of groups, based on their similarities.**

2. **Add your business to one of the groups.**

3. **Looking at each group carefully, try to come up with the basic criteria that you used to make your selections.**

4. **Take a hard look at the group in which you put your business.**

   Are these competitors really closest to you in terms of their characteristics and the criteria that you identify?

5. **Ask a few trusted customers to look over your groups and see whether they agree.**

   Viewing the world through your customers' eyes is always worthwhile and can sometimes be a real eye-opener.

6. **Adjust the groups, if necessary, and work on additional criteria that may point to other strategic groupings.**

WARNING

Strategic groups are relevant and useful in many industries; they often provide a means of organizing competitors in ways that can simplify the competitive landscape. But keep in mind that all industries don't play by the same rules. If the mobility barriers aren't very high, for example, businesses can adjust their capabilities and change strategies quickly, limiting the usefulness of long-term strategic groups. In addition, acquisitions and alliances between companies can change the composition of groups very rapidly. Make sure that the groups you identify in your industry are real and won't dissolve before you have a chance to analyse them.

Focusing on future competition

Always remember that new competition can come from anywhere. So keep an eye out for emerging competitors. Determine who they are and how seriously to worry about them. The following are the most likely sources of new competition:

>> **Market expansion:** For example, a business that operated successfully for years outside your geographic region decides to expand into your territory.

>> **Product expansion:** For example, a business decides to take advantage of its brand name, technology, or distribution system and creates a new product line in direct competition with yours.

>> **Backward integration:** In-house grocery store brands, such as President's Choice, are a perfect example of a packaged goods customer becoming a direct competitor.

>> **Forward integration:** Your business buys many products from many suppliers. One day, one of those suppliers decides that it can bring all the pieces together as well as you can.

>> **Change in fortune:** Out of the blue, a major company purchases a minor competitor. With access to new resources (financing, marketing, and distribution), the minor competitor becomes a major player.

REMEMBER

Keeping track of your future competitors is as important as tracking your current ones. So, keep your eyes and ears open, and don't be shy about asking your customers and suppliers about competitors on a regular basis.

Tracking your competitors' actions

Suppose that you're armed with a fresh, up-to-date list of competitors. You rank which of those competitors you have to watch most carefully and tag them as head-to-head competitors, first-tier competitors, or indirect competitors. (The earlier section "Identifying your real competitors" discusses separating companies into groups.) Maybe you even put them into strategic groups, singling out the competitors in your group for special attention.

So, what's next? First, decide which competitors on your list to spend more time with. Remember — you probably can't find out everything about each competitor. Keeping track of competitors' actions involves looking at both what the companies are capable of doing and what they plan to do.

Determining competitors' capabilities

The capabilities that you're most interested in tell you something about your competitors' ability to react when your industry changes. How quickly they can react — and how much they can do to change themselves — says a great deal about the competitive danger they pose.

To determine your competitors' capabilities, start with this list of important business functions and areas. Get going with the following questions:

» **Management:** What do you know about the background and experience of the competitor's chief bigwigs? What about the board of directors? Do any managers hail from another industry? If so, what are their past track records?

» **Organization:** How structured and centralized is the competitor's organization? Does it promote from within or hire from the outside? How would you describe the corporate culture?

» **Customer base:** What's the competitor's share of the market? Is it growing? How loyal are its customers? Are customers concentrated in one segment, or do the competitor's products appeal to several segments?

» **Research and development:** Is the competitor known for innovation and technology? Is it even involved in R&D (research and development)? How often does it come out with new products? Does it have patents and copyrights to rely on? How stable and committed are the members of its technical staff? Does the competitor draw on outside expertise?

» **Operations:** How modern are the competitor's facilities? What about capacity? Can the company count on its suppliers? What's the general attitude of the workforce? Does the competitor have a history of labour disputes?

» **Marketing and sales:** How strong are the competitor's products? How broad is the product line? Does the competitor have a reputation for quality? How about brand-name recognition? Does the competitor put a large amount of its resources into advertising and promotion? Is it known for its customer service? Are the salespeople aggressive and well trained?

» **Distribution and delivery:** How many distribution channels does the competitor sell through? Does it have a good relationship with its distributors? Is it quick to take advantage of new distribution opportunities?

>> **Financial condition:** Is the competitor's revenue growing? How about profits? Does it manage costs well? Are profit margins steady or growing? What's the cash-flow situation? Is its long-term debt manageable? Does the competitor have ready access to cash?

TIP

Jot down a half–page corporate bio on each competitor. Each bio should capture the competitor's defining traits, including the following:

>> Capability to respond quickly

>> Willingness to change

>> Determination to compete

>> Capacity to grow

Assessing competitors' strategies

Your competitors' capabilities tell you something important about their capacity to get things done right now in your business. But what about the future?

To answer that question, you need to assess their capabilities strategically. The following three strategies are sometimes called *generic strategies* because they've been tried many times before and because they work well in almost any market or industry:

>> **Low cost:** The first generic strategy comes from a basic economic principle: If you can offer a product or service at the lowest price in the market, customers are naturally going to buy from you. This strategy assumes, of course, that you can also produce your product at a low-enough cost so that the company makes a profit over time. The strategy also assumes that your product or service is similar enough to the competition's that a lower price can entice customers and clinch the sale.

>> **Something different:** This strategy is based on the simple notion that if you can come up with something different or unique in the products you offer or the services you provide, customers will beat a path to your company door. These customers are likely to become good customers, loyal customers, and customers that aren't terribly sensitive to price because you offer them special benefits that they can't find anywhere else.

>> **Focus:** The last generic strategy is about the kinds of customers you decide to serve. Instead of positioning yourself everywhere in the market and trying to sell products and services to everyone, carefully choose your customers.

You win these customers over as a group by focusing on understanding their needs better than the competition does and by providing them with the benefits that they look for, be it cost savings or something unique.

Competitors often combine strategies. A business that follows a focused strategy may find success in serving a particular market segment simply because its products or services are different from those of the competition.

Put together a short summary of what strategies you think your competitors may be coming up with. Review their capabilities and past actions, considering the following questions:

>> What generic strategies has each competitor adopted in the past?

>> Have the strategies generally been successful?

>> Are changes in the industry forcing competitors to change their strategies?

>> What kinds of change is each competitor capable of making?

>> How fast can each competitor change?

Usually, you find that a long-term strategy requires time and the total commitment of the business. So knowing a little about your competitors' history is very useful in understanding their strategies. It also helps you keep in mind what you think your competitors are capable of in the future. Remember, you can use the concept of strategic groups to simplify this process. (See the earlier section "Spotting strategic groups" to find out more about this concept.)

Predicting your competitors' moves

Trying to predict where your competitors are headed isn't easy, of course; looking into the future never is. But where your competitors plan to be in the months and years to come certainly depends on where they are today, as well as on their capabilities and the strategies that they've set in motion.

Many companies intentionally (or accidentally) send market signals about how they may behave. Some businesses, for example, always lower their prices in response to a competitor. Looking at the past actions of competitors can provide you with an indication of what they may do next. Predicting your competitors' actions also requires a little insight into what they think and how they think — their goals and the assumptions that they make about the industry.

Figuring out competitors' goals

Your competitors' mission, vision, and values statements tell you a great deal about what they expect of themselves in the future. (Chapter 1 of Book 3 talks about these statements.) These documents aren't top-secret; they communicate a business's intentions to all its stakeholders, and you should take advantage of them. You don't have to read your competitors' minds. All you have to do is read what they say about themselves and what they plan to do.

To discover the details about your competitors' plans, take the following steps:

1. **Select a short list of competitors.**

2. **Dig up as much information as you can find on each competitor's values, vision, and mission statements, as well as any stated business goals and objectives.**

3. **Ask customers, suppliers, your salespeople (if you have any), and maybe even your competitors' former employees for information about each of your competitor's long-term plans.**

4. **Write down your educated estimation of your competitors' financial and strategic goals.**

   Don't forget to read between the lines. In particular, look for the following:

   - Market-share goals
   - Revenue targets
   - Profitability targets
   - Technology milestones
   - Customer-service goals
   - Distribution targets
   - Changes in leadership or senior management

Uncovering competitors' assumptions

What your competitors plan to do is usually related to their assumptions about themselves, about you and other businesses like you, and about your industry — how they think and the way in which they see the world. Sometimes, you can get important clues about your competitors' assumptions by going back over their goals and objectives. Businesses can't easily make a statement about where they want to go without giving something away about where they think they are today. You can often come up with valuable insights by comparing your competitors' assumptions about the industry with what you know (and think) is true.

WARNING

Assumptions aren't always true — which is what makes them assumptions in the first place. False assumptions can be very dangerous for business, especially when they lead to so-called conventional wisdom or blind spots:

>> **Conventional wisdom:** Prevailing assumptions in an industry often become so ingrained that businesses mistake them for the gospel truth. Conventional wisdom is almost always proved wrong when an unconventional competitor comes along. Watch your competitors for signs that they take their assumptions too seriously and have forgotten the importance of asking, "Why?"

>> **Blind spots:** Missing the significance of events or trends in an industry is all too easy, especially if they run counter to prevailing notions and conventional wisdom. A competitor's worldview often dictates what that company sees and doesn't see. While you track your competitors, look closely for actions and reactions that may point to blind spots and a misreading of what's happening in the marketplace.

Competing to Win

The more you get to know your competitors, the better off you are when it comes to understanding their actions and anticipating their moves.

TIP

But remember — the more you discover about your competitors, the more they probably discover about you. You probably put out as much information about your company and its intentions as your competitors do, so listening to yourself is just as important as listening to your competition. Put yourself on your list of competitors. Interpret your actions from a competitor's point of view. That way, you understand the implications of your competitive behaviour in the industry as well as you understand your competitors' behaviours.

If you're serious about the competition, you can't do all this analysis one time, wash your hands, and be finished. You have to monitor your competitors in a systematic way. If you're good at observing your competitors, you can choose the competitive battles that you want to win. You don't get ambushed in competitive situations where you're bound to lose.

Organizing facts and figures

To find out what really makes your competitors tick, take advantage of data from all sorts of places. Start your search by using the power of the Internet.

You can usually find facts and figures on the competition included in the following resources:

>> Business, trade, and technical publications

>> Trade shows

>> Company documents

>> Stock-market analyses

>> Management speeches

>> Suppliers and distributors

>> Customer feedback

>> Your employees

TIP

The last item on the list deserves a special note. Your employees (if you have any at this point) are an invaluable source of data when it comes to the competition. When you look inside your business, start with your salespeople, who are smack-dab in the middle of the information stream. They talk with customers, deal with distributors, and occasionally run into competitors. They hear all the gossip, rumours, and news flashes that flow through your industry. Take advantage of their position and figure out how to capture what they know — and how to use it to your advantage.

WARNING

You have to be a little careful about gathering information from employees other than your salespeople. In many industries, people move from job to job and company to company. Brainstorming about what a competitor may be up to is harmless, but warning flags should go up if someone pulls out documents marked Top Secret. Such behaviour isn't only wrong, it's illegal. You can't use certain pieces of information that a former employee may have about a competitor — anything that may be construed as proprietary information or trade secrets. (Read more about intellectual property in Book 2.) High-tech companies are forever exchanging threats and lawsuits over alleged violations of trade secrets laws.

TIP

You need a way to organize the facts and figures that you collect from your many sources so that you can turn the pieces into useful competitive information. Long ago, filing cabinets and file folders did the trick nicely. Now, however, setting up a computer-based system to keep track of the data probably makes more sense. When you set up the system, keep in mind that information about your competitors won't fall in your lap in the next two days — instead, it trickles in over weeks, months, and years.

More than likely, you already have bits and pieces of data about your key competitors stashed away. You just need to develop a procedure that keeps the bits and pieces coming in and brings them together to create a useful, up-to-date profile of the competition. The following steps help you develop such a procedure:

1. **Start with a pilot procedure for tracking competitors.**

2. **Set up a company-wide system for tracking competitors.**

3. **Make someone responsible for competitor analysis.**

4. **Make it your priority to see that the system is carried out.**

Choosing your battles

The more thoroughly you understand your competitors — what they did in the past, what they do now, and what they may do in the future — the better you can plan for and choose the competitive battles that you want to take part in.

REMEMBER

Naturally, you want to go after markets in which you have a strategy and the capability to succeed. But you have to keep your eyes wide open because you're never alone in any marketplace for long. By embracing the competition, rather than ignoring it, you have the added advantage of knowing where the competition is weakest. Choose each battleground by pitting your strengths against areas where the competition has weaknesses so that you win half the battle before it begins.

Chapter **3**

Weighing Your Business's Prospects

We've all looked at a snapshot of ourselves or listened to our voices on the outgoing voice mail messages and said, *That sure doesn't look like me!* or *Is that what I really sound like?*

If your business is already up and running, you likely have difficulty seeing clearly and objectively when you take on the task of measuring your business's internal strengths and weaknesses. If you're just starting up a business, this chapter shows you what to think about soon enough because successful business planning absolutely requires that you always know where you stand.

This chapter helps you get a handle on your business's strengths and weaknesses in relation to the opportunities and threats that you face. You find out how the critical success factors (CSFs) in your industry come into play to determine which of those capabilities and resources are strengths and which aren't. You pull all the pieces of the puzzle together into a SWOT analysis to create a complete picture. You also create a strategic balance sheet so you can track where you stand, what you should do, and when you should do it. And finally, you discover how to develop and sustain a business model so you can make money now and in the long term.

Identifying Strengths and Weaknesses

Assessing yourself isn't easy. You have to measure strengths and weaknesses relative to the situations at hand; a strength in one circumstance may prove to be a weakness in another. Leadership and snap decision-making, for example, may serve you well in an emergency. But the same temperament may be a liability when you're a part of a team that must navigate delicate give-and-take negotiations.

REMEMBER

Your business's *strengths* are the capabilities, resources, and skills that you can draw upon to carry out strategies, implement plans, and achieve the goals that you set for the business. Your business's *weaknesses* are any lack of skills or a deficiency in your capabilities and resources relative to the competition that may stop you from acting on strategies and plans or from accomplishing your goals.

To capture your first impressions of your business, complete the Business Strengths and Weaknesses Questionnaire (see Figure 3-1). On the right side of the questionnaire, assess your capabilities and resources in each area. On the left side, rate the importance of these elements to your industry.

Company Strengths and Weaknesses Questionnaire

Importance to Industry			Business Area	Your Capabilities and Resources			
Low	Moderate	High		Poor	Fair	Good	Excellent
❑	❑	❑	Management	❑	❑	❑	❑
❑	❑	❑	Organization	❑	❑	❑	❑
❑	❑	❑	Customer base	❑	❑	❑	❑
❑	❑	❑	Research and development	❑	❑	❑	❑
❑	❑	❑	Operations	❑	❑	❑	❑
❑	❑	❑	Marketing and sales	❑	❑	❑	❑
❑	❑	❑	Distribution and delivery	❑	❑	❑	❑
❑	❑	❑	Financial condition	❑	❑	❑	❑

FIGURE 3-1: Fill out the questionnaire to get a quick take on your business's strengths and weaknesses in major business areas.

© John Wiley & Sons, Inc.

Getting other points of view

Completing the questionnaire in Figure 3-1 gives you a beginning list of your business's strengths and weaknesses. To be objective, however, you need to go beyond first impressions and look at your business assets from more than one point of view. Different frames of reference offer the advantage of smoothing out biases that creep into a single viewpoint. They also offer the best chance of making your list as complete as it can be. Consider these three independent viewpoints:

>> **Internal view:** Draw on the managerial experience inside your business (use your own experience or that of your friends and former co-workers if you're self-employed) to come up with a consensus on your business strengths and weaknesses.

>> **Outside view:** Perhaps you identify business strengths as assets only because your competitors haven't reacted yet, or maybe you ignore real weaknesses because everybody else has them, too. You need an objective outside assessment of what's happening in your business, and consultants can assist.

>> **Competitive view:** Beware of becoming too self-absorbed in this analysis. Step back and look around, using your competitors as yardsticks, if you can. Your competitors do business in the same industry and marketplace, and they show strength or weakness in all the key areas that interest you. If your list is going to mean anything when the time comes to apply it to your business situation, you have to measure your strengths and weaknesses against your competitors'. (Refer to Chapter 2 of Book 3 for more about how sizing up your competitors helps you.)

TIP

If you don't have a management team that can conduct a situation analysis, bring together one of the informal groups that you rely on for some of your other planning tasks. Ask the group members to analyse strengths and weaknesses. Make sure that the group looks at your business's situation from various perspectives, using the different frames of reference in the preceding list.

Defining capabilities and resources

In putting together a list of your business's capabilities and resources, cast your net as widely as possible. Start by reviewing all the business areas introduced in the Business Strengths and Weaknesses Questionnaire (refer to Figure 3-1). In each area, try to identify as many capabilities and resources as possible by using different frames of reference (see the preceding section). At the same time, assess how relevant each capability or resource is in helping you carry out your plans and achieve your business goals.

Management: Setting direction from the top

Your business's management team brings together skills, talent, and commitment. You want team members to find their direction from your business's mission, values, and vision statements, as well as from the business goals and objectives that you plan to achieve. Top-notch managers and owners are particularly important in industries that face increasing competition or fast-changing technologies. Try to think of an industry that doesn't fit into one of these two categories.

REMEMBER

Management determines what your business does in the future. Senior managers are officially charged with setting the direction and strategy for your business and laying the foundation for a new business, but all managers indirectly set a tone that encourages certain activities and discourages others. Frank Stronach, the founder of automotive-parts giant Magna International, has always believed employees should own a piece of the business, share in its profits, and receive excellent benefits without the help of a labour union. Therefore, Magna International employees receive this vested involvement in the business, and the business has the speed and flexibility of much smaller rivals. Edmonton-based BioWare Corp, a world leader in video-game design, ranks close to the top of the Best Employer list when it comes to providing a healthy workplace and recognizing good performance. Because of this culture, the business attracts highly qualified people who want to work in a business environment that values both personal and corporate responsibility. These capabilities point to great strengths of both companies.

The following list gives you some key questions to ask about the management and/or ownership of your business:

>> How long have managers been around at various levels in your business? (Alternatively, what variety of experiences do you have as an owner?)

>> Does your business plan to hire from the outside or promote from within?

>> What's the general tone set by you and your business's management?

>> Do you have a management-development program in place? (Alternatively, how do you plan to develop your own skills, if you're a sole proprietor?)

>> What background do you or your managers have?

>> How do you measure management performance in your business?

>> How would you rate the general quality of your skills or those of your management team?

Organization: Bringing people together

The people who make up your business and its workforce represent a key resource, both in terms of who they are and how you organize them. Although human resources are important to all companies, they play an especially key role for companies in service industries, in which people are closely tied to the product.

Your organization starts with who your employees are, and that characteristic depends first on how well you select and train them. Beyond that, the work environment and your business's incentive systems determine who goes on to become a dedicated, hard-working employee and who gets frustrated and finally gives up. The setup of your organization (its structure and how it adapts) can be just as important as who your employees are when it comes to creating a business team — even a small one — that performs at the highest levels, year in and year out.

Many industries, such as financial services, experience high employee turnover at a cost of millions of dollars a year. So, it's no wonder that the key expressions of employee engagement and retention dance on the lips of human resources managers. Excellence Canada (EC) knows this and not only provides a menu of solutions for its members, but also recognizes outstanding results through its Canada Awards of Excellence (CAE). By implementing healthy workplace programmes, some award winners have reduced employee turnover by an outstanding 99 percent — obviously becoming "employers of choice."

The following list includes some key questions about your organization that you may want to consider:

>> What words best describe the overall structure of your organization?

>> How many reporting levels do you have between a front-line employee and your CEO?

>> How often does your business plan to reorganize?

>> What are your employees' general attitudes about their jobs and responsibilities?

>> How long does the average employee stay with your business?

>> Does your business plan to have ways to measure and track employees' attitudes and morale?

>> What does your business plan to do to maintain morale and positive job performance?

Customer base: Pleasing the crowds

Your business success depends, to a great extent, on the satisfaction and loyalty of your customers. In Chapter 2 of Book 3, you discover who those customers are and what makes them tick. Understanding your customers and satisfying their wants and needs are critical to the future of your business.

Nordstrom is a Seattle, Washington–based department store chain that appeals to upscale shoppers. The business bases its reputation on the simple idea that the customer is always right. And the business means it. As one story goes, some time ago, a disgruntled customer stormed into the back loading dock of a Nordstrom store, demanding the immediate replacement of defective tires that he recently purchased. The store managers were extremely polite. They quickly discovered that the man was indeed one of their best customers, and they arranged an immediate reimbursement for the full price of the tires. In a better mood, the customer decided that he'd rather have a new set installed. When he asked where he should take the car, the managers informed him that Nordstrom doesn't sell tires. Obviously, this man became a satisfied customer — and a Nordstrom advocate for life.

Is the story true? Maybe, maybe not. The point is that this often-repeated account highlights the customer-focused mentality of the department store chain. Nordstrom customers receive thank you cards for shopping. A knowledgeable sales staff handles unusual requests with aplomb. Employees have hand-delivered special orders to customers' homes and even obtained specialty merchandise from competing stores to satisfy customer requests. And merchandise returns are never challenged when the items clearly have not come from Nordstrom stock.

The following list gives you some key questions to consider when you study your customer base:

>> What does your business do to create loyal customers?

>> How much effort do you put into tracking customers' attitudes, satisfaction, and loyalty?

>> What do you offer customers that keeps them coming back?

>> How easy and economical is it for your business to acquire new customers?

>> How many years does a typical customer stay with you?

>> How many markets does your business serve?

>> Are you either number one or number two in the markets in which you compete?

Research and development: Inventing the future

Research and development (R&D) often plays an important role in the long-term success of a business. R&D is particularly critical in industries where new and better products come along all the time. But your research and product-development efforts must align with your business strategy and planning to make the investments pay off.

Operations: Making things work

The operations side of your business is obviously critical if you're a manufacturing business. The products that you make (and the way that they work, how long they last, and what they cost) depend entirely on the capabilities and resources of your production facilities and workforce. But you can easily forget that operations are equally important to businesses in the service sector. Customers demand value in all markets today, and they simply won't pay for inefficiencies. Whether you make autos or anoraks, produce cereal boxes or serial ports, run a bank, or manage a hotel, operations are at the heart of your enterprise.

Operations in your business are driven, to some extent, by costs on one side and product or service quality on the other. The tension between controlling costs and improving quality has led many companies to explore new ways to reduce costs and increase quality at the same time. One way is to involve outside suppliers in certain aspects of your operations, if those suppliers have resources that you can't match. Another way to achieve both goals is to streamline parts of your operations (through automation, for example).

Automation can also be a source of growth and may even create new business opportunities for your business. The airline industry is as big as it is today because of the computer revolution: Computers enable airlines to track millions of passenger reservations and itineraries at the same time. Imagine the lines at airports if airlines still issued tickets by hand and completed passenger flight lists by using carbon paper.

Business operations are often at the heart of major corporate success stories. Wal-Mart's relentless rise to become the world's largest company is based largely on its continuously improving ability to handle, move, and track merchandise. Wal-Mart uses its operations efficiency for one strategic goal: to bring the lowest possible prices to its customers. And the company now does more business than HBC, Sears, and a number of major U.S. retailers combined.

Airlines have tried to streamline their business operations by offering online reservations systems and installing do-it-yourself check-in kiosks at major airports. They even want to do away with the hassle and expense of paper tickets, so they now offer electronic tickets, which customers can print out themselves.

The following list gives you some questions to mull over about the operations side of your business:

>> Does your business have programs for controlling costs and improving quality?

>> Has your business taken full advantage of new technologies?

- » Are your production costs in line with those of the rest of the industry?

- » How quickly can you boost production or expand services to meet new demand?

- » Does your business use outside suppliers?

- » Is your operations workforce flexible, well trained, and prepared for change?

- » Can you apply your operations expertise to other parts of the business?

Sales and marketing: Telling a good story

The best product or service in the world won't take your business far if you don't successfully market and sell it to all the potential customers. Your sales and marketing people are your eyes and ears, giving you feedback on what customers think about and look for. They're also your voice, telling your business's story and putting your products in context, offering solutions, satisfying needs, and fulfilling wants in the marketplace. (Flip to Book 6 for much more on marketing.)

What could a marketing department possibly do to package and promote a boring old chemical such as sodium bicarbonate? It turns out that such a department can do quite a bit, if it happens to be part of Arm & Hammer, which markets sodium bicarbonate as Arm & Hammer baking soda. Their marketing strategy created an indispensable product for baking, cleaning, bathing, and even medicinal purposes. The familiar yellow box is in thousands of refrigerators, open and ready to remove unpleasant odours. The business also created a successful market for baking soda–based toothpaste. And in another pitch, Arm & Hammer now touts baking soda as the best way to ensure that your fresh fruits and vegetables are as clean as they can possibly be. All this from a common, readily available chemical salt.

Lately, drug makers have also begun to tell good stories about their products to polish up their images and to encourage patients to ask their doctors about specific drugs. Some tell the inspirational stories of patients whose lives have been saved by cancer treatment and support programs, such as *Canada AM's* Beverly Thomson, whose photograph was included in the global Breast Friends initiative that was sponsored by a pharmaceutical business. Others show happy families enjoying a summer picnic, thanks to new allergy medicines.

The following list includes a few key questions to ask about the marketing of your product line:

- » How broad is your business's product or service line?

- » Do consumers identify with your business's brand names?

>> Are you investing in market research and receiving continuous customer feedback?

>> Are you using all the marketing resources you have at your disposal?

>> Is your business's sales force knowledgeable, energetic, and persuasive?

Distribution and delivery: Completing the cycle

To be successful, you have to get your products and services to their final destinations and into your customers' hands. Distribution and delivery systems must come into play. No matter how good your products are, your customers have to be able to get them when and where they want them.

Your business most likely distributes its products and services through *traditional channels* — time-tested ways in which you and your competitors have always reached customers. On top of that, your distribution and delivery costs may represent a significant part of your total expenses. The standard costs often include warehouse operations, transportation, and product returns. If you operate in retail, you can end up paying for expensive shelf space, as well. Supermarkets routinely ask for money up front before they stock a new item, and you pay more for the best locations. After all, supermarkets control what customers see — and buy — as harried shoppers troop down the aisles with kids and carts in tow.

REMEMBER

How — and where — customers shop is often just as important as what they buy, so when a different way to deliver products and services comes along, the new system revolutionizes a marketplace or even an entire economy. The Internet offers companies a new and powerful way to reach out to their customers more directly, increasing business clout and, at the same time, lowering distribution costs. So consider *alternate channels* and *multichannels* (more than one type of channel) as you plan your distribution and delivery strategy going forward.

Many innovative products and companies succeed because of their novel approaches to the costs and other hurdles associated with traditional distribution networks. In the '80s, Canada Post was mandated by the federal government to improve its operations, reduce losses, and perhaps (just perhaps) make a profit, despite being a Crown corporation. Canada Post revisited its mission and values (refer to Chapter 1 of Book 3), and claimed its vision prepared it to be a world leader in providing innovative physical and electronic delivery systems, creating value for customers, employees, and all Canadians. One approach was to cut cost and improve service. It accomplished that by franchising some of its postal outlets, increasing their number, and making them more accessible to customers through new locations, such as in convenience stores. These privately owned outlets have longer hours and a wider range of services than government-owned locations. Canada Post also increased the number of stamp retailers by 75 percent and provided electronic postage service through its website.

The following list gives you some questions about the distribution and delivery of your product or service:

>> What are the costs associated with your business's inventory system?

>> Can you reduce inventories by changing the way that you process orders?

>> How much time does it take you to fill a customer order, and can you reduce the time?

>> How many distribution channels does your business use?

>> What are the relative costs in various channels, and which are most effective?

>> How much control do your distributors have over your business?

>> Can you use any new channels to reach your customers more directly?

Financial condition: Keeping track of money

The long-term financial health of your business determines the overall health of your business, period. You simply can't survive in business for long without having your financial house in order. Come to think of it, the expenses that you have to track when looking at business finances aren't all that different from the issues that you face in running your own household.

If you're just starting in business, for example, how much money your business can get its hands on up front (your *initial capital*) is a key to survival. (Does this sound like trying to buy and furnish your first house?) When your business is up and running, you need to make sure that more money comes in than goes out (a *positive cash flow*) so that you can pay all your bills. (Remember those times when the mortgage and utility bills were due, but payday hadn't come yet?)

REMEMBER

Figuring out how to keep your business financially fit is critical to planning your business. When you take the time to look over your important financial statements periodically, you give your business the benefit of a regular financial checkup. The checkup is usually routine, but every once in a while, you uncover an early warning — lower-than-expected profits, for example, or an out-of-line promotional expense. Your financial vigilance pays off.

The following list includes questions to ask about your business's financial health:

>> Are your revenue and profits growing?

>> Are you carefully monitoring your business's cash flow?

>> Does your business have ready access to cash reserves?

>> Does your business — and every business unit or area — have a budget for the coming year?

>> Do you consistently track key financial ratios for the business?

>> How does your business's financial picture compare with that of the competition?

If you don't know how to answer the questions in the preceding list, carve out some time to spend with Book 4.

Monitoring critical success factors

Not all your capabilities are equally important. Some may be critical to success. Others may be nice to have but not especially relevant to your business. You must decide whether your capabilities and resources represent business strengths that you can leverage or weaknesses you have to correct as you plan for the future. To make those decisions, you have to be clear about what's important to your industry and the marketplace. The *critical success factors* (CSFs) are the general capabilities and resources that absolutely have to be in place for any business in your industry to succeed over the long haul.

You may have already prepared a list of CSFs (if you haven't, take a look at Chapter 2 of Book 3). Along with a CSF list, you need a list of your business's capabilities and resources. You can use the two lists to construct a grid, which in turn allows you to compare your capabilities and resources with those that your industry thinks are important. In a perfect world, the lists match up exactly, but that seldom occurs. The completed grid helps you identify your business's current strengths and weaknesses (see Figure 3-2).

To complete a grid similar to the one in Figure 3-2, keep the following in mind:

>> The capabilities and resources that you place on the left side of the grid are in your industry's must-have category. They represent CSFs.

>> The capabilities and resources that you place in the top-left corner of the grid are CSFs in which your business is good or excellent. They represent your strengths.

>> The capabilities and resources that you place in the bottom-left corner of the grid are CSFs in which your business is only fair or even poor. They represent your weaknesses.

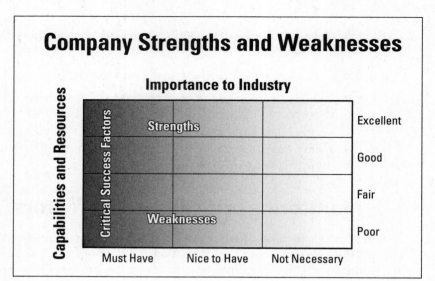

FIGURE 3-2: Compare your capabilities and resources with the critical success factors (CSFs) in your industry.

© John Wiley & Sons, Inc.

REMEMBER

You can easily find value in the capabilities that your business already excels in, and you can just as easily underestimate the importance of things that your business doesn't do very well. Admitting that you devote valuable resources to areas that don't affect you as much is hard, as is admitting that you may neglect key business areas. Try to be as objective as you can.

Measuring Your Business against Competitors

You must be prepared to take advantage of your business's strengths and minimize its weaknesses, which means that you have to know how to recognize opportunities when they arise and prepare for threats before they overtake you. Timing is everything here, and it represents another major dimension that you need to think about.

Getting a glance at competitors

Create strengths-and-weaknesses grids for two or three of your most intense competitors. (Refer to Figures 3-1 and 3-2 for grid info and Chapter 2 in Book 3 for a refresher on exactly who your competitors are and what information you have about them.) You don't know as much about your competitors as you know about yourself, of course, so the grids can't be as complete as they may be for your business. But what you *do* know tells you a great deal.

REMEMBER

Comparing the strengths and weaknesses of competitors with your own can help you see where competitive opportunities and threats to your business may come from. Opportunities often arise when your business has a strength that you can exploit in a critical area in which your competition is weak. And you can sometimes anticipate a threat when you see the reverse situation — when a competitor takes advantage of a key strength by making a move in an area where you're weak. Because the competitive landscape always changes, plan to monitor these grids on a regular basis.

Completing your SWOT analysis

A *SWOT* analysis (an analysis of your strengths, weaknesses, opportunities, and threats) allows you to construct a strategic balance sheet for your business. In the analysis, you bring together all the internal factors, including your business's strengths and weaknesses. You weigh these factors against the external forces that you identify, such as the opportunities and threats that your business faces due to competitive forces or trends in your business environment. How these factors balance out determines what your business should do and when it should do it. Follow these steps to complete the SWOT analysis grid (and check out Figures 3-1 and 3-2 for info on coming up with a strength/weakness grid):

1. Divide all the strengths that you identify into two groups, based on whether you associate them with potential opportunities in your industry or with latent threats.

2. Divide all the weaknesses the same way — one group associated with opportunities and the other with threats.

3. Construct a grid with four quadrants.

4. Place your business's strengths and weaknesses, paired with industry opportunities or threats, in one of the four boxes (see Figure 3-3).

SWOT Analysis

Internal

2 **Capitalize on These**	**3** **Improve These**	Opportunities
4 **Monitor These**	**1** **Eliminate These**	Threats

External

Strengths   Weaknesses

FIGURE 3-3:
The SWOT grid balances your business's internal strengths and weaknesses against external opportunities and threats.

SWOT analysis provides useful strategic guidance, mostly through common sense. First, fix what's broken and address imminent threats. Next, make the most of the business opportunities that you see. Only then do you have the luxury of tending to other business issues and areas. Be sure to address each of the following steps in your business plan:

1. Eliminate any business weaknesses that you identify in areas in which you face serious threats from your competitors or unfavourable trends in a changing business environment.

2. Capitalize on any business opportunities that you discover where your business has real strengths and your competitors may have weaknesses.

3. Work on improving any weaknesses that you identify in areas that may contain potential business opportunities.

4. Monitor business areas in which you're strong today so that you aren't surprised by any latent threats that may appear.

REMEMBER

Change is the only constant in your business, your industry, and your marketplace. Constant change means that you have to revise the grid regularly while your business grows and the environment around you changes. Think of your SWOT analysis as a continuous process — something that you do repeatedly as an important part of your business-planning cycle.

Evaluating the Value Chain and What You Do Best

When customers are making decisions on what to buy and where to shop, they continually weigh various combinations of product or service benefits against price. This calculation is referred to as the *value equation* (refer to Chapter 2 of Book 3). But what does having the best value actually mean? If you want to be successful in your marketplace, you need to know exactly where and how your products add value in the eyes of your customers. In the customers' minds, their perception is reality.

The upcoming sections look at creating customer value around products and services. The approach is called the *value chain,* and you use it to identify which parts of your business are responsible for adding the greatest value for customers. You find out how to put together a value proposition for your customers and how you can use it as the basis for your *business model,* or plan for making money. You also find out how to use your value chain to help explain why you may have a competitive advantage in the marketplace, and you discover how you can maintain that competitive advantage over the long term. Finally, you see how to make the most of your business's human and financial resources while you put your business plan and business model to work.

Describing what you do best

Describing what your business does best — summarizing your key business activities in a few well-chosen sentences or in a clear diagram — should be easy, shouldn't it? It's not. (Refer to Chapter 1 of Book 3 for help capturing your business in 50 words or less.) From the inside of your business looking out, you may have difficulty pushing away the everyday details and getting at the core of what actually keeps you in business from one day to the next.

Due to this difficulty, business consultants do a bang-up business. They may have fancy names for the services they offer, but the essence of what they do is simple: They help you describe what you do. Their little secret, of course, is that they don't really possess more valuable knowledge than you. Consultants seem to have a clearer view of your business because they view it from the outside looking in.

You have a built-in understanding of your business and what really makes your business successful — you just need to unlock what you already know.

Looking at the links in a value chain

A business constructs its *value chain* from the sequence of activities that it engages in to increase the value of its products and services in the eyes of its customers (see Figure 3-4). The chain shows where a business may have an advantage over its competitors, and it connects a business to the marketplace, making sure that it doesn't stray too far from the customers it plans to serve.

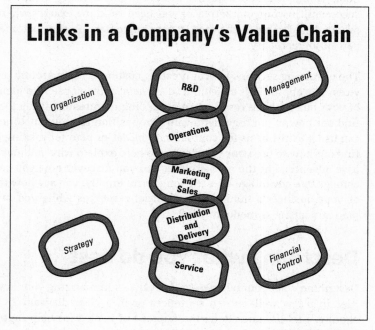

FIGURE 3-4: A business's value chain has two types of links: Primary activities and support activities.

The links in a value chain — both primary and supporting — help you better understand your business activities.

Primary links in the value chain are the business functions representing the heart of what your business does. Primary links are usually sequential. They're the essential stages that your business goes through in developing, producing, and getting products to market, and they often involve the following:

» Research and development

» Operations

» Marketing and sales

>> Distribution and delivery

>> Service

Supporting links in the value chain contribute to the overall success of the business by strengthening your business's primary links. Supporting links are often spread throughout an organization. They assist and tie together all the primary business functions, as well as support one another. The activities often involve the following:

>> Management

>> Organization

>> Strategy and planning

>> Financial control

Forging your value chain

To develop your business's value chain — the sequence of activities that you go through in the process of adding value to your products and services — you need a list of your business's capabilities and resources. Read the earlier sections of this chapter if you need help.

You can construct a framework for your value chain by creating a grid that divides your business into value-creating areas (see Figure 3-5). You place activities in the grid based on whether they act as part of your primary business functions or you associate them with supporting areas.

Follow these steps to create the grid that shapes your value chain:

1. **List all the key business areas that work to put together your business's products and services and get the products and services out to customers.**

Include such departments as R&D (research and development), operations, marketing, sales, distribution, delivery, and service. (Refer to the earlier section "Defining capabilities and resources" for more details on these areas.)

2. **Arrange a list of key business areas in order, from the first good idea R&D produces to the finished product or service.**

3. **List the general business areas in your business that support the primary business functions.**

   Include such supporting areas as management, organization and human resources, strategy and planning, and financial control.

4. **Construct a grid similar to the one you see in Figure 3-5, using your lists of primary and supporting business areas.**

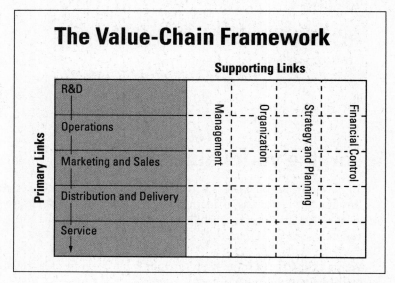

FIGURE 3-5: The value-chain framework.

TIP

Your value chain may not look exactly like all those organization charts you see floating around your business. The primary and supporting business functions that add customer value may be framed differently, depending on whom you ask, so you should talk to customers and co-workers. Ask your customers to describe your business as they see it — they may have a better vantage point.

To fill in the value-chain grid, you have to fill in all the specific value-adding activities — the capabilities and resources that your business uses to increase the value of your products and services. Follow these steps:

1. **Go through the lists of capabilities and resources, and make a first pass at placing them in the value-chain grid.**

2. **In the boxes on the left side of the value-chain grid, place value-adding activities that directly contribute to your primary business functions.**

   These activities make up the primary links in your value chain.

3. **Place value-adding activities that you associate with supporting functions in grid boxes to the right of the primary functions that they support.**

   These activities make up the supporting links in the value chain.

4. **On the grid, include a description of the customer value that the various links add, as well as how they add that value.**

REMEMBER

The value chain offers you a unique look at your business through your customers' eyes. Every link in the value chain is something that you do as a business. Every link is an activity that you spend money on. The value chain allows you to see exactly what value customers get out of each link. It gives you a relatively clear picture of why you stay in business, as well as where you could do a better job.

Creating your value proposition

During a recent business trip, a woman pulled into a small town to look for a gas station. She had two choices, and the gas prices were exactly the same. One station had several cars at the pumps; the other was empty. When she asked the manager of the busy station whether he could explain the popularity of his station compared with the one across the street, the man didn't miss a beat:

> *Oh, they're in a different business. They're a filling station; we're a service station.*

This canny businessman had a real feeling for why his station was successful. You can develop that same feeling by taking the value chain that you put together for your business (see the preceding section) and boiling it down into a clear statement of what benefits you provide your customers and what real value your customers place on those benefits.

Business people refer to the preceding statement as the *value proposition* — fancy jargon for a simple idea. A value proposition may be similar to your business's mission statement (flip to Chapter 1 of Book 3 for the details on mission statements), but the proposition is more narrowly focused on customers — what you provide them and what they take away. At first glance, a business's value proposition seems pretty obvious:

>> Giant Tiger Discount Stores offer the cheapest prices around on a wide range of merchandise.

>> Canadian Automobile Association (CAA) offers travel and motoring services at home and around the world.

But companies often provide their customers with more value than first meets the eye — even more value than the businesses themselves may realize.

Putting Together a Business Model

Business models don't have to be complex or elaborate. In fact, when management types talk about them — as in, "So what's your business model?" — they intend to ask a very direct and basic question: How do you plan to make money? Your answer should be at the very heart of your business plan and reflected in each of its sections.

Where's the money?

Whether you like it or not, at some point, you have to get down to the nitty-gritty details of your business's finances — income statements, balance sheets, cash flow, budgeting, and all that stuff. (Check out Book 4 for details.) In this chapter, you need to ponder something much more basic: coming up with the money. Not literally, of course (just yet). But you need to know how you expect to make money in your business.

Simple, you say. Your customers give you money in exchange for the valuable products and services you provide, right? Well, much like the value chains that support them (refer to the earlier section "Evaluating the Value Chain and What You Do Best" for more on value chains), business models aren't always that obvious or straightforward. Businesses often make a profit on areas outside the main product or service — areas that customers don't focus on. These areas can bring great success. Here are some surprising examples:

>> Given the price of a good meal out, you may think that successful restaurants rake in the dough. And many of them do. But they make the bulk of their profits not on those delicious appetizers and entrees, but on the mixed drinks and wine that they serve before, during, and after the meal.

>> Luxury vacation fractional ownership is all the rage for the about-to-be-retired set. The prices sound reasonable, and who wouldn't enjoy owning a piece of a condo or villa overlooking the Rockies, the ocean, or a pristine Muskoka lake? It turns out that fractional-ownership real estate companies make their profits not on that primo real estate, but on all the maintenance fees they tack on to the contract — fees that every fractional owner must pay on an ongoing basis.

>> Some companies happily sell their products at break-even prices — and then make their real money on the so-called *consumables* (products you use up). Hewlett-Packard, for example, doesn't mind selling its printers at close to cost, knowing that the business makes its real profits on ink and toner cartridges. As long as HP can keep customers satisfied with their total printing experience, the money flows in month after month, year after year.

How's your timing?

How you expect to make your money is only one part of your business model. An equally important piece relates to *when* you get the cash. You may like the idea that the loonies are going to start pouring in tomorrow; however, reality suggests that your business may begin incurring costs and spending money months (or maybe even years) before a revenue stream begins to flow. In the case of pharmaceuticals, for instance, a company can spend years and millions of dollars developing and testing a drug before the first patient — or insurance company — pays a penny to buy it. If your business must spend money before it starts sending out those invoices, your business model must include a timeline that takes the following factors into account:

» The up-front costs you expect when you set up your business

» The source of funds to pay for your up-front costs

» A schedule showing when you expect cash to pour in (For more information on cash flow, see Book 4.)

The question of timing is as important for both small and large businesses. Many retail businesses that operate year-round actually take in most of their revenue during one season — the Christmas holiday rush, for example. In some cases, retailers rake in half of their annual revenues during late November and December. Timing for these establishments is quite literally a make-or-break affair.

At Harris Hatch Inn, a bed and breakfast in St. Andrews-by-the-Sea, New Brunswick, the tourist season begins at the end of May and ends in September. Except for a few hardy souls who go there for holiday weekends — Thanksgiving, Christmas, and New Year's — virtually all Harris Hatch's revenue comes in during those three summer months. The inn's business model must ensure that the money coming in during that short period is enough to pay for fixed costs — mortgage, utilities, taxes, salaries, and upkeep — throughout the entire year. If not, the innkeeper could wake up one morning to the sound of creditors knocking on the door.

Making Your Business Model Work

Companies don't stay in business year after year by accident. Oh, maybe a manager somewhere gets lucky occasionally, making a brilliant move without knowing its significance. But that kind of luck never lasts long, especially when the competition is intense. Companies succeed over the long haul because they understand what their customers value the most, and they figure out how to make money by providing products and services that consistently meet or exceed customer expectation, often at the expense of unsuspecting competitors. By capturing this information in your business plan, you improve the odds of your business model continuing to work in the future.

Searching for a competitive advantage

Most people who take car trips have a special produce stand, a favourite diner, or a certain ice-cream place along the way that they never miss. Why do these travellers develop such affection for specific stops on their route when hundreds of other places are available? What makes particular establishments so unique?

These travellers could come up with all sorts of reasons. They may tell you that they've stopped at the same places for years, they love the food, they like the atmosphere, they know the owners, they can count on the service . . . whatever. No doubt, all these things are true. But if you take a careful look at the value chain for many of these businesses, one important link likely jumps right out at you: location. Distances and driving times likely are the major reasons why many customers find these businesses in the first place; the storefronts literally happen to be in the right place at the right time. Customers choose the business based on location and stay for the value added in other business areas. Location provides a significant competitive advantage in this on-the-move marketplace.

Competitive advantage means exactly what it says; a business has some sort of advantage over the competition. Where does it come from? Usually, out of the distinct and special value that the business can offer its customers — and from the premium that customers place on that value. Ask yourself this basic question:

> *Why do customers choose my business and its products when other competitors in the industry have more-or-less similar offerings?*

You can find the answer in the strongest links of your value chain (covered earlier in this chapter) — the links that produce the bulk of your customer value. Location, service, image, and product features are some of the links that create a competitive advantage in the marketplace.

In 1975, Microsoft was a partnership of two: Bill Gates and Paul Allen. They started out competing against a host of bright young entrepreneurs like themselves and eventually had to go head-to-head with IBM. Today, Microsoft has tens of thousands of employees and billions of dollars in revenue, and it offers a wide array of software products, ranging from word processing programs and spreadsheet applications, to language tools and operating systems, to games and smartphone applications. You can find Microsoft's competitive advantage in these areas:

>> **Standards:** Microsoft's programs pretty much set standards in the PC world. Microsoft offers the standard operating system and the standard suite of office applications. Although other companies sell better products here and there, customers see Microsoft as the safe and sensible choice across the board, a distinctive image advantage over the competition.

>> **Compatibility:** Microsoft programs promise to work with one another and with the operating system. You don't have to worry about your favourite application becoming an outcast or somehow misbehaving on your computer.

>> **Product range:** You name it, and Microsoft probably has a product that can do it — from word processing to picture editing, from managing your money to keeping track of your e-mail. The company continues to aggressively develop new software to meet the needs of rapidly changing markets. The company even targeted Internet users with a host of new products, including its flagship Internet site, www.msn.com.

>> **Service and support:** With Microsoft, you know what you're getting. If a product doesn't work, the company tries hard to fix it quickly. Microsoft devotes tremendous resources to product support and provides a wide range of service options, including online knowledge bases, news groups, chat rooms, e-mail, and (of course) telephone support.

Discount Car & Truck Rentals is by far Canada's largest privately owned international car-rental agency. The company has more than 300 rental locations in Canada and Australia. But Discount faces competition at all levels, from the mom-and-pop rental outlets at popular vacation spots to regional agencies and global companies, including Avis, Hertz, and National. Here's how Discount finds a competitive advantage:

>> **Free pickup and return:** When you call Discount to book a vehicle, a representative picks you up at your home, office, or travel location. Discount also takes you where you need to go after you return the rental unit.

>> **National presence:** No matter which major Canadian city you visit, Discount can rent you what you need.

>> **Peace of mind:** With Discount, you don't have to worry about the car not being there, the rate doubling, or that you'll end up paying for an old rent-a-dent.

>> **Rewards for loyalty:** As a loyal Discount customer, the company rewards you with membership in a club that provides notification of low-rate specials; a rent two weekends, get one free deal; and frequent-user points that you can redeem toward free rental days.

Focusing on core competence

You create your competitive advantage in the marketplace. Your advantages have everything to do with your customers — with the relative value that they place on your products and services, and with the purchase decisions that they finally make. What internal capabilities and resources do you have, and what business activities do you engage in that lead directly to your competitive advantage? You must make sure to capture these in your business plan.

Go back to your business's value chain (which is discussed in the earlier section "Evaluating the Value Chain and What You Do Best") and focus on the links that provide your competitive advantage. When you do, you come face to face with something that the gurus call your core competence. Simply defined, *core competence* is your business's special capability to create a competitive advantage in the marketplace. In almost all cases, this gift is specific to your business. Think of core competence as being corporate DNA. Unlike your personal genetic code, however, your business's core competence is something you can build on — or lose, depending on how attentive you are to your marketplace and your business.

The preceding section examines two well-known companies: Microsoft and Discount.

Microsoft's core competence consists of

- » **Visionary executives:** The executive team has a broad vision of the future, enabling the company to forge today's software standards and shape tomorrow's.

- » **Top-notch development team:** The company supports a dream-team corps of developers and programmers who create and maintain a state-of-the-art product line.

- » **Management of complexity:** Microsoft manages a complex related set of software products that all have to behave and work together.

- » **Capability to change direction:** The company has the capacity to redirect resources and energies when the fast-moving marketplace shifts course and the rules of the game suddenly change.

Microsoft's first two core competence factors lead to the others because success and profit allow for more capabilities and value.

Discount's core competence includes

>> **Information systems:** A sophisticated computer database allows the company to keep track of customer profiles and match them against an ever-changing supply of rental cars and special rates.

>> **National logistics:** The company can track, distribute, arrange, and rearrange a huge fleet of vehicles in all shapes and sizes on a regional and national basis.

>> **Scale of operations:** The company uses its sheer size and business volume to negotiate favourable terms on new-car purchases and even insurance premiums.

>> **Relationships and tie-ins:** Discount has the resources to work closely with corporate clients, travel agencies, and the travel industry to create new business by expanding car-rental options and opportunities.

TIP

A business's core competence can point the way toward new market opportunities. Honda, for example, used a core competence in designing engines to expand its markets. The company created product lines in lawn mowers, snow throwers, snowmobiles, motorcycles, and all-terrain vehicles, to name just a few of its motor-based businesses. Honda benefits from a related competitive advantage (state-of-the-art engines) in each of these distinct markets. Take another look at your business's core competence to see if you can come up with any new business directions based on your already successful business areas.

Sustaining an advantage over time

Every organization that manages to stay in business has some sort of competitive advantage and core competence to draw upon; otherwise, it simply can't exist. But here comes the million-dollar question: How can you renew and sustain that competitive advantage over years and even decades? Customers and their needs shift over time, competition gets more intense, and industries evolve, so your competitive advantage and the core competence that supports it aren't guaranteed to stay around. You rent them; you don't own them. You want to make sure that you keep a long-term lease on both.

Sustained competitive advantage — the business world's Holy Grail — is a business's capability to renew competitive advantages over and over again in the face of a constantly changing business environment and marketplace. But, if you want to sustain competitive advantages over time, you need a long-term strategy.

Think about ongoing strategies that your business can use to see that you preserve your core competence. How can you sustain the competitive advantage that your business already has? Get a blank sheet of paper and jot down answers to these key questions:

>> Where will changes in your business most likely come from?

>> How will those changes likely affect your business's competitive advantage?

>> What can your business do to maintain core competence in the face of change? Is it consistent with your values and mission statements? (Refer to Chapter 1 of Book 3 for more about values and for information about your mission statement.)

Focus on each of the major forces that fuel change in your industry:

>> Your customers and their changing needs and requirements

>> Your competitors and their changing capabilities, strategies, and goals

>> Your business, its value chain, and its shifting strengths and weaknesses

When you create your business plan, make sure that you continue to track these forces so that they don't threaten the core competence that you work so hard to achieve.

Earmarking resources

The value chain paints a portrait of your business as your customers see it. (Find out about the value chain in the earlier section "Evaluating the Value Chain and What You Do Best.") Links in the chain reflect the value that customers place on aspects of your products and services. The strongest links capture your competitive advantage in the market and define your core competence as a business.

Because the value chain is so good at helping you weigh the importance of your business decisions, it comes in handy when you put together your business plan. In particular, the value chain is invaluable for earmarking scarce resources toward specific business activities.

At almost any major racetrack, a group of regulars hangs around the stands or clusters at the fence. These people are serious about horse racing. They spend time poring over track sheets and newspapers — circling this, checking that, and pacing back and forth.

When they finally place bets, they don't rely on Lady Luck alone. They use all the information available — the condition of the track, the horse's racing history and bloodlines, the jockey's record, and the betting odds — to place their cash on the wagers most likely to result in the best payoffs and the biggest winnings.

Betting on the horses is a serious business for these committed professionals. And they can show you something about how to divvy up your working assets. Is it sensible to spread your business's limited resources equally among all the areas that make up your business? Probably not. Each time you set aside time and money for a particular business activity, you place a bet on your business plan. You bet that the resources you commit are going to contribute to your business, add value to what you do, and eventually come back around to generate revenue and profits.

TIP

So, how do you know where to place your bets? You guessed it: You go back to your business's value chain. Follow these simple steps to check your resource allocation based on your value chain:

1. **Look at where your business currently spends money.**

   Make a quick-and-dirty estimate of how you divvy up yearly expenses among business activities — from R&D to delivery and service — and jot the numbers down on your value-chain grid (refer to Figure 3-5). To keep things simple, use percentages. Make sure that the numbers add up to 100 percent.

2. **Look at where your customers think that you provide them value.**

   Take the total value that customers think you provide and divvy it up among your business activities. If customers pay $100 to buy your widget, for example, how much of that do they pay for features, how much for service, and how much for convenience? Again, use percentages and jot the numbers on the same value-chain grid. Make sure that the numbers add up to 100 percent.

3. **As a reminder, highlight the boxes on the value-chain grid that represent your core competence and account for your competitive advantage in the marketplace.**

4. **Analyse the completed grid.**

   If the percentages line up and are concentrated in the highlighted boxes, you're in good shape. But if you find a glaring mismatch in where you spend money, what your core competence is, and where your customers think that your products give them value, you need to reassess where you direct your resources.

4

Bookkeeping and Accounting

Contents at a Glance

Chapter 1

Basic Bookkeeping: What It Is and Why You Need It

All businesses need to keep track of their financial transactions — that's why bookkeeping and bookkeepers are so important. Without accurate books and records, how can you tell whether your business is making a profit or taking a loss?

Keeping the books of a business can be a lot more difficult than maintaining a personal chequebook. You must carefully record each business transaction to make sure that it goes into the right account. This bookkeeping gives you an effective tool for figuring out how well the business is doing financially.

This chapter covers the key parts of bookkeeping by introducing you to the language of bookkeeping, familiarizing you with how bookkeepers manage the accounting cycle, and showing you how to understand the most difficult type of bookkeeping — double-entry bookkeeping.

This chapter also tells you how to set up the Chart of Accounts, which is a roadmap to help you determine where to record the effect of all your transactions. It includes many different accounts. Here, you find out about the types of transactions you enter into each type of account to track the key parts of any business — assets, liabilities, equity, revenue, and expenses.

Bookkeepers: The Record Keepers of the Business World

Bookkeeping, the methodical way in which businesses track their financial transactions, is rooted in accounting. *Accounting* is the total structure of records and procedures used to record, classify, and report information about a business's financial transactions. Bookkeeping involves the recording of that financial information into the accounting system while maintaining adherence to solid accounting principles.

Bookkeepers are the ones who toil day in and day out to ensure that transactions are captured and accurately recorded in the accounts making up the books and records. Books and records are made up of individual *accounts* that keep track of increases and decreases by the amounts recorded. Bookkeepers need to be very detail-oriented and must love to work with numbers, because numbers and the accounts they go into are just about all these people see all day. Bookkeepers don't need to have a professional accounting designation.

Many small-business owners who are just starting their businesses serve as their own bookkeepers until their businesses grow large enough that they can hire someone dedicated to keeping the books. Few small businesses have accountants on staff to check the books and prepare official financial reports; instead, they have a bookkeeper on staff who serves as the outside accountant's eyes and ears. Most businesses seek an accountant who has a professional designation to perform all the necessary duties and responsibilities as required by the business owners and by the different Canadian laws.

In many small businesses today, a bookkeeper enters the business transactions on a daily basis while working inside the business. At the end of each month or quarter, the bookkeeper sends summary reports to the accountant, who checks the transactions for accuracy and completeness and then prepares financial statements. (Find out more about financial statements in Chapters 2 and 4 of Book 4.)

In most cases, an accountant initially helps set up the accounting system so that the business owner can be sure it uses solid accounting principles. That accountant periodically stops by the office and reviews how the business uses the system to be sure the business is handling transactions properly.

REMEMBER

Creating accurate financial reports is the only way you can know how your business is doing. The business develops these reports by using the information you, as the bookkeeper, enter into your accounting system. If that information isn't accurate, your financial reports are meaningless.

Wading through Basic Bookkeeping Lingo

Before you can take on bookkeeping and start keeping the books, you must get a handle on some key accounting terms. The following sections include lists of terms that all bookkeepers use on a daily basis.

Accounts for the balance sheet

Here are a few terms you need to know to understand the common elements of all balance sheets:

>> **Balance sheet:** The financial statement that presents a snapshot of the business's financial position (assets, liabilities, and equity) as of a particular date in time. It's called a *balance sheet* because the things owned by the business (assets) must equal the claims against those assets (liabilities and equity). Sometimes, accountants call this statement the statement of financial position, which gives more emphasis to the fact that the amounts presented are a snapshot of a particular point in time.

On a proper balance sheet, the total assets should equal the total liabilities plus the total equity. If your numbers fit this formula, the business's books are in balance. (The balance sheet is discussed in greater detail in Chapters 2 and 4 of Book 4.)

>> **Assets:** All the things a business owns in order to successfully run, such as cash, accounts receivable, inventory, buildings, land, tools, equipment, vehicles, and furniture.

>> **Liabilities:** All the debts the business owes, such as bank loans, credit card balances, and unpaid bills.

>> **Equity:** All the money invested in the business by its owners. In a small business owned by one person, the owner's equity appears in a single Capital account named after the owner. In a partnership, you need several Capital accounts — one for each partner. In a larger business that's incorporated, owners' equity appears in shares, usually referred to as common shares and *Retained Earnings*. Retained Earnings track all the profits and losses of prior years that the owners of the business have chosen to reinvest into the business, instead of paying out to the business's shareholders. Small, unincorporated businesses track money paid out to owners in Drawings accounts, whereas incorporated businesses dole out money to owners by paying *dividends,* which are tracked in a Dividends account.

Accounts for the income statement or statement of earnings

Here are a few terms that you should know related to the income statement:

>> **Income statement:** The financial statement that presents a summary of the business's financial activity over a certain period of time, such as a month, quarter, or year. The statement starts with revenue earned, subtracts the costs of goods sold and expenses, and ends with the bottom line — net profit or loss. This end result is where most people get the term profit and loss, or *P&L,* for this statement. (You find out how to develop an income statement in Chapters 2 and 4 of Book 4.)

>> **Revenue:** All money earned in the process of selling the business's goods and services. Those who are in the business of selling goods generally use the term *sales*. Besides providing a good or service, some businesses also earn revenue through other means, such as rents or earning interest by offering short-term loans to other businesses.

>> **Costs of goods sold:** All money spent to purchase or make the goods or services that a business plans to sell to its customers.

>> **Expenses:** All money spent on business operations this is not directly related to the sale of individual goods or services.

>> **Gains and losses:** Transactions recorded as gains and losses rather than revenues and expenses to indicate that they did not result from the main activities of the business. Selling assets that the business no longer needs is an example of this type of transaction.

Other common terms

Some other common bookkeeping terms include the following:

» **Accounting period:** The time during which you track financial information. Most businesses track their financial results on a monthly basis, so each accounting period equals one month. Some businesses choose to do financial reports on a quarterly basis, so the accounting periods are three months. Other businesses look at their results only on a yearly basis, so their accounting periods are 12 months. Businesses that track their financial activities monthly usually also create quarterly and *annual reports* (a year-end summary of the business's activities and financial results) based on the information they gather.

» **Accounts Receivable:** The account used to track all customer sales that are made on credit (or on account). The terms *credit sales* and *sales on account* do not refer to credit card sales. Customers establish credit with the business directly and promise to pay for their purchases at an agreed-upon date.

» **Accounts Payable:** The account used to track all outstanding bills from vendors or suppliers, contractors, consultants, and any other companies or individuals from whom the business buys goods or services on credit.

» **Depreciation:** An accounting method used to track the aging and use of property, plant, and equipment assets. Accountants use the term *property, plant, and equipment* for a category of assets that the business finds useful for more than one year. For example, if you own a car, you know that its book value is reduced each year you use the car. Every major asset a business owns ages, gets used up, and eventually needs to be replaced, including buildings, factories, equipment, and other key assets.

» **General Ledger:** Where all the business's accounts are summarized. The General Ledger is the granddaddy of the bookkeeping system.

» **Interest:** The money that a business needs to pay if it borrows money from a bank or other business, in addition to the original sum borrowed. For example, when you buy a car by using a car loan, you must pay not only the amount you borrowed but also additional money (interest) based on a percent of the amount you borrowed and have not yet repaid.

» **Inventory:** The account that tracks all products that you plan to sell to customers.

» **Journals:** Where bookkeepers keep records (in chronological order) of daily business transactions. Each of the most active accounts — including Cash, Accounts Payable, and Accounts Receivable — has its own journal.

>> **Payroll:** The way a business pays its employees. Managing payroll is a key function of the bookkeeper and involves reporting many aspects of payroll to the government, including taxes and benefits to be paid on behalf of the employee for Canada Pension Plan, Employment Insurance (EI), and worker's compensation premiums.

>> **Trial balance:** How you determine whether the books are in balance before you pull together information for the financial reports and close the books for the accounting period.

Pedalling through the Accounting Cycle

A bookkeeper does her work by completing the tasks of the *accounting cycle*. It's called a cycle because the workflow is circular: entering transactions, adjusting the account balances, closing the books at the end of the accounting year, and then starting the entire process again for the next accounting cycle.

The accounting cycle has eight basic steps, which you can see in Figure 1-1.

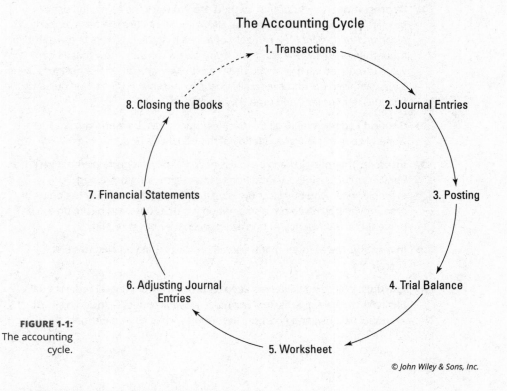

FIGURE 1-1:
The accounting cycle.

© *John Wiley & Sons, Inc.*

Here's a breakdown of each step in this cycle:

1. **Transactions:** Financial transactions start the process. Transactions can include the sale or return of a product, the purchase of supplies for business activities, or any other financial activity that involves the exchange of the business's assets, the establishment or payoff of a debt, or the deposit from or payout of money to the business's owners. All sales and expenses are transactions that you must record.

2. **Journal entries:** You list the transaction in the appropriate journal, maintaining the journal's chronological order of transactions. (Accountants also call the journal the *book of original entry,* and it's the first place you record a transaction.)

3. **Posting:** You post each transaction to the account that is affected by the transaction. These accounts are part of the General Ledger, where you can find a summary of all the business's accounts.

4. **Trial balance:** At the end of the accounting period (which may be a month, quarter, or year, depending on your business's practices), you prepare a trial balance from the General Ledger. (Your accounting software may produce this trial balance automatically. Flip to Chapter 3 of Book 4 for more about software options.)

5. **Worksheet:** Unfortunately, if you're preparing a trial balance manually, your first result may show that the books aren't in balance. If that's the case, you must first look for errors and make any necessary corrections. Some bookkeepers find that using a worksheet is a good way to come up with all the necessary corrections and adjustments to the trial balance. You don't need to record the adjusting entries in the General Ledger until you have arrived at the adjusted trial balance on the worksheet. If, on the other hand, you opted to skip using a worksheet, you need to post your adjusting journal entries directly into the General Ledger.

6. **Adjusting journal entries:** After your trial balance is in balance, you need to record additional transactions called *adjustments,* which you can track on a worksheet. (You can skip using a worksheet if only a few adjusting entries are needed.) You make adjustments directly to the accounts affected in the General Ledger. Typical adjustments include recording the depreciation of assets and adjusting for one-time payments (such as insurance) at the end of an accounting cycle. These adjustments are needed to more accurately match monthly expenses with monthly revenues. You may also make adjustments to record revenues that the business has earned by performing services for which the business hasn't yet billed customers. After you make and record adjustments, you prepare another trial balance to make sure the accounts remain in balance. (Some bookkeepers and accountants feel that this last step can be optional if you record the adjusting journal entries directly into the General Ledger.)

7. **Financial statements:** You prepare the balance sheet and income statement by using the corrected General Ledger account balances.

8. **Closing:** You close the books for the Revenue, Expense, and Drawings (or Dividends for incorporated businesses) accounts, and then begin the entire cycle again with zero balances in those last three types of accounts.

REMEMBER

As a businessperson, you want to be able to gauge your profit or loss on month-by-month, quarter-by-quarter, and year-by-year bases. Revenue, Expense, and Drawings (or Dividends) accounts must start with zero balances at the beginning of each year. In contrast, you carry over Asset, Liability, and Equity account balances from year to year because the business doesn't start with nothing at the beginning of each year. Assets, Liabilities, and Equity account balances carry forward and continue into the next year. Accounts receivable get collected, outstanding bills and debt get paid, and so on. You carry forward the balances of these three types of accounts from year to year until you sell the business or wind it up.

Exploring Cash and Accrual Accounting

Small businesses often run their operations on a *cash basis,* meaning they never buy or sell on credit (often referred to as *on account*). Some owners essentially measure their financial performance based on how much money they have in the bank account. Although cash basis provides a simple business model, it doesn't take long before it isn't practical. The other danger is that not all transactions are taken into account. When the business starts to send out invoices on account, or when it starts to deal with suppliers on credit, you need to adopt accrual accounting. The following sections look at both methods.

Cash-basis accounting

With *cash-basis accounting,* you record all transactions in the books when cash changes hands, meaning when the business receives cash payment from customers or pays out cash for purchases or other services. Cash receipt or payment can be in the form of cash, cheque, credit card, debit card, electronic fund payments, or other means used to pay for an item.

You can't use cash-basis accounting if your store sells products on account and bills the customer, who then pays at a later date. The cash-basis accounting method has no means to record and track money due from customers.

With the cash-basis accounting method, the business records the purchase of supplies or goods that you plan to sell only when you pay cash for those supplies or goods. If you buy goods on credit, which you plan to pay later, you don't record the transaction until you pay out the cash.

WARNING

Although cash-basis accounting is easy, the Canada Revenue Agency (CRA) doesn't like it, allowing only certain select businesses to use it for reporting taxable income. Businesses involved in farming and the fishing industries and self-employed commission agents can report income on a cash basis. All other businesses must follow the accrual accounting method described in the next section. Go to www.canada.ca/en/revenue-agency/services/tax/businesses/small-businesses-self-employed-income/business-income-tax-reporting/accounting-your-earnings.html for more information and the forms for the cash method.

WARNING

Cash-basis accounting does a good job of tracking cash flow, but it does a poor job of matching revenues earned with expenses incurred. You may find this deficiency a problem if, as it often happens, your business buys products in one month and sells those products in the next month. For example, suppose you buy products in June with the intent to sell, and you pay $1,000 cash for those products. You don't sell the products until July, and that's when you receive cash for the sales. When you close the books at the end of June, you have to show the $1,000 expense with no revenue to offset it, meaning you have a loss that month. When you sell the products for $1,500 in July, you have a $1,500 profit. So, your monthly report for June shows a $1,000 loss, and your monthly report for July shows a $1,500 profit, when in actuality, you had net revenues of $500 over the two-month period.

REMEMBER

This book concentrates on the accrual accounting method. If you choose to use cash-basis accounting, don't panic: You can still find most of the bookkeeping information in here useful, but you don't need to maintain some of the accounts listed, such as Accounts Receivable and Accounts Payable, because you don't record transactions until cash changes hands. If you're using a cash-basis accounting system and sell things on credit, though, you need to have a way to track what people owe you — particularly for tax-reporting purposes.

Accrual accounting

With *accrual accounting,* you record all transactions in the books when those transactions occur, even if no cash changes hands. For example, if you sell on account, you record the transaction immediately and enter it into an Accounts Receivable account until you receive payment. If you buy goods on account, you immediately enter the transaction into an Accounts Payable account until you pay out cash.

Accrual accounting is based on the *generally accepted accounting principles* (GAAP), the authoritative standards and rules that govern financial accounting and financial reporting. GAAP is very important to businesses, and users of financial information such as lenders and CRA. Businesses that are incorporated and intend to have their shares traded on a stock market (such as the Toronto Stock Exchange (TSX) must follow the GAAP rules based on the International Financial Reporting Standards (IFRS) and have their financial statements audited every year. The GAAP for all businesses, not just public companies, maintain that accrual accounting presents a fairer picture of the financial performance of a business than cash-basis accounting. (Refer to the preceding section for a look at the problems that crop up when you use cash-basis accounting.)

WARNING

Like cash-basis accounting, accrual accounting has its drawbacks. It does a good job of matching revenues and expenses within the same accounting period, but it does a poor job of getting you to pay attention to cash. Because you record revenue when the transaction occurs and not when you collect the cash, your attention may be diverted from the all-important cash collection. If your customers are slow to pay, you may end up with a lot of revenue and little cash.

TIP

Many businesses that use the accrual accounting method monitor cash flow on a weekly basis to be sure that they have enough cash on hand to operate the business. If your business is seasonal, such as a landscaping business that has little to do during the winter months, you can establish short-term lines of credit through your bank to maintain cash flow through the lean times.

Seeing Double with Double-Entry Bookkeeping

All businesses use double-entry bookkeeping to keep their books. A practice that helps minimize errors and increases the chance that your books balance, *double-entry bookkeeping* gets its name because you enter all transactions with two sides, using a minimum of two accounts.

REMEMBER

When it comes to double-entry bookkeeping, the key formula for the balance sheet (Assets = Liabilities + Equity) plays a major role. Accountants call this formula the *accounting equation*.

To adjust the balance of accounts in the bookkeeping world, you use a combination of debits and credits. You may think of a *debit* as a subtraction because debits usually mean a decrease in your bank balance. On the other hand, you've probably been excited to find unexpected *credits* in your bank account or on your credit card, which mean you've received more money in the account. Now, forget all that you've ever heard about debits or credits. In the world of bookkeeping, their meanings aren't so simple.

The only definite thing when it comes to debits and credits in the bookkeeping world is that a debit is on the left side of a transaction and a credit is on the right side of a transaction. Everything beyond that can get muddled. You get the basics of debits and credits in this chapter, but don't worry if you're finding this concept difficult to grasp. You get plenty of practice in using these concepts throughout this book.

Here's an example of the practice in action. Suppose you purchase for your office a new desk that costs $1,500. This transaction has two parts: You spend an asset — cash — to buy another asset — furniture. So, you must adjust two accounts in your business's books: the Cash account and the Furniture account. Here's what the transaction looks like in a bookkeeping entry:

Account	Debit	Credit
Furniture	$1,500	
Cash		$1,500

To purchase a new desk for the office with cash.

In this transaction, you record the accounts affected by the transaction. The debit increases the amount of the Furniture account, and the credit decreases the amount in the Cash account. For this transaction, both affected accounts are asset accounts, so if you look at how the balance sheet is affected, you can see that the only changes are to the asset side of the balance sheet equation:

Assets = Liabilities + Equity

Furniture increase

Cash decrease

= No change to this side of the equation

In this case, the books stay in balance because the dollar amount that increases the amount of your Furniture account decreases the amount of your Cash account. At the bottom of any journal entry, you should include a brief explanation of the purpose for the entry. In the first example, this entry was "To purchase a new desk for the office with cash."

How do you record a transaction if it affects both sides of the balance sheet equation? Here's an example that shows how to record the purchase of inventory on account. Suppose that you purchase $5,000 worth of widgets on credit. These new widgets add more costs to your Inventory asset account and also add to your obligations in your Accounts Payable account. (Remember, the Accounts Payable account is a Liability account in which you track bills that you need to pay at some point.) Here's how the bookkeeping transaction for your widget purchase looks:

Account	Debit	Credit
Inventory	$5,000	
Accounts Payable		$5,000

Purchase on account widgets for sale to customers.

Here's how this transaction affects the balance sheet equation:

Assets = Liabilities + Equity

Inventory increases = Accounts Payable increases + No change

In this case, the books stay in balance because both sides of the accounting equation increase by $5,000.

REMEMBER

You can see from the two preceding example transactions how double-entry bookkeeping helps to keep your books in balance — as long as you make sure each entry in the books is balanced. Balancing your entries may look simple here, but bookkeeping entries can get complex when the transaction affects more than two accounts. (Don't worry; you don't have to understand transactions totally now. You're just getting a quick overview to introduce the subject right now.)

Differentiating Debits and Credits

Because bookkeeping's debits and credits are different than the ones you encounter in everyday life, you're probably wondering how you're supposed to know whether a debit or credit will increase or decrease an account. Believe it or not, identifying the difference becomes second nature when you start making regular entries in your bookkeeping system. But to make things easier for you, here is Table 1-1, a chart that's commonly used by all bookkeepers and accountants. Yep, everyone needs help sometimes.

TIP

Copy Table 1-1 and post it on an index card at your desk when you start keeping your own books. It can help you keep your debits and credits straight.

TABLE 1-1

How Credits and Debits Affect Your Accounts

Account Type	Debits	Credits
Assets	Increase	Decrease
Liabilities	Decrease	Increase
Equity	Decrease	Increase
Drawings	Increase	Decrease
Revenue	Decrease	Increase
Expenses	Increase	Decrease

Getting to Know the Chart of Accounts

The *Chart of Accounts* is the roadmap that a business creates to organize its financial transactions. After all, you can't record a transaction until you know where to put it! Essentially, this chart is a list of all the accounts a business has, organized in a specific order. Each account has a description that includes the type of account and the types of transactions that should be entered into that account. Every business creates its own Chart of Accounts based on how the business is operated, so you're unlikely to find two businesses with the exact same Chart of Accounts.

However, some basic organizational and structural characteristics are common to all Charts of Accounts. The organization and structure are designed around two key financial statements: the *balance sheet*, which shows what your business owns and what it owes, and the *income statement*, which shows how much money your business took in from sales and revenue, and how much money it spent on expenses to generate those sales. (You can find out more about balance sheets and income statements in Chapters 2 and 4 of Book 4.)

The Chart of Accounts starts first with the balance sheet accounts, which include:

>> **Current Assets:** All accounts that track things that the business owns and expects to use in the next 12 months, such as cash, accounts receivable (money not yet collected from customers), and inventory.

>> **Long-Term Assets:** All accounts that track things that the business owns with a lifespan or usefulness to the business of more than 12 months, such as buildings, furniture, equipment, intangible assets, and long-term investments.

>> **Current Liabilities:** All accounts that track debts that the business must pay over the next 12 months, such as accounts payable (bills from vendors and suppliers, contractors, and consultants), interest payable, credit cards payable, and any amounts owing from payroll transactions, such as amounts subtracted from employees' pay for income taxes.

>> **Long-Term Liabilities:** All accounts that track debts that the business must pay over a period of time longer than the next 12 months, such as mortgages payable and long-term bank loans.

>> **Equity:** All accounts that track the owners' transactions directly with the business and their claims against the business's assets, which include any money invested in the business, any money taken out of the business, and any earnings that the owners have reinvested in the business.

Income statement accounts, which follow, fill the rest of the chart:

>> **Revenues:** All accounts that track sales of goods and services, as well as revenue generated for the business by other means, such as lending money

>> **Cost of Goods Sold:** All accounts that track the direct costs of goods the business has sold (only used by businesses selling goods)

>> **Expenses:** All accounts that track expenses related to running the business that aren't directly tied to the sale of individual products or services

When developing the Chart of Accounts, start by listing all the Asset accounts, the Liability accounts, the Equity accounts, the Drawings accounts (if applicable for unincorporated businesses), the Revenue accounts, and finally, the Expense accounts. All these accounts come from two places: the balance sheet and the income statement.

TIP

The rest of this chapter reviews the key account types found in most businesses, but this list isn't cast in stone. You need to develop an account list that makes the most sense for operating your business and that provides the financial information you want to track. Although you explore the various accounts that make up the Chart of Accounts in this chapter, you find out how the structure may vary for different types of businesses.

REMEMBER

The Chart of Accounts is a money-management tool that helps you track your business transactions, so set it up in a way that provides you with the financial information you need to make smart business decisions. You'll probably end up tweaking the accounts in your chart annually, and you may add accounts during the year if you find something for which you want more detailed tracking.

Starting with Balance Sheet Accounts

The first part of the Chart of Accounts is made up of balance sheet accounts, which break down into the following three categories:

» **Asset:** These accounts track what the business owns. Assets include cash on hand, inventory, furniture, buildings, vehicles, and so on.

» **Liability:** These accounts track what the business owes, or more specifically, the claims that lenders have against the business's assets. For example, mortgages on buildings and lines of credit with the bank are two common types of liabilities.

» **Equity:** These accounts track what the owners put into the business and the claims that the owners have against the business's assets. For example, shareholders are business owners who have claims against the business's assets.

REMEMBER

The balance sheet accounts, and the financial report they make up, are so-called because they have to *balance* out. The reported book value of the assets must be equal to the claims made against those assets. (These claims are liabilities made by lenders and equity belonging to owners.)

The balance sheet, including how you prepare and use it, is discussed in greater detail in Chapters 2 and 4 of Book 4. The following sections examine the basic components of the balance sheet, as reflected in the Chart of Accounts.

Tackling assets

First on the chart are always the accounts that track what the business owns — its assets. The two types of Asset accounts are Current Assets and Long-Term Assets.

Current assets

Current assets are the key assets that your business uses up during a 12-month period, so those assets likely won't be available the next year — or, at least, will be replaced by new assets by that time. The accounts that reflect current assets on the Chart of Accounts follow:

» **Cash in Chequing:** Any business's primary account is the chequing account used for operating activities, to deposit revenues collected, and to pay expenses and debt. Some businesses have more than one operating account in this category; for example, a business that has many divisions or locations may have an operating account for each division or location.

>> **Cash in Savings:** This account is used for surplus cash. Any cash for which the business has no immediate plan is deposited in an interest-earning savings account so that it can at least earn interest while the business decides what to do with it.

>> **Cash on Hand:** This account tracks any cash kept at retail stores or in the office. In retail stores, cash must be kept as floats in registers to provide change to customers. In the office, businesses often keep petty cash around for immediate cash needs that pop up from time to time. The Cash on Hand account helps you keep track of the cash held by the business outside a bank.

>> **Accounts Receivable:** If you offer your products or services to customers on account (meaning on *your* credit system), you need this account to track the customers who buy on your dime.

You don't use Accounts Receivable to track purchases made by customers on a bank credit card such as Visa because your business gets paid directly by the bank, not by the customers.

>> **Inventory:** This account tracks the cost of products that you have on hand to sell to your customers. The cost of the assets in this account varies, depending on the cost formula you decide to use to track the flow of inventory into and out of the business.

>> **Prepaid Insurance:** This account tracks insurance you paid earlier in the year in advance. Later, you reduce the prepaid insurance each month with a credit to show that month's insurance coverage as an insurance expense because the portion of the asset has been used up.

Depending on the type of business you're setting up, you may have other Current Asset accounts that you decide to track. For example, if you're starting a service business, you may want to have a Supplies account.

Long-term assets

Long-term assets are assets that your business plans to use for more than 12 months. This list includes some of the most common long-term assets, starting with the key accounts related to buildings and factories owned by the business:

>> **Land:** This account tracks the land owned by the business. The value of the land is based on the cost of purchasing it. Land value is tracked separately from the value of any buildings standing on that land because land doesn't depreciate in the books, but buildings do. *Depreciation* is an accounting method that shows an asset is being used up.

>> **Buildings:** This account tracks the value of any buildings that a business owns. Like with land, the value of the building is based on the cost of

purchasing it. The key difference between buildings and land is that the accountant depreciates the building.

>> **Accumulated Depreciation — Buildings:** This account tracks the cumulative amount the accountant has recorded as depreciation for a building over its useful lifespan.

>> **Leasehold Improvements:** This account tracks the value of long-lasting improvements made to buildings or other facilities that a business leases, rather than purchases. Frequently, when a business leases a property, the business must pay for any improvements necessary in order to use that property the way the business needs to use it. For example, if a business leases a store in a strip mall, the space leased is probably either an empty shell or filled with shelving and other items that may not match the particular needs of the business. Like with buildings, the accountant depreciates leasehold improvements while the asset gets used up.

>> **Accumulated Depreciation — Leasehold Improvements:** This account tracks the cumulative amount by which the accountant depreciates leasehold improvements.

Your business may also have extra cash that it invests in the shares of other businesses, in long-term investments in land, or in other types of assets that may earn some interest income. If your business intends to hold these assets for a long time, you must add another title and subtotal for long-term investments, as part of the required classification of accounts inside your balance sheet. You also need to create and track additional accounts in the General Ledger.

The following list includes the types of accounts for small long-term assets, such as vehicles and furniture:

>> **Vehicles:** This account tracks any cars, trucks, or other vehicles owned by the business. You list the initial book value of any vehicle in this account based on the total cost paid to put the vehicle in service. Sometimes, this book value can become greater than the purchase price if you make alterations or additions so that the vehicle is usable for your business. For example, if a business provides transportation for people with disabilities and must add equipment to the vehicle to serve the needs of its customers, the business adds that additional equipment cost to the book value of the vehicle. Vehicles depreciate through their useful lifespan.

>> **Accumulated Depreciation — Vehicles:** This account tracks the depreciation of all vehicles owned by the business.

>> **Furniture and Fixtures:** This account tracks any furniture or fixtures purchased for use in the business. The account includes the value of all chairs,

desks, store fixtures, shelving, and so on needed to operate the business. You base the value of the furniture and fixtures in this account on the cost of purchasing these items. These items depreciate during their useful lifespan.

>> **Accumulated Depreciation — Furniture and Fixtures:** This account tracks the accumulated depreciation of all furniture and fixtures.

>> **Equipment:** This account tracks equipment that you purchase for use for more than one year, such as computers, copiers, tools, and cash registers. You base the value of the equipment on the cost to purchase these items. Equipment depreciates over time, until the asset reaches the point where you must replace it.

>> **Accumulated Depreciation — Equipment:** This account tracks the accumulated depreciation of all the equipment.

The following accounts track the long-term assets that you can't touch but that still represent things of value owned and used by the business, such as patents and copyrights. These assets are called *intangible assets*, and the accounts that track them include the following:

>> **Patents:** This account tracks the costs associated with *patents,* which are grants made by governments that guarantee to the inventor or the owner of the patent of a product or process the exclusive right to make, use, and sell that product or process over a set period of time. Patent costs are amortized. You base the value of this asset on the expenses that the business incurs to get the right to patent the product or the cost of purchasing that patent. (Find out more about the patent process in Chapters 1 and 2 of Book 2.)

>> **Accumulated Amortization — Patents:** This account tracks the accumulated amortization of a business's patents. Amortization is much like depreciation, but amortization is a term used for intangible assets whereas depreciation is typically used for tangible, depreciable long-term assets.

>> **Copyrights:** This account tracks the costs incurred to establish *copyrights,* the legal rights given to an author, a playwright, a publisher, or any other distributor of a publication or production for a unique work of literature, music, drama, or art. This legal right expires after a set number of years, so amortization is recorded only up until the business reaches that limit or when a choice is made to stop using the copyright, whichever comes first. (See Chapter 3 in Book 2 for an introduction to copyrights.)

>> **Goodwill:** You need this account only if your business buys another business for more than the fair value of its *net assets* (assets minus liabilities). Goodwill reflects the intangible value of this purchase for assets not on the balance sheet of the seller, such as business reputation, store locations, customer base, and other items that increase the value of a business bought as a going concern.

TIP

If you hold a lot of assets that don't fit in the categories listed in this section, you can also set up an Other Assets account to track those assets. While time goes by, the purpose of owning a particular asset may change. For example, say you purchase some land with the intention of building a factory. Before construction, economic changes cause you to revise your plans, and you now need to put the land up for sale. The asset may then rightfully belong to another asset category. If that happens, you can move that asset to the appropriate category or group. So, in this example, the land goes from the Land account classified under long-term assets to the Land Available for Sale account because the land has become an investment. Your change in the intended use of the asset may mean that you need to add another account to your Chart of Accounts to accommodate this change.

Laying out your liabilities

After you cover assets, the next stop on the bookkeeping highway consists of the accounts that track what your business owes to others. These others can include vendors and suppliers from whom you buy products or supplies on account, banks from which you borrow money, and anyone else who lends money to your business or to whom the business needs to make a payment to settle an obligation, such as credit card companies, employees, or the Canada Revenue Agency (CRA). Like assets, liabilities are lumped into two types: current liabilities and long-term liabilities (sometimes also called *long-term debt*).

Current liabilities

Current liabilities are debts due to be paid in the next 12 months. Some of the most common types of Current Liabilities accounts that appear on the Chart of Accounts are:

>> **Accounts Payable:** This account tracks money owed that the business must pay in less than a year to vendors, contractors, suppliers, and consultants. The business must pay most of these liabilities in 30 to 60 days from the date of their invoices, depending on the terms you have negotiated.

>> **Goods and Services Tax Payable and Retail Taxes Payable:** You may not think of goods and services tax (GST), harmonized sales tax (HST), and provincial sales tax (PST) as liabilities. But because your business collects taxes from your customers and doesn't pay those taxes immediately to the government entities, the taxes collected become a liability tracked in these accounts. A business usually charges the sales tax throughout the month, and then pays the tax to the appropriate provincial or federal government on a monthly basis.

>> **Payroll Taxes:** This account tracks payroll taxes collected from employees to pay combined federal and provincial income taxes, as well as Canada Pension Plan (CPP) and Employment Insurance (EI) contributions. Businesses don't have to pay these taxes to the government entities immediately, so depending on the size of the payroll, businesses may pay payroll taxes on a monthly or quarterly basis.

>> **Credit Cards Payable:** This account tracks all accounts with credit card companies to which the business owes money. Most businesses use credit cards as short-term debt and pay the balance owed at the end of each month. Some smaller businesses carry credit card balances over a longer period of time. Because credit cards often have a much higher interest rate than lines of credit, most businesses transfer any credit card debt that they can't pay entirely at the end of a month to a line of credit at a bank. When it comes to your Chart of Accounts, you can set up one Credit Card Payable account, but you may want to set up a separate account for each card your business holds to improve your ability to track credit card usage.

How you set up your current liabilities and how many individual accounts you establish depend on how detailed you want to make each type of liability tracking. For example, you can set up separate current liability accounts for major vendors if that approach provides you with a better money-management tool. Suppose that a small hardware retail store buys most of the tools it sells from Snap-On Tools. To keep better control of its purchases from Snap-On Tools, the bookkeeper sets up a specific account called Accounts Payable — Snap-On Tools, which she uses for tracking invoices and payments to only that vendor. In this example, the bookkeeper tracks all other invoices and payments to other vendors and suppliers in the general Accounts Payable account.

Long-term liabilities

Long-term liabilities are debts due in more than 12 months. The number of long-term liability accounts you maintain in your Chart of Accounts depends on your debt structure. The two most common types of long-term liability accounts are

>> **Loans Payable:** This account tracks any long-term loans, such as a mortgage on your business building. Most businesses have separate Loans Payable accounts for each of their long-term loans. For example, you could have Loans Payable — Mortgage for your building and Loans Payable — Car for your vehicle loan.

>> **Notes Payable:** Some businesses borrow money from other businesses using *promissory notes,* a method of borrowing that doesn't require the business to put up an asset as collateral, which you need to do with a mortgage on a building. The promissory note documents a formal promise to repay the loan, plus interest, at a specified future date. The Notes Payable account tracks any notes due.

Eyeing equity

Every business is owned by somebody. *Equity accounts* track owners' contributions to the business, as well as their share of ownership. For a corporation, you track ownership by the sale of individual shares because each shareholder owns a portion of the business. In smaller businesses that are owned by one person or a group of people, you track equity by using Capital and Drawings accounts. Here are the basic Equity accounts that appear in the Chart of Accounts:

>> **Common Shares:** This account reflects the book value of outstanding shares sold to investors. The amount in this account corresponds to the amount paid by the original investors. Only corporations need to establish this account. If an original investor resells his shares to another investor, that transaction does not affect the recorded value in the Common Shares account of the corporation.

>> **Retained Earnings:** This account, exclusive to corporations, tracks the profits or losses accumulated since a business opened. At the end of each year, the profit or loss calculated on the income statement is closed to this account. For example, if your business made a $100,000 profit in the past year, you increase the Retained Earnings account by that amount; if the business lost $100,000, you subtract that amount from this account.

>> **Capital:** Only unincorporated businesses need this account. The Capital account reflects the amount of initial money the business owner contributed to the business, as well as owner contributions made after the initial start-up. You base the book value of this account on cash contributions and other assets contributed by the business owner, such as equipment, vehicles, or buildings invested at their fair market value. If a small business has several different partners, each partner gets her own Capital account to track her contributions. Similar to Retained Earnings, the Capital account increases for profits and decreases for any losses accumulated since the business opened.

>> **Drawings:** Only businesses that aren't incorporated need this account. The Drawings account tracks any money or other assets that a business owner takes out of the business. If the business has several partners, each partner gets his own Drawings account to track what he takes out of the business.

REMEMBER

Drawings by an owner are not a salary. Owners often make the mistake of thinking that the cash they draw from their business is the amount on which they have to pay income taxes. Not so. The amount reported on the personal income tax return of the owner of an unincorporated business is the amount of the owner's share of profit of that business.

Tracking Income Statement Accounts

Two types of accounts make up the income statement:

>> **Revenues:** These accounts track all money coming into the business, including sales, services rendered, rents, dividends from investments, interest earned on savings, and any other methods used to generate income.

>> **Expenses:** These accounts track all money that a business spends to earn revenues. You include in expenses the depreciation that doesn't directly involve cash spent during the year.

The bottom line of the income statement shows whether your business made a profit or suffered a loss for a specified period of time. You find out how to prepare and use an income statement in Chapters 2 and 4 of Book 4. The following sections examine the various accounts that make up the income statement portion of the Chart of Accounts.

Recording the money you make

First up in the income statement portion of the Chart of Accounts are accounts that track revenue. If you choose to offer discounts, accept merchandise returns, or possibly grant allowances, that activity also falls within the revenue group. The most common income accounts follow:

>> **Sales and Service Revenue:** These accounts, which appear at the top of every income statement, track all the money that the business earns by selling its products, its services, or both.

>> **Sales Discounts:** Because most businesses offer discounts to encourage quick payments, this account tracks any reductions to the full price of merchandise.

>> **Volume Discounts:** This account keeps track of reductions in your selling price to foster relationships with key customers or to encourage large orders from your customers. Some computer software packages don't keep track of volume discounts.

>> **Sales Returns and Allowances:** This account tracks transactions related to *returns* — when customers bring products back to your business because they're unhappy with them for some reason — and *allowances* — which are reductions to the price of goods that you make because of defects in the products. With allowances, the customer doesn't return the goods.

TIP

When you examine an income statement from a business other than the one you own or are working for, you usually see the previous accounts summarized as one line item called either Revenue or Net Revenue.

Because sales of products or services don't generate all income, other income accounts that may appear on a Chart of Accounts include the following:

>> **Other Income:** If a business takes in income from a source other than its primary business activity, you record that income in this account. For example, a business that encourages recycling and earns income from the items recycled records that income in this account.

>> **Interest Income:** This account tracks any income earned by collecting interest on a business's savings accounts, promissory notes receivable, or long-term investments. If the business loans money to another business and earns interest on that money, you record that interest in this account.

>> **Rent Revenue:** Occasionally, a business may have extra office or warehouse space that it rents to tenants. Although this source of cash might not represent a large amount of revenue, you need to track it in its own account in your bookkeeping.

>> **Gain or Loss on Disposal of Fixed Assets:** Any time your business sells a *fixed asset,* such as a car or furniture, you record in this account any gain or loss made from the sale. A business should record only revenue remaining after subtracting the accumulated depreciation from the original cost of the asset. The CRA calculates and taxes these gains and losses in a different way from other revenues, so identifying what the amounts are every year is important.

Tracking the cost of sales

Of course, before you can sell a product, you must spend some money to either buy or make that product. The type of account used to track the money spent is called a Cost of Goods Sold account. The most common Cost of Goods Sold accounts follow:

>> **Purchases:** This account tracks the purchases of all items you plan to sell.

>> **Purchase Discount:** This account tracks the discounts you may receive from vendors if you pay for your purchase quickly. For example, a business may give you a 2 percent discount on your purchase if you pay the bill in 10 days, rather than wait until the end of the 30-day payment term originally negotiated.

>> **Purchase Returns and Allowances:** If you're unhappy with a product you buy, record the cost of any items you return to the vendor in this account. You use this account also to record any *purchase allowances* — allowances given to you by the vendor as reductions in the purchase price you pay for defective goods that you're willing to keep.

>> **Freight-In Charges:** You track any charges related to shipping items that you purchase for later sale in this account.

Acknowledging the money you spend

Expense accounts take the cake for the longest list of individual accounts. Any money you spend on the business that you can't tie directly to the sale of an individual product falls under the Expense account category. For example, advertising a storewide sale isn't directly tied to the sale of any one product, so the costs associated with advertising go into an Expense account.

REMEMBER

The Chart of Accounts mirrors your business operations, so deciding how much detail you want to keep in your Expense accounts is up to you. Most businesses have expenses unique to their operations, so your list is probably longer than the one presented here. However, you may find that you don't need some of the accounts suggested here.

On your Chart of Accounts, the Expense accounts don't have to appear in any specific order, so they are listed here alphabetically. The most common Expense accounts are:

>> **Advertising and Promotion:** This account tracks all expenses involved in promoting a business or its products. You record money spent on newspaper, television, Internet, magazine, and radio advertising in this account, as well as any money spent to print flyers and mailings to customers.

>> **Automotive Expenses:** This account tracks expenses related to the operation of business vehicles.

>> **Bank Service Charges:** This account tracks any charges made by a bank to service a business's bank accounts.

>> **Depreciation and Amortization:** These accounts track the cost of property, plant, and equipment, as well as intangible assets that the business uses.

>> **Dues and Subscriptions:** This account tracks expenses related to memberships, professional associations, or subscriptions to magazines for the business.

- **» Equipment Rental:** This account tracks expenses related to renting equipment for a short-term project. For example, a business that needs to rent a truck to pick up some new fixtures for its store records that truck rental cost in this account.

- **» Interest:** This account tracks all interest paid by the business on borrowed money.

- **» Insurance:** This account tracks any money paid for insurance. Many businesses break down insurance costs into several accounts, such as Insurance — Casualty, which tracks the coverage for any damages to property, or Insurance — Officers' Life, which tracks money spent to buy insurance to protect the lives of key business managers or officers. Businesses often insure their key executives because an unexpected death, especially for a small business, may mean facing many expenses to keep the business's doors open. In such a case, you can use the insurance proceeds to cover those expenses.

- **» Legal and Accounting:** This account tracks any money that a business pays for legal or accounting advice.

- **» Maintenance and Repairs:** This account tracks any payments to keep the property, plant, and equipment, or the rented premises, in good working order.

- **» Miscellaneous Expenses:** A catchall account for expenses that don't fit in one of a business's established accounts. If certain miscellaneous expenses occur frequently, a business may choose to add an account to the Chart of Accounts to better keep track of the particular expense. The bookkeeper then moves the related expenses into that new account by subtracting all related transactions from the Miscellaneous Expenses account and adding them to the new account. If you do this shuffle, you need to carefully balance out the adjusting transaction to prevent any errors or double counting.

- **» Office Expense:** This account tracks the cost of items used to run an office. For example, office supplies used (such as paper, pens, or business cards) fit in this account. As with the Miscellaneous Expenses, a business may choose to track some office expense items in their own accounts. For example, if your office uses a lot of copy paper and you want to track that separately, you would set up a Copy Paper Expense account. Just be sure you really need the detail, because the number of accounts can get unwieldy and hard to manage.

- **» Payroll Benefits:** This account tracks any payments for employee benefits, such as the employer's share of Canada Pension Plan (CPP), Employment Insurance (EI), and worker's compensation.

>> **Postage and Delivery:** This account tracks any money spent on stamps, express package shipping, and other shipping. If a business does a large amount of shipping through vendors such as FedEx, UPS, or Purolator, it may want to track that spending in separate accounts for each vendor. This option is particularly helpful for small businesses that sell over the Internet.

Don't confuse the delivery costs tracked here with the freight costs paid to purchase inventory for resale. The preceding section explains that freight-in costs get grouped with purchases to become Costs of Goods Sold.

>> **Rent Expense:** This account tracks rental costs for a business's office, storage, or retail space.

>> **Salaries and Wages:** This account tracks any money paid to employees as salary or wages. You may want a separate account to track vacation pay.

>> **Supplies Expense:** This account tracks any business supplies used that don't fit into the category of office expenses. For example, you track supplies needed for the operation of retail stores, such as shopping bags, by using this account. You can also create separate Supplies Expense accounts for services that your business provides. An example would be grease used by a business providing oil changes for vehicles.

>> **Travel and Entertainment:** This account tracks money spent for business purposes on travel or entertainment. Some businesses separate these expenses into several accounts such as Travel and Entertainment — Meals; Travel and Entertainment — Travel; and Travel and Entertainment — Entertainment, to keep a closer watch on these costs.

>> **Telephone and Internet:** This account tracks all business expenses related to using telephones and the Internet.

>> **Utilities:** This account tracks money paid for utilities, such as electricity, gas, and water.

Setting Up Your Chart of Accounts

You can use the lists of accounts provided in this chapter to get started setting up your business's own Chart of Accounts. You don't need to know a secret method to make your own chart — just make a list of the accounts that apply to your business.

REMEMBER

When first setting up your Chart of Accounts, don't panic if you can't think of every type of account you may need for your business. You can easily add to the Chart of Accounts at any time. Just add the account to the list and distribute the revised list to any employees who use the Chart of Accounts for recording transactions into the bookkeeping system. (Even employees not involved in bookkeeping need a copy of your Chart of Accounts if they are responsible for telling the bookkeeper to which account transactions should be recorded.)

The Chart of Accounts usually includes at least three columns:

>> **Account:** Lists the account names

>> **Type:** Lists the types of accounts — Asset, Liability, Equity, Revenue, Cost of Goods Sold, or other Expenses

>> **Description:** Contains a description of the type of transaction you should record in the account

Many businesses also assign numbers to the accounts that you can use for coding charges. If your business is using a computerized system, the computer automatically assigns the account number. Otherwise, you need to plan your own numbering system. The most common number system follows:

>> **Asset accounts:** 1,000 to 1,999

>> **Liability accounts:** 2,000 to 2,999

>> **Equity accounts:** 3,000 to 3,999

>> **Sales accounts:** 4,000 to 4,999

>> **Cost of Goods Sold accounts:** 5,000 to 5,999

>> **Expense accounts:** 6,000 to 6,999

This type of numbering system matches the one used by computerized accounting systems, making it easy for a business to transition if at some future time it decides to automate its books by using a computerized accounting system. (See Chapter 3 in Book 4 for computer software options.)

One major advantage of using a computerized accounting system is that most accounting software can be customized with different Charts of Accounts based on the type of business you plan to run. When you get your computerized system, whichever accounting software you decide to use, review the list of business-type chart options included with that software, delete any accounts you don't want, and add any new accounts that fit your business plan.

TIP

If you're setting up your Chart of Accounts manually, be sure to leave a lot of room between accounts to add new accounts. For example, number your Cash account 1,000 and your Accounts Receivable account 1,100. That numbering leaves you plenty of room to add other accounts that track cash.

Figure 1-2 is a sample Chart of Accounts for H.G.'s Cheesecake Shop, which was developed by using QuickBooks. Note that in QuickBooks, the General Ledger accounts aren't necessarily assigned account numbers. Also note the column for the type of account to which each General Ledger account belongs. For example, when you select Long-Term Liability as the type for a loan, the principal payments on the loan will come due in more than 12 months, as described previously in this chapter. This selection determines where QuickBooks places the debt on your balance sheet. You find out how to prepare a balance sheet in Chapters 2 and 4 of Book 4.

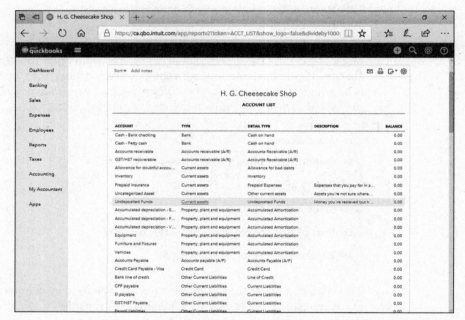

FIGURE 1-2:
The top portion of a sample Chart of Accounts.

Chapter **2**

Financial Statements and Accounting Standards

I n the world of bookkeeping and accounting, the three primary business financial statements are the income statement, the balance sheet, and the statement of cash flows. The purpose of financial statements is to communicate information that is useful to their readers. Financial statement readers include the managers of the business and its lenders and investors. These constitute the primary audience for financial statements.

Think of yourself as a shareholder in a business. What sort of information would you want to know about the business? The answer to this question should be the touchstone for the accountant in preparing the financial statements. This chapter introduces the basic information components of each type of financial statement.

This chapter also briefly discusses financial accounting and reporting standards. Businesses comply with established rules for recording revenue, gains, expenses, and losses; for putting values on assets and liabilities; and for presenting and disclosing information in their financial reports. The basic idea is that all businesses should follow uniform methods for measuring and reporting profit performance, and reporting financial condition and cash flows. Consistency in accounting from business to business is the goal. This chapter explains who makes the rules and discusses two important developments: the internationalization of accounting standards, and the increasing divide between financial reporting for public and private companies.

Introducing the Information Content of Financial Statements

This chapter focuses on the basic *information components* of each financial statement reported by a business. It does not address the classification, or grouping, of these information packets within each financial statement. The first step here is to get a good idea of the information content reported in financial statements. The second step is to become familiar with the architecture, rules of classification, and other features of financial statements.

Setting up the business example

To better illustrate the three primary financial statements, we need a realistic business example. The information content of its financial statements depends on the line of business a company is in — in other words, which types of products and services it sells. The financial statements of a movie theatre chain are different from those of a bank, which are different from those of an airline, which are different from an automobile manufacturer. This chapter uses a fairly common type of business example with these particulars:

- >> It sells products, mainly to other businesses.

- >> It sells on credit, and its customers take a month or so before they pay.

- >> It holds a fairly large stock of products awaiting sale (its inventory).

- >> It owns a wide variety of long-term operating assets that have useful lives from 2 to 30 years or longer (a building, machines, tools, computers, office furniture, and so on).

- >> It's been in business for many years and has made a steady profit over the years.

- >> It borrows money for part of the total capital it needs.

>> It's organized as a corporation and pays federal and provincial income taxes on its annual taxable income.

>> It has never been in bankruptcy and is not facing any immediate financial difficulties.

Upcoming figures present the company's annual income statement for the year just ended, its balance sheet at the end of the year, and its statement of cash flows for the year. Dollar amounts in the three financials are rounded off to the nearest thousand, which is not uncommon. Dollar amounts can be reported out to the last dollar, or even the last penny for that matter. But too many digits in a dollar amount are hard to absorb, so many businesses round off the dollar amounts in their financial statements.

REMEMBER

These financial statements are stepping-stone illustrations that are concerned mainly with the basic information components in each statement. The financial statements in this chapter do not include all the information you see in actual financial statements. Also, these financial statements use descriptive labels for each item rather than the terse and technical titles you see in actual financial statements. And subtotals that you see in actual financial statements are stripped out because they are not necessary at this point. So, with all these conventions in mind, let's get going.

First, here's a quick heads-up on a few characteristics of financial statements. Financial statements are stiff and formal. No slang or street language is allowed. Seldom do you see any graphics or artwork in a financial statement itself, although you do see a fair number of photos and graphics elsewhere in the annual reports of public companies. And virtually no humour appears in financial reports.

The income statement

The *income statement* is the all-important financial statement that summarizes the profit-making activities of a business over a period of time. Its more formal name is the *statement of financial performance*. Figure 2-1 shows the basic information content for an external income statement: one released outside the business to its owners and lenders. The income statement in Figure 2-1 shows six lines of information: sales revenue on the top line, four types of expenses that are deducted from sales revenue, and finally bottom-line net income. Virtually all income statements disclose at least the four expenses shown in Figure 2-1. The first two expenses (cost of goods sold and selling, general, and administrative expenses) take a big bite out of sales revenue. The other two expenses (interest and income tax) are relatively small as a percentage of annual sales revenue but important enough in their own right to be reported separately.

Company's Name
Income Statement
for Most Recent Year
(Dollar amounts in thousands)

Sales revenue	$10,400
Cost of goods sold expense	6,240
Selling, general, and administrative expenses	3,235
Interest expense	125
Income tax expense	280
Net income	$520

TIP

Instead of one amount for all selling, general, and administrative expenses, a business may separate out certain expenses from this broad category. For example, a business could disclose separate expenses for advertising and sales promotion, depreciation, salaries and wages, research and development, and delivery and shipping — though reporting these expenses is not common. Businesses do not disclose the compensation of top management in their external financial reports.

Inside most businesses, an income statement is called a *P&L (profit and loss) report*. These internal profit performance reports to the managers of a business include a good deal more detailed information about expenses as well as about sales revenue. Reporting just four expenses to managers (as shown in Figure 2-1) would not do.

Sales revenue is from the sales of products and services to customers. *Other revenues and gains* refer to amounts earned by a business from sources other than sales; for example, a real estate rental business receives rental income from its tenants. (In the example, the business has only sales revenue.) As mentioned, businesses report the expenses shown in Figure 2-1 — cost of goods sold expense, selling and general expenses, interest expense, and income tax expense. Further breakdown of expenses is at the business's discretion.

Net income, being the bottom line of the income statement after deducting all expenses from sales revenue (and gains, if any), is called, not surprisingly, the *bottom line*. It is also called *net earnings*. A few companies call it *profit* or *net profit*.

The income statement gets the most attention from business managers, lenders, and investors (not that they ignore the other two financial statements). The much abbreviated versions of income statements that you see in the financial press or on financial Internet sites report the top line (sales revenue), the bottom line (net income), and not much more. Refer to Chapter 4 in Book 4 for more information on income statements.

The balance sheet

Figure 2-2 shows the basic information components of a typical balance sheet. One reason the balance sheet is called by this name is that its two sides balance, or are equal in total amounts. In the example, the $5.2 million total of assets equals the $5.2 million total of liabilities and owners' equity. The balance, or equality, of total assets on the one hand and the sum of liabilities plus owners' equity on the other hand is expressed in the accounting equation, which is discussed in Chapter 1 of Book 4.

Company's Name
Balance Sheet
at End of Most Recent Year
(Dollar amounts in thousands)

Assets	
Cash	$1,000
Receivables from sales made on credit	800
Inventory of unsold products, at cost	1,560
Long-term operating assets, at cost less cumulative amount charged off to depreciation expense	1,840
Total assets	$5,200

Liabilities and Owners' Equity	
Non-interest-bearing liabilities from purchases on credit and for unpaid expenses	$650
Interest-bearing debt	2,080
Owners' equity capital invested in business plus profit earned and retained in business	2,470
Total liabilities and owners' equity	$5,200

© John Wiley & Sons, Inc.

FIGURE 2-2: Basic information components of the balance sheet.

In general, five or more assets are reported in a typical balance sheet, starting with cash, and then receivables, and then cost of products held for sale, and so on down the line. Generally five or more liabilities are disclosed, starting with trade credit liabilities (from buying on credit), then unpaid expenses, and then proceeding through the interest-bearing debts of the business. Two or more owners' equity accounts are generally reported. In summary, you'll find 12 or more lines of information in most balance sheets. Each of these information packets is called an *account* — so a balance sheet has a composite of asset accounts, liability accounts, and owners' equity accounts.

Most businesses need a variety of assets. You have *cash,* which every business needs, of course. Businesses that sell products carry an *inventory* of products awaiting sale to customers. Businesses need long-term resources that are generally called *property, plant, and equipment;* this group includes buildings, vehicles, tools, machines, and other resources needed in their operations. All these and more go under the collective name *assets.*

As you'd suspect, the particular assets reported in the balance sheet depend on which assets the business owns. Figure 2-2 includes just four basic assets. These are the hardcore assets that a business selling products on credit would have. In this example, the business owns *fixed assets.* They are *fixed* because they are held for use in the business's operations and are not for sale, and their usefulness lasts several years or longer.

So, where does a business get the money to buy its assets? Most businesses borrow money on the basis of interest-bearing bank loans, promissory notes, or other credit instruments for part of the total capital they need for their assets. Also, businesses buy many things on credit and at the balance sheet date owe money to their suppliers, which will be paid in the future. These operating liabilities are never grouped with interest-bearing debt in the balance sheet. Note that liabilities are not intermingled among assets — this is a definite no-no in financial reporting. You cannot subtract certain liabilities from certain assets and report only the net balance.

Could a business's total liabilities be greater than its total assets? Well, not likely — unless the business has been losing money hand over fist. In the vast majority of cases, a business has more total assets than total liabilities. Why? For two reasons:

>> Its owners have invested money in the business, which is not a liability of the business.

>> The business has earned profit over the years, and some (or all) of the profit has been retained in the business. Making profit increases assets; if not all the profit is distributed to owners, the company's assets increase by the amount of profit retained.

WARNING

In the example (refer to Figure 2-2), owners' equity is about $2.5 million, $2.47 million to be exact. Sometimes this amount is referred to as *net worth,* because it equals total assets minus total liabilities. However, net worth is not a good term because it implies that the business is worth the amount recorded in its owners' equity accounts. The market value of a business, when it needs to be known, depends on many factors. The amount of owners' equity reported in a balance sheet, which is called its *book value,* is not irrelevant in setting a market value on the business but is usually not the dominant factor. The amount of owners' equity in a balance sheet is based on the history of capital invested in the business by its owners and the history of its profit performance and distributions from profit.

TIP

A balance sheet could be whipped up anytime you want — say, at the end of every day. Typically, preparing a balance sheet at the end of each month is adequate for general management purposes, although a manager might need to take a look at the business's balance sheet in the middle of the month. In external financial reports (those released outside the business to its lenders and investors), a balance sheet is required at the close of business on the last day of the income statement period. Say the annual or quarterly income statement ends September 30; the business would reports its balance sheet at the close of business on September 30.

The balance sheet could more properly be called the *statement of assets, liabilities, and owners' equity*. Its more formal name is the *statement of financial position*. Just a reminder: The profit *for the most recent period* is found in the income statement; periodic profit is not reported in the balance sheet. The profit reported in the income statement is before any distributions from profit to owners. The cumulative amount of profit over the years that has not been distributed to its owners is reported in the owners' equity section of the company's balance sheet.

TIP

By the way, note that the balance sheet in Figure 2-2 is presented in two formats, either of which is acceptable:

>> Report format is a top and bottom format (also called portrait mode).

>> Account format is a left and right side format (also called landscape mode).

See Chapter 4 in Book 4 for more about balance sheets.

The statement of cash flows

To survive and thrive, business managers fulfil three financial imperatives:

>> Make an adequate profit

>> Keep the financial condition out of trouble and in good shape

>> Control cash flows

The income statement reports whether the business made a profit. The balance sheet reports the business's financial condition. The third imperative is reported on in the *statement of cash flows,* which presents a summary of the business's sources and uses of cash during the income statement period.

Smart business managers hardly get the words *net income* (or profit) out of their mouths before mentioning *cash flow*. Successful business managers tell you that they have to manage both profit *and* cash flow; you can't do one and ignore the other. Business is a two-headed dragon in this respect. Ignoring cash flow can pull the rug out from under a successful profit formula. Still, some managers are preoccupied with making profit and overlook cash flow.

For external financial reporting, the cash flows of a business are divided into three categories, which are shown in Figure 2-3.

Company's Name
Statement of Cash Flows
for Most Recent Year
(Dollar amounts in thousands)

(1) Cash effect during period from operating activities (collecting cash from sales and paying cash for expenses)	$400
(2) Cash effect during period from making investments in long-term operating assets	(450)
(3) Cash effect during period from dealings with lenders and owners	200
Cash increase during period	150
Cash at start of year	850
Cash at end of year	$1,000

© John Wiley & Sons, Inc.

FIGURE 2-3:
Basic information components in the statement of cash flows.

In the example, the company earned $520,000 profit during the year (see Figure 2-1). One result of its profit-making activities was an increase of $400,000 in cash, which you see in part 1 of the statement of cash flows (see Figure 2-3). This still leaves $120,000 of profit to explain. The actual cash inflows from revenues and outflows for expenses run on a different timetable than the recording of the sales revenue and expenses for determining profit. It's like two different trains going to the same destination — the second train (the cash flow train) runs on a different schedule than the first train (the recording of sales revenue and expenses in the business's accounts). The next section presents a scenario that accounts for the $120,000 difference between cash flow and profit.

The second part of the statement of cash flows sums the long-term investments made by the business during the year, such as constructing a new production plant or replacing machinery and equipment. If the business sold any of its long-term assets, it reports the cash inflows from these disposals in this section of the statement of cash flows. The cash flows of other investment activities (if any) are reported in this part of the statement as well. As you can see in part 2 of the statement of cash flows (see Figure 2-3), the business invested $450,000 in new long-term operating assets (trucks, equipment, tools, and computers).

The third part of the statement sums the dealings between the business and its sources of capital during the period — borrowing money from lenders and raising new capital from its owners. Cash outflows to pay debt are reported in this section, as well as cash distributions from profit paid to the business's owners. As you can see in part 3 of the statement of cash flows (see Figure 2-3), the result of these transactions was to increase cash by $200,000. Note that in this example, the business did not make cash distributions from profit to its owners. It could have, but it didn't — which is an important point discussed later in the chapter (see the section "Why no cash distribution from profit?").

TIP

As you see in Figure 2-3, the net result of the three types of cash activities was a $150,000 increase during the year. The increase is added to the cash balance at the start of the year to get the cash balance at the end of the year, which is $1 million. Note that the $150,000 increase in cash during the year (in this example) is never referred to as a cash flow *bottom line,* or any such thing. The term *bottom line* is strictly reserved for the last line of the income statement, which reports net income — the final profit after all expenses are deducted.

The statements of cash flows reported by most businesses are frustratingly difficult to read. Figure 2-3 presents the statement of cash flows for the business example as simply as possible. Actual cash flow statements are much more complicated than the brief introduction to this financial statement that you see in Figure 2-3.

REMEMBER

Imagine you have a highlighter in your hand, and the three basic financial statements of a business are in front of you. What are the most important numbers to mark? Financial statements do not come with headlines, like newspapers. You have to find your own headlines. Bottom-line profit (net income) in the income statement is one number you should mark. Another key number is *cash flow from operating activities* in the statement of cash flows.

How Profit and Cash Flow from Profit Differ

The income statement in Figure 2-1 reports that the business in the example earned $520,000 in net income for the year. However, the statement of cash flows in Figure 2-3 reports that its profit-making, or operating, activities increased cash only $400,000 during the year. This gap between profit and cash flow from operating activities is not unusual. So, what happened to the other $120,000 of profit? Is some accounting sleight of hand going on? Did the business really earn $520,000 net income if cash increased only $400,000? These are good questions.

Here's one scenario that explains the $120,000 difference between profit (net income) and cash flow from operating activities:

>> Suppose the business collected $50,000 less cash from customers during the year than the total sales revenue reported in its income statement. (Remember that the business sells on credit and its customers take time before paying the business.) Therefore, a cash flow lag happens between booking sales and collecting cash from customers. As a result, the business's cash inflow from customers was $50,000 less than the sales revenue amount used to calculate profit for the year.

>> Also suppose that during the year the business made cash payments connected with its expenses that were $70,000 higher than the total amount of expenses reported in the income statement. For example, a business that sells products buys or makes the products, and then holds the products in inventory for some time before it sells the items to customers. Cash is paid out before the cost of goods sold expense is recorded. This is one example of a difference between cash flow connected with an expense and the amount recorded in the income statement for the expense.

In this scenario, the two factors cause cash flow from profit-making (operating) activities to be $120,000 less than the net income earned for the year. Cash collections from customers were $50,000 less than sales revenue, and cash payments for expenses were $70,000 more than the amount of expenses recorded to the year.

REMEMBER

At this point the key idea to hold in mind is that the sales revenue reported in the income statement does not equal cash collections from customers during the year, and expenses do not equal cash payments during the year. Cash collections from sales minus cash payments for expenses gives cash flow from a company's profit-making activities; sales revenue minus expenses gives the net income earned for the year. Cash flow almost always is different from net income.

Gleaning Key Information from Financial Statements

The point of reporting financial statements is to provide important information to people who have a financial interest in the business — mainly its outside investors and lenders. From that information, investors and lenders can answer key questions about the business's financial performance and condition. This section discusses some of these key questions.

How's profit performance?

Investors use two important measures to judge a company's annual profit performance. Here, we use the data from Figures 2-1 and 2-2 (the dollar amounts are in thousands):

» **Return on sales** = profit as a percentage of annual sales revenue:

$520 bottom-line annual profit (net income) ÷ $10,400 annual sales revenue = 5.0%

» **Return on equity** = profit as a percentage of owners' equity:

$520 bottom-line annual profit (net income) ÷ $2,470 owners' equity = 21.1%

Profit looks pretty thin compared with annual sales revenue. The company earns only 5 percent return on sales. In other words, 95 cents out of every sales dollar goes for expenses, and the company keeps only 5 cents for profit. (Many businesses earn 10 percent or higher return on sales.) However, when profit is compared with owners' equity, things look a lot better. The business earns more than 21 percent profit on its owners' equity. You probably don't have many investments earning 21 percent per year.

Is there enough cash?

Cash is the lubricant of business activity. Realistically, a business can't operate with a zero cash balance. It can't wait to open the morning mail or look at the bank account online to see how much cash it will have for the day's needs (although some businesses try to operate on a shoestring cash balance). A business should keep enough cash on hand to keep things running smoothly even when interruptions occur in the normal inflows of cash. A business has to meet its payroll on time, for example. Keeping an adequate balance in the chequing account serves as a buffer against unforeseen disruptions in normal cash inflows.

At the end of the year, the business in the example has $1 million cash on hand (refer to Figure 2-2). This cash balance is available for general business purposes. (If restrictions exist on how it can use its cash balance, the business is obligated to disclose those restrictions.) Is $1 million enough? Interestingly, businesses do not have to comment on their cash balance.

The business has $650,000 in operating liabilities that will come due for payment over the next month or so (refer to Figure 2-2). So, it has enough cash to pay these liabilities. But it doesn't have enough cash on hand to pay its operating liabilities and its $2.08 million interest-bearing debt (refer to Figure 2-2 again). Lenders don't expect a business to keep a cash balance more than the amount of debt; this condition would defeat the purpose of lending money to the business, which is to have the business put the money to good use and be able to pay interest on the debt.

Lenders are more interested in the business's capability to control its cash flows so that when the time comes to pay off loans it will be able to do so. They know that the business's other, non-cash assets will be converted into cash flow. Receivables will be collected, and products held in inventory will be sold and the sales will generate cash flow. So, you shouldn't focus just on cash; throw the net wider and look at the other assets as well.

Taking this broader approach, the business has $1 million cash, $800,000 receivables, and $1.56 million inventory, which adds up to $3.36 million of cash and cash potential. Relative to its $2.73 million total liabilities ($650,000 operating liabilities plus $2.08 million debt), the business looks in pretty good shape. On the other hand, if it turns out that the business is not able to collect its receivables and is not able to sell its products, it would end up in deep trouble.

TIP

One other way to look at a business's cash balance is to express its cash balance in terms of how many days of sales the amount represents. In the example, the business has an ending cash balance equal to 35 days of sales, calculated as follows:

$10,400,000 annual sales revenue ÷ 365 days = $28,493 sales per day

$1,000,000 cash balance ÷ $28,493 sales per day = 35 days

The business's cash balance equals a little more than one month of sales activity, which most lenders and investors would consider adequate.

Can you trust the financial statement numbers?

Whether the financial statements are correct or not depends on the answers to two basic questions:

>> Does the business have a reliable accounting system in place and employ competent accountants?

>> Has top management manipulated the business's accounting methods or deliberately falsified the numbers?

WARNING

Many businesses don't put much effort into keeping their accounting systems up to speed, and they skimp on hiring competent accountants. In short, a risk exists that the financial statements of a business could be incorrect and seriously misleading.

To increase the credibility of their financial statements, many businesses hire independent auditors to examine their accounting systems and records and to express opinions on whether the financial statements present fairly the reality of the company's performance and conditions and the preparation of the statement conforms to established accounting standards. In fact, some business lenders insist on an annual audit by an independent public accounting firm as a condition of making the loan. The outside, non-management investors in a privately owned business could vote to have annual audits of the financial statements. Public companies have no choice; a public company is required to have annual audits by an independent public accounting firm.

Two points: Audits are not cheap, and these audits are not always effective in rooting out financial reporting fraud by high-level managers.

Why no cash distribution from profit?

In this chapter's example, the business did not distribute any of its profit for the year to its owners. Distributions from profit by a business corporation are called *dividends*. (The total amount distributed is divided up among the shareholders, hence the term *dividends*.) Cash distributions from profit to owners are included in the third section of the statement of cash flows (refer to Figure 2-3). But in the example, the business did not make any cash distributions from profit — even though it earned $520,000 net income (refer to Figure 2-1). Why not?

The business realized $400,000 cash flow from its profit-making (operating) activities (refer to Figure 2-3). In most cases, this would be the upper limit on how much cash a business would distribute from profit to its owners. So you might very well ask whether the business should have distributed, say, at least half of its cash flow from profit, or $200,000, to its owners. If you owned 20 percent of the business's ownership shares, you would have received 20 percent, or $40,000, of the distribution. But you got no cash return on your investment in the business. Your shares should be worth more because the profit for the year increased the company's owners' equity. But you did not see any of this increase in your wallet.

REMEMBER

Deciding whether to make cash distributions from profit to shareholders is in the hands of the directors of a business corporation. Its shareowners elect the directors, and in theory the directors act in the best interests of the shareholders. Evidently the directors thought the business had better uses for the $400,000 cash flow from profit than distributing some of it to shareholders. Generally, the main reason for not making cash distributions from profit is to finance the business's growth — to use all the cash flow from profit for expanding the assets needed by the business at the higher sales level. Ideally, the business's directors would explain their decision not to distribute any money from profit to the shareholders. But, generally, no such comments are made in financial reports.

Keeping in Step with Accounting and Financial Reporting Standards

The unimpeded flow of capital is absolutely critical in a free-market economic system and in the international flow of capital between countries. Investors and lenders put their capital to work where they think they can get the best returns on their investments consistent with the risks they're willing to take. To make these decisions, they need the accounting information provided in financial statements of businesses.

Imagine the confusion that would result if every business were permitted to invent its own accounting methods for measuring profit and for putting values on assets and liabilities. What if every business adopted its own individual accounting terminology and followed its own style for presenting financial statements? Such a state of affairs would be a Tower of Babel.

Recognizing Canadian and international standards

The authoritative standards and rules that govern financial accounting and reporting by businesses based in Canada are called *generally accepted accounting principles* (GAAP). When you read the financial statements of a business, you're entitled to assume that the business has fully complied with GAAP in reporting its cash flows, profit-making activities, and financial condition — unless the business makes clear that it has prepared its financial statements using some other basis of accounting or has deviated from GAAP in one or more significant respects.

WARNING

If GAAP are not the basis for preparing its financial statements, a business should make clear which other basis of accounting is being used and should avoid using financial statement titles that are associated with GAAP. For example, if a business such as a farm uses a simple cash receipts and cash disbursements basis of accounting — which falls way short of GAAP — it should not use the terms *income statement* and *balance sheet.* These terms are part and parcel of GAAP, and their use as titles for financial statements implies that the business is using GAAP.

You don't need a lengthy historical discourse on the development of accounting and financial reporting standards in Canada. The general consensus (backed up by law) is that businesses should use consistent accounting methods and terminology. Of course, businesses in different industries have different types of transactions, but the same types of transactions should be accounted for in the same way. That is the goal.

Around 4,000 publicly owned corporations have their shares traded on the Toronto Stock Exchange (TSX). Now, do you really think that all these businesses should use the same accounting methods, terminology, and presentation styles for their financial statements? The correct answer is that all businesses *should* use the same rulebook of GAAP. However, the rulebook permits alternative accounting methods for some transactions. Furthermore, accountants have to interpret the rules as they apply GAAP in actual situations. The devil is in the details.

REMEMBER

In Canada, as in the majority of countries around the globe, GAAP, which include international standards, constitute the gold standard for preparing financial statements of business entities. The presumption is that any deviations from GAAP would cause misleading financial statements. If a business honestly thinks it should deviate from GAAP — to better reflect the economic reality of its transactions or situation — it should make clear that it has not complied with GAAP in one or more respects. If the business does not disclose the deviations from GAAP, the business may have legal exposure to those who relied on the information in its financial report and suffered a loss attributable to the misleading nature of the information.

CANADIAN VERSUS US ACCOUNTING STANDARDS

There are many commonalities between USA and Canada as they are among the most integrated trading partners around the globe, with massive amounts of international commerce conducted on a daily basis. Since many companies operate in both nations, it is important for accounting professionals to understand the differences in Canada and US accounting standards.

Here are a few important points about Canada and USA accounting:

- GAAP USA is often used by Canadian companies that frequently conduct international business and or investors.

- Both the USA and Canada have their own process for certifying accountants. CPA is used both in USA and Canada and they cannot be interchanged.

- When issuing financial statements, Canada does not require IFRS standards of reporting as the USA does.

- Canada and the USA also differ on matters related to reporting assets and liabilities on the companies balance sheets. Canadian GAAP follows the same protocols as the IFRS, which allows assets to be recorded as either date of trade or date of settlement.

Getting to know the Canadian, U.S., and international standard setters

Okay, so everyone reading a financial report is entitled to assume that GAAP have been followed — unless the business clearly discloses that it is using another basis of accounting.

REMEMBER

The basic idea behind the development of GAAP is to measure profit and to value assets and liabilities *consistently* from business to business — to establish broad-scale uniformity in accounting methods for all businesses. The idea is to make sure that all accountants are singing the same tune from the same hymnal. The purpose is also to establish realistic and objective methods for measuring profit and putting values on assets and liabilities. The authoritative bodies write the tunes that accountants have to sing.

Who are these authoritative bodies? Canada has two bodies setting standards for businesses.

>> The main authoritative accounting standards setter is the International Accounting Standards Board (IASB), which is based in London. The standards set by this body are called International Financial Reporting Standards (IFRS) and they have been adopted by Canada for all publicly traded companies. These standards can be found in Part 1 of the *CPA Canada Handbook.*

>> The second body making pronouncements on Canadian GAAP for private enterprises and for keeping these accounting standards up-to-date is the Accounting Standards Board (AcSB) of CPA Canada. The standards set by this body are called Accounting Standards for Private Enterprises (ASPE) and can be found in Part 2 of the *CPA Canada Handbook.*

The body in the United States is the Financial Accounting Standards Board (FASB). Unlike in Canada, the U.S. federal Securities and Exchange Commission (SEC) has broad powers over accounting and financial reporting standards for publicly traded companies.

All GAAP (Canadian, U.S., and international) also include minimum requirements for *disclosure,* which refers to how information is classified and presented in financial statements and to the types of information that have to be included with the financial statements, mainly as notes.

Some people think the rules have become too complicated and far too technical. If you flip through the many parts of the *Handbook,* you'll see why people come to this conclusion. However, if the rules are not specific and detailed enough, different accountants will make different interpretations that will cause inconsistency from one business to the next regarding how profit is measured and how assets and liabilities are reported in the balance sheet. The AcSB was between a rock and a hard place. Consequently, two sets of GAAP were put into place — one for public companies (IFRS) and one for private companies (ASPE). For the most part the AcSB issues rules that are detailed and technical but take care of the major concerns of most businesses.

Going worldwide

Although it's a bit of an overstatement, today the investment of capital knows no borders. Canadian capital is invested in European and other countries, and capital from other countries is invested in Canadian businesses. In short, the flow of capital has become international. Recognizing the need, the AcSB joined the IASB and adopted IFRS for public companies.

The need to make GAAP uniform globally (at least for public companies) also applies to the United States. Of course, political issues and national pride come into play in trying to achieve this goal. The term *harmonization* is favoured, which sidesteps difficult issues regarding the future roles of the FASB and IASB in the issuance of international accounting standards.

One major obstacle deterring the goal of worldwide accounting standards concerns which sort of standards should be issued:

>> The FASB follows a *rules-based* approach. Its pronouncements have been detailed and technical. The idea is to leave little room for differences of interpretation.

>> The IASB favours a *principles-based* method. Under this approach, accounting standards are stated in fairly broad general language and the detailed interpretation of the standards is left to accountants in the field.

The two authoritative bodies have disagreed on some key accounting issues, and the road to convergence of accounting standards will be rocky.

In Canada and internationally, the guidelines are more flexible. Accountants use their professional judgment and experience to decide which method is best in situations where different options for how to account for transactions are available. Accountants use additional sources of GAAP outside the *Handbook* to decide which accounting practice to follow.

No country's economy is an island to itself. The stability, development, and growth of an economy depend on securing capital from both inside and outside the country. The flow of capital across borders by investors and lenders gives enormous impetus for the development of uniform international accounting standards. Stay tuned; in the coming years, there may be more and more convergence of accounting standards in the remaining countries that have not yet adopted IFRS.

Noting a divide between public and private companies

Up until the adoption of IFRS for public companies, GAAP and financial reporting standards were viewed as equally applicable to public companies (generally large corporations) and private (generally smaller) companies. People witnessed a growing distinction between accounting and financial reporting standards for public versus private companies. Although most accountants don't like to admit it, there has always been a de facto divergence in financial reporting practices by private companies compared with the more rigorously enforced standards for public companies.

REMEMBER

It's probably safe to say that the financial reports of most private businesses measure up to GAAP standards in all significant respects. At the same time, however, little doubt exists that the financial reports of some private companies fall short. Private companies do not have many of the accounting problems of large, public companies. For example, many public companies deal in complex derivative instruments, issue stock options to managers, provide highly developed defined-benefit retirement and health benefit plans for their employees, enter into complicated inter-company investment and joint venture operations, have complex organizational structures, and so on. Most private companies do not have to deal with these issues.

Finally, note that smaller private businesses do not have as much money to spend on their accountants and auditors. Big companies can spend big bucks and hire highly qualified accountants. Furthermore, public companies are legally required to have annual audits by independent public accountants. The annual audit keeps a big business up-to-date on accounting and financial reporting standards. Frankly, smaller private companies are somewhat at a disadvantage in keeping up with accounting and financial reporting standards.

Recognizing how income tax methods influence accounting methods

Generally speaking, the income tax accounting rules for determining the annual taxable income of a business are in agreement with GAAP. In other words, the accounting methods used for figuring taxable income and for figuring business profit before income tax are in general agreement. Having said this, several differences do exist. A business may use one accounting method for filing its annual income tax returns and a different method for measuring its annual profit both internally for management reporting and externally for preparing its financial statements to outsiders.

Many people argue that certain income tax accounting methods have had an unhealthy effect on GAAP. If a particular accounting method is allowed for determining annual taxable income, the path of least resistance is for a business to use the same method for preparing its financial statements. For example, the income tax laws permit accelerated methods for depreciating long-lived operating assets — software, computers, tools, and autos and trucks. (Even the cost of buildings can be depreciated over shorter life spans than the actual lives of most buildings.) Other depreciation methods might be more realistic, but many businesses use accelerated depreciation methods both in their income tax returns and in their financial statements.

Following the rules and bending the rules

An often repeated accounting story concerns three people interviewing for an important accounting position. They are asked one key question: "What's 2 plus 2?" The first candidate answers, "It's 4," and is told, "Don't call us, we'll call you." The second candidate answers, "Well, most of the time the answer is 4, but sometimes it's 3 and sometimes it's 5." The third candidate answers: "What do you want the answer to be?" Guess who gets the job. This story exaggerates, of course, but it does have an element of truth.

The point is that interpreting GAAP is not cut and dried. Many accounting standards leave a lot of wiggle room for interpretation. *Guidelines* would be a better word to describe many accounting rules. Deciding how to account for certain transactions and situations requires seasoned judgment and careful analysis of the rules. Furthermore, many estimates have to be made. Deciding on accounting methods requires, above all else, *good faith.*

WARNING

A business might resort to creative accounting to make profit for the period look better, or to make its year-to-year profit less erratic than it really is (which is called *income smoothing*). Like lawyers who know where to find loopholes, accountants can come up with inventive interpretations that stay within the boundaries of GAAP. These creative accounting techniques are also called massaging the numbers. Massaging the numbers can get out of hand and become accounting fraud, also called cooking the books. Massaging the numbers has some basis in honest differences for interpreting the facts. Cooking the books goes way beyond interpreting facts; this fraud consists of *inventing* facts and good old-fashioned chicanery.

Chapter **3**

Computer Options for Your Bookkeeping

A very few small-business owners who have been around awhile still do things the old-fashioned way — keep their books in paper journals and ledgers. However, in this age of technology and instant information, the vast majority of today's businesses computerize their books.

Not only is computerized bookkeeping easier than the pen-and-paper method, but it also minimizes the chance of errors because most of the work that you do to a computerized system's ledgers and journals involves inputting data for transactions on forms that even someone without training in accounting or bookkeeping can understand. The person entering the information doesn't need to know whether something is a debit or a credit (Chapter 1 in Book 4 has an explanation of the difference) because the computerized system takes care of everything.

This chapter explores the two top accounting software packages for small businesses, discusses the basics of setting up your own computerized books, talks about how you can customize a program for your business, and gives you some pointers on converting your manual bookkeeping system to a computerized one.

Surveying Your Software Options

More than 50 different types of accounting software programs are on the market, and all are designed to computerize your bookkeeping. The more sophisticated ones target specific industry needs, such as construction, food services, or utilities, and they can cost thousands of dollars. A quick Internet search unearths the options available to you. Several sites offer demos of their software packages.

Luckily, as a small-business owner, you probably don't need all the bells and whistles offered by the top-of-the-line programs. Instead, two software programs reviewed in this chapter can meet the needs of most small businesses. They may not be fancy, but basic computerized accounting software can do a fine job of helping you keep your books. And you can always upgrade to a more expensive program, if needed, while your business grows.

Software suppliers are slowly phasing out desktop versions of their software in favour of online versions. If you need payroll software, you may find that payment-based cloud versions are a better value because payroll software is an expensive addition to desktop versions of accounting packages.

Online software also provides added security and peace of mind with automated backups stored offsite, in the cloud. QuickBooks Online has iPhone/iPad and Android application for mobile devices. You can link your software to your bank.

The two programs that meet any small business's basic bookkeeping needs are Sage 50cloud Pro and QuickBooks Online by Intuit, which cost around $30 to $50 per month. Both software providers offer a 30-day trial.

Sage 50cloud Pro and QuickBooks Online Essentials include a General Ledger, which allows you to prepare a full trial balance and financial statements. They also include GST/HST and PST for all Canadian provinces. If you are looking at a different software package, make sure it too offers these features. In addition, you can add your accountant to your Quickbooks, so they can pull the information directly to monitor and help prepare your taxes.

REMEMBER

Accounting software packages are updated almost every year because tax laws and laws involving many other aspects of operating a business, such as payroll, change so often. In addition, computer software companies are always improving their products to make computerized accounting programs more user-friendly, so be sure that you always buy the most current version of an accounting software package.

Sage 50cloud and QuickBooks Online offer add-ons and features that you're likely to need, such as the following examples:

>> **Tax updates:** If you have employees and want up-to-date tax information and forms to do your payroll by using your accounting software, you need to buy an update each year, unless you are using the online version. The software suppliers or their distributors charge you a monthly fee for the online package, which gives you access to the updates when you need them.

>> **EFT Direct:** Sage 50 Accounting EFT Direct lets you quickly and easily transfer data to your bank. You can do employee and vendor direct deposits as well as customer pre-authorized debits.

>> **Intelligence Reporting:** Sage 50 Accounting allows you to get customized Microsoft Excel–based business accounting reports, automatically updated with real-time data. With this feature you don't have to export, consolidate, or cut and paste data.

Before you sign on for one of the add-ons, make sure you understand what fees you have to pay. Usually, the software supplier or a distributor advises you of the additional costs whenever you try to do anything that incurs extra fees.

Receipt tracking

Keeping track of receipts is important for business owners so they can ensure they're correctly reporting business expenses to ease their tax burden. Today, using an app and going digital is the best way to organize your receipts. Use your phone to take a picture from an app, and it can be automatically uploaded to software and stored in the cloud. A bonus is that many receipts apps connect to popular accounting software, such as QuickBooks and Sage 50, which are both widely used in Canada.

If you search **receipt app** online, you will get tons of choices. Following are three of the most popular apps:

>> Neat (http://neat.com)

>> Expensify (www.expensify.com)

>> Zoho Expense (http://zoho.com)

Get in the habit of taking a photo of a receipt with the app and then weekly moving them to your folders you created for your system. Then, annually, when you do your taxes you can quickly delete by year, month, and so on, and they will never build up. Most of the apps keep the receipts in the cloud so there is no need to keep the physical copy. If you feel safer keeping a copy on your hard drive, that can also be an option.

Sage 50 Accounting

Sage 50 Accounting used to be known as Simply Accounting Pro. Sage 50 is available in several versions (visit www.sage.com) and is a cost-effective choice for bookkeeping software if you're just starting and don't have sophisticated bookkeeping or accounting needs. This program caters to the bookkeeping novice and even provides an option that lets you avoid accounting jargon by using words such as *purchase* and *vendor* in the icon list, rather than *accounts payable,* when you want to record a purchase of goods from a vendor. The program includes several accounting templates for documents such as sales orders, quotes, receipts, and other basic needs for a variety of industries, including medical/dental, real estate, property management, and retail firms.

Sage 50 Accounting has an integrated feature that allows you to do Employee Direct Deposit or electronic funds transfers (EFTs) for payroll.

If you're working with another software system to manage your business data and want to switch to Sage 50 Accounting, you may be able to import that data directly into your new system. (The program includes information on how to import data.) You can import data from software such as Microsoft Excel (a spreadsheet program) and Access (a database program).

QuickBooks Online

QuickBooks Online offers the best of both worlds: an easy user interface (for the novice) and extensive bookkeeping and accounting features (for the experienced bookkeeper or accountant). More small-business owners today use QuickBooks than any other small-business accounting software package. For additional information on this software, check out https://quickbooks.intuit.com/ as well as the latest edition of *QuickBooks Online For Dummies* by Elaine Marmel (Wiley).

QuickBooks Online Easy Start, priced around $30 per month, takes care of billing and cash transactions for small businesses. If you want to track inventory, create and use budgets, download your online banking info, or integrate your bookkeeping with a point-of-sale package, which integrates cash-register sales, you need to get QuickBooks Online Plus, which will set you back around $50+ a month. You'll need to upgrade even further if you want to create purchase orders, track back orders, and forecast sales and expenses. Determining what version of QuickBooks is best for you really depends on your business needs.

TIP

QuickBooks is the most versatile software if you plan to use other software packages along with it, because it can share data with countless popular business software applications. You can easily share sales, customer, and financial data, too, so you don't have to enter that information twice. To find out whether QuickBooks can share data with the business software applications you're currently using or plan to use, contact Intuit directly at www.intuit.ca.

Setting Up Your Computerized Books

Setting up your software package will probably take less time than you spent researching your options and choosing your software. Both packages discussed in the preceding section have good start-up tutorials to help you set up the books.

Sage 50 Accounting and QuickBooks both produce a number of sample Charts of Accounts, which you can use as starting points to save time. Begin with one of the charts offered by the software, and then tweak the sample chart by adding and deleting accounts to suit your business's needs. Or, if you want, you can start from scratch.

Starting with the basics

In QuickBooks, you start creating your company profile by clicking the gear icon in the top menu bar and choosing Account and Settings. The screen shown in Figure 3-1 appears. Click Company (on the left), and enter all the basic information, including your business address and business number (BN). This information will then appear in other applications, such as your customer invoices. You also enter the tax form and industry in which you operate.

Next, choose Advanced (on the left) and select the first month of your fiscal year (see Figure 3-2). If the calendar year is your accounting period, you don't have to change anything. But if your business is incorporated, which means it can have a fiscal year other than the calendar year (such as September 1 to August 31), you must enter that information. The software will recognize the fiscal year for the part of the accounting cycle that involves closing the books.

TIP

Many retail businesses don't close their books at the end of December because the holiday season isn't a good time for those businesses to close out for the year. Because of gift cards and other new ways to give gifts, retail businesses can see active purchases after the holidays. Therefore, many retail businesses operate on a fiscal year of February 1 to January 31, closing the books well after the holiday season ends.

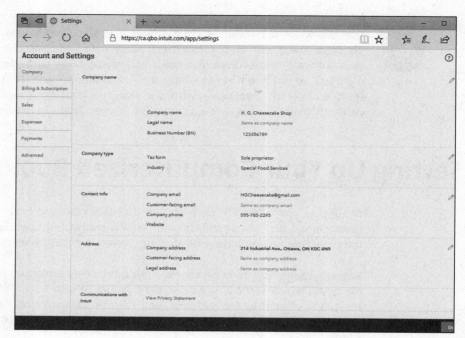

FIGURE 3-1:
As part of the initial setup in QuickBooks, record your basic company information.

Source: QuickBooks

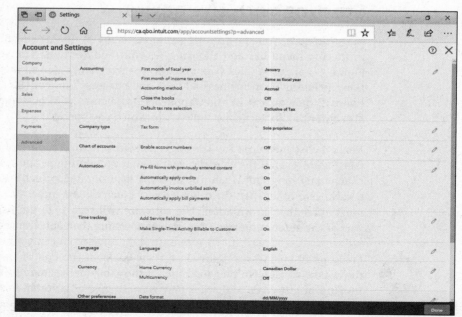

FIGURE 3-2:
Choose your fiscal year, accounting method, and tax default setting in Account and Settings.

Source: QuickBooks

WARNING

If you don't change your accounting period to match your fiscal year when you first record your company's information in your accounting software, you'll have to delete the business from the system and start over.

When using the QuickBooks Advanced command from Account and Settings, choose which accounting method you are using and which default setting you want applied on transactions such as invoicing.

Your choices in the Company and Advanced screens guide QuickBooks to create a preliminary Chart of Accounts for your business, saving you a lot of work. To view this Chart of Accounts, click the gear icon in the top menu bar and select Chart of Accounts. The screen shown in Figure 3-3 appears.

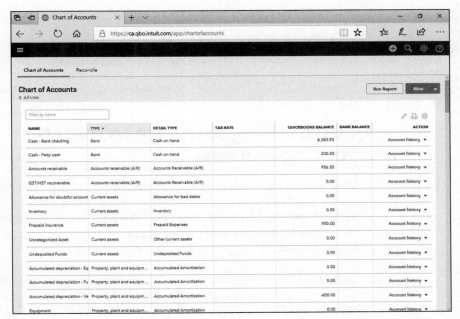

FIGURE 3-3:
Your Chart of Accounts in QuickBooks.

Source: QuickBooks

From here, you can make edits, delete accounts, and run transaction reports by clicking the blue Account History button for any account in your chart.

To add an account to your Chart of Accounts, click the green New button in the upper right. Figure 3-4 shows you the pop-up screen that appears, with an account called Credit Card Visa. You use the Account Types drop-down list to decide which group of accounts this new liability account belongs. Your account type choice determines where this account will appear in your financial reports. (See Chapter 1 in Book 4 for a discussion of the Chart of Accounts.)

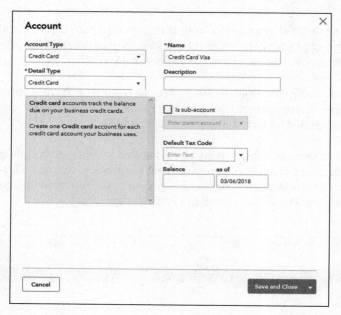

Source: QuickBooks

FIGURE 3-4:
Add accounts in your Quick-Books Chart of Accounts.

Customizing software to match your operations

After you set up the basics (see the preceding section), you can customize the software to fit your business's operations. For example, you can choose the type of invoices and other business forms that you want to use. Where available, you can control the format of forms as they appear on the screen. You access these commands by clicking the gear icon on individual input screens.

You can also input information about your bank accounts and other key financial data. Then you can add opening balances to accounts for customers and suppliers so that you can track future cash transactions. Make your main business bank account the first account listed in your software program, labelled as either Cash — Bank Chequing or just Cash.

After you enter your bank and other financial information, you can enter data unique to your business. If you want to use the program's budgeting features, you enter your budget information before entering other data. Then you add your supplier and customer accounts so that when you start entering transactions, you already have the supplier or customer information in the system. If you don't have any outstanding bills or customer payments due, you can wait and enter supplier and customer information when the need arises.

TIP

If you have payments that you need to make or money that you need to collect from customers, be sure to input that information so that your system is ready when it comes time to pay the bills or input a customer payment on account. Also, you don't want to forget to pay a bill or collect from a customer!

You may be able to import data about your customers, suppliers, and employees from the software package that you're currently using, such as Microsoft Excel or Access. Full instructions for importing data come with the software program you choose.

REMEMBER

Don't panic about entering everything into your computerized system right away. All programs make it easy to add customers, suppliers, and employees at any time.

You need to enter information about whether you collect GST/HST and provincial sales taxes from your customers and, if you do, the sales tax rates. Your software also lets you choose a format for your invoices, set up payroll data, and make arrangements for how you want to pay bills.

Converting your manual bookkeeping to a computerized system

If you're converting a manual bookkeeping system to a computerized system, the conversion takes a bit more time than just starting fresh because you need to be sure that your new system starts with information that matches your current books. The process for entering your initial data varies, depending on the software you choose, so this section doesn't go into detail about that process. To ensure that you properly convert your bookkeeping system, use the information that comes with your software — read the manual, use the online tutorials, review the start-up suggestions that the software makes while you set up the system, and choose the methods that best match your style of operating.

TIP

The best time to convert your pen-and-paper books to computerized versions is at the end of an accounting period. That way, you don't have to do a lot of extra work adding transactions that already occurred during a period. For example, if you decide to computerize your accounting system on March 15, you have to add all the transactions that occurred between March 1 and March 15 into your new system. You may even have to go back to the beginning of the fiscal year. You can make the process much easier by waiting until April 1 to get started, even if you buy the software on March 15. Although you can convert to a computerized accounting system at the end of a month, the best time to do the conversion is at the end of a calendar or fiscal year. Otherwise, you have to input data for all the months of the year that have passed.

Whenever you decide to start your computerized bookkeeping, use the data from the trial balance that you used to close the books at the end of the last fiscal year. In the computerized system, enter the balances in your trial balance for each of the accounts. Asset, Liability, and Equity accounts should have carry-over balances, but Revenue and Expense accounts should have zero balances.

Of course, if you're starting a new business, you don't have a previous trial balance. In that case, you just enter any balances you may have in your Cash accounts, any assets your business may own when it starts, and any liabilities that your business may already owe relating to start-up expenses. You also add any contributions owners made to get the business started in the Equity accounts. You enter these balances in the Journal Entry screen in your software.

TIP

After you enter all the appropriate data, run a series of financial reports, such as an income statement (called Profit and Loss in QuickBooks) and a balance sheet, to be sure that you entered the data correctly and that the software formats the data the way you want. If, for example, you need subtotals in financial statements, you can add that feature to your computerized financial statements or reports right away.

REMEMBER

You need to be sure that you've entered the right numbers, so verify that the new accounting system's financial reports match what you created manually. If the numbers are different, now is the time to figure out why. Otherwise, the reports you do at the end of the accounting period will have the wrong information. If the numbers don't match, don't assume that the error can be in only the data entered. You may find that you made an error in the reports you developed manually. Of course, check your entries first, but if the income statement and balance sheet still don't look right, double-check your old trial balances, as well.

accounts

» **Choosing a balance sheet format**

» **Drawing conclusions from your balance sheet**

» **Sorting out the elements and format of an income statement**

» **Keeping an eye on expenses**

» **Using percentages and ratios**

» **Digging into the income statement details**

Chapter **4**

Reporting Results

eriodically, you want to know where your business stands. Therefore, at the end of each accounting period, you take a snapshot of your business's condition. This snapshot, which is called a *balance sheet* (or sometimes called a *statement of financial position*), gives you a picture of where your business stands — how much it has in assets, how much it owes in liabilities, and how much the owners have invested in the business at a particular point in time.

This chapter explains the key ingredients of a balance sheet and tells you how to pull them all together. You can also find out how to use some analytical tools called *ratios* to see how well your business is doing.

But that's not all you find here. Without one important financial report tool, you'd never know for sure whether your business made a profit. This tool is called the *income statement*, and most businesses prepare one on a monthly basis, as well as quarterly and annually, to get feedback on how well the business is doing financially.

Analysing the income statement and the details behind it can reveal a lot of useful information that can help you make decisions to immediately improve your profits and your business overall. This chapter covers the parts of an income statement, how you develop one, and examples of how you can use it to make business decisions.

Beginning with the Balance Sheet

Basically, creating a balance sheet is like taking a picture of the financial aspects of your business. You put the business name, the title of the statement, and the ending date for the accounting period on which you're reporting at the top of the balance sheet.

REMEMBER

Insert the proper name of the business in the titles of your financial statements. When outside readers look at your reports, they want to know who they're dealing with, and your business's name tells them a lot. For example, an incorporated business has one of the following at the end of its name: Limited (Ltd.), Corporation (Corp.), or Incorporated (Inc.).

Although a balance sheet doesn't tell the entire story about a business, it gives the outside readers some idea of the business's financial position and how it's financed at a particular point in time. For example, a bank needs to decide whether to lend your business some money. Your balance sheet reveals that you already owe a lot of money to other banks and mortgage companies, and so the bank decides that your business is too high a risk and declines your loan request. Here's another example: An outside reader may be someone interested in buying your business. In this case, the reader looks at the balance sheet to help determine the value of the business so that she can decide on a fair purchase price.

The rest of the report summarizes the following:

>> **The business's assets:** Including everything the business owns to stay in operation

>> **The business's debts:** Including any outstanding bills and loans that the business must pay

>> **The owners' equity:** Basically, how much the business owners have invested directly and indirectly in the business

REMEMBER

Assets, liabilities, and equity probably sound familiar — they're the key elements that show whether your books are in balance. If your liabilities plus equity equal assets, your books are in balance. All your bookkeeping efforts are an attempt to keep the books in balance based on this equation, which is covered in Chapter 1 of Book 4.

Gathering Balance Sheet Ingredients

You can find most of the information you need to prepare a balance sheet on your adjusted trial balance, which you can get from your worksheet or from running a trial balance with your computerized accounting system after you have calculated and recorded any necessary adjusting journal entries. (Flip to Chapter 3 in Book 4 for help with choosing computer software options for your bookkeeping.)

To keep this example somewhat simple, we assume that H.G.'s Cheesecake Shop, a fictitious business, has no adjustments for the balance sheet as of June 30, 2020. In the real world, every business needs to adjust something (you usually need to record depreciation) every month, at a minimum.

To prepare the balance sheet illustrations in this chapter, we use the key accounts listed in Table 4-1; these accounts and dollar amounts come from the H.G.'s Cheesecake Shop's trial balance.

TABLE 4-1

Balance Sheet Accounts

Account Name	Balance in Account
Cash	$2,500
Petty Cash	500
Accounts Receivable	1,000
Allowance for Doubtful Accounts	(100)
GST/HST Recoverable	50
Inventory	1,200
Equipment	5,050
Vehicles	30,000
Furniture	5,600
Accumulated Depreciation	(5,000)
Accounts Payable	2,200
GST/HST Payable	250
Bank Line of Credit	600
Bank Loans Payable	20,650
H.G. Capital	17,100

Dividing and listing your assets

The first part of the balance sheet is the Assets section. The first step in developing this section involves dividing your assets into two categories: current assets and non-current assets.

Placing the accounts from your trial balance into groups onto your balance sheet is called *classification*. After you give the proper classification to the individual accounts, you can organize your financial statements into groups of accounts, which enables you to create subtotals (such as current assets) on your balance sheet. These key subtotals allow you and your readers to make a quick comparison to other figures or subtotals in a financial statement or to another financial statement.

For example, an owner may compare the amount of profit on the income statement to the total equity appearing on his business's balance sheet to decide whether he's getting enough of a financial reward or return (profit) for his investment (equity). (You find out how to perform this calculation later in this chapter.)

REMEMBER

The grouping of current and non-current assets and liabilities on the balance sheet is the most valuable classification provided to outside readers. The reader can compare current assets to current liabilities to quickly and easily measure your business's liquidity. In turn, your business's liquidity is defined as your business's ability to pay the debts and liabilities that are due in the next 12 months (current liabilities) with the current assets. You discover how to calculate some key liquidity ratios later in this chapter.

Current assets

Current assets are things your business owns that you can easily convert to cash and that you expect to use in the next 12 months to pay your bills, your employees, and any other debt that comes due. Current assets include cash, *accounts receivable* (money due from customers, net of any allowance for doubtful accounts), short-term investments (including money market mutual funds, share investments, and bond investments), GST/HST recoverable, inventory, and prepaid expenses.

The Cash line item on a balance sheet includes what you have on hand in the cash register, as a float; what you have in the bank, including chequing accounts and savings accounts; and what's in your petty cash box. In most cases, you simply list all these accounts as one item, Cash, on the balance sheet.

H.G.'s Cheesecake Shop's current assets follow:

Cash	$2,500
Petty Cash	500
Accounts Receivable	1,000
Allowance for Doubtful Accounts	(100)
GST/HST Recoverable	50
Inventory	1,200

The bookkeeper totals the Cash and Petty Cash accounts, giving her $3,000, which she lists on the balance sheet as a line item called Cash.

Non-current assets

Non-current assets are things your business owns that you expect to have for more than 12 months. Non-current assets include land, buildings, equipment, furniture, vehicles, and anything else that you expect to have for longer than a year.

Following are H.G.'s Cheesecake Shop's non-current assets:

Equipment	$5,050
Vehicles	30,000
Furniture	5,600
Less: Accumulated Depreciation	(5,000)

Most businesses have more items in the Property, Plant, and Equipment category in the non-current assets section of a balance sheet than H.G.'s Cheesecake Shop. For example, a manufacturing business that has a lot of tools, dies, or moulds created specifically for its manufacturing processes would have a line item called Tools, Dies, and Moulds in this asset group on its balance sheet.

Similarly, if your business owns one or more buildings, you should have a line item labelled Land and another labelled Buildings. And if you lease equipment under certain conditions that resemble a purchase, you classify that equipment as Equipment under Lease.

Some businesses lease their business space and then spend a lot of money fixing that space up. For example, a restaurant may rent a large space and then furnish it according to a desired theme. Money spent on fixing up the space becomes an asset called Leasehold Improvements that you list on the balance sheet in the Property, Plant, and Equipment category of non-current assets.

Everything mentioned so far in this section — land, buildings, capitalized leases, leasehold improvements, and so on — is a *tangible asset,* which is an item that you can touch or hold. Another type of non-current asset is the intangible asset. *Intangible assets* aren't physical objects; common examples are patents, copyrights, and trademarks (all of which are rights granted by the government). Besides these intangible assets, you may also own goodwill. All intangibles assets are useful to the business in earning revenue and have the following descriptions:

>> **Patents:** Give businesses the right to dominate the markets for patented products. When a patent expires, competitors can enter the marketplace for the product that was patented, and the competition helps to lower the price for consumers. For example, pharmaceutical companies patent all their new drugs and therefore are protected as the sole providers of those drugs. When your doctor prescribes a brand-name drug, you're getting a patented product. Generic drugs are products whose patents have run out, meaning that any pharmaceutical business can produce and sell its own version of essentially the same product. See Chapters 1 and 2 in Book 2 for more about patents.

>> **Copyrights:** Protect original works — including books, magazines, articles, newspapers, television shows, movies, music, poetry, and plays — from being copied by anyone other than their creators. For example, this book is copyrighted, so no one can make a copy of any of its contents without the permission of the publisher, John Wiley & Sons, Inc. Flip to Chapter 3 in Book 2 for more about copyrights.

>> **Trademarks:** Give companies ownership of distinguishing words, phrases, symbols, or designs. For example, check out this book's cover to see the registered trademark, *For Dummies,* for this brand. Trademarks can last forever, as long as a business continues to use the trademark and files the proper paperwork periodically with the governments in the countries in which it operates. Consequently, because this type of asset can have a limitless useful life, you may not record any depreciation or amortization. See Chapter 4 in Book 2 for more about trademarks.

>> **Goodwill:** Exists only in relation to a business as a whole. A bookkeeper records goodwill in the books only if someone has purchased the business. Goodwill is somewhat of a specialized asset and has some unique accounting rules surrounding it. If it comes up in your Chart of Accounts, consult your business's accountant to find out what you need to know to properly deal with it.

REMEMBER

To show in financial statements that the book values of non-current assets reduce over time, you either depreciate or amortize them. You depreciate tangible assets in the category of Property, Plant, and Equipment, with the exception of land. You amortize intangible assets, such as patents and copyrights (amortization is similar to depreciation). Each patent or copyright asset has a lifespan based on the number of years the government grants the rights for it. After recording an initial cost for the intangible asset, a business then divides that cost by the number of years it has government protection and writes the resulting amount off each year as an amortization expense, which appears on the income statement. If, for some reason, the business doesn't feel like the asset will be useful during all of its legal life, then you reduce the amount of years used in the calculation to a lower, more reasonable number. You place the sum of the amortization or depreciation expenses that your business has written off to expense during the life of the asset on the balance sheet in a line item called Accumulated Depreciation or Accumulated Amortization (whichever is appropriate for the type of asset).

Acknowledging your debts

The Liabilities section of the balance sheet comes after the Assets section (see the earlier section "Dividing and listing your assets") and shows all the money that your business owes to others, including banks, vendors, governments, financial institutions, mortgage companies, or individuals. Like assets, you divide your liabilities into two categories on the balance sheet:

>> **Current Liabilities:** All bills and debts that you plan to pay within the next 12 months. Accounts appearing in this section include any demand bank loan for an operating line of credit, accounts payable (bills due to vendors and others), GST/HST payable, credit cards payable, all the payroll withholding liability accounts, and the current portion of any long-term debt (for example, if you have a mortgage on your store, the amount of any principal payments due in the next 12 months appear in the current liabilities section).

Whenever a business has a demand bank loan, the business has to include the unpaid principal balance of this loan with current liabilities. (With a *demand bank loan,* if at any time the bank doesn't feel comfortable with your financial position or if you overstep the limits set down in the loan agreement, the bank can demand a full principal repayment within an extremely short period of time.) Because the business has the looming possibility that it may have to repay this loan balance quickly, accounting rules require that the business groups the loan with current liabilities.

>> **Non-current Liabilities:** All debts you owe to lenders that your business is required to pay with due dates beyond 12 months. Mortgages payable (for the principal amount due beyond the next 12 months), loans payable, and notes and bonds payable are common accounts in the non-current liabilities section of the balance sheet.

TIP

Most businesses try to minimize their current liabilities that carry interest charges because the interest rates on short-term loans, such as credit cards, are usually much higher than those on loans that have long terms. While you manage your business's liabilities, always look for ways to minimize your interest payments by seeking long-term loans that have lower interest rates than you can get on a credit card or short-term loan.

H.G.'s Cheesecake Shop's balance sheet has the following accounts in its liabilities section:

Current Liabilities:

Accounts Payable	$2,200
GST/HST Payable	250
Bank Line of Credit	600

Non-current Liabilities:

Bank Loans Payable	20,650

Naming your owners' investments

Every business has investors. Even a small mom-and-pop grocery store requires money up front to get the business on its feet. You report investments that individuals or other businesses make into the business on the balance sheet as *equity*. The line items that appear in a balance sheet's Equity section vary, depending on whether the business is incorporated. (Businesses incorporate primarily to minimize the owners' personal legal liabilities.)

If you're preparing the books for a sole-proprietorship business, the Equity section of your balance sheet should contain a single Capital account for the owner. If the business is a partnership, you need to list a Capital account for each partner, with the partner's name as part of the account title. Capital accounts record all money or other assets invested by the owners to start up the business, as well as any additional contributions they make after the start-up phase. You also have a Drawings account for each owner, which tracks all money that each owner takes out of the business during the year. You don't list the Drawing accounts on the balance sheet but you do reduce the Capital account by the amount of the Drawings account to arrive at a net investment by the owner reported on the balance sheet.

For a business that's incorporated, the Equity section of the balance sheet should contain the following accounts, at a minimum:

>> **Common Shares:** Portions of ownership in the business, purchased as investments by business owners. The units of ownership are *shares.* Each share carries a voting right for the owner of the share.

>> **Retained Earnings:** All profits that shareholders have reinvested in the corporation.

Because H.G.'s Cheesecake Shop is a sole proprietorship, a single account appears in the Equity section of its balance sheet:

H.G. Capital	$17,100

This amount represents the balance in the owner's Capital account after you close the income statement accounts and the Drawings account at the end of the year. The Capital account increases by the net profit and decreases by any drawings taken by the owner during the year.

Pulling Together the Final Balance Sheet

After you group together all your accounts (see the earlier section "Gathering Balance Sheet Ingredients"), you're ready to produce a balance sheet. Businesses usually choose between two common formats for their balance sheets: the Account format or the Report format. The same line items appear in both formats; the only difference is the way in which you lay out the information on the page.

TIP

If you use a computerized accounting system, you can take advantage of its report function to automatically generate your balance sheets. These balance sheets give you a snapshot of the business's financial position, but they may require adjustments before you prepare your financial statement for external use. One key adjustment you'll likely have to make involves your Inventory account. If you're using a periodic inventory system, your computer software isn't keeping track of all the ins and outs of the purchases and sales transactions involving your inventory. You must adjust your Inventory balance sheet account to the amount left on hand after you do a physical count.

Account format

The Account format is a two-column layout that has Assets on one side, and Liabilities and Equity on the other side. Here's how the balance sheet of H.G.'s Cheesecake Shop on June 30, 2020, looks by using the Account format:

H.G.'s Cheesecake Shop

Balance Sheet

June 30, 2020

Current Assets		Current Liabilities	
Cash	$3,000	Accounts payable	$2,200
Accounts receivable (net)	900	Bank loan payable	600
GST/HST receivable	50	GST/HST payable	250
Inventory	1,200		
Total current assets	$5,150	Total current liabilities	$3,050
Non-current Assets		**Non-current Liabilities**	
Equipment	$5,050	Loans payable	$20,650
Furniture	5,600	Total liabilities	$23,700
Vehicles	30,000		
Accumulated depreciation	(5,000)	**Equity**	
Total non-current assets	$35,650	H.G. Capital	$17,100
Total assets	$40,800	Total liabilities and equity	$40,800

Report format

The Report format is a one-column layout that shows assets first, then liabilities, and then equity.

Here's the balance sheet of H.G.'s Cheesecake Shop on June 30, 2020, using the Report format:

H.G.'s Cheesecake Shop

Balance Sheet

June 30, 2020

Current Assets		
Cash	$3,000	
Accounts receivable (net)	900	
GST/HST receivable	50	
Inventory	1,200	
Total current assets		$5,150
Non-current Assets		
Equipment	$5,050	
Furniture	5,600	
Vehicles	30,000	
Accumulated depreciation	(5,000)	
Total non-current assets		$35,650
Total assets		$40,800
Current Liabilities		
Accounts payable		$2,200
Bank line of credit		600
GST/HST payable		250
Total current liabilities		$3,050
Non-current Liabilities		
Bank loans payable		$20,650
Total liabilities		$23,700
Equity		
H.G. Capital		$17,100
Total liabilities and owner's equity		$40,800

Putting Your Balance Sheet to Work

With a complete balance sheet in your hands, you can analyse the numbers through a series of ratio tests to check your cash status and track your debt. Because banks and potential investors use these types of tests to determine whether to loan money to or invest in your business, run these tests yourself before you seek loans or investors. Ultimately, the ratio tests in the following sections can help you determine whether your business is in a strong position.

Testing your liquidity

When you approach a bank or other financial institution for a loan, you can expect the lender to use two ratios to test your liquidity position: the current ratio and the acid test ratio (also known as the *quick ratio*). A business has a good liquidity position when it can show that it has the ability to pay off its bills when they're due without experiencing a serious cash crunch.

Current ratio

This ratio compares your current assets to your current liabilities. It provides a quick glimpse of your business's capability to pay its bills.

The formula for calculating the current ratio is:

Current assets ÷ Current liabilities = Current ratio

The following equation calculates the current ratio for H.G.'s Cheesecake Shop:

$5,150 ÷ $3,050 = 1.69

REMEMBER

Lenders usually look for current ratios of 1.20 to 2.00, so any bank would consider a current ratio of 1.69 a good sign. A current ratio less than 1.00 is considered a danger sign because it indicates the business doesn't have enough current assets to pay its current bills.

WARNING

A current ratio greater than 2.00 may indicate that your business isn't investing its assets well and may be able to make better use of its current assets. For example, if your business holds a lot of cash, you may want to invest that money in some non-current assets, such as additional equipment, that you need to help grow the business.

Acid test (quick) ratio

The acid test ratio uses only the financial figures in your business's Cash, Short-Term Investments, and Accounts Receivable accounts. Although the acid test ratio is similar to the current ratio in that it examines current assets and liabilities, the acid test ratio is a stricter test of your business's liquidity. The assets part of this calculation doesn't include inventory because you can't always convert inventory to cash as quickly as other current assets and because, in a slow market, selling your inventory may take a while.

REMEMBER

Many lenders prefer the acid test ratio when determining whether to give you a loan because of this ratio's strictness.

Follow these steps to calculate your business's acid test ratio:

1. **Determine your quick assets:**

Cash + Short-term investments + Accounts receivable = Quick assets

2. **Calculate your quick ratio:**

Quick assets ÷ Current liabilities = Quick ratio

The following calculations give you an example of an acid test ratio:

$3,000 + $900 + $50 = $3,950 (quick assets)

$3,950 ÷ $3,050 = 1.30 (acid test ratio)

REMEMBER

Lenders consider a business that has an acid test ratio around 1.0 to be in good condition. An acid test ratio less than 1.0 indicates that the business may have to sell some of its short-term investments or take on additional debt until it can sell more of its inventory.

Assessing your debt

Before you even consider whether to take on additional debt, you should always check out your present debt condition. One common ratio that you can use to assess your business's debt position is the *debt-to-equity ratio.* This ratio compares what your business owes to what your business owns.

Follow these steps to calculate your debt-to-equity ratio:

1. **Calculate your total debt:**

Current liabilities + Non-current liabilities = Total debt

2. **Calculate your debt-to-equity ratio:**

Total debt ÷ Equity = Debt-to-equity ratio

The following calculation gives you the debt-to-equity ratio for H.G.'s Cheesecake Shop on June 30, 2020:

$2,200 + $600 + $250 + $20,650 = $23,700 (total debt)

$23,700 ÷ $17,100 = 1.39 (debt-to-equity ratio)

REMEMBER

Lenders like to see a debt-to-equity ratio close to 1.0 because it indicates that the amount of debt is equal to the amount of equity. Because H.G.'s Cheesecake Shop has a debt-to-equity ratio of 1.39, most banks probably wouldn't loan it any money until either it lowered its debt levels or the owners put more money into the business.

Introducing the Income Statement

Did your business make any money? You can find the answer in your *income statement*, the financial report that summarizes all the sales and revenue activities, costs of producing or buying the goods or services sold, and expenses incurred to run the business.

Income statements summarize the financial activities of a business during a particular accounting period (which can be a month, quarter, year, or some other period of time that makes sense for a business's needs).

REMEMBER

Often, bookkeepers include three accounting periods on an income statement: the current period and two prior periods. So, a monthly statement shows the current month and the two previous months; a quarterly statement shows the current quarter and the two previous quarters; and an annual statement shows the current year and the two previous years. Providing this much information gives income statement readers a view of the business's earning trends.

Organizing the accounts from your trial balance and placing them into groups in your income statement is called *classification*. Deciding which expenses belong in a particular group depends on what you want to emphasize and what the people looking at the financial statement want to see. Although you don't have to, you may choose to classify your business's expenses by either their nature or their function.

The Employee Benefit Costs item on an income statement provides an example of the classification of an expense based on its nature. On the other hand, you can group this expense with others in the more general Administrative Expenses item, classifying the employee benefits costs as an expense, in accordance with their function.

The classification and grouping of accounts allows you to create subtotals that your readers can use to make easy comparisons within a financial statement or with another financial statement. These number comparisons often result in ratios, which managers or bankers, for example, use as tools for analysis because they want a quick measure of the performance of the business. We look at some key ratios in the later section "Testing Profits."

The seven key lines that make up an income statement classified by function are

>> **Net Sales or Revenue:** The total amount of money taken in from selling the business's goods or services. You calculate this amount by totalling all the sales or revenue accounts, less any sales returns. You label the top line of the income statement as either Sales or Revenues; either is okay.

>> **Cost of Goods Sold:** How much a business spent to buy or make the goods that it sold during the accounting period in review. We show you how to calculate cost of goods sold in the later section "Finding cost of goods sold."

>> **Gross Profit:** How much a business made before taking into account operations expenses, calculated by subtracting the Cost of Goods Sold figure from the Net Sales or Revenue figure. Gross profit is a subtotal and doesn't represent an account in the General Ledger.

>> **Operating Expenses:** How much the business spent on operations. Qualifying expenses include administrative fees, salaries, advertising, utilities, rent, and other operations expenses. You add all the Expense accounts that appear on your income statement to get this total.

>> **Other Income:** How much a business has earned in rental revenue or interest income from some of its savings or investments.

>> **Other Expenses:** How much the business spent on financing (in the form of interest costs).

>> **Profit or Loss:** Whether the business made a profit or loss during the accounting period in review, calculated by subtracting total operating expenses from gross profit, adding any other income, and subtracting other expenses.

Figure 4-1 shows you the kind of detailed income statements (referred to as Profit and Loss statements by QuickBooks) that can be generated automatically in different formats by your QuickBooks software. See Chapter 3 in Book 4 for more about QuickBooks and other computer software for bookkeeping.

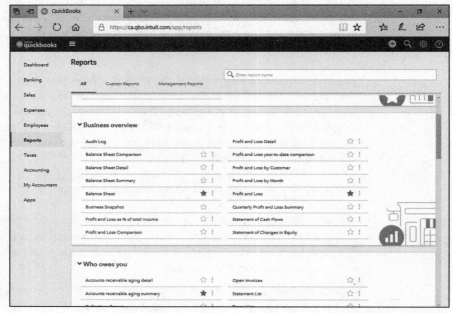

FIGURE 4-1:
The QuickBooks Reports menu lets you choose from several financial statement formats.

Source: QuickBooks

Formatting the Income Statement

Before you create your business's income statement, you have to choose a format in which to organize your financial information. You have two options to choose from: the single-step format or the multistep format. They contain the same information but present it in slightly different ways.

The *single-step format* groups all data into two categories: revenue and expenses. The *multistep format* divides the income statement into several sections and gives the reader some key subtotals, which make analysing the data easier.

REMEMBER

The single-step format allows readers to calculate the same subtotals that appear in the multistep format, but those calculations mean more work for the reader. Therefore, most businesses that sell inventory choose the multistep format so that people inside and outside the organization can more easily analyse the business's income statement.

Here's an example of a basic income statement prepared in the single-step format for H.G.'s Cheesecake Shop using imaginary amounts:

Revenues		
Net sales	$28,500	
Interest income	150	
Total revenues		$28,650
Expenses		
Cost of goods sold	16,300	
Depreciation	1,200	
Rent	1,000	
Salaries	3,500	
Supplies	300	
Interest expense	250	
Total expenses		22,550
Profit		**$6,100**

Using the same numbers, here's a basic income statement prepared in the multistep format:

Revenues		
Net sales	$28,500	
Cost of goods sold	16,300	
Gross profit		$12,200
Operating expenses		
Depreciation	1,200	
Rent	1,000	
Salaries	3,500	
Supplies	300	
Total operating expenses		6,000
Profit from operations		6,200

Other income		
Interest income		<u>150</u>
		6,350
Other expenses		
Interest expense		<u>250</u>
Profit		$6,100

Preparing the Income Statement

Before you can prepare your income statement, you have to calculate net sales and cost of goods sold by using information that appears on your worksheet, or preferably on the computerized trial balance. The following sections use the amounts reported on the H.G.'s Cheesecake Shop worksheet that appears in Figure 4-2.

Finding net sales

Net sales is a total of all your sales minus any sales discounts, returns, and allowances. To calculate net sales, you look at the worksheet's line items regarding sales, discounts, and any sales returns and allowances. H.G.'s Cheesecake Shop's worksheet lists Sales of $21,600 and $150 for Sales Returns and Allowances given to customers. To find your net sales, you subtract the sales discounts from your total sales amount; so, H.G.'s Cheesecake Shop has $21,450 net sales.

Finding cost of goods sold

Cost of goods sold is the total amount your business spent to buy or make the goods that you sold. To calculate this amount for a business that buys its finished products from another business to sell them to customers, you start with the book value of the business's *opening inventory* (the amount in the Inventory account at the beginning of the accounting period), add all purchases of new inventory (net of any purchase discounts or returns and allowances, and adding freight-in), and then subtract any *ending inventory* (inventory that's still on the store shelves or in the warehouse; it appears on the balance sheet, which is explained earlier in this chapter).

H. G.'s Cheesecake Shop Worksheet Month ended June 30, 2020						
	Trial Balance		Income Statement		Balance Sheet	
Account	Debit	Credit	Debit	Credit	Debit	Credit
Cash - Petty Cash	500				500	
Cash - Bank Chequing	2,500				2,500	
Accounts Receivable	1,000				1,000	
Allowance for Doubtful Accounts		100				100
GST/HST Recoverable	50				50	
Inventory	1,200				1,200	
Equipment	5,050				5,050	
Vehicle	30,000				30,000	
Furniture	5,600				5,600	
Accumulated Depreciation		5,000				5,000
Accounts Payable		2,200				2,200
GST/HST Payable		250				250
Bank Line of Credit		600				600
Bank Loans Payable		20,650				20,650
H.G. Capital		19,200				19,200
H.G. Drawings	4,000				4,000	
Sales		21,600		21,600		
Sales Returns & Allowances	150		150			
Purchases	12,300		12,300			
Purchase Returns & Allowances		180		180		
Automobile Expense	370		370			
Computer & Internet Expenses	220		220			
Depreciation Expense	600		600			
Insurance Expense	400		400			
Interest Expense	70		70			
Office Supplies Expense	140		140			
Payroll Benefits Expense	270		270			
Rent Expense	1,000		1,000			
Salaries and Wages Expense	3,600		3,600			
Telephone Expense	310		310			
Utilities Expense	450		450			
Totals	69,780	69,780	19,880	21,780	49,900	48,000
Net income			1,900			1,900
Total	69,780	69,780	21,780	21,780	49,900	49,900

FIGURE 4-2:
This sample worksheet shows the first step in developing a business's financial statements.

The following is a basic cost-of-goods-sold calculation with imaginary amounts:

Opening inventory + Purchases = Goods available for sale

$100 + $1,000 = $1,100

Goods available for sale – Ending inventory = Cost of goods sold

$1,100 – $200 = $900

To simplify the example for calculating cost of goods sold, assume that the book values for opening inventory (the book value of the inventory at the beginning of the accounting period) and ending inventory (the book value of the inventory at the end of the accounting period) are the same. So, to calculate H.G.'s Cheesecake Shop's cost of goods sold, you need only two key lines of its worksheet: the Purchases made and the Purchase Returns and Allowances received to lower the purchase cost:

Purchases – Purchases returns and allowances = Cost of goods sold

$12,300 – $180 = $12,120

Drawing remaining amounts from your worksheet

After you calculate net sales and cost of goods sold (see the preceding sections), you can use the rest of the numbers from your worksheet to prepare the income statement.

Showing three accounting periods on an income statement is standard practice (refer to the earlier section "Introducing the Income Statement"), so Table 4-2 shows what an income statement spanning three months looks like (but shows actual numbers for only one month).

TABLE 4-2   **H.G.'s Cheesecake Shop's Monthly Income Statement for June 2020**

Months Ended	June	May	April
Revenues			
Net sales	$21,450		
Cost of goods sold	12,120		
Gross profit	9,330		
Operating expenses			
Automobile expense	370		
Computer and Internet expenses	220		
Depreciation expense	600		

Insurance expense	400		
Office supplies expense	140		
Payroll benefits expense	270		
Rent expense	1,000		
Salaries and wages expense	3,600		
Telephone expense	310		
Utilities expense	450		
Total operating expenses	7,360		
Profit from operations	1,970		
Other expenses			
Interest expense	<u>70</u>		
Profit	$1,900		

TIP

You and anyone else in-house are likely to want to see the type of detail shown in the example in Table 4-2, but most business owners prefer not to show all their operating details to outsiders. Note that the more information you give to outsiders, the more they know about how your business operates and the more easily they can come up with strategies to compete with your business. Therefore, consider summarizing the Expense section in income statements that you plan to distribute externally. For external statements, many businesses group all advertising and promotions expenses into one line item and all administrative expenses into another line item.

Gauging your cost of goods sold

Businesses that make their own products, rather than buy them for future sale, must track inventory at three different levels:

>> **Raw Materials:** Purchases of all items used to make your business's products. For example, a fudge shop buys all the ingredients to make the fudge it sells, so the cost of any inventory on hand that the business hasn't yet used to make fudge should appear in the Raw Materials line item.

>> **Work-in-Process Inventory:** The book value of any products that your business is making but can't yet sell. A fudge shop probably wouldn't have anything in this line item, considering fudge doesn't take more than a few

hours to make. However, many manufacturing companies take weeks or months to produce products and therefore usually have some portion of the inventory book value in this line item.

>> **Finished-Goods Inventory:** The value of inventory that a business has ready for sale. (For a business that doesn't make its own products, Finished-Goods Inventory is the same as the Inventory line item.)

TIP

If you keep the books for a business that manufactures its own products, you can use a computerized accounting system to track the various inventory accounts described in the preceding list. However, your basic accounting system software can't cut it — you need an advanced package to track multiple inventory types. See Chapter 3 in Book 4 for an introduction to computer software options for bookkeeping.

Deciphering Gross Profit

Business owners must carefully watch their gross profit trends on monthly income statements. Gross profit trends that appear lower from one month to the next can mean one of two things: Sales revenue is down, or cost of goods sold is up (or both).

If revenue is down month-to-month, you may need to quickly figure out why and fix the problem to meet your sales goals for the year. Or, by examining sales figures for the same month in previous years, you may determine that the drop is just a normal sales slowdown given the time of year, so you don't need to hit the panic button.

WARNING

If a downward profit trend at a particular time of year isn't normal for your business, it may be a sign that a competitor's successfully drawing customers away from your business, or it may indicate that customers are dissatisfied with some aspect of the goods or services you supply. Whatever the reason, preparing a monthly income statement gives you the ammunition you need to quickly find and fix a problem, thereby minimizing any negative hit to your yearly profits.

TIP

In addition to sales revenue, cost of goods sold can also be a big factor in a downward profit trend. For example, if the amount you spend to purchase products that you then sell goes up, your gross profit goes down. As a business owner, you need to do one of five things if the costs of goods sold are reducing your gross profit:

- >> Find a new supplier who can provide the goods more cheaply.

- >> Increase your prices, as long as you don't lose sales because of the increase.

- >> Increase your volume of sales so that you can sell more products and meet your annual profit goals.

- >> Reduce other expenses to offset the additional product costs.

- >> Accept the fact that your annual profit will be lower than expected.

The sooner you find out that you have a problem with costs, the faster you can find a solution and minimize any reduction in your annual profit goals.

Monitoring Expenses

The Expenses section of your income statement gives you a good summary of all the money you spent to keep your business operating that didn't directly relate to the sale of an individual good or service. For example, businesses usually use advertising both to bring customers in and with the hopes of selling many different types of products. So you should list advertising as an expense, rather than a cost of goods sold. After all, rarely can you link an advertisement to the sale of an individual product. You also can't directly connect the administrative expenses that go into running a business — such as rent, wages and salaries, office costs, and so on — with specific sales.

REMEMBER

A business owner watches her expense trends closely to be sure that costs don't creep upwards and lower the business's bottom line. Any cost cutting that you can do on the expense side can definitely increase your bottom-line profit.

Using the Income Statement to Make Business Decisions

Many business owners compare their income statement trends by using percentages, rather than the actual numbers. You can calculate these percentages easily enough — simply divide each line item by the Net Sales appearing at the top of the income statement. Table 4-3 shows a business's percentage breakdown for one month.

TABLE 4-3

H.G.'s Cheesecake Shop's Monthly Income Statement for June 2020 with Percentage of Net Sales

Month Ended	June	
Revenues		
Net sales	$21,450	100.0%
Cost of goods sold	12,120	56.5%
Gross profit	9,330	43.5%
Operating expenses		
Automobile expense	370	1.7%
Computer and Internet expenses	220	1.0%
Depreciation expense	600	2.8%
Insurance expense	400	1.9%
Office supplies expense	140	0.7%
Payroll benefits expense	270	1.3%
Rent expense	1,000	4.6%
Salaries and wages expense	3,600	16.8%
Telephone expense	310	1.4%
Utilities expense	450	2.1%
Total operating expenses	7,360	34.3%
Profit from operations	1,970	9.2%
Other expenses		
Interest expense	70	0.3%
Profit	$1,900	8.9%

Looking at this percentage breakdown, you can see that H.G.'s Cheesecake Shop had a gross profit of 43.5 percent in June, and its cost of goods sold was 56.5 percent. If the prior month's cost of goods sold was only 52 percent, for example, the business owner would need to find out why the cost of the goods used to make his product likely went up. If the owner doesn't take action to change the trend of increasing cost of goods sold, the business will make a lot less profit.

You may want to see how your income statement results compare to industry trends for similar businesses that have similar revenues; this process is called *benchmarking.* By comparing results, you can find out whether your costs and expenses are reasonable for the type of business you operate, and you can identify areas in which you have room to improve your profitability. You also may spot some red flags related to line items for which you spend much more than the average.

WARNING

You may find locating financial information truly comparable to yours that you can use for benchmarking more difficult than you may expect. The vast majority of small businesses are privately owned, so you don't find their information readily available. Some of the information that you can find concerns businesses that are much larger than yours and can consequently achieve huge economies of scale for some of their expenses. Take any information that you find with a grain of salt and use it only as a guide, rather than a rule.

TIP

To obtain industry trends for businesses similar to yours, for a fee, visit www.bizminer.com. For free business statistics and financial ratios, visit www.bizstats.com or visit the Government of Canada site for Canadian Industry Statistics at www.ic.gc.ca/app/scr/app/cis/search-recherche?lang=eng. To use the statistics tool on these website, select the industry that best matches the one your business operates in, such as Retail: Vehicle Dealers, and review the resulting average profitability and expense percentages for businesses in the same industry.

Testing Profits

With a completed income statement, you can do a number of ratio calculations of your business's profitability. You certainly want to know how well your business did in comparison to other similar businesses. You also want to be able to gauge your *return* on your business.

Three common tests are return on sales (ROS), return on assets (ROA), and return on equity (ROE). These ratios have much more meaning if you can find industry averages for your particular type of business so that you can compare your results.

TIP

When you're looking at the profit of a small, owner-managed business, ask yourself this question: Did the owner get paid for her work? Many mom-and-pop operations have few, if any, employees. The owners don't take a salary from the business. Instead, they live off the profits of the business. If that's the case for your business, you need to make some adjustments to the numbers to make a comparison with another business that has employees (or vice versa). You want to level out the playing field between the two businesses in your comparison. You can either add a salary to the non-salaried business or reduce the wages and salaries expenses from the business that has employees.

When looking at apparently comparable income statements, watch for another line item: Income Taxes. If one of the businesses is incorporated and therefore must pay income taxes, and the other business isn't incorporated (so it doesn't pay income taxes), you can't compare the results of the two businesses. If you want to compare your unincorporated business with an incorporated one, use that business's subtotal of profit before taxes to make your comparisons (or compare your incorporated business's subtotal with an unincorporated business's total profit).

Return on sales

The return on sales (ROS) ratio tells you how efficiently your business runs its operations. Some accountants and investors use the term *profit margin,* which is essentially the same ratio. Using the information on your income statement, you can measure how much profit your business produced per dollar of sales and how much extra cash you brought in per sale.

You calculate ROS by dividing profit (before income taxes) by net sales. H.G.'s Cheesecake Shop had a profit of $1,900 and net sales of $21,600. (If your business isn't a corporation, you don't have to factor in any business income taxes because only corporations pay income taxes.) Here's H.G.'s Cheesecake Shop's calculation of ROS:

Profit before income taxes ÷ Net sales = Return on sales

$1,900 ÷ $21,450 = 8.86%

As you can see from this calculation, H.G.'s Cheesecake Shop made approximately 9 cents on each dollar of sales. To determine whether the ROS that you calculate for your business calls for celebration, you need to find the ROS ratios for similar businesses.

Return on assets

The return on assets (ROA) ratio tests how well your business uses its assets to generate profits. If your business's ROA is the same as or higher than similar companies' ROA ratios, you're doing a good job managing your assets.

To calculate ROA, you divide profit by total assets. H.G.'s Cheesecake Shop has on its balance sheet and in its worksheet total assets of $40,800. The business's profit was $1,900. Here's H.G. Cheesecake Shop's calculation of ROA:

Profit ÷ Total assets = Return on assets

$1,900 ÷ $40,800 = 4.66%

This calculation shows that H.G.'s Cheesecake Shop made approximately 4.6 cents or 4.66 percent on each dollar of assets it held.

REMEMBER

ROA can vary significantly, depending on the type of industry in which you operate. For example, if your business requires you to maintain a lot of expensive equipment, such as a manufacturing firm, you have a much lower ROA than a service business that doesn't need as many assets. ROA can range from less than 5 percent for manufacturing companies that require a large investment in machinery and factories to as high as 20 percent or even higher for service companies that have few assets.

Return on equity

To measure how successfully your business earned money for its owners or investors, calculate the return on equity (ROE) ratio. This ratio almost always looks better than the return on assets (refer to the preceding section) because ROE doesn't take debt into consideration.

You calculate ROE by dividing profit by shareholders' or owner's equity. The balance of the H.G. Capital account, which represents the only owner's equity on H.G.'s Cheesecake Shop's balance sheet of June 30, 2020, can be obtained by adding the beginning balance of $19,200 and the profit for June of $1,900 less drawings of $4,000 to get $17,100. As was the case for the revenue and expense accounts used for preparing the income statement, these amounts appear in the worksheet. The following shows H.G.'s Cheesecake Shop's calculation of ROE:

Profit ÷ Shareholders' or owners' equity = Return on Equity

$1,900 ÷ $17,100 = 11.11%

The ROE for H.G.'s Cheesecake Shop is 2.4 times larger than the ROA, demonstrating a relatively high level of liabilities compared to equity on its balance sheet.

Branching Out with Income Statement Data

REMEMBER

The income statement you produce for external use — banks and investors — may look very different from the one that you produce for in-house use by owners or managers. Most business owners prefer to provide the minimum amount of detail necessary to satisfy external users of their financial statements. For instance, they prefer to deliver summaries of expenses, rather than line-by-line expense details;

a net sales figure without reporting all the detail about discounts, returns, and allowances; and a cost of goods sold figure without reporting all the detail about how you calculated that figure.

Internally, the contents of the income statement are a different story. With more detail, a business's managers can better make accurate business decisions. Most businesses develop detailed reports based on the data collected to develop the income statement. Bookkeepers commonly pull items such as discounts, returns, and allowances out of income statements and break them down into further detail:

>> **Discounts:** Reductions on the retail price as part of a special sale. Discounts may also be in the form of volume discounts provided to customers who buy large amounts of the business's products. For example, a store may offer a 10 percent discount to customers who buy 20 or more of the same item at one time. To put their net sales numbers in perspective, business owners and managers must track how much they reduce their revenues to attract sales.

>> **Returns and allowances:** Transactions in which a significant reduction in price is granted to resolve a dispute or in which items are returned by your customer for any reason — not the right size, damaged, defective, and so on. If a business's number of returns increases dramatically, a larger problem may be the cause; therefore, business owners need to track these numbers carefully to identify and resolve any problems with the items that they sell.

Another section of the income statement that you're likely to break down into more detail for internal use is the Cost of Goods Sold line item. Basically, you present the detail collected to calculate that line item — including beginning inventory, ending inventory, purchases, freight-in costs, purchase discounts, and purchase returns and allowances — in a separate report. (Find out how to calculate the cost of goods sold in the earlier section "Finding cost of goods sold.")

TIP

You can generate an unlimited number of internal reports from the detail that goes into your income statement and other financial statements. For example, many businesses design a report that looks at month-to-month trends in revenue, cost of goods sold, and income. In fact, you can set up your computerized accounting system (if you use one; see Chapter 3 in Book 4) to automatically generate this report and other custom-designed reports. Using your computerized system, you can produce these reports at any time during the month if you want to see how close you are to meeting your month-end, quarter-end, or year-end goal.

TIP

Many businesses also design a report that compares actual spending to the budget. On this report, each of the income statement line items appears with its planned budget figures and the actual figures. When you review this report, you flag any line item that's significantly higher or lower than expected, and then research that item to find a reason for the difference.

5

Human
Resources

Contents at a Glance

Chapter **1**

Recruiting the Right People

Recruiting and hiring good employees is arguably the most critical of all the areas you're responsible for overseeing in your business. And it's not a simple matter of filling job openings. More than ever, successful hiring is a multidimensional process. It is rooted, above all, in your ability to know your business's strategic needs; you may need to change the way you view the hiring process, and take a step back and take a long-term view of your specific business needs so you can find the right combination of resources.

A lot is riding on choosing the right candidate — but don't panic. Most bad hiring decisions are avoidable, assuming that you and others in your business approach the process with respect, understanding, and discipline. This chapter is full of information. It takes you through the steps of recruiting, from drafting the job description to conducting effective interviews and making the final offer of employment.

Thinking about Hiring in a New Way

The traditional hiring notion of "finding the best people to fill job openings" has been replaced by a much more dynamic concept. It's generally referred to as *strategic staffing*, which means putting together a combination of human resources — both internal and external — that are strategically keyed to the needs of the business and the realities of the labour market. This hiring approach is based on the immediate and long-term needs of the business, as opposed to the specs of a particular job.

Table 1-1 shows the difference between the traditional approach to hiring and the strategic staffing model.

TABLE 1-1 **Paradigms: Old and New**

Old Staffing Paradigm	Strategic Staffing
Think "job."	Think tasks and responsibilities that are keyed to business goals and enhance a business's ability to compete.
Create a set of job "specs."	Determine which competencies and skills are necessary to produce outstanding performance in any particular function.
Find the person who best "fits" the job.	Determine which combination of resources — internal or external — can get the most mileage out of the tasks and responsibilities that need to be carried out.
Look mainly for technical competence.	Find people who are more than simply "technically" qualified but can carry forward your business's mission and values.
Base the hiring decision primarily on the selection interview.	View the selection interview as only one of a series of tools designed to make the best choice of hiring.
Hire only full-time employees.	Consider a blend of full-time and temporary workers to meet variable workload needs.

REMEMBER

True, setting the strategic direction of your business is not normally an HR function, but as a small-business owner, you need to look at your business's overall priorities and determine their staffing implications. Equally important, you need to make sure that any staffing decision clearly supports these business priorities. You're not simply "filling jobs." You're constantly seeking to bring to your business the skills and attributes that it needs to meet any challenge. To do so, you must look beyond the purely functional requirements of the various positions in your business and focus instead on what skills and attributes employees need to perform those functions exceptionally well.

Grasping the big picture

Strategic staffing begins with an effort to reassess your human resources needs in the context of your business priorities. It's a mindset rather than a process. The idea is to begin thinking in terms of need rather than job, long term rather than short term, and big picture rather than immediate opening. This approach ties directly into the changing role of the HR professional from administrator to strategist. To succeed, you need to gain a firm understanding of your business's major goals and priorities.

REMEMBER

Unless you head an extremely small organization, you can't adopt a strategic staffing approach all by yourself. Make it a priority to introduce the concept to managers in your organization. Get their input to better understand business and departmental priorities. In turn, you can help them through the process and adopting this mindset as well.

Together, you'll need to identify everything that may affect the efficiency and profitability of your business's operations — and not just in the short term, either. To get you started, here are some of the key questions that you and other people in your business should answer before you make your next move:

>> What are your business's long-term strategic goals or those of departments seeking your assistance in hiring employees?

>> What are the key competitive trends in your industry? (In other words, what factors have the greatest bearing on competitive success?)

>> What kind of culture currently exists in your business? And what kind of culture do you ultimately want to create? What are the values you want the business to stand for?

>> What knowledge, skill sets, and attributes (in general) are required to keep pace with those goals and, at the same time, remain true to your business values?

>> How does the current level of knowledge, skill sets, and attributes among your present employees match up with what will be necessary in the future?

>> How reasonable is it for you to expect that with the proper support and training, your current employees will be able to develop the skills they're going to need for your business to keep pace with the competition?

>> What combination of resources (rather than specific people) represents the best strategic approach to the staffing needs you face over the near-term and the long-term?

Recruiting the Right People

REMEMBER

Strategic staffing is not just about hiring more employees. It involves making the best staffing choices available to address core business needs. If you're thinking of filling an existing position, consider how the business's most critical needs have changed since the last time the job was open, rather than immediately searching for a candidate to fill the vacant position. Is a full-time individual still required in this role? And should a potential replacement have the same skills and experience as the predecessor? Or does the position need to be re-filled at all and the duties handled in other ways?

Analyse the business's daily activities to better understand how current resources are allocated. Identify the frequency and timing of workload peaks and valleys and look for predictable patterns. Consider the impact of shifts in business priorities and what eventual effect these are likely to have on your business. This thought process allows you to spot any shortfalls in human resources for upcoming initiatives.

Reassessing goals annually

TIP

Change is the name of the game in business. Business priorities will undoubtedly shift over time as you seek ways to keep your business competitive. As a result, you and any managers should consider performing your needs assessments on an annual basis to ensure that you're still on track with the assumptions that are guiding your staffing strategy.

Finding New Employees

You can look for new employees in two general places: inside or outside your organization. Looking inside your business is the easier of the two approaches, simply because it's a finite universe (although if your business is still very small, this option won't work for you). But before you get into the specifics of your hiring strategy, you should have a general idea of what you stand to gain — or lose — when you focus your staffing efforts inside your organization or look outside for new talent.

Inner peace: Filling jobs from within the organization

The rule in successful staffing has always been to do your best to fill new job openings from within before looking for outside candidates. Here are the key reasons:

>> Increased efficiency

>> Increased morale

>> Shorter period of adjustment

New horizons: Looking for staff outside the company

For all its virtues, a staffing strategy that's built almost entirely around promoting from within isn't always the best way to go — especially if your business has never taken the time and effort to develop a well-structured employee development program. Here are the basic arguments for looking outside the business to fill certain positions:

>> A broader selection of talent

>> The "new blood" factor

>> The diversity factor

Diversity doesn't mean that you have to include employees from every possible background, which is impossible. However, a commitment to diversity means that you create a workplace environment supportive of a wide range of perspectives.

Outsourcing: The role of HR

Outsourcing is the practice of turning over an entire function (shipping, payroll, benefits administration, security, computer networking) to an outside specialist. In many cases, the outside firm's employees or consultants work side by side with a company's regular employees. In some cases, a function may be moved to a remote location away from your office — even occasionally out of the country. This latter approach, often referred to as *offshoring,* has grabbed headlines and generated much economic and political debate in recent years.

Of course, outsourcing is hardly a new concept. Small businesses and mom-and-pop businesses have been outsourcing for a long time. What's new is the emergence of outsourcing as an increasingly useful staffing strategy for businesses that have historically used their own personnel.

Businesses usually outsource to save time and money, either because of one of two factors:

>> **Necessity:** This is the driving factor when a company's business demands outstrip its ability to handle a particular function without investing heavily in new equipment (or a new facility) or bringing in a large number of new employees.

>> **Choice:** This is the driving factor when businesses want to focus all their internal energies on those operations that contribute directly to their competitive advantage — and outsource those that may only be necessary for a discreet period of time or specific function.

In your HR role, you need to grasp the implications of outsourcing so that you can help provide strategic counsel throughout any hiring process — and contribute to decisions about whether to use this alternative in the first place. After all, any outsourcing effort inherently carries a demand not just for one discreet hire, but for many people — and knowing how to conduct an effective search for skilled contractors or consultants is extremely valuable.

Another reason to be aware of the outsourcing trend is that it affects the HR function itself: Businesses are increasingly outsourcing some of their HR services. But no matter which business process is involved, your ability to apply hiring principles can play a major role in ensuring that any outsourcing effort is implemented as efficiently as possible.

Building Competency Models

Many businesses today are using a process called *competency modelling* to help target the characteristics that distinguish top performers. Businesses can then use this information in the hiring process to seek and evaluate prospective employees.

Competency modelling is a matter of determining, as accurately as you can, what particular mix of skills, attributes, and attitudes produce superior performance in those operational functions that have the most bearing on your business's competitive strength. This strategic recipe becomes the basis not only of your hiring decisions but also of your training and development strategies.

Suppose, for example, that your business sells home security systems. One way that you market your service is to solicit potential customers by phone. The basic job of a telemarketer, of course, is to generate leads by calling people on the phone. Some telemarketers, however, are clearly much better at this task than others. They're better at engaging the interest of the people they call. They don't allow repeated rejections to wear down their spirits. In other words, they possess certain attributes that contribute to superior performance in this job. And these attributes (as opposed to the actual tasks of the job) are the basis of the competency model.

REMEMBER

You can apply the concept of competency modelling to virtually any function in your business. The basic objective is always the same: To determine as precisely as you can what combination of skills and attributes are required to excel at that function. You can then identify with greater precision any skill deficits — gaps between the requirements of the job and the qualifications of the candidate. And you can frequently close these gaps through training and coaching.

The following suggestions can help you gain insights:

>> **Interview your own "top" performers.** Sit down with your key people to determine what makes them so successful. Try to answer the following questions:

- What special skills do these star performers possess that the others don't?

- What type of personality traits do they share?

- What common attitudes and values do they bring to their jobs?

>> **Talk to your customers.** One of the best ways to find out who in your business can provide the basis for your competency modelling is to talk to your customers. Find out which employees your customers enjoy dealing with the most, and, more important, what those employees do to win the affection of these customers.

Understanding the ABCs of Job Descriptions

After you've determined the qualities that are most important to specific functions and positions in your business (see the preceding section), you're ready to use these competency models to create hiring criteria. Your first stop is the job description.

Done correctly, a well thought-out job description delivers the following benefits:

>> Ensures that everyone who has a say in the hiring decision agrees on what the job entails.

>> Serves as the basis for key hiring criteria.

>> Ensures that candidates have a clear idea of what to expect if, indeed, you hire them.

>> Serves as a reference tool during the evaluation process.

>> Serves as a benchmark for performance after you hire the candidate.

The job description needs to communicate as specifically but concisely as possible what responsibilities and tasks the job entails and to indicate the key qualifications of the job — the basic requirements (specific credentials or skills) — and, if possible, the attributes that underlie superior performance.

REMEMBER

Following is a quick look at the categories that make up a well-written job description:

>> Title of the position

>> Department (if applicable)

>> Direct report (to whom the person directly reports)

>> Responsibilities

>> Necessary skills

>> Experience required

Looking at a sample job description

The following job description is a good model to follow, regardless of what job you're describing. Notice the following:

>> A distinction exists between overall responsibility and specific areas of responsibility.

>> The experience requirement is separated from skills and attributes.

>> The language is easy to understand.

Position title Senior Mailroom Clerk

Department Operations

Reports to Building Services Supervisor

Overall responsibility Supervise mailroom staff and interface with all levels of management regarding mail and supply deliveries

Key areas of responsibility

» Maintain established shipping/receiving procedures

» Sort and distribute all mail on a timely basis

» Maintain all photocopiers and postage meters

» Order, store, and distribute supplies

» Facilitate all off-site storage, inventory, and records-management requests

» Document current policies and procedures in the COS Department as well as implement new procedures for improvement

» Oversee the use of a company van when needed

» Ensure that water and paper is available for customers on a continuous basis

Skills and attributes

» Strong sense of customer service

» Good organizational skills

» Ability to lift a minimum of 25 pounds

Experience requirement

» Supervisory experience in a corporate mailroom environment

» Good driving record

Keeping tasks and qualifications straight

A *task* is what the person or people you hire actually do: take orders over the phone, deliver pizzas, keep your computer network up and running, and so on. *Qualifications* are the skills, attributes, or credentials a person needs to perform

each task, such as possess a driver's licence, have an upbeat personality, be familiar with computer networking, and so on.

TIP

Do your best to avoid the common pitfall of blurring this distinction. Discipline
yourself to clarify the actual tasks and responsibilities before you start to think
about what special attributes the person needs to carry out those tasks and fulfill
those responsibilities.

Being flexible

Credentials such as degrees and licences are formal acknowledgements that a
candidate has passed a particular test or completed a specific field of study. Credentials are absolute necessities in some jobs. (The person who delivers pizza for
you, for example, must have a driver's licence.)

REMEMBER

At the same time, stay flexible. What you prefer in a candidate — such as an
advanced degree — may not necessarily be what's required for the position, particularly when you take into account a candidate's various work experiences and
accomplishments. This advice is particularly true when hiring for middle and
senior-level managers. The thing that you want to make sure of most of all is
that the credentials you establish have a direct bearing on a candidate's ability to
become a top performer.

Considering soft skills

Don't overlook those broad but telling aspects of a candidate known as *soft skills.*
These skills include an aptitude for communicating with people; the ability to
work well in teams; and other factors, such as a strong sense of ethics and a talent for efficient and creative problem-solving. Candidates who are weak in these
areas may prove unable to grow with your business.

Being specific

You don't need to be William Shakespeare to write a solid job description, but you
definitely need to appreciate the nuances of the language. And you want to make
sure that the words you choose actually spell out what the job entails. Table 1-2
provides a handful of examples of task descriptions that are far too general,
coupled with suggested rewrites.

TABLE 1-2   **Good and Bad Task Descriptions**

Too general	Specific
Handles administrative chores	Receives, sorts, and files monthly personnel action reports
Good communication skills	Ability to communicate technical information to nontechnical audiences
Computer literate	Proficient with Microsoft Word, Excel, and QuickBooks

WARNING

Apart from everything else, a job description is generally regarded as a legal document. As such, any references to race, colour, religion, age, sex, national origin or nationality, or physical or mental disability can expose your company to a possible suit.

Setting a salary range

Before you start the recruiting process and look at options for how and where you'll find the ideal candidate for the job you're designing, you should establish a salary range for the position. See Chapter 2 of Book 5 for details of salary and benefits and what constitutes an effective compensation structure.

Determining a job title

WARNING

Now that so many jobs involve multitasking, job titles are no longer a reliable indicator of the responsibilities of any particular job and, as such, can be tricky to handle. Even so, you need to give some attention to what you're actually calling the job. An inaccurate or overblown job title can create false expectations and lead to resentment, disappointment, or worse.

Resourceful Recruiting

The obvious objective of a recruiting effort is to attract as large a pool of qualified candidates as possible. Two considerations, however, are less obvious but no less important. For one thing, the measure of a successful recruiting effort isn't only numbers; it's also about quality. Keep in mind as well that everything you do as a recruiter is making a statement about your business, and, in the process, shaping your company's reputation.

Clearly, recruiting is probably the most challenging stage of the hiring process. The following list covers some of the general guidelines that you want to bear in mind:

>> **Make recruitment an ongoing process.** Businesses known for their ability to attract and hire good employees are always recruiting — even if they have no current openings. At the very least, keep an active database of the names and resumes of qualified people you've met, sent you letters, or contacted you online.

>> **Create a plan.** Always have a general idea before you start any recruiting effort of how you intend to conduct and manage the process: various candidate sources, the deadline for filling the position, how you are going to post or advertise the position, etc.

>> **Be systematic.** Before you start the search, set up a *protocol* for processing process applications, resumes, and cover letters. If you're using an outside recruiter (see the later section "Working with Recruiters" for details), make sure that someone in your business has a direct line to the individual who's handling the search. If you're seeking candidates through the Internet, have secure and streamlined systems in place. If you intend to use a variety of publications or websites for your classified ads, think about setting up some sort of database of basic information so you don't need to re-educate yourself every time you run a new ad.

>> **Keep tabs on your progress.** Monitor your recruiting efforts on a daily basis and evaluate your progress on the quality of inquiries.

>> **Be flexible.** Be prepared to revisit the job description or even explore the possibility of restructuring the job — breaking it into two part-time jobs, perhaps — in an effort to attract more (or better) candidates.

Recruiting from within Your Business

If your business has enough employees to fill a position from within, the advantages of doing so are well known and well documented. Promoting from within helps keep morale and motivation levels high. And, assuming that your internal search is successful, you don't need to worry about the employee fitting into your culture; that person already knows the territory.

The drawbacks? Only two, really.

>> The most obvious one is that limiting your search to internal candidates limits the candidates to choose from, and you may end up hiring someone who's not up to the challenge of the job.

>> The second drawback is that, whenever you recruit from within, you always run a risk that otherwise important and valuable employees who don't get the job may become resentful and even decide to quit.

Your only real defense is to go out of your way to ensure that everyone understands the scope and basic duties of the job plus the hiring criteria you're using. You also must make sure that everyone gets a fair shot at the opening.

Following are the key procedures that you need to initiate in setting up a successful internal hiring process:

>> Create a means to post jobs internally

>> Spell out the criteria

>> Establish procedures for applying

TIP

If you see yourself hiring internally, setting up an employee skills inventory can be a great help. This inventory is exactly what the name implies: a catalog of the individual skills, attributes, credentials, and areas of knowledge that currently exist. You may assume that this practice is one that is suitable for only big businesses and that the process isn't worth the bother. Even if your company is relatively small, it still may be worth the time and effort to develop an employee skills inventory.

The key to developing a practical, user-friendly employee skills inventory lies in how you organize various categories of information. Try to keep the number of fields to a reasonable minimum and make sure that they're job-related. A typical employee skills inventory form may incorporate the following fields, including conventional job history data:

>> Skills/knowledge areas

>> Second-language skills

>> Special preferences

>> Educational background

>> Job history at your business

>> Previous job history

>> Training courses and seminars

>> Skills, aptitude, and other test results

>> Licences, credentials, and affiliations

Note: The preceding list is meant to be a set of recommendations. You can incorporate into your own employee skills inventory anything that you consider relevant.

Writing a Good Job Ad

Whether you plan to post a job ad in the newspaper, on your company website, or on a job board, you're not going to have much luck if it doesn't concisely convey what you're offering potential applicants. Writing a good job ad is a critical step in the hiring process. You're trying to attract the right candidates!

Keep in mind the following two considerations in writing a job ad:

>> The goal of a job ad is not only to generate responses from qualified applicants, but also to prevent candidates who are clearly unqualified from applying for the position.

>> You're advertising your company. Every aspect of your ad must seek to foster a favourable impression of the organization.

Your next step is to actually compose the ad. If you've done a good job of writing the job description (see the earlier section "Understanding the ABCs of Job Descriptions" for more about developing a quality job description), then you've already accomplished this task. In fact, think of the ad as a synopsis of the existing job description.

As for the ad itself, the following list describes the elements you need to think about as you compose the ad:

>> **Headline:** The headline almost always is the job title.

>> **Job information:** A line or two about the general duties and responsibilities of the job.

>> **Company information:** Always include a few words on what your company does.

>> **Qualifications and hiring criteria:** Specify the level of education and experience and relevant attributes and skills required to do the job.

>> **Response method:** Let applicants know the best way to get in touch with you: e-mail, regular mail, phone, or in person.

TIP

This is an ad that takes into consideration the criteria of a good job ad.

ADMINISTRATIVE ASSISTANT, LAW OFFICE

Busy, growing law office specializing in entertainment and intellectual property seeks well-organized individual to support staff of five lawyers and two paralegals. Responsibilities include processing correspondence, maintaining schedules and client files, and updating publications. College diploma preferred. Must be bilingual and familiar with Microsoft Office. Competitive salary and benefits. AA job@ lawfirm.com or Bing, Bong, and Bang, P.O. Box 999, Overbrook, ON K1K M3P.

Using the Internet as a Recruitment Tool

The Internet has revolutionized the recruiting process. It has created countless new opportunities for employers and job seekers alike. Specialized and general job sites abound, and today even the smallest of businesses has a website describing what the business does and, often, the advantages of working for the business.

No doubt, you're already familiar with many of the benefits of the Internet as a recruiting tool: access to a much larger potential candidate base and a relatively low-cost way to manage the process of hiring and continually attracting future employees.

WARNING

One of the web's huge appeals is its ability to help you locate qualified candidates at extremely low costs. More candidates for less money? Sounds like a hiring manager's dream. But hang on. It can also become a nightmare if not managed properly. For starters, the Internet has the potential of dramatically increasing the number of responses to your job ads. Many HR managers report they have great difficulty even keeping track of submissions. Even small businesses can receive hundreds of resumes from a single ad, depending on the position and job market. Some HR professionals, or their staff members, still manually read through or at least scan each resume.

The Internet has greatly facilitated applicants' research. Your website is a great place to communicate your unique culture and most appealing characteristics. Well executed, your site can give job seekers a glimpse into the employee experience — what it's like to work in your company. In addition, the proliferation of social media such as Facebook and LinkedIn allow candidates to research and share information and perspectives on your company.

With information now so much more accessible than ever, you want to make sure that your company's website accurately showcases your firm's strengths and range of capabilities. Don't be surprised at how well prepared candidates are today when you get to the interview process. You'll also need to be prepared and raise your expectations for the discussion. The topics you cover can relate more specifically to business priorities and issues affecting your industry.

TIP

Establish a system to keep track of your recruiting success from various websites and publications. How many candidates did each source produce? How qualified and skilled was each applicant? These metrics can help you determine the return on your investment in a variety of recruiting channels.

Working with Recruiters

Recruiters can be an invaluable part of your search arsenal. And if you know how to maximize their services, recruiters can more than pay for themselves. Using outside recruiters has several key advantages — namely, the following:

>> Outside recruiters generally have access to a large pool of applicants — after all, continually locating quality candidates is their job.

>> They handle such cumbersome administrative details of recruiting as placing ads, skills evaluation, and preliminary interviews.

REMEMBER

In the course of their evaluation process, staffing firms typically check selected references from their candidates' past employers to gather skill proficiency information and job performance history, but employers should perform their own reference checks as well.

>> They're often a valuable source of staffing advice.

Looking at the types of recruiters

If you're not sure what makes a *headhunter* different from a *recruiter* and an *employment agency* different from a *search firm*, you're not alone. The difference between the various specialists in this large and growing industry is primarily how they charge and on which segment of the labour market they focus.

The following list offers you a rundown on how these players differ on the recruiting field:

>> **Employment agencies, staffing firms, and contingency search firms:** These are companies you engage to find job candidates for specific positions. What they all have in common is that you pay them a fee — but only after

they find you someone you eventually hire. These firms recruit candidates in virtually every industry, and businesses call on them to fill positions at all levels of the corporate ladder. They typically charge you a percentage of the new employee's first year's salary. It can range from 15 percent to 30 percent, depending on the level of the position you're filling and the skills required.

The trend toward specialization is good news for you because firms that specialize have a strong sense of the marketplace in a given field. Among other things, they make sure that the package you're offering is competitive. Many of the larger staffing firms offer an expanded variety of services, including preliminary reference checks, as well as refunds or replacement guarantees if the new employee doesn't work out.

>> **Executive search firms, or headhunters:** These types of recruiters focus on higher-level executives, up to and including CEOs. Unlike employment agencies, most executive search firms charge a retainer whether they produce results or not. You can also expect to pay, in addition to expenses, a commission of 25 percent — or even a third — of the executive's annual salary if the firm's successful in its search. The main value comes into play if you're seeking someone for a high-level job that's most likely to be filled by an executive who's already working for another company.

Knowing when to use a recruiter

Most businesses that rely on outside recruiters to fill positions do so for one of two reasons:

>> They don't have the time or the expertise to recruit effectively on their own.

>> The recruiting efforts they've put forward to date have yet to yield results.

Finding the "right" recruiter

You choose a recruiter the same way that you choose any professional services specialist: You look at what services are available. You ask colleagues for recommendations. You talk to different recruiters. The following list provides some reminders that can help you make a wise choice:

>> Check out recruiters personally.

>> Be explicit about your needs.

>> Clarify fee arrangements in writing.

>> Ask about replacement guarantees.

>> Express your concerns openly. If you aren't happy about any aspect of the arrangement you've struck with a recruiter, speak up. Tell the recruiter exactly what your concerns are. If you don't feel comfortable expressing your concerns with the recruiter you've chosen, you're probably dealing with the wrong company.

Recruiting on campus

TIP

If you're recruiting for an entry-level position, college or university campuses can be a good place to look. Smaller firms without well-organized college/university recruiting programs have always been at something of a disadvantage. If you're one of the "smaller guys," get to know the folks in the placement office, because campus recruiting is usually coordinated by the college/university placement office. The best way to build a strong relationship with placement office personnel is to pay them a personal visit — or better still, invite them to your company to see what you have to offer.

Surveying other recruiting sources

Aside from some of the traditional recruiting options discussed earlier in this chapter, the following resources may help you in your search for qualified candidates:

>> Employee referrals

>> Job fairs

>> Open houses

>> Professional associations and unions

>> Non-profit employment services

Assessing Potential Employees

Just about everybody agrees that the job interview is the most important element of the hiring process. But what many otherwise savvy business people often forget is that one of the keys to effective interviewing is effectively evaluating candidates. You don't want to inadvertently weed out candidates who clearly deserve a second look. Just as bad, your process may fail to accomplish its fundamental purpose: making sure that you're not wasting your time and effort on candidates who are clearly unqualified for the position you're seeking to fill.

No set rules exist for evaluating job applicants — other than common sense. Having some kind of evaluation system or protocol in place is important — before resumes begin to arrive.

Keep in mind the following three key questions at all times:

>> What are the prerequisites for the position?

>> What are the special requirements for your business, such as certifications or special education?

>> What qualifications and attributes are critical to performing well in this particular position?

REMEMBER

If you haven't answered these three questions, you're not ready to start evaluating potential employees.

Here's an overview of the evaluation process:

1. **Scan applications or resumes first for basic qualifications.**

2. **Look for key criteria.**

TIP

   Begin the evaluation process by setting a high standard (for example, the resume must meet a certain high percentage of the criteria), but if your reject pile is growing and you haven't "cleared" anyone, you may need to lower the bar somewhat.

3. **Flag and identify your top candidates.**

4. **Contact top candidates for a phone or in-person interview.**

Reading Resumes Effectively

Based on resumes alone, you'd think that all your candidates are such outstanding prospects that you could hire them sight unseen. And no wonder. People write their resumes to put themselves in the best light possible. And those who don't know how to write a great resume can hire people who do know.

Why, then, take resumes seriously? Because resumes, regardless of how "professional" they are, can still reveal a wealth of information about the candidate — after you crack the code.

Mastering the basics

Here's what you probably know already: Basically, job candidates submit only two types of resumes:

>> **Chronological,** where all the work-related information appears in a time-line sequence

>> **Functional,** where the information appears in various categories (skills, achievements, qualifications, and so on)

In the past, the general rule was that candidates trying to hide something, such as gaps in their work history, wrote functional resumes. But because a well-rounded background (in conjunction with one's specialty area) can prove an asset in today's job market, the functional resume is now more acceptable. The key point is to be open to either type of resume.

REMEMBER

Some applicants use a combination of the two formats, presenting a capsule of what they believe are their most important qualifications and accomplishments, together with a chronological work history. If a resume is short on work history, look for skills that may be transferable to your position. Identifying these skills will be much easier if you've weighted the application questions to tie certain types of experience or skills with success in the job.

Before diving into that pile of resumes, consider the following observations:

>> No sane job applicant is going to put derogatory or detracting information on a resume.

>> Many resumes are professionally prepared, designed to create a winning, but not necessarily accurate, impression.

>> Reviewing resumes is tedious, no matter what. You may need to sift through the stack several times.

>> If you don't review resumes yourself or delegate it to the wrong person, you're likely to miss that diamond-in-the-rough, that ideal employee who unfortu-nately has poor resume-drafting skills.

Reading between the lines

Now that more and more people are using outside specialists or software packages to prepare their resumes, getting an accurate reading of a candidate's strengths simply by reading a resume is more difficult than ever. Even so, here are some of the resume characteristics that generally (although not always) describe a candidate worth interviewing:

>> **Lots of details:** Though applicants are generally advised to avoid wordiness, the more detailed they are in their descriptions of what they did and accomplished in previous jobs, the more reliable (as a rule) the information is.

>> **A history of stability and advancement:** The applicant's work history should show a steady progression into greater responsibility and more important positions. Be wary of candidates who have bounced from one company to the next, but do be open to the possibility that these candidates had good reasons for the career moves.

>> **A strong, well-written cover letter:** Assuming that the candidate wrote the letter, the cover letter is generally a good indication of the candidate's overall communication skills.

Watching out for red flags

WARNING

Resume writing is a good example of the Law of Unintended Consequences. Sometimes what's not in a resume or what's done through carelessness or mistake can reveal quite a bit about a candidate. Following are some things to watch out for:

>> Sloppy overall appearance

>> Unexplained chronological gaps

>> Static career pattern

>> Typos and misspellings

>> Vaguely worded job descriptions

>> Potentially misleading wording

>> Job hopping

>> Overemphasis on hobbies or interests outside of work

Performing Short Phone Interviews

After sorting through resumes and selecting the most promising candidates, conducting a brief telephone interview can help you narrow down the list of individuals to interview in person. Before calling a candidate, review the resume and cover letter carefully, noting questions to ask. You'll likely see a pattern emerge among the applicants who are a good fit for your business. Here are a few good questions to ask:

>> "Tell me a little about yourself and your work history."

>> "What interests you about this job?"

>> "What skills can you bring to the job?"

>> "What sort of work environment brings out your best performance?"

Estimate how long you'll need to effectively conduct a telephone interview with job applicants, say 15 to 30 minutes.

Interviewing Effectively Face to Face

Conducting a job interview seems easier than it is. As a result, many people take interviewing for granted. They don't invest the time, effort, and concentration that effective job interviewing requires. And, above all, they don't prepare enough for interviews, so often little correlation exists between the "positive reports" that emerge from the typical job interview and the job performance of the candidates who receive those glowing reports. This correlation goes up dramatically whenever interviewing becomes a structured, well-planned process — one that's well integrated into a business's overall staffing practices.

The upcoming sections take a look at interviewing, with a focus on the things you need to know and do to get the most out of the interviewing process.

Knowing the goals

Job interviews enable you to perform the following four tasks that, combined with other steps you take, are essential to making a sound hiring decision:

>> Obtain firsthand information about the candidate's background, work experience, and skill level that clarifies what you need to confirm from the resume or previous interviews.

>> Get a general sense of the candidate's overall intelligence, aptitude, enthusiasm, and attitudes, with particular respect to how those attributes match up to the requirements of the job.

>> Gain insight — to the extent possible — into the candidate's basic personality traits and motivation to tackle the responsibilities of the job and become a part of the business.

>> Estimate the candidate's ability to adapt to your business's work environment.

Setting the stage

Your ability to get the most out of the interviews you conduct depends on how well prepared you are. Here's a checklist to follow before you pop the first interview question:

>> Thoroughly familiarize yourself with the job description, especially its hiring criteria.

>> Review everything the candidate has submitted to date.

>> Set up a general structure for the interview.

>> Write down the questions you intend to ask.

>> Make arrangements to hold the interview in a room that's private and reasonably comfortable.

WARNING

Try not to schedule job interviews in the middle of the day. The reason: You're not likely to be as relaxed and as focused as you need to be, and you may have a tough time fighting off interruptions and distractions. The ideal time to interview candidates is early morning, when the workday starts. You're fresher then, and so is the candidate. If you have no choice, give yourself a buffer of at least half an hour before the interview so that you can switch gears and prepare for the interview in the right manner.

Meeting the candidate

Your priority in meeting a candidate face-to-face for the first time is to put the candidate at ease. Disregard any advice anyone has given you about doing things to create stress just to see how the individual responds. Those techniques are rarely productive, and they put both you and your business in a bad light. Instead, view the first minutes of the meeting as an opportunity to build a rapport with the candidate. The more comfortable the candidate is, the more engaging the interview will be, and the more you'll learn about your potential employee.

TIP

If you're seated at your desk as the candidate walks in, a common courtesy is to stand and meet the individual halfway, shake hands, and let the candidate know that you're happy to be meeting. (Basic stuff, but easy to forget.) You don't need to cut to the chase right away with penetrating questions. Skilled job interviewers usually begin with small talk — a general comment about the weather, transportation difficulties, and so on — but they keep it to a minimum.

Minding the Q&As

The Q&A is the main part of the interview. How you phrase questions, when you ask them, how you follow up — each of these aspects can go a long way toward affecting the quality and usability of the answers you get. Here are the key practices that differentiate people who've mastered the art of questioning from those who haven't. (See the later section "Asking Fifteen Solid Questions and Interpreting the Answers" for even more guidance.)

>> **Have a focus.** Even before you start to ask questions, you want to have a reasonably specific idea of what information or insights you're expecting to gain from the interview based on your research and the hiring criteria in the job description. Whatever the need, decide ahead of time what you want to know more about and build your interview strategy around that goal.

>> **Make every question count.** Every question you ask during a job interview must have a specific purpose. The general rule: If the question has no strategic significance, think twice before asking it. Again, tie questions to the job criteria defined in the job description.

>> **Pay attention.** In a job interview situation, you find yourself drawing conclusions before the candidate has finished answering a question, or begin rehearsing in your mind the next question while the candidate is still talking. Fight those tendencies. Write down your questions and then concentrate completely on the candidate.

>> **Don't hesitate to probe.** Nothing's wrong with asking additional questions to draw out more specific answers. Too many interviewers let candidates "off the hook" in the interest of being "nice." That practice, however, can prove counterproductive — the candidate may give you valuable background on specific abilities if your questions are more penetrating.

>> **Give candidates ample time to respond.** Give the candidate time to come up with a thoughtful answer. If the silence persists for more than, say, ten seconds, ask if the candidate would like you to clarify the question. Otherwise, don't rush things. Use the silence to observe the candidate and to take stock of where you are in the interview.

WARNING

Tread carefully whenever you come across a candidate who seems flat and disinterested during the job interview. If a candidate can't demonstrate any real enthusiasm during the interview, don't expect any enthusiasm on the job.

>> **Suspend judgments.** Try to keep your attention on the answers you're getting instead of making interpretations or judgments. You're going to have plenty of time after the interview to evaluate what you see and hear.

TIP

>> **Take notes.** Memory can be tricky, leading people to ignore what actually happened during an interview and to rely instead on general impressions. Taking notes helps you avoid this common pitfall. Make sure that you give yourself a few moments after the interview to review your notes and put them into some kind of order.

Varying the style of questions

You can usually divide interview questions into four categories, based on the kinds of answers you're trying to elicit: closed-ended, open-ended, hypothetical, and leading.

Closed-ended

Definition: Questions that call for a simple, informational answer — usually a yes or no.

Examples: "How many years did you work for the circus?" "Did you enjoy it?" "What cities did you tour?"

When to use them: Closed-ended questions work best if you're trying to elicit specific information or set the stage for more complex questions.

Pitfall to avoid: Asking too many of them in rapid-fire succession without tying them back to the job criteria makes candidates feel as though they're being interrogated.

Open-ended

Definition: Questions that require thought and oblige the candidate to reveal attitudes or opinions.

Examples: "Describe for me how you handle stress on the job." "Can you give me an illustration of how you improved productivity at your last job?"

When to use them: Most of the time, but interspersed with closed-ended questions. Because this approach requires candidates to describe how they've handled real tasks and problems, it can be very useful and revealing.

Pitfalls to avoid: Not being specific enough as you phrase the question and not interceding if the candidate's answer starts to veer off track.

Hypothetical

Definition: Questions that invite the candidate to resolve an imaginary situation or react to a given situation.

Examples: "If you were the purchasing manager, would you institute an automated purchase-order system?" "If you were to take over this department, what's the first thing you'd do to improve productivity?"

When to use them: Useful if framed in the context of actual job situations.

Pitfall to avoid: Putting too much stock in the candidate's hypothetical answer. (You're usually better off asking questions that force a candidate to use an actual experience as the basis for an answer.)

Leading

Definition: Questions asked in such a way that the answer you're looking for is obvious.

Examples: "You rarely fought with your last boss, right?" "You know a lot about team-building, don't you?" "You wouldn't dream of falsifying your expense accounts, would you?"

When to use them: Rarely, if ever.

Knowing what you can't ask

Employers must respect the dignity of their employees and must make sure that their actions and workplaces are free of harmful discrimination. Human rights laws across Canada prohibit employers from discriminating against individuals in hiring, firing, or the terms and conditions of employment because of certain personal characteristics (unless it is for a valid job requirement). With some exceptions, workers in Canada are protected from discrimination based on the following factors:

» National or ethnic origin, race, ancestry, place of origin, colour

» Disability (physical and/or mental)

» Religion, creed, political belief, association

» Sex, sexual orientation, pregnancy

» Age (with exceptions for minors and seniors in some cases)

» Marital or family status

WARNING

Become familiar with the rules and regulations in your province and avoid interview questions related to the preceding factors. If you ask any of these questions in an interview and do not hire the candidate, you are presumed to have discriminated against the candidate. This can lead to any number of unwanted outcomes such as having to offer the candidate a job, compensating the candidate, or being subject to a discrimination suit.

Considering multiple and panel interviews

It's not unusual for more than one employee to interview a candidate to provide a variety of opinions, especially if the candidate will play a key role in the organization. In fact, sometimes these meetings are carried out simultaneously through an interviewing panel made up of the hiring manager plus other members of the management team or work group, usually no more than three to five people.

Panel interviews are beneficial when you want to quickly get a promising hire through multiple interviews in a timely manner. It's best for the hiring manager to conduct one-on-one interviews with applicants first, however, choosing only a few finalists for panel interviews. This saves panelists' time and ensures that the hiring manager is presenting only those candidates that may ultimately be hired. Panel interviews are most successful when the hiring manager distributes job criteria to the interview team in advance along with specific questions. This ensures panel members will be able to compare candidates in a consistent way using the same criteria.

Ending the interview on the right note

With only a few minutes to go, you can bring the session to a graceful close by following these steps:

1. Offer the candidate a broad-brushstroke summary of the interview.

2. Let the candidate ask questions.

3. **Let the candidate know what comes next.**

4. **End the interview on a formal, but sincere note.**

TIP

As soon as possible after the candidate's departure, take a couple of moments to collect your thoughts and write your impressions and a summary of your notes. You don't need to make any definitive decisions at this point, but recording your impressions while they're still fresh in your mind will help you immeasurably if the final choice boils down to several candidates with comparable qualifications.

Asking Fifteen Solid Questions and Interpreting the Answers

What makes an interview question "good"? The answer, simply, is that a "good question" does two things:

>> It gives you the specific information you need to make a sound hiring decision.

>> It helps you gain insight into how the candidate's mind and emotions work.

Avoid timeworn, cliché questions, such as "What are your strengths and weaknesses?" or "Where do you see yourself in the next five years?" or "If you were an animal, which one would it be?" Instead develop a list of questions designed to elicit responses that will be most helpful in evaluating a candidate's suitability for the position and your business. You can ask hundreds of such questions, but following are 15 to get you started, along with ideas on what to look for in the answers:

>> **Can you tell me a little about yourself?** Most interview strategy books describe this one as the "killer question." You can bet the farm that a well-prepared candidate has a well-rehearsed answer. A confident applicant can give a brief summary of strengths, significant achievements, and career goals. Your main job? To make sure that the answers are consistent with the applicant's resume.

>> **What interests you about this job, and what skills and strengths can you bring to it?** Nothing tricky here, but it's a solid question all the same. Note that the question is not "What are your skills and strengths?" but "What skills and strengths can you bring to the job?" The answer is yet another way to gauge how much interest the applicant has in the job and how well prepared the person is for the interview. Stronger candidates should be able to correlate their skills with specific job requirements.

>> **Can you tell me a little about your current job?** Strong candidates should be able to give you a short and precise summary of duties and responsibilities. How they answer this question can help you determine their passion and enthusiasm for their work and their sense of personal accountability. Be wary of applicants who bad-mouth or blame their employers.

>> **In a way that anyone could understand, can you describe a professional success you are proud of?** This question is especially good when you're interviewing someone for a technical position, such as a systems analyst or tax accountant. The answer shows the applicant's ability to explain what they do so that anyone can understand it.

>> **How have you changed the nature of your current job?** A convincing answer here shows adaptability and a willingness to "take the bull by the horns," if necessary. An individual who chose to do a job differently from other people also shows creativity and resourcefulness.

>> **What was the most difficult decision you ever had to make on the job?** Notice the intentionally vague aspect of this question. It's not hypothetical. It's real. What you're looking for is the person's decision-making style and how it fits into your company culture. Someone who admits that firing a subordinate was difficult demonstrates compassion, and those who successfully decided to approach a co-worker over a conflict may turn out to be great team players. Individuals who admit a mistake they've made exhibit honesty and open-mindedness.

>> **Why did you decide to pursue a new job?** This question is just a different way of asking, "What are you looking for in a job?" Some candidates come so well rehearsed they are never at a loss for an answer. Sometimes by phrasing the question in a different way, you can cause them to go "off script."

>> **I see that you've been unemployed for the past few months. Why did you leave your last job, and what have you been doing since then?** This question is important, but don't let it seem accusatory. Generally speaking, people don't leave jobs voluntarily without another one waiting in the wings, but it happens. Try to get specific, factual answers that you can verify later. Candidates with a spotty employment history, at the very least, ought to be able to account for all extended periods of unemployment and to demonstrate whether they used that time productively — getting an advanced degree, for example.

>> **Who was your best boss ever and why? Who was the worst, and looking back, what could you have done to make that relationship better?** These two are more penetrating questions than you may think. Among other things, the answers give you insight into how the candidate views and responds to supervision. A reflective, responsive answer to the second part of the question

may indicate a loyal employee capable of rising above an unpleasant supervisory situation and/or learning from past mistakes, both highly desirable qualities. A bitter, critical answer may indicate someone who holds grudges or simply can't get along with certain personality types.

» **Which do you enjoy the most: working alone with information or working with other people?** The ideal answer here is "both." People who say they like working with information are obviously a good choice for technical positions, but it may be a red flag if they don't also mention that they like communicating and collaborating with others, which is increasingly a function of even technical jobs. An excellent candidate might say the different perspectives within a group produce more innovative ideas than one person working alone can, but without information, a team can't get very far.

» **What sort of things do you think your current (past) company could do to be more successful?** This one is a great "big picture" question. You're probing to find out whether the candidate has a clear understanding of a current or past employer's missions and goals and whether the candidate thinks in terms of those goals.

» **Can you describe a typical day at work in your last job?** Strong candidates can give you specific details that you can later verify, but the main point of this question is to see how the applicant's current (or most recent) routine compares with the requirements of the job in question. How interviewees describe their duties can prove highly revealing.

» **What sort of work environment do you prefer? What brings out your best performance?** Probe for specifics. You want to find out whether this person is going to fit in at your business. If your corporate culture is collegial and team-centred, you don't want someone who answers, "I like to be left alone to do my work." You may also uncover unrealistic expectations or potential future clashes. People rarely, if ever, work at their best in all situations. Candidates who say otherwise aren't being honest with themselves or with you.

» **How do you handle conflict? Can you give me an example of how you handled a workplace conflict in the past?** You want candidates who try to be reasonable but nonetheless stand up for what's right. While some people may be naturally easygoing, candidates who say that they never get into conflict situations are either dishonest or delusional.

» **How would you respond if you were put in a situation you felt presented a conflict of interest or was unethical? Have you ever had this experience in previous positions?** How individuals approach this question and anecdotes they relay can offer valuable insights as to how they may respond if faced with such a situation.

TIP

In addition to an opportunity to showcase their qualifications, savvy candidates also use the interview to find out as much as they can about the position and company, so don't be surprised if they come prepared with questions of their own. Don't interpret questions as disruptive to your agenda: They're a show of interest and professionalism. In fact, you can address many of their concerns by proactively "selling" your company during the interview. Just as candidates try to show how their skills are a match with the position, you can also point out programs and policies that fit the needs of promising applicants and promote your firm as a great place to work.

Making the Final Hiring Decision

The moment of truth in the hiring process is choosing who will get the job. Because hiring mistakes can be costly, a lot is riding on your ability to select the best people for your available positions.

Coming to grips with the decision-making process

Stripped to its essentials, the decision-making process in the final stages of hiring is no different than buying a car or deciding on your vacation destination. You look at your options, weigh the pros and cons of each, and then you make a choice.

You can never be absolutely certain that the decision you make is right. You can improve your chances significantly, however, if you manage the decision-making process in a reasonably disciplined, intelligent way, which means that you consistently focus on the key hiring criteria you established at the outset of the process (covered earlier in this chapter) and perform the following tasks:

>> You do a thorough job early on in the hiring process of identifying your needs and drawing up a job description that pinpoints the combination of skills, attributes, and credentials that a particular position requires.

>> You gather enough information about each candidate — through interviewing, testing, and observation — so that you have a reasonably good idea of the candidates' capabilities, personalities, strengths, and weaknesses.

>> You remain objective in evaluating candidates. Your personal biases don't steer your focus away from your hiring criteria.

>> You develop methods to evaluate your strategies, such as using a particular recruiter or running a classified ad, so that, the next time around, you can repeat practices that produce good results and modify those that lead to hiring mistakes.

The simplest method is to think back on the process that led to the hiring of your top employees, and compare that process with how you handled things with candidates who were eventually let go.

>> You "sell" the candidates on the job, and they're enthusiastic about the position.

Using the "tools" of the trade

Your available resources in making hiring decisions are usually fairly limited, so you need to use them well. The following list takes a brief look at those tools and what you need to keep in mind as you're tapping each one:

>> **Past experience:** A long-time truism in successful hiring is the concept that the best indicator of a candidate's future performance is past performance.

The only caveat to this usually reliable principle: The conditions that prevailed in the candidate's last job need to closely parallel the conditions in the job the candidate's seeking. Otherwise, you have no real basis for comparison. No two business environments are identical.

>> **Interview impressions:** Impressions you pick up during an interview almost always carry a great deal of weight in hiring decisions.

>> **Test results:** Some people regard test results as the only truly reliable predictor of future success. The argument goes as follows: Test results are quantifiable. In most tests, results aren't subject to personal interpretation. With a large enough sample, you can compare test scores to job-performance ratings and, eventually, use test scores as a predictor of future performance.

>> **Firsthand observation:** Call it the proof-in-the-pudding principle. Watching candidates actually perform some of the tasks for which you're considering hiring them is clearly the most reliable way to judge their competence.

Using a system to make your selection

Decision-makers in businesses with good track records of making successful hires use their intuition, but they don't use intuition as the sole basis for their judgments. The following list describes what such decision-makers rely on:

>> **They have in place some sort of** *system* — a well-thought-out protocol for assessing the strengths and weaknesses of candidates and applying those assessments to the hiring criteria.

>> **The system that they use, regardless of how simple or elaborate, is weighted** — that is, it presupposes that certain skills and attributes bear more on job performance than do others and takes those differences into account.

>> **They constantly monitor and evaluate the effectiveness of the system** — always with an eye toward sharpening their own ability and the ability of others to link any data they obtain during the recruiting and interviewing process to the on-the-job performance of new hires. If a particular type of testing mechanism is used in the selection process, the validity of the test (how closely the test results correlate with successful on-the-job performance) is monitored regularly.

Setting up your own scale

These are the fundamental steps you must go through for selecting your next hire:

1. **Isolate key hiring criteria.**

By this point in the hiring process, you should know what combination of skills and attributes a candidate needs to perform the job well and fit your business's pace and culture.

2. **Set priorities.**

You can safely assume that some of your hiring criteria are more important than others. To take these differences into account, set up a scale that reflects the relative importance of any particular skill or attribute.

3. **Evaluate candidates on the basis of the weighted scale you established in Step 2.**

Instead of simply looking at the candidate as a whole, you look at each of the criteria you set down, and you rate the candidate on the basis of how the person measures up in that particular category.

Say, for example, that one candidate's strength is the ability to work as part of a team. The candidate's rating on that particular attribute may be a 5, but the relative importance of teamwork to the task at hand may be anywhere from 1 to 5, which means that the overall ranking may end up as low as 5 (5 times 1) or as high as 25 (5 times 5).

All in all, a weighted system gives you an opportunity to see how well candidates measure up against one another and how closely their skills and attributes match the job requirements. You must be careful, however. The effectiveness of this system depends on two crucial factors: the validity of your hiring criteria and the objectivity of the judgments that underlie any ratings you assign to each candidate.

Factoring in the intangibles

The really tough part of any evaluation procedure is attaching numerical ratings to the *intangibles* — those attributes that you can measure only through your observations. The following sections cover those intangible factors that you commonly find in the criteria for most jobs, along with suggestions on how to tell whether the candidate measures up.

Industriousness and motivation

Definition: Candidates' work ethic — how hard they're willing to work and how important they feel it is to perform to the best of their ability.

When important: All the time.

How to measure: Verifiable accomplishments in their last jobs. Evaluation of past employers and co-workers. Track records of successful jobs that go back to college/university or even earlier.

Intelligence

Definition: Mental alertness, thinking ability, capability to process abstract information.

When important: Any job that requires the ability to make decisions (and not just follow instructions).

How to measure: Evidence of good decision-making ability in previous jobs. Also through testing. (Make sure, however, that the tests aren't in any way discriminatory.)

Temperament and ability to cope with stress

Definition: General demeanour — whether the candidate is calm and level-headed or hyper or hot-headed.

When important: In any job where the stress level is high or in any work environment where people must interact and rely on one another.

How to measure: Personality testing can sometimes prove reliable, but the best way to measure these criteria is to ask during the interview about stress levels in candidates' previous jobs and how they feel they performed.

Creativity and resourcefulness

Definition: The ability to think *outside the box* — to come up with innovative solutions to problems.

When important: In jobs that require imagination or problem-solving skills that don't rely on set procedures.

How to measure: Examples of previous work (graphic-design work, writing samples, and so on). Specific examples of situations in which the candidate had come up with an innovative solution to a problem. Previous accomplishments or awards. Outside interests.

Teamwork abilities

Definition: The ability to work harmoniously with others and share responsibility for achieving the same goal.

When important: Any task with a strong need for employees to work closely and collaboratively.

How to measure: Previous work experience. (Did candidates work on their own or with groups?) Team successes mentioned during the interview. Evidence of ability to work within project team rules, protocols, and work practices. Support for co-workers. Willingness to ask for help.

Hiring right

Bad hiring decisions rarely happen by accident. In retrospect, you can usually discover that you didn't do something you should have. The following list covers the key principles to follow in order to hire the right person:

>> Anchor yourself to the hiring criteria.

>> Take your time.

>> Cross-verify whenever possible.

>> Get help, but avoid the "too many cooks" syndrome.

>> Don't put a "good" employee in the "wrong" job.

>> Avoid the "top-of-mind" syndrome, choosing the last interviewed candidate.

Checking References

References and other third-party observations are useful and necessary components of the hiring process. Selected references from past employers help you separate those with good employment records from others who have a less positive job performance history. Not taking these steps can increase your risk of making a hiring mistake and putting your business at a disadvantage. If you succeed in matching up the candidate and the credentials presented to you, however, you may have found a new productive and valuable member of your team. Conduct reference checks or other checks yourself if you'll be the one working with the employee.

Many businesses, increasingly aware of the pitfalls of failing to adequately evaluate applicants before bringing them on board, are conducting background checks on candidates. *Background checks* take reference checks a step further, and businesses use them because they feel they're a way to gain more assurance that the people they hire are what they seem to be. In other words, where reference checks allow you to verify with former employers a potential hire's accomplishments and personal attributes (see the preceding section), background checks attempt to delve into additional aspects of a candidate's activities and behaviour.

Background checks can take many forms, depending on the position and what the employer considers most important in evaluating job candidates. The principal measures in use today include the following:

>> Criminal background checks

>> Education records/academic degree verification

>> Certifications and licences (such as CPA)

>> Credit checks

>> Driving histories

>> Medical exams

>> Drug tests

>> Workers' compensation reports

Making Offers They Can't Refuse

After you make your final choice, you may think that you and the other decision-makers can just sit back and relax. Not just yet. You still must make the offer official, and if you don't proceed carefully, one of two things can happen: You can lose the candidate, or, even if the candidate comes aboard, you can start the relationship off on a bumpy note. The following sections tell you what to bear in mind.

Avoiding delays

REMEMBER

After you make up your mind about a candidate, make the offer immediately, especially if you're in a tight labour market. Even a day or two delay can cost you the employee of choice.

Putting your offer on the table

Give the person you want to hire all the details about salary, benefits, and anything extra. Most businesses make job offers verbally by phone and then follow up with an official letter.

WARNING

Never back down on anything you promise at any stage in the recruiting or hiring process. ("You misunderstood. I didn't say, 'We're giving you a car,' I asked whether you 'had' a car.") That's a sure way to scare off an employee, and it may land you in legal trouble as well.

You should establish a salary range for the position before you begin recruiting. In addition, make sure that you have a standard job offer letter as a template that you can customize and that you clear the template with legal counsel.

Also, remind the individual of the benefits of joining your business. Augment the discussion about the financial aspects of the offer by highlighting positives, such as a supportive work environment and the chance to work on a variety of assignments.

REMEMBER

Consult your lawyer for advice on employment contracts and to create a contract template if you go in this direction. An employment contract doesn't need to be a 20-page legal document. It can take the form of a one-page letter that specifies the job title, duties, responsibilities and obligations, conditions of employment, and, most important, severance arrangements if things don't work out.

Setting a deadline

Give candidates a reasonable amount of time to decide whether to accept the offer. What's "reasonable" generally depends on the type of job. The time frame for an entry-level job may be a few days, but for a middle- or senior-level candidate in a competitive market or for a position that involves relocation, a week isn't excessive.

Staying connected

While a candidate is considering an offer, you, the hiring manager, or people from the interview panel should stay in touch with the candidate. The purpose is for you to reinforce your excitement about the candidate potentially joining your team. This could involve keeping in touch by phone or e-mail, or even asking the candidate to have lunch with you or visit the office during work hours.

Negotiating salary

After receiving a candidate's response to your offer, you must be prepared to negotiate. Job seekers today have access to an abundance of information on salary negotiation through websites and books, so most will enter the meeting ready to haggle. To reach a fair deal, you need to be equally prepared.

Decide how far you're willing to go

If the candidate suggests a higher figure than you've offered, you can choose to raise the amount of your proposal and wait for the candidate to respond or give a counteroffer. Then, ideally, you arrive at an agreement that's within the salary range you've set for the position.

If the candidate keeps pushing, whether you want to exceed the established range generally depends on two factors: one, how badly you want the individual; and two, the policies and precedents in your company. Ask yourself these three questions before you bring in the heavy artillery:

>> Are other, equally qualified candidates available if the applicant says no?

>> Has the job been particularly hard to fill, or are market conditions making finding and recruiting suitable candidates difficult? If the answer is yes, the leverage rests with the candidate.

>> Will a stronger offer be significantly out of line with existing pay levels for comparable positions in your business?

Recognize that if you decide to go beyond the firm's pay scale to win a really stellar candidate, you risk poor morale among existing staff if they learn that a new hire in the same role is making more money. And the best-kept secrets often do get out.

Think creatively

If you're not able to match a candidate's salary request, consider expanding other components of the package. Applicants are often willing to compromise on base compensation if concessions are made in other areas.

Flexible scheduling is one candidate-pleasing option that will cost you little to nothing. Providing additional time off or opportunities to telecommute may also be acceptable to a candidate in lieu of higher wages. Also consider a signing bonus or a performance-based bonus after a specified period of time.

Knowing when to draw the line

Some HR experts insist that you shouldn't push too hard if a candidate isn't interested. Probing a bit in order to find out why a candidate is being hesitant isn't a bad idea, though. Try to identify the source of the problem and make reasonable accommodations. But don't get so caught up in negotiations that you lose sight of what is appropriate for your business. Sometimes you just have to walk away.

Clarify acceptance details

Some businesses ask candidates to sign a duplicate copy of the job-offer letter to show they accept the offer. The signature confirms that the candidate understands the basic terms of the offer. If you're making a job offer contingent on reference checking or a physical examination and/or drug and alcohol testing, or background checks, make sure that the candidate understands and accepts this restriction.

Checking in

Even after a candidate accepts your offer and you agree on a starting date, keeping in touch with the new employee is still a good idea. Two to three weeks is the customary time between an acceptance and start date. Most people who are changing jobs give a standard two-weeks' notice to their former employer. For those who want to take a few days off before starting their new job, a three-week interval is not unusual. Use the transition period to mail off all those informational brochures and employment forms and to schedule a lunch or two, if appropriate.

IN THIS CHAPTER

» **Creating an effective compensation system**

» **Making a positive work environment**

» **Offering flexible working arrangements**

» **Preventing employee burnout**

» **Checking the pulse of your workforce**

» **Exploring training and development**

Chapter **2**

Retention: Critical in Any Business Environment

The compensation system you establish for employees is one of the main engines that drives your business. If your business is like most, payroll is an expensive engine to maintain — probably even your number one expense.

But payroll is not just an expense. How much you pay your employees and the factors you use to establish pay scales and award raises, bonuses, and incentives can profoundly affect the quality of your workforce. The way you compensate people plays a key role in your ability to attract and retain a productive, reliable workforce.

In this chapter, you find out about how to build well-planned compensation system so your employees will stick around. You also see how to be a people-friendly business, check out different work arrangements, and look at the benefits of training and developing your workforce for the benefit of your business and employees.

Ensuring an Effective Compensation Structure

Your business's compensation and benefits package should be competitive enough to keep your top employees from being wooed away by businesses that claim to offer better total compensation packages.

REMEMBER

Get the sound advice of your lawyer when making decisions about compensation. A lawyer can assist you in setting up policies and wage structures that can help you avoid problems, legal and otherwise.

Speaking the language of employee compensation

Unless you specialize in employee compensation, terminology can get confusing. So, to start you out, the following list offers a quick rundown of key terms in the field, along with their definitions:

>> **Compensation:** You use this term to define all the rewards that employees receive in exchange for their work, including base pay, bonuses, and incentives.

>> **Base salary:** The base salary is simply the salary or wage — before deductions and incentives — that employees receive for the work they do.

>> **Raises:** This term refers to increases in base salary, as opposed to one-time or periodic awards.

>> **Bonuses and incentives:** These two terms may seem like synonyms. To some degree, they are. What both have in common is the objective of making employees feel appreciated and valued.

REMEMBER

But the terms also have key differences. A *bonus* is a reward for a job well done. Though usually financial, bonuses also can include rewarding with time off, a free membership to a local health club, or discounts on merchandise. In contrast, an *incentive* is a tool used to boost productivity. In other words, an incentive programme sets a goal — "Contact ten new customers within a month" — and rewards employees who attain it. An easy way to remember the distinction: An incentive comes *before* work is done; a bonus comes *after*.

>> **Benefits:** Benefits are also items that you offer to employees in addition to their base wage or salary. Examples include health insurance, stock options, and retirement plans.

>> **Commission:** This term refers to a percentage of the sales price of a service or product that salespeople receive in addition to (or in lieu of) salary. Commission arrangements are sometimes *straight commission* (with no salary), sometimes combined with a base salary, and sometimes part of an arrangement in which the salesperson receives a set amount (known as a *draw*) on a regular basis, regardless of how much commission is actually earned during that period, with adjustments made at set intervals.

Being consistent and flexible

When you're establishing total compensation packages, you need to be both consistent and flexible. The two may sound contradictory, but they actually go hand in hand.

>> *Consistency* means that you have a logical plan and structure for compensation and benefits so you don't inadvertently create employee discord by giving the impression that you're showing favouritism or acting capriciously.

>> *Flexibility* means that you're doing your best — within reason — to adapt to the individual needs and desires of your employees.

By balancing these two factors, you get a wage-and-salary structure that not only gives your employees equitable compensation, but also focuses on the market realities of your business.

Basing compensation and benefits on a scale

The compensation and benefits aspect of the human resources function is very detail oriented. And the bigger the business, the more complicated maintaining the required paper trail can be. But benefits and compensation is also one of the more engaging areas of human resources. Businesses have become much more creative in the ways they reward employees, from performance-based pay to stock options. Your business's overall compensation package plays a major role in your ability to recruit and retain employees. You don't need an advanced degree in economics to know that your business could wind up in big financial trouble if you ignore compensation and benefits.

It's all about scale. For a one-person business, decisions regarding wages, private health coverage, sick leave, retirement, and educational assistance aren't likely to bring a flood of red ink to your bottom line. You can give yourself a raise, take a few extra vacation days, add special areas to your medical coverage without losing sleep over whether these extra expenditures will put you out of business.

REMEMBER

You enter an entirely new phase of operation when you hire your first full-time or part-time employee. When you're responsible for someone else's well-being, you must become more structured in your basic approach to compensation and benefits — and, for that matter, to all HR issues. And that's not particularly easy. Even a seemingly routine decision, such as whether or not to offer private health and dental insurance, becomes complex. The same principle holds true for all decisions regarding such benefits as overtime, holidays, vacations, and so on.

Setting the Foundation for an Effective Compensation System

When thinking about compensation, think *system*. Creating an effective compensation system requires thinking strategically — that is, with a constant eye toward the long-term needs and goals of your business. Your goal is to establish a well thought-out set of practices that helps to ensure the following results:

>> Employees receive a fair and equitable salary (from their perspective) for the work that they perform.

>> Payroll costs are in line with the overall financial health of your business.

>> Your employees clearly understand your basic philosophy of compensation.

>> The pay scale for the various jobs in the business reflects the relative importance of the job and the skills that those jobs require.

>> Pay scales are competitive enough so that you're not constantly seeing competitors hire your top employees away from you.

>> Compensation policies are in line with provincial and federal laws involving minimum wage, vacation pay, and so forth.

>> Compensation policies are keeping pace with the changing nature of today's labour market — particularly in recruiting and retaining your business's top performers.

REMEMBER

Federal and provincial laws require employers to pay employees on time and at regular periods. The laws also regulate what employers must and may deduct from an employee's paycheque.

Setting pay levels in your organization

One of the fundamental tasks in creating an equitable and effective wage and compensation system is to develop a consistent protocol for setting pay levels for each job in your organization. The more essential a job is to the fundamental mission of your business, the higher its pay range is likely to be.

TIP

The following procedure can help you come up with some preliminary guidelines:

1. **Make a list of all the jobs at your business, from the most senior to the least senior employee.**

2. **Group the jobs by major function — management, administrative, production, and so on.**

3. **Rank the jobs according to their relationship to your business's mission.**

   You wind up with two major categories — those jobs that contribute directly to the mission and those jobs that provide support for those mission-critical jobs. Ask yourself the following questions to help make this particular distinction:

   - How closely does the job relate to our mission?

   - How indispensable is the job?

   - How difficult is the job — that is, does it require special skills or training?

   - Does the position generate revenue or support revenue-producing functions?

   - Do political or other factors make this job important?

   Eventually, you produce a ranking or hierarchy of positions. Keep in mind that you're not rating individuals. You're rating the relative importance of each job with respect to your business's mission and strategic goals.

In setting the actual pay scale for specific jobs, you have several options, as the following sections describe.

Job evaluation and pay grading

How this approach works: You look at each job in your business and evaluate it on the basis of several factors, such as relative value to the bottom line, complexity, hazards, required credentials, and so on.

The rationale: In large businesses, you must use a reasonably structured approach to deciding what pay range to apply to each job. Otherwise, you invite chaos.

The more systematic you are as you develop that structure, the more effective the system is likely to be.

The downside: Creating and maintaining a structure of this nature takes a lot of time and effort.

The going rate

How this approach works: You look at what other businesses in your industry (and region) pay people for comparable jobs and set up your pay structure accordingly. You can obtain this data from government and industry websites and publications.

Rationale: The laws of supply and demand directly affect salary levels, as do geographic factors such as cost of housing and living, among others.

The downside: Comparing even apples to apples can be difficult in today's job market. Many new jobs that businesses are creating today are actually combinations of jobs in the traditional sense of the word and, as such, can prove difficult to price.

Management fit

How this approach works: The owner decides arbitrarily how much each employee is paid.

Rationale: The owner of a business has the right to pay people whatever that owner deems appropriate.

The downside: Inconsistent wage differentials often breed resentment and discontent. Lack of a reasonable degree of internal equity diminishes the spirit of teamwork and fairness.

Collective bargaining

How this approach works: In unionized workplaces, formal bargaining between management and labour representatives sets wage levels for specific groups of workers, based on market rate and the employer's resources available to pay wages.

The rationale: Workers should have a strong say (and agree as a group) on how much the business pays them. This system, of course, is (arguably) the ultimate form of establishing internal equity.

The downside: Acrimony arises if management and labour fail to see eye to eye. In addition, someone else — the union — plays a key role in your business decisions. Also, in this system, employees who perform exceptionally well can feel less rewarded because their wages are then the same as less proficient colleagues in similar positions.

Accounting for individuals

You pay people, not positions. So, sooner or later, you must program into your salary decisions those factors that relate solely to the individual performing the job. The following list describes the key "people factors" that you may want to consider in defining your pay–scale structure.

>> Experience and education

>> Job performance

>> Seniority

>> Potential

The bottom line on overtime

Employees in many industries depend on the extra money they make in overtime wages to support their standard of living. No one disputes that overtime certainly makes sense in many situations. The question you need to ask yourself is whether overtime is the best option for your business in any given situation. The question doesn't lend itself to a from–the–hip answer, but the following list describes basic truths about overtime:

WARNING

>> Responding to increased demand by putting existing workers on overtime is less expensive than hiring new employees.

>> Of course, cost savings from using overtime are true only for a short period of time. A steady diet of overtime to increase production can have negative long-term consequences. Numerous studies have demonstrated that excessive, long-term overtime can increase the rate of on-the-job accidents, erode employee morale, and cause family pressures.

>> You're best off viewing overtime as a stop-gap strategy, reserving it for short-term situations, such as when people call in sick or take vacations, or when the workload increases in the short term. If the need becomes constant, consider adding a new employee.

Reviewing the Basics of Raises, Bonuses, and Incentives

Offering competitive compensation is key in attracting top talent to your organization, but once employees are on board, salary levels don't stay competitive for long. As staff develop new skills and increase their knowledge of your business, they become more and more valuable to you — and their value in the marketplace increases as well, meaning that they become attractive targets for other businesses. To keep your best and brightest, you need to figure out fair (and affordable) ways to augment what you pay them. Most businesses enhance their compensation through raises, bonuses, and incentives designed to retain their best workers and give them a reason to stay on.

Employers structure effective bonus and incentive programmes around the following main principles:

>> **Results-oriented:** Employees must accomplish something to receive a bonus.

>> **Fair:** The rules for bonuses are clear, and you enforce them equitably.

>> **Competitive:** The programme rewards extra effort and superior performance.

Pay raises

Traditional pay systems often link raises to *tenure* (that is, time spent in that grade or position). Other systems frequently tie raises to performance. The most common types of raises include the following:

>> Seniority

>> Merit raise

>> Productivity increases

>> Cost of living adjustments

Bonuses

Bonuses are one-shot payments that you always key to results: the business's, the employee's, or those of the employee's department. They come in a variety of flavours:

>> **Annual and bi-annual bonuses:** These bonuses are one-shot payments to all eligible employees, based on the business's results, individual performance, or a combination thereof.

>> **Spot bonuses:** Spot bonuses are awarded in direct response to a single instance of superior employee performance (an employee suggestion, for example). Employees receive the bonus on the spot — that is, at the time of, or immediately thereafter, the action that has earned the bonus.

>> **Retention bonuses:** You make such payments to persuade key people — top managers or star performers — to stay with your business. These bonuses are common in industries that employ hard-to-recruit specialists.

>> **Team bonuses:** These bonuses are awarded to group members for the collective success of their team.

Incentives

Incentives are like bonuses in that they don't increase base pay. The difference is that most incentive programmes, unlike bonuses, are often long term in nature to cement employee loyalty or spur productivity. The following sections outline some common incentive programmes.

Profit-sharing plans

Profit-sharing plans enable the business to set aside a percentage of its profits for distribution to employees. If profits go up, the employees get more money. You can focus these programmes very sharply by allocating the profit sharing on a department or business-unit basis.

Stock

Stock in the business is an incentive that publicly traded firms (or firms planning to go public) may choose to offer their employees. *Stock option* plans give employees at publicly held companies the right to purchase shares in the business at a time of their own choosing, but at a price that is set at the time the option is awarded. Employees are under no obligation to exercise that option, but should the stock go up, employees can buy the stock at the cheaper price and either hold on to it or sell it for the current value, thereby earning a profit.

Stock options have also given small, growing businesses a way to attract top talent without having to pay high salaries.

REMEMBER

If your business is thinking about offering stock options as part of your overall benefits package, everyone must be aware of certain aspects of the process. If you're a privately held business, for example, your employees need to recognize that a stock option plan isn't likely to mean anything to them unless your business goes public or is acquired. If you're publicly held, you need to make sure that you have an organized plan and some mechanisms in place that will not dilute the value of the stock to non-employee stock-holders. Bear in mind, too, that these programmes must comply with tax and security laws.

What's fair versus what works

The easiest way to start a mutiny among your employees is to institute a raise or bonus process that people don't clearly understand and that neither managers nor employees buy into. The following list offers guidelines to help you avoid this all-too-common pitfall:

>> Set clear rules.

>> Set specific targets or goals that you can quantify.

>> Make the goal worthwhile.

>> Don't ask for the impossible.

>> Don't make promises you can't keep.

Communicating Your Compensation Policies

Many businesses unfortunately spend a lot of time and effort designing a pay system and then leave it to the paycheque alone to communicate their pay philosophy and administration. You need to thoroughly brief managers and supervisors in particular on your business's pay systems so that they can effectively explain, administer, and support your policies. Managers and supervisors need to possess the following information:

>> Your business's pay philosophy

>> How to conduct a performance appraisal

>> How to handle and refer employee pay complaints

>> Legal implications of all compensation policies

You need to advise employees of the business's pay policies and how these policies affect them individually. You also need to communicate and fully explain any changes in these policies promptly. Employees need to possess the following information:

>> The job's rating system, how it works, and how it affects them

>> How the performance-appraisal and incentive systems work

>> How they can raise their own income through performance and promotion

>> How to voice complaints or concerns

You must keep your compensation system competitive and up-to-date. The key steps in doing so are as follows:

>> Obtain and review competitive data at regular intervals.

>> Review — and adjust if necessary — salary ranges at least annually.

>> Review job descriptions regularly and make adjustments based on disparities between actual work performance and the formal description.

>> Evaluate the performance-appraisal system. One common problem is that too many employees get superior ratings.

>> Review salary systems in terms of your business's financial condition to determine whether the system is in line with the business's financial health and is tax-effective and efficient.

>> Periodically measure and rate productivity and determine whether any links exist between productivity increases (or declines) and pay policies.

Creating an Employee-Friendly Work Environment

A wise man once said that the mark of an outstanding mind is the ability to hold two seemingly opposing ideas at the same time. Consider two aspects of contemporary business: On the one hand, in order to thrive, your organization must be diligent, competitive, and keenly focused on bottom-line results. But at the same time, most businesses that earn respect and profits know that nothing is more critical to attaining their goals than a workforce that feels not just engaged, but valued. Businesses that are appropriately attuned to creating a supportive, nurturing work environment stand the best chance for long-term growth. What appear to be opposite ideas — unwavering attention to business results, coupled with an employee-friendly environment — go together like bees and honey. Your skill in linking the two can go a long way toward building a first-rate organization.

A number of organizations and publications regularly select lists of best employers and best employment practices. While the criteria sometimes differ and the approaches vary, all would agree that the best employers do the following to create a people-friendly workplace:

>> Foster employee well-being

>> Are reasonably committed to job security

>> Provide people-friendly facilities

>> Are sensitive to work-life balance issues

>> Allow for a high degree of employee autonomy

>> Ensure open communication

>> Create a sense of belonging among employees

Establishing Alternate Work Arrangements

Broadly speaking, an alternate work arrangement is any scheduling pattern that deviates from the traditional Monday-through-Friday, nine-to-five workweek.

Alternate work arrangements are an approach that employees really care about. Flexibility is the basic idea behind alternate work arrangements. You give employees some measure of control over their work schedules to help them manage non-job-related responsibilities. The business rationale behind the concept is that by supporting employees to deal with pressures on the home front, they'll be more productive when they're on the job — and less likely to jump ship if one of your competitors offers them a little more money.

Alternate work arrangements are generally grouped into the following general categories:

>> Flextime

>> Compressed workweek

>> Job-sharing

» Telecommuting

» Permanent part-time arrangements

In theory, alternate work arrangements offer a win-win situation. Many studies have shown that flexible scheduling policies improve morale and job satisfaction, reduce absenteeism, cut down on turnover, and minimize burnout — with no measurable decline in productivity.

REMEMBER

But these arrangements don't work for every business at every level, and thus the practices may have to be carefully implemented with some legally sound ground rules. In addition, instituting a policy of alternate work arrangements involves a good deal more than simply giving your employees a broader selection of scheduling options. The process needs to be carefully thought out. It must be implemented with consistency, patience, and discipline because you can easily ruin a good thing.

Follow these guidelines if you're thinking of setting up a flexible scheduling policy in your business:

» Be willing to rethink processes.

» Establish guidelines.

» Pay attention to legal implications.

» Get managerial buy-in.

Looking at Telecommuting

Telecommuting is one of the fastest-growing alternate work arrangements. Strictly speaking, *telecommuters* are employees who regularly work out of their homes or other locations all or part of the workweek. The key word in the previous definition is *regularly*. The structured aspect of the arrangement is what differentiates telecommuters as a group from employees who routinely take work home from the office.

Telecommuting arrangements vary. In some cases, employees never come into the office except for special events. More typically, though, a business's telecommuters spend part of the week — one or two days, usually — working out of their homes and the rest of the week in the office.

Identifying prime candidates for telecommuting

Candidates for a successful telecommuting arrangement might include those who

>> Perform a function that doesn't require extensive interaction with other employees or the use of equipment found only on business premises.

>> Have a compelling personal reason (a long commute, for example, or family responsibilities) for working from home part of the time.

>> Have the temperament and the discipline to work alone.

>> Can be absent from the office without creating an inconvenience for others in the business.

These factors are just a few to consider when selecting telecommuting candidates. You should also take into account a number of sticky legal and operational aspects.

Home office expenses

The basic question is simple: Who pays for what? The answer isn't simple and can depend on any number of factors, including the safety and health of the employee. The general guideline is that if the expense involves a piece of equipment that an employee must use to perform the job and that the employer would routinely be responsible for if the employee were working on business premises, your business should consider paying for it.

This guideline doesn't mean that you're obliged to replicate the working conditions at your business (the corporate gym, for example) in the telecommuter's home office. But most businesses view basic resources — at least one dedicated phone line, a computer with a high-speed Internet connection, a scanner, and a photocopier — as business expenses. Common sense needs to prevail.

Viability of service contracts

Some office equipment vendors provide service only at the employer's office locations. If your business intends to furnish a telecommuter's home office with equipment that would normally be covered by a service contract, double-check with the service provider to make sure that your policy covers residential visits.

Security

REMEMBER

The mere fact that telecommuters are working out of the office — well outside the sphere of normal business security procedures — creates a hornet's nest of potential security problems. Technology-driven security measures, such as access codes, passwords, and firewalls, can reduce but never eliminate the chance that confidential business information will end up in the wrong hands, particularly when the Internet is an integral part of many people's jobs. At the very least, have a written agreement with all telecommuters that spells out the business's confidentiality policies and sets down specific guidelines.

Local zoning issues

Many communities have zoning restrictions against conducting certain business activities in residential neighbourhoods. While these rules generally are loosely enforced, the restrictions can create legal problems. Somebody — either the employee or employer — should take the initiative to investigate the situation before a problem arises.

Temperament and discipline

Unquestionably, telecommuting provides many opportunities and rewards. It's a highly productive way for certain employees to get their work done. It's also a good way to draw on the skills of talented, high-performing employees who may otherwise be unable to work for your business under a standard scheduling arrangement. This advantage makes it a compelling recruiting strategy.

But you should also take into account other factors before permitting someone to telecommute. For example, consider the temperament and discipline of the telecommuter. Can the individual continually work effectively in relative isolation? How does the employee's work fit into a broader team environment — not just now, but as you look ahead to future growth? What is the impact of the telecommuting arrangement on others? If the telecommuter is a manager, for example, supervising people even part of the time by telephone and e-mail is not always productive.

Setting up an agreement for a telecommuter

Consider preparing a formal agreement with any employee who is going to be telecommuting. The agreement, at the very least, should spell out the following:

>> The specific scheduling terms — that is, how much time the employee spends at home or at the office.

>> The specific equipment the business is willing to provide, and how the equipment is to be installed and maintained.

>> Reporting requirements: How often should the telecommuter send e-mail updates? Should the employee be part of a weekly departmental conference call? What kind of voice mail setup will the employee have (on both the business home office line and cellphone)?

>> How proprietary information is to be controlled and handled.

Avoiding Burnout

The Japanese have a word for it: *karoshi*. The term means, literally, "death from overwork." *Karoshi* may not be a major cause of death in Canada, but almost everywhere you look in today's lean and mean environment — even in businesses with employee-friendly policies — you sometimes hear complaints and concerns about employee burnout. Often it relates to the psychological, social, and physical problems that result when workers literally "wear down" from stress and become unable to cope with workday demands.

Most psychologists explain burnout as the convergence of two forces:

>> High job demand

>> Low job control

In a typical burnout situation, employees not only feel tremendous pressure to extend themselves, but they also perceive that they lack the ability or the resources to meet the demands. Whether this latter perception is justified doesn't really matter. As long as employees believe they're both overworked and under-resourced, the potential for employee burnout exists.

Recognizing employee burnout

Employee burnout can manifest itself any number of ways. Among the most obvious signs are the following:

>> Noticeable increase in staff absenteeism or tardiness

>> Any obvious change (for the worse) in the general mood of the workplace

>> Uncharacteristic emotional outbursts from employees who are normally calm

>> Increased customer complaints about the quality of goods and services

REMEMBER

Burnout doesn't happen overnight; it's a gradual process. However, if you can become sensitive to the warning signs of burnout, you can frequently avert a crisis. Your managers and supervisors are your first line of defense against burnout and the workplace problems it causes. Make sure that they're trained to recognize burnout symptoms before the situation gets out of hand.

Being sensitive to extended periods of excessive workload

The prime cause of employee burnout is overwork, or, to be more precise, sustained periods of overwork. Most successful businesses, of course, run into periods of peak workloads from time to time, and expecting good employees to rise to the occasion isn't unreasonable. But even if you're giving your regular employees extra income to meet the increased demand, at some point even the most dedicated employees will reach their physical, emotional, and mental limits. When they reach this point, you have two options:

>> Hire additional full-time employees.

>> Hire supplemental workers to ease the burden.

Giving employees more day-to-day job autonomy

Productive, happy employees generally feel that they're making unique contributions that provide a sense of personal pride. Peter Drucker, the prominent management scholar, repeatedly emphasized the importance of personal ownership. If you've haven't already done so, take a look at the responsibilities your employees have, make sure that they have the necessary resources, and then be certain to provide them with plenty of independence.

REMEMBER

You've no doubt heard of or experienced the dreaded micromanager. And perhaps you've found moments when you yourself have taken on some of those characteristics and suffered the consequences. You don't need to abandon demanding accountability (such as weekly update meetings or written reports), but think how much you like it when your own supervisors display ample trust in your ability to get your work done. Nothing is more important to wedding productivity and an employee-friendly culture than encouraging self-reliance and the accompanying spirit of trust.

Providing help

No matter how good your work environment, some employees will develop personal problems that have nothing to do with your business but that they nonetheless bring to work. The most damaging effects include behaviour and attitudes that hinder their ability to do their jobs. The HR professional has a responsibility to offer resources to assist employees in addressing these issues.

In the HR world, programs that help workers cope with personal difficulties are known as *Employee Assistance Programs* (EAPs). EAPs include such activities as confidential counselling or seminars for employees seeking to better handle job pressures. Employees need to know that help is available and that their careers will not suffer if they seek it.

Keeping Tabs on Morale

In many cases, particularly if your business has fewer than 50 employees, you don't have a hard time getting a good read on the general atmosphere in the workplace. You're able to personally make your way around offices and work areas enough to observe how employees interact with one another, how they feel about the way they're treated by senior management, and whether morale is rising or falling.

If your business is larger — over 50 employees — periodically conduct a rigorous employee survey. Here are some tips on how to proceed:

>> Watch your timing. Don't conduct surveys during holidays when many employees may be taking days off. And avoid exceptionally heavy workload periods.

>> Think carefully about your objectives before crafting your survey questions. What do you want to find out? What do you intend to do with the information?

>> Share survey objectives with employees, but do so in language that's relevant to them. In other words, instead of using HR terms such as "We want to assess employee attitudes," tell them that "We want to hear your thoughts since we merged with Company X."

>> Before you unveil your survey to the entire business, test it out on a small group of employees to see whether your questions are appropriate and what you can refine.

>> A key step: Assure employees that their comments are confidential.

>> Communicate to employees the results of the survey on a timely basis and take action, as appropriate, when employees make recommendations. Let employees know how their input has affected policies.

TIP

When you're trying to "take the temperature" of the organization, some of the most candid employees are often those who are leaving your business. To gain valuable ideas about improving your working conditions and making the workplace more inviting, consider conducting exit interviews with employees who have resigned or are otherwise voluntarily leaving your business. (People you've had to fire, while potentially the most candid of all, are not good subjects for two reasons: They're unlikely to cooperate and, if they do, their input will probably be overly negative rather than constructive.)

Providing Training and Development

In a perfect world, every employee you hire would already possess the knowledge, skills, and background to perform every facet of the job flawlessly. However, employees can always discover something that can help improve their performance. This simple, universally acknowledged principle underlies the HR function, and is generally known as employee training and development.

Broadly speaking, *employee training and development* refers to a wide range of educational and learning-based tools. These activities aren't inherently built into job functions, but generally produce some positive change in the way employees handle their work. These activities can range from a live seminar, to digital content that employees listen to while commuting, to an online instructional session they participate in at home or at their desks.

REMEMBER

No matter what the nature of your business, you won't stay on top unless you help your people stay ahead of emerging trends and changing needs. Increasing the knowledge of your workforce not only enhances your business's ability to compete, but also makes for more satisfied employees. Even in lean times, cutting back on training to reduce expenses can be "shooting yourself in the foot," both in terms of business success and employee retention.

Knowing the benefits of training

The biggest change in training is the degree to which it has become intertwined with other HR functions (hiring, promotions, and so on) and the business's long-term goals. Because businesses and employees alike value training, it's become a big business in its own right, with a wide range of products, services, seminars, and materials available for businesses of all sizes.

If you're responsible for training in a growth-oriented business, you're working more closely than ever with senior managers, supervisors, and employees. You're making sure that a logical connection exists between the programmes being offered and the skill sets necessary to keep your business competitive. Here are key factors:

>> **The "learning" route to competitive advantage:** Profitable organizations recognize that in today's highly competitive and changeable business environment, what employees currently know does not shape the business's future; what they must *eventually* know is most important. That's why one major objective of training is to increase each employee's intellectual capacity for acquiring the knowledge and skills needed to thrive amid the increasing demands and pressures of a global marketplace.

>> **The need to attract and keep talented employees:** The degree to which your business is genuinely committed to developing the skills of your employees is critical for attracting and keeping high-performing employees. Businesses that provide their employees with opportunities to learn and grow have an edge when recruiting.

>> **The competition for skilled labour:** Simply put, the "shape up or ship out" approach to managing is no longer feasible in most industries, even for entry-level positions. In response to the realities of the workplace, businesses are investing more time and money in training, mentoring, and developing other employee activities.

>> **The disappearance of hierarchies and the emergence of team play:** The ability to communicate effectively and build a spirit of teamwork is important in today's workplace.

Assessing your training needs

A growing number of consulting companies and individuals specialize in helping businesses identify their training needs. If your business is large enough and you don't have the time or resources to engage in this process yourself, consider hiring one of these outside sources. If you do decide to manage this process yourself, consider exploring the options in the upcoming sections.

REMEMBER

Keep in mind that some options work better at larger businesses, while others are more effective in smaller businesses.

Employee focus groups

Generally implemented at larger firms, *employee focus groups* often represent the ideal first step to a needs-assessment process. You pull together a group of employees from various departments or levels of your organization. If time permits, you spend a day or two (possibly off-site) discussing as a group what your business needs to do to achieve its strategic goals and what skills are required to meet this challenge. If you don't have much time, even a two- to three-hour session in a conference room at your office can be illuminating.

TIP

No matter how much time you're able to take, keep in mind these two keys to make sure that this process is productive:

>> **The make-up of the group:** The group should include representatives from a wide cross section of departments and experience levels.

>> **The ability of the facilitator:** It can be either you or someone else, but the facilitator needs to promote open discussion and keep the focus group from disintegrating into a "gripe session."

Surveys and questionnaires

Surveys and questionnaires are standard tools in the needs-assessment process. Depending on the size of your business, surveys may represent the most cost-effective approach to needs assessment.

If you intend to survey employees in this way, also gathering feedback from supervisors is a good idea. Each group may offer a unique perspective. You can also use a questionnaire to get some survey feedback from customers.

WARNING

Employees may well have an accurate sense of what they need to improve in order to perform more effectively, but these areas may not necessarily connect directly to the strategic objectives of the business. The goal is to view the information you gather from employees as simply one tool in a process.

Observation

Simply observing how employees are performing on the job and taking note of the problems they're experiencing can often give you insight into their training needs. Just be careful about the conclusions you draw. When observing employees who are struggling, you may be tempted to attribute the difficulty to a single cause — some problem that you can solve by scheduling a training programme or by sending them to a seminar.

TIP

One way to avoid the common pitfall of jumping to conclusions is to speak directly with the employees you've observed and give them the opportunity to explain why their performance may be falling short.

Tying training needs to strategic goals

Whatever approach (or approaches) you take to evaluate your training requirements, the needs-assessment process should be strategically driven. After you've gathered the data — regardless of how you've gathered it (see the preceding section for ideas) — you need to process it within the framework of the following questions:

>> What are the strategic goals of this business — both long term and short term?

>> What competencies do employees need to achieve these goals?

>> What are the current strengths and weaknesses of the workforce relative to those competencies?

>> What improvements can training be expected to offer that differ from day-to-day supervision?

>> What kind of a commitment — in money, time, and effort — is your business willing and able to make to provide necessary training?

Deciding whether to train or not to train

The basic question you need to ask is whether a training program represents the best and most cost-effective approach to reducing the gap between job demands and employee capabilities. How do you determine whether or not to train a group of employees, and how do you determine how much time and money to invest? No simple answers exist, but certain factors can help guide you:

>> State of the labour market

>> Current workload in the business

>> Internal resources and budget

Noting the principles of first-rate training

Fortune 100 companies like General Electric spend in excess of $1 billion a year on training. Though your business does not likely have that kind of budget, you can still show your employees you support their ongoing professional development. Training your employees does, of course, require spending money, but what matters most is the level of your commitment. Here are just a few ways your business can "walk the walk":

>> A progressive tuition reimbursement policy

>> A scheduling policy that doesn't oblige employees to attend training sessions during non-working hours

>> Excellent communication channels between HR professionals involved in training and line managers

>> Performance appraisal systems that take into account what managers have done to enhance the individual development of the employees they manage

>> A mentoring programme that gives employees the chance to learn from and interact with others in the business who might not necessarily be that employee's immediate supervisor (find out more about mentoring later in this chapter)

>> If possible, comfortable, well-equipped on-site facilities (a library or training room, for example) where employees have access to books, periodicals, research studies, digital content, and self-administered courses — and, of course, to the extent possible, this information should also be available through the company's intranet

Evaluating training options

After conducting the needs-assessment process, the biggest challenge you face is setting up an effective training programme. What follows is a brief look at the range of approaches that are possible today, along with the pros and cons.

In-house classroom training

With *in-house classroom training*, the traditional and most familiar form of training, a group of employees gathers in a classroom and is led through the programme by an instructor. These sessions occur on-site or off-site and can be facilitated by trainers who are either employees themselves or outside specialists.

Pros: The main advantage to classroom training (apart from its familiarity) is that it provides ample opportunities for group interaction and gives instructors a chance to motivate the group and address the individual needs of students.

Cons: In-house classroom training requires considerable administrative support. This form of training can also entail major expense (travel and lodging, for example), which is not directly connected to the learning experience.

Public seminars

You can encourage employees to attend topic-specific workshops that are organized and run by training companies. These public seminars are usually held at a public site, such as a hotel or conference centre.

Pros: Public seminars require little or no administrative support. The per-person cost is reasonable.

Cons: Most public seminar offerings are, by necessity, generic. Topics covered don't necessarily have direct relevance to your particular business. The quality of seminars may also vary from one to the next.

Executive education seminars

Seminars and workshops offered by universities and business schools are targeted, in most cases, to middle and upper-level managers. Typically they cover a wide range of both theoretical ideas and practical pointers for putting these principles into practice.

Pros: Instructors are usually faculty members with a high level of expertise. These kinds of seminars are a good opportunity for attendees to network and share ideas.

Cons: Courses at the more prestigious schools can take the executive away from the office for more days than desired. They're also expensive, in some cases as much as $5,000 (including room and board) for a five-day course. Make sure that events cover management concepts and techniques that are relevant or applicable to your business's focus and culture.

E-learning

E-learning has gained rapid acceptance throughout corporate North America. The concept of learning from sources based far away is, of course, hardly new. Correspondence courses were popular long before the Internet entered the workplace. But the great payoff of e-learning is its flexibility and speed, delivering the real-time immediacy of classroom instruction without the need to actually be present in a classroom.

Pros: E-learning has a number of important benefits:

» Vastly increases the scope and reach of a corporate training effort

» Eliminates, or greatly reduces, ancillary, non-learning expenses of training, such as travel and lodging costs for participants

» Enables students to work at their own pace and convenience so they avoid production downtime

» Enables participants to not only experience training in real time but also to store and retrieve information transmitted through the course

» Enables students to set up individualized objectives and to establish milestones to mark different levels of achievement

» Liberates you or your training staff from classroom presentations, enabling more one-on-one consultations

Cons: The downside of e-learning is that lack of human interaction and direct instructor involvement might not work well for people who are not self-motivated.

REMEMBER

Don't forget you've got to monitor and manage e-learning if it's to be successful. If you simply upload a slew of training courses and tell employees to "have at it," it won't do much good. But e-learning is easy to monitor. In fact, one of the benefits of e-learning is that you can track its usage to make sure that employees are engaged in the learning and are actively participating and completing the required workshops and courses. Encourage — and maybe even offer incentives (read more about incentives earlier in this chapter) — to employees who complete training. Set aside specific times for training so that employees feel comfortable temporarily stopping their day-to-day tasks to complete an online course.

REMEMBER

E-learning is a productive training technique, but also one that requires careful attention. You need to determine which mix of approaches best matches your real needs. Create a team consisting of yourself, technology experts, and line managers to figure out the best possible set of solutions. For example, the time and money required to set up an effective system of intranet-based training makes sense only when you have a lot of potential students — and only when your long-term strategy is to make your intranet your primary training delivery system.

Considering mentoring as a training tool

TIP

Some skills, such as interpersonal abilities, are not easily taught in the classroom or through online courses. In fact, some skills aren't taught well in groups at all. Enter employee mentors. Just as appointing a more experienced employee to serve as a mentor for a new employee can help the new person acclimate to your work environment, well-chosen mentors can likewise assist staff at any stage of their careers with longer term developmental learning.

In a mentoring role, an employee who excels in a given area — customer service, for example — can help fellow employees discover how to more smoothly interact with customers and colleagues or develop additional skills that require more long-term and individualized attention than a classroom or online course can offer. Regarding interpersonal, or people skills, employees who are paired with an appropriate manager can pick up such abilities as persuasiveness and diplomacy.

Mentors can also serve as valuable training facilitators for high-potential employees you may want to groom to eventually take over key roles. Mentoring programmes are among the most effective ways to transfer tacit knowledge from seasoned leaders to aspiring ones. As businesses prepare to lose their most experienced employees due to the retirement of many baby boomers, such arrangements may become important for passing on valuable know-how to less experienced workers and preparing them take on greater responsibility.

Deciding on a training programme

Learning is a highly individual process, and because of that you must remain leery of taking the "one-size-fits-all" approach. In general, here are some of the factors that most often influence the effectiveness of a programme, regardless of which form it takes:

>> Receptivity level of students

>> Applicability of subject matter

>> The overall learning experience and the variety of learning tools

>> Quality of instructor

>> Reinforcement of class concepts at work

Measuring the results of training efforts

HR professionals have long wrestled with the problem of quantifying the results of training — a process that doesn't readily lend itself to quantifiable measures. For example, one of the primary benefits of employee training is that it enhances morale. But how do you measure the bottom-line benefits of morale? Not easily, to be sure.

Yet another problem with measuring the results of training is that the skills and knowledge that people bring to a task represent only one factor in job performance. In many situations, factors that are independent of an employee's knowledge and skills will either impede or enhance job performance.

These issues aside, following are four generally accepted practices for measuring the results of training:

>> **Initial employee reaction:** The most common way to gather feedback from participants immediately following a training session is to distribute a questionnaire to each one at the end of the session. The answers give you a general idea of whether your employees thought the training was worthwhile. Post-training surveys measure initial reactions, but offer little insight into how effective the training was in the long run.

Employees' answers to the following survey questions can help you gauge the effectiveness of your training sessions:

- Did the course meet your expectations, based on the course description?

- Were the topics covered in the course directly relevant to your job?

- Was the instructor sensitive to the needs of the group?

- Were the instructional materials easy to follow and logical?

- Would you recommend this programme to other employees?

- Were the facilities adequate?

TIP

E-mail allows you to measure the effectiveness of training in a timely manner. You can quickly send surveys to large groups of employees. If you want, you can distribute them and ask for responses within a few days or even hours of the session's conclusion. You can also record survey responses online, with results organized into databases and available to HR and managers.

>> **Effectiveness of learning:** You can measure the learning that takes place during programmes that focus on well-defined technical skills (using software programmes, for example) by administering tests before and after the training and comparing the results. Keep in mind, though, that the subject matter of many training programmes (leadership skills, for example) doesn't lend itself to specific metrics. One way around this limitation is to observe the accomplishments or behaviour of employees in the weeks and months after soft skills training.

>> **Impact on job performance:** Determining whether training has had a positive impact on actual job performance depends on the nature of the training and the specific tasks. The problem? Performance in most jobs is

influenced by variables that may have little bearing on what was taught in a workshop. Participants might bring new skills back to their jobs, but run into resistance from supervisors when they try to put their new skills into practice. That's why educating business managers about the advantages training sessions bring to their employees is important.

WARNING

» **Cost/benefit analysis:** Training simply doesn't easily lend itself to familiar cost/benefit analysis. The costs are easy enough to quantify. The problem lies with attaching a dollar value to the many indirect benefits that training brings, which may include reduced absenteeism and turnover, reduced employee grievances, a less stressful workplace (with fewer medical problems), and the need for less supervision.

» Choosing and launching your appraisal system

» Ensuring appraisal meetings are effective

» Avoiding wrongful dismissal claims

» Setting up a progressive discipline procedure

» Firing or laying off employees

Chapter **3**

Monitoring Ongoing Performance

You've moved mountains to hire the best staff in the world, and you are offering them the most comprehensive and cost-effective benefits package known to man. But you have to keep the machines well oiled, turbocharge them occasionally, and fix them when they break down. From assessing the way your team is handling their jobs and inspiring them to achieve even more, to handling the not-so-fun aspects of HR, this chapter shows you how to keep it all together.

Assessing Employee Performance

Few management practices are more basic or prevalent than *performance appraisals* — the mechanism through which managers or supervisors evaluate the job performance of their employees. Yet, as common as the practice may be, many businesses, both large and small, experience difficulty in structuring and managing the process.

Effective managers have to monitor the performance of direct reports, note the areas of job performance need to be improved, and then communicate assessments to them in a positive and constructive way. How else would you determine how people get promoted, if they deserve salary increases, and how much they should be making?

The problem seems to be not with the concept, but with the format and mechanics.

>> In many businesses today, managers as well as employees aren't convinced of the value of appraisal systems. To many supervisors, they simply represent additional work, and some employees remain skeptical and apprehensive regarding the process.

>> In addition, traditional approaches to performance appraisals aren't necessarily well suited to today's flatter management structures, which de-emphasize direct supervision, promote employee autonomy, and often involve collaboration with many different employees from a wide range of disciplines. In fact, many younger businesses were created with the goal of intentionally *not* resembling older command-and-control corporations and, as a result, are reluctant to create formal employee performance evaluation procedures.

>> Yet another problem with performance appraisals in today's workplace is that the difficulty in finding highly skilled employees, coupled with the fear of litigation, has made some managers gun-shy about being too critical of staff.

REMEMBER

These problems notwithstanding, performance appraisals are a vital management function, and your business must implement a structured and systematic programme that takes into account the realities of today's workplace — and the nuances of your business's unique culture.

TIP

Here's a list of questions to ask yourself about your business's current programme. If you can answer "yes" to all the questions, you can probably relax. A "no" answer may indicate an aspect of your programme that needs to be re-examined.

>> Are all performance criteria job-related?

>> Is the focus on results, as opposed to personal traits?

>> Do your employees understand how the process works and how appraisals tie into other aspects of their jobs?

>> Have managers been adequately trained to implement the system?

>> Do employees thoroughly understand the programme?

>> Have all relevant employee behaviours been documented?

>> Have promises of confidentiality been kept?

>> Are all subsequent HR decisions consistent with employee evaluations?

>> Are follow-up plans built into appraisals?

>> Have you reviewed all elements of your programme with legal counsel?

Reaping the Benefits of Performance Appraisals

Creating and implementing a structured performance appraisal process is a challenge. For one thing, performance appraisals invariably create additional work for supervisors. The process also puts pressure on employees by forcing everyone to establish specific goals and identify the behaviours necessary to achieve those goals, which some may view in the short term as simply "busy work."

What's more, the very nature of appraisal systems puts both employees and supervisors into situations that most people find uncomfortable. Being, in effect, "graded" makes many employees feel as though they're back in school. And most managers, even those who've been involved with an evaluation process for many years, find being candid and constructive difficult when they're conducting an appraisal session that involves negative feedback.

REMEMBER

Why, then, should you put in the time and effort to create and implement this process? The answer is that the long-term benefits of an effectively structured and administered performance appraisal process far outweigh the time and effort the process requires. Here's what a well-designed, well-implemented performance appraisal system does for your business:

>> Creates criteria for determining how well employees are truly performing — and, to that end, clarifies how their job descriptions and responsibilities fit in with business and departmental priorities

>> Provides an objective — and legally defensible — basis for key human resources decisions, including merit pay increases, promotions, and job responsibilities

>> Verifies that reward mechanisms are logically tied to outstanding performance

>> Motivates employees to improve their job performance

- ≫ Enhances the impact of the coaching that is already taking place between employees and their managers
- ≫ Establishes a reasonably uniform set of performance standards that are in sync with the business's values
- ≫ Confirms that employees possess the skills or attributes needed to successfully fulfil a particular job
- ≫ Irons out difficulties in the supervisor-employee relationship
- ≫ Gives underperforming employees the guidance that can lead to better performance
- ≫ Keeps employees focused on business goals and objectives
- ≫ Helps employees clarify career goals
- ≫ Validates hiring strategies and practices
- ≫ Reinforces corporate values
- ≫ Assesses training and staff development needs
- ≫ Motivates employees to upgrade their skills and job knowledge so that they can make a more meaningful contribution to your business's success

Deciding on a Performance Appraisal System

All performance appraisal systems are driven by the same objective: to establish a systematic way of evaluating performance, providing constructive feedback, and enabling employees to continually improve their performance.

The basic ingredients in all systems are pretty much the same: setting performance criteria, developing tracking and documenting procedures, determining which areas should be measured quantitatively, and deciding how the information is to be communicated to employees. Methods vary in the following areas:

- ≫ The degree to which employees are involved in establishing performance evaluation criteria
- ≫ How employee performance is tracked and documented
- ≫ How performance is rated and how it's aligned with corporate priorities, objectives, and goals

>> The specific types of appraisal tools used — in some cases, for example, certain approaches are more appropriate for evaluating managers and professionals than other employees

>> The amount of time and effort required to implement the process

>> How the results of the appraisal are integrated into other management or HR functions

>> How the actual appraisal session is conducted

The following sections offer a brief description of performance appraisal methods most commonly used today.

Goal-setting, or management by objectives

In a typical management by objectives (MBO) scenario, an employee and a manager sit down together at the start of an appraisal period and formulate a set of statements that represent specific job goals, targets, or *deliverables.*

TIP

What makes MBO so powerful is its direct link to organizational objectives and priorities. In the case of MBO, goals, targets, and deliverables should be as specific and measurable as possible. For example, instead of "improve customer service" (too vague), try something like "reduce the number of customer complaints by 5 percent." And instead of "increase number of sales calls" (too vague), go with "increase the number of sales calls by 5 percent without changing current criteria for prospects."

This list of targets becomes the basis for an action plan that spells out what steps need to be taken to achieve each goal. At a later date — six months or a year later — the employee and the manager sit down again and measure employee performance on the basis of how many of those goals were met.

Essay appraisals

The *essay approach* can be useful for a supervisor to periodically compose statements that describe an employee's performance. The statements are usually written on standard forms, and they can be as general or as specific as you want. A supervisor may describe an employee's performance in terms of "the employee's ability to relate to other team members." These written statements can either be forwarded to the HR department or used as one element in an appraisal session. Any written evaluation also needs to include more measurable evaluation tools, such as rating scales applied to specific objectives, tasks, and goals.

Critical incidents reporting

The *critical incidents method* of performance appraisal is built around a list of specific behaviours, generally known as *critical behaviours*, that are deemed necessary to perform a particular job competently. Performance evaluators use a critical incident report to record actual incidents of behaviour that illustrate when employees either carried out or didn't carry out these behaviours. You can use these logs to document a wide variety of job behaviours, such as interpersonal skills, initiative, and leadership ability.

Job rating checklist

The *job rating checklist* method of performance appraisal is the simplest method to use and lends itself to a variety of approaches. To implement this approach, you supply each evaluator with a prepared list of statements or questions that relate to specific aspects of job performance. The questions typically require the evaluator to write a simple "yes" or "no" answer or to record a number (or some other notation) that indicates which statement applies to a particular employee's performance.

Behaviourally anchored rating scale

Behaviourally anchored rating scale (BARS) systems are designed to emphasize the behaviour, traits, and skills needed to successfully perform a job. A typical BARS form has two columns. The left column has a rating scale, usually in stages from very poor to excellent. The right column contains behavioural anchors that are the reflections of those ratings.

If the scale were being used, for example, to evaluate a telephone order taker, the statement in one column may read "1–very poor," and the statement in the right column may read, "Occasionally rude or abrupt to customer" or "Makes frequent mistakes on order form."

Forced choice

Forced-choice methods generally come in two forms: paired statements and forced ranking.

>> In the *paired statements method,* evaluators are presented with two statements and must check the one that best describes the employee; it's either one or the other.

» In the *forced ranking method,* a number of options are listed, allowing the evaluator to select a description that may fall somewhere in between the two extremes.

The following example illustrates how each version may be used to cover the same aspect of job performance for a field service representative.

Paired statements:

____ Provides sufficient detail when filling out trip reports

____ Doesn't provide sufficient detail when filling out trip reports

Forced ranking:

____ Provides sufficient detail when filling out trip reports

____ Exceptional

____ Above average

____ Average

____ Needs improvement

____ Unsatisfactory

Ranking methods

Ranking methods compare employees in a group to one another. All involve an evaluator who asks managers to rank employees from the "best" to the "worst" with respect to specific job performance criteria. The three most common variations of this method are as follows:

» **Straight ranking:** Employees are simply listed in order of ranking.

» **Forced comparison:** Every employee is paired with every other employee in the group, and in each case, the manager identifies the better of the two employees in any pairing. The employees are ranked by the number of times they're identified as the best.

» **Forced distribution:** The employees are ranked along a standard statistical distribution, the so-called *bell curve.*

Multi-rater assessments

Multi-rater assessments are also called *360-degree assessments.* The employee's supervisors, co-workers, subordinates, and, in some cases, customers are asked to complete detailed questionnaires on the employee. The employee completes the same questionnaire. The results are tabulated, and the employee then compares the self-assessment with the other results.

Launching an Appraisal Programme

When you set up a new performance appraisal system, you need to gather input from both senior management and employees and also make sure that the programme is workable and well communicated throughout the organization. Use the following general guidelines in setting up and launching your performance appraisal system:

>> Enlist the support of senior management.

>> Give employees a say in establishing performance criteria.

>> Choose performance measures with care.

>> Develop a fair and practical tracking mechanism.

>> Devise a workable evaluation method.

>> Keep it simple.

>> Develop a communication game plan.

WARNING

Regardless of how much time you take to gather feedback and incorporate it into a new performance appraisal system, you may still face objections. Some employees approach appraisals with skepticism and even trepidation. Some supervisors may not appreciate the reasons for the additional work. And the senior management of some younger businesses, eager not to mimic what they perceive as the harsh, judgmental cultures of older corporations, resists the idea of conducting performance appraisals at all. Show your team that, for businesses to grow, they must evaluate what's working, what isn't, and what can be improved.

When making the case for performance appraisal systems, here's what you can expect — and what to do about it:

>> **Employee resistance:** Employees often feel threatened by appraisal systems, and some employees actively dislike being appraised. Respond by communicating as clearly and as openly as possible the purpose and mechanics of the new appraisal system and that it was built with their input. Make sure that employees understand what role the appraisal will play in influencing the things they care about: raises, promotions, and so on. Spell out the role they're expected to play in the process.

>> **Supervisor resistance:** Appraisal systems require extra work by supervisors and managers, as well as create additional paperwork and administrative overhead. Try to keep forms and paperwork to a minimum, but provide forms for continuing tasks such as critical incidents reporting. Train evaluators and audit their performance to see whether follow-up training is needed.

Getting the Most Out of the Performance Appraisal Meeting

When you're creating a performance appraisal process, you have to address the "people" component — what happens when managers and employees sit down together to set goals or to discuss work performance during the appraisal period. The following sections help you maximize the effective of a performance appraisal meeting.

Preparing for the meeting

Managers should be thoroughly briefed on what they need to do prior to holding a performance appraisal session. The key point is that they must be ready: that is, not wait until the last minute before thinking about how the session is going to be handled. Managers should have a clear idea before the meeting begins of what specific behaviours are going to be the focal point of the session. Other points to stress include the following:

>> Give employees sufficient time to prepare for the session.

>> Allot sufficient time to conduct a productive session.

>> Have all documentation ready prior to the meeting.

>> Choose a suitable place (private, quiet, relaxing, with no interruptions) for the meeting.

Conducting the session

If more than a handful of managers are involved in the performance appraisal process, training sessions on how to conduct an effective appraisal session may be beneficial. Whether you conduct this training yourself or bring in an outside company, here are the points to stress:

>> The appraisal meeting should always be a two-way conversation, not a one-way lecture.

>> Positives should always be emphasized before negatives are discussed.

>> The emphasis should be always on what needs to be done to improve and not what was done wrong.

>> Employees should be encouraged to comment on any observations managers share with them.

>> Managers should know how to explain to employees the difference between *effort* (how hard employees are working) and *quality results* (whether the results of those efforts are contributing significantly to business objectives).

Giving constructive feedback

If your business is like most, the toughest thing about the appraisal meeting will be to talk about performance areas in which the employee is lacking. Working in advance with your managers (or on your own, if you're conducting the appraisals) is a good idea, so that they're sufficiently prepared to handle this undeniably tricky aspect of the process. Here are the points to emphasize:

>> **Focus on why candor is important.** Failing to focus on the negative aspects of employee performance when necessary not only does the employee a disservice, but can also harm your business. The employee can't very well improve if no one communicates the need. Additionally, if firing an employee becomes necessary (as covered later in this chapter), failing to mention the employee's weakness in a performance appraisal can jeopardize the business's ability to defend the firing decision.

>> **Stress the importance of documentation.** Always be prepared to back up critical comments with specific, job-related examples. Gather documentation for these examples prior to the meeting.

>> **Highlight the importance of careful wording.** How a criticism is worded is every bit as important as what behaviour is being described. Focus on the behaviour itself and not on the personality quality that may have led to the behaviour. For example, instead of saying, "You've been irresponsible," be

sure to describe the specific event that reflects the irresponsibility, as in "For the past few weeks, you've missed these deadlines."

>> **Encourage employee feedback.** Employees should be given the opportunity to comment on points of criticism. Given a chance, employees will often admit to their shortcomings and may even ask for help.

>> **End on a positive note.** No matter how negative the feedback may be, performance appraisal meetings should end on a positive note and with a plan for improvement.

Preparing for a negative reaction

In a well-managed business, most employees are probably performing adequately or better, but some people don't take criticism well, no matter how minimal or appropriately delivered. In any performance appraisal meeting, an employee whose work is being criticized has the potential to become agitated, confrontational, verbally abusive, and, in very rare instances, violent. Anyone conducting appraisals must be aware of this possibility and have a strategy for response. Here's some advice on handling these difficult situations:

>> **Within reason, let the employee blow off steam.** Don't respond, comment on, or challenge the employee while the employee is agitated or angry. In certain situations, a calm, nonthreatening demeanour can defuse a situation.

>> **Don't fake agreement.** The worst thing to say in this sort of situation is "I can see why you're upset." It can very well set the employee off again.

>> **When the storm passes, continue the meeting.** A lack of response usually ends most outbursts, and the employee quickly realizes the gravity of the mistake. Accept the apology and move on.

WARNING

>> **If any hint arises that the employee may become violent, leave the room immediately and seek help.** Call an in-house security guard, 911 for the police, or, if necessary, other nearby employees.

Choosing areas for further development

What's most important after giving any constructive criticism is a mutual effort between employees and managers to initiate changes that will help staff perform at a higher level. As part of the appraisal meeting, supervisors should recommend areas for improvement and, together with employees, build a set of workable performance-development activities.

Prior to the meeting, the one doing the appraisal should create a concise, one-page list of potential developmental activities for the employee. The list can include

» Recommended readings, both current and ongoing, that the employee can learn from and that are devoted to the topics where development is suggested.

» Possible classroom or online courses that may help the employee.

» People within the business who may offer useful input. ("John became a supervisor last year, so you can talk with him about the challenges of managing people.")

REMEMBER

Employee development isn't just for underperformers, of course. (Refer to Chapter 2 of Book 5 for more about training and development for employees.) Even the very best employees have room to improve and further develop themselves. For any professional, appraisal time is the ideal opportunity to tie a look backward with a look forward.

Performance-development activities are a means to help employees better achieve their job objectives set at the start of the appraisal period. (See the earlier section "Goal-setting, or management by objectives.") As a result, the employee and manager should revisit these objectives during this phase of the appraisal meeting to ensure that they're still on target. Many businesses require an annual goal-setting meeting, and the appraisal meeting may be a good time to tackle that task. You certainly don't want to establish developmental activities around goals that will soon be changing.

Making appraisal follow-up ongoing

The performance appraisal meeting is not the conclusion of the appraisal process. The truth is, the days following this session are extremely important. Providing adequate follow-up is key, including regular monitoring of employee progress toward performance-development goals. Without sustained follow-up — both formal and informal — any input an employee receives is unlikely to be effective in the long run.

The employee and supervisor should have both short- and long-term methods to review progress on the improvement areas discussed and schedule specific dates to do so. Many businesses advise managers to conduct interim meetings after six months, but the interval can be shorter or longer depending on the situation. Between these sessions, supervisors should be encouraged to remain easily accessible so that employees can share thoughts, concerns, or suggestions on any of the topics covered during the appraisal. Real benefits exist to providing input to staff throughout the year: If feedback is ongoing, nothing in the performance appraisal should come as a surprise to employees.

TIP

At the end of any appraisal process, evaluate your own performance as the one who created and implemented the process. Were you able to thoroughly explain the evaluation approach to line managers? Did employees feel the session was conducted appropriately, with their supervisors providing enough time for discussion? Did you recommend specific actions to take following the appraisal — courses, reading, or contacts within the organization who may offer a different perspective? Being a "business strategist" requires extensive attention to these very human, delicate matters. Doing so can be quite rewarding — for the business, for employees, and for your own personal growth.

Handling Difficult Situations

Regardless of how good a job you've done in organizing the human resources function in your business, and regardless of how diligently you handle your day-to-day challenges, you're engaging in wishful thinking if you expect your organization to be entirely free of personnel-related concerns. Even your best employees are going to make mistakes. So are your best supervisors. Even the most closely knit and harmonious group of employees is going to get into occasional squabbles. And unpleasant though the prospect may seem, inevitably, you or the managers in your business will be obliged to take some sort of corrective action — including termination — against an employee whose job performance or conduct falls short of business expectations.

You must ensure that job performance and workplace conduct issues are handled promptly, intelligently, and fairly — and in a way that doesn't diminish productivity, accelerate turnover, or deplete employee morale. And most important perhaps, you have to make sure that your business's disciplinary and termination policies minimize exposure to wrongful dismissal lawsuits.

WARNING

This area is not one where you can afford to be your own lawyer. Employee disciplinary action, termination, and layoffs are matters that require advice tailored to your particular business and situation. Hire a lawyer.

Establishing an ethical culture

The best overall way to reduce the number of difficult situations you have to deal with is to prevent them from happening in the first place. You can never hope to avert all employee improprieties, poor judgments, and disputes, but establishing a culture based on ethical behaviour can go a long way in diminishing these situations.

REMEMBER

From the "tone at the top" on down, become a business that emphasizes the critical importance of employees' ethical behaviour in all interactions, whether externally with customers and vendors or internally among each other. People will always find ways and excuses for wrongdoing just as they will always be capable of making honest mistakes. But including integrity and consideration of others as one of your core values not only prevents many unpleasant situations from occurring, but also helps you develop a reputation as a business people want to work for. (Chapter 1 in Book 3 talks more about your business's values.)

WARNING

Managers must be every bit as accountable as employees. Your business should have a formal code of conduct that is not buried on a shelf, but actively reinforced by all managers. When employees hear one set of values but see another enforced — or, for that matter, neglected — by managers, the inconsistent messages confuse them or, cause them to question your commitment to your basic principles. As a result, they will likely become less committed to the overall organization.

Staying out of court

REMEMBER

The last thing you want is to have to defend a wrongful dismissal case in court. It will cost you a substantial amount of money. It will take time and take you away from managing your business. How do you protect yourself? In short, protection comes from preventive action. Here are seven key principles to bear in mind:

>> Have your lawyer review all business recruiting and orientation literature to ensure that no statements could be misconstrued or used against you.

>> Establish and document specific, easy-to-understand performance standards for every position in your business and make sure that every employee is aware of those standards.

>> Train managers to maintain careful, detailed records of all performance problems and the disciplinary actions that have been taken in response to those problems.

>> Make sure that all disciplinary and dismissal procedures are handled "by the book."

>> Make sure that all the managers and supervisors in your business are well-versed in your business's disciplinary and termination procedures.

>> Seek legal advice whenever you are uncertain about any aspects of your business's disciplinary or legal policy.

>> Be sensitive to the possibility that an employee who leaves your business voluntarily as a result of a change in assignment or work practices may be able to convince a jury that the change represented a deliberate attempt on your business's part to force the employee to quit.

Developing Disciplinary Procedures

Some businesses like a formalized disciplinary process, one that reasonably and systematically warns employees when performance falls short of expectations.

A formal disciplinary procedure works best in businesses that are highly centralized, where personnel decisions for the entire business are made within one department (most likely HR), which makes sure that each step of the disciplinary process is implemented properly. The advantage is that the rules and regulations of job performance are consistently communicated to everyone. The disadvantage, however, is that if your business doesn't abide by these self-imposed rules, not even a lawyer can help you.

On the other hand, some businesses don't like such a process. Using a formalized disciplinary process doesn't work as well for organizations that are decentralized, where personnel decisions are made within each office or department on a case-by-case basis in accordance with a business's general expectations. In these situations, ensuring that each office or department follows the same disciplinary procedure is difficult.

Formal disciplinary processes can vary, but most practices are structured along similar lines. To some degree, they all mirror the following phases:

1. **Initial notification:** The employee's manager typically delivers this initial communication verbally in a one-on-one meeting. Details from this and all later conversations should also be documented. The report needn't be lengthy; a few bullet points highlighting the main topics are perfectly acceptable.

2. **Second warning:** This phase applies if the performance or conduct problems raised in the initial phase worsen or fail to improve. The recommended practice is for the manager to hold yet another one-on-one meeting with the employee and accompany this oral warning with a memo that spells out job performance areas that need improvement. At this stage in the process, the manager needs to make the employee aware of how the employee's behaviour is affecting the business and what the consequences are for failing to improve or correct the problem. The manager needs to work with the employee to come up with a written plan of action that gives the employee concrete, quantifiable goals and a timeline for achieving them.

3. **Last-chance warning:** The "last-chance" phase of discipline usually takes the form of a written notice from a senior manager or, in smaller business, from the owner or president. The notice informs the employee that if the job performance or workplace conduct problems continue, the employee will be subject to termination. What you're doing here is applying the heat.

4. **Corrective action:** Corrective action is some form of discipline administered prior to termination. In union contracts, for example, this action may take the form of a suspension, mandatory leave, or possibly a demotion. In small businesses, disciplinary actions become a little trickier to implement — so much so, that corrective action can become termination itself.

5. **Termination:** Termination is the last step in the process — the step taken when all other corrective or disciplinary actions have failed to solve the problem. (See the next section for more on firing employees.)

REMEMBER

These progressive disciplinary steps serve as general guidelines and aren't intended as a substitute for legal counsel.

REMEMBER

However you decide to structure your disciplinary plan, the process itself — apart from being fair — should meet the following criteria:

>> Clearly defined expectations and consequences

>> Early intervention

>> Consistency

>> Rigorous documentation

REMEMBER

Certain employee infractions and misdeeds are so blatant that you can generally terminate the employee (see the next section) without going through the normal disciplinary channels. Your orientation literature should spell out the offences that lead to immediate dismissal. Here's a list to get you started:

>> Stealing from the business or from other employees

>> Possession or use of illegal drugs

>> Distribution or selling of illegal drugs

>> Blatant negligence that results in the damage to or loss of business machinery or equipment

>> Falsifying business records

>> Violation of confidentiality agreements

>> Misappropriation of business assets

>> Making threatening remarks to other employees or managers

>> Engaging in activities that represent a clear case of conflict of interest

>> Lying about credentials

Firing Employees Is Never Easy

Even when you have ample cause for doing so, firing employees is always a cause for heartache — not only for the employees losing their jobs and the supervisors making the decision, but the co-workers as well.

You can do only so much to ease the pain and disruption that firings create. You can do a great deal, however, to help ensure that your business's approach to firing meets two criteria:

>> It protects the dignity and the rights of the employee being terminated.

>> It protects your business from retaliatory action by a disgruntled former employee.

The standard (and recommended) practice in most businesses is for the immediate supervisor to deliver the termination notice. The message should be delivered in person and in a private location. Depending on the circumstances, include a third person, such as another supervisor or member of the human resources department, at the meeting. Do not involve co-workers.

Regardless of why an employee is leaving your business, keep the termination meeting as conclusive as possible, which means you need to prepare prior to the meeting. The following list covers some issues to consider:

>> **Final payment:** Ideally, any employee being dismissed should walk out of the termination meeting with a cheque that covers everything the employee is entitled to, including severance, money due from accumulated vacation, sick days, expense reimbursements, and so forth.

>> **Security issues:** Think about the security of the business, including keys, access cards, and company credit cards. If the employee has been using a password to access the business's files, ask your IT department or consultant (or whoever sets up your computers) to change it on the system. Do the same with credit-card privileges.

>> **Business-owned equipment:** The employee should return any business-owned equipment immediately. If the equipment is off-site (a computer in the employee's home, for example), arrange for its pickup.

>> **Notification of outplacement or other support mechanisms:** If your business has set up outplacement arrangements (or any other services designed to help terminated employees find another job), provide all the relevant information. In some businesses, the outplacement counsellor is already on the premises and is the first person the terminated employee talks to following the meeting.

Following post-termination protocol

If your business hasn't developed one, work with your management to develop a disciplined, clearly defined procedure for what happens after you discharge an employee. Make the break as clean as possible — albeit with respect to the feelings and the dignity of the person being fired. Harsh and humiliating though the practice may seem, accompany the dismissed employee back to the employee's office or workstation to collect personal belongings and escort the employee out the door. If the business has confidentiality agreements, remind employees — in writing — of their legal obligations. Also advise employees that they're no longer authorized to access the business's computer systems and any online accounts.

TIP

Generally speaking, holding the meeting early in the week (not the weekend) and at the end of the workday works best. If you conduct the termination meeting on Monday or Tuesday, you make it easier for the dismissed employee to get started immediately on a job search and for you to begin searching for another employee. By delivering the news as late in the day as possible, you spare the employee the embarrassment of clearing out his or her office in front of co-workers.

Using a waiver of rights

Some businesses ask a discharged employee to sign a statement that addresses confidential agreements and also releases the business from legal liabilities. Often called a *severance agreement*, businesses require employees to sign this document and return it by a specified date before they receive a severance payout. Note that this payout is separate from any compensation regulated by federal or provincial law.

REMEMBER

The value of this practice is obvious. Although some people believe that employers who present waivers of rights while terminating employees can communicate that they're worried about the legality of their actions, it's common practice and a useful business tool. Have your legal counsel review such a document; encourage the employee to consult legal counsel as well. In fact, a good practice is to discourage employees from signing the document during the exit interview. This is because an argument may be made later that the employee signed the document under duress. Telling the employee to take time to consider the document and to consult legal counsel helps further dispel the notion that the business is trying to hide something.

Easing the trauma of layoffs

Layoffs differ from firings in a variety of ways, but one critical aspect comes to mind: The people being let go haven't done anything to warrant losing their jobs. Layoffs occur for a number of reasons, such as the following:

>> Seasonal shifts in the demand for a business's products or services

>> An unexpected business downturn that requires the business to make drastic cost reductions

>> A plant/company closure

>> An initiative that restructures work practices, leaving fewer jobs

>> A merger or acquisition that makes certain positions redundant

Monitoring Ongoing Performance

Generally, when someone is *laid off*, no expectation exists that the person will be returning to work. Some businesses use the term in a different sense, however. When business is slow and they don't need the entire current workforce, some organizations (particularly those operating in a unionized environment) notify workers that they will be placed on *furlough* for a period of time and will be offered the opportunity to return to work on a certain date or in stages. Some businesses (especially seasonal businesses and those for which losing a major project creates a significant worker surplus) call this arrangement a "layoff" even though they plan to bring people back to work if and when conditions allow.

Whatever the reason for a layoff, the pressure on the HR function is the same. You need to help your business navigate this difficult turn of events with as few long-term repercussions as possible. Keep the following points in mind to guide you through the process:

>> View layoffs as a last resort.

>> Know the law around layoffs.

>> Think through the layoff criteria.

>> Ease the burden of layoffs with severance packages.

>> Hire outplacement specialists.

>> Help former employees take advantage of staffing and placement services.

>> Address the concerns of those who remain.

TIP

If the purpose of the layoff is to cut down on costs (as opposed to reduce redundancy), you may want to explore options that, at the very least, can reduce the number of people who need to be let go:

>> **Temporary pay cuts:** Reducing salary costs is probably the simplest and most direct way to cut staffing costs without cutting staff. The key to this strategy is to ensure that everyone — including senior managers — shares the pain. Many businesses, in their efforts to ensure equality, vary the percentage of reduction according to the amount of salary an employee is earning, with higher-salaried workers surrendering a higher percentage of their regular paycheques than their lower-salaried counterparts.

Downside: No matter how justified the cuts and how many jobs you save, some workers will resent losing pay — and the decision to cut back on pay may induce your best and most mobile workers to quit. Keep in mind, too, that employees who agree to pay cuts will expect the salary to be restored — and then some, when the business turns around. If your business doesn't meet that expectation, you'll likely soon encounter decreased employee commitment and, down the road, a higher turnover rate than desired. Though no legal limit applies to the duration of a temporary pay cut, the sooner you can communicate when wages will be restored, the more positive the impact on morale.

>> **Workweek reductions:** This option is worth exploring for businesses that have large numbers of hourly workers. You maintain the same hourly rates, but employees work fewer hours. As an inducement to accept the lower take-home pay, most businesses pledge to maintain benefits at full-time levels.

Downside: Reducing hours has no effect on salaried employees and managers who are not paid by the hour.

>> **Early retirement:** An often-used method of reducing payroll costs is to encourage early retirement, generally through financial incentives. Because senior employees are usually the most highly paid, trimming their ranks can result in significant savings.

Downsides: Senior employees are often your most valued, and losing too many of them at one time can significantly weaken the leadership of your business. Note, too, that you cannot discriminate against a person because of age and it is therefore not usually possible to force anyone to retire.

In addition, in order to avoid charges of age discrimination, early retirement offers usually have to be extended to wide classes of employees rather than selected individuals. This option can sometimes backfire when large numbers of employees you may want to keep accept the offer.

6
Building Your Marketing Strategy

Contents at a Glance

Chapter **1**

Researching Your Customers, Competitors, and Industry

O ne of the biggest mistakes any marketer can make is to assume. As a marketer, you need to be aware of assuming that you know what your customers think about your brand, products, overall category, and what inspires them to purchase or not. Just as dangerous is assuming that your customers are just like you. Chances are they're not. Making assumptions about the marketplace, trends, and your competition is also not a good idea.

The foundation of any successful marketing plan is a solid research programme, and with all the technologies and sources available today, it's easier and more affordable than ever. Your research plan is your guide to how your customers decide what they like or don't like about your brand, expectations they have for products and customer service, their level of potential loyalty or attrition, and so on. It should also include insights about your category, local markets, and competitive landscape.

Regularly conducting surveys among your customers and prospects is essential to staying on top of what drives your customers to purchase from and stay loyal to you and how likely they are to refer others, which is critical to any company's success.

In addition, reviewing secondary research such as consumer trend reports, white papers on emerging technology, and market analyses and projections should all be part of your body of knowledge as you craft your product and marketing strategies.

This chapter outlines some tips and tactics for surveying customers to gain a better understanding of what really inspires your customers to act, how they process information, and what matters most to them. You also find suggestions for researching your competitors and determining how best to use your resources.

Knowing When and Why to Do Research

Research provides valuable insights about your customers, competition, and industry to help you make informed and thus better decisions about your brand positioning, messaging, offers, engagement activities, media purchases, and more. You can also use various methods to help you test your marketing campaign ideas and their likelihood to succeed before spending a lot of money on execution.

Following are some guidelines for gathering insights, information, and expectations about your market and consumers that will help you make wise decisions and communicate with spot-on relevance for your various consumer segments.

Monitoring social chatter to better understand your customers

In a world where trends change almost daily, or so it seems, so do the demands, expectations, and interests of consumers. The good news is that with all the social media outlets that capture consumers' thoughts, likes, shares, and other expressed interests, you can monitor the issues, attitudes, ideas, inspirations, and aspirations that are most on the minds of your consumers. This kind of information can stimulate your own imagination and new strategies while helping you see new business opportunities.

Don't fall into the trap of doing all your customer research online. Make a point of talking to people face to face, in groups and individually. Carry an idea notebook in your pocket or purse and try to collect a few insights from people every day. This habit gets you asking salespeople, employees, customers, and strangers on the street for their ideas and suggestions. You never know when a suggestion may prove valuable and lead to another.

Popular social media outlets

Get started by identifying the social channels your customers most use and follow in general as well as your subsegments. And follow them yourself. The most common among young and more mature adult audiences include

>> Facebook (www.facebook.com)

>> Twitter (www.twitter.com)

>> Pinterest (www.pinterest.com)

>> LinkedIn (www.linkedin.com)

>> Instagram (www.instagram.com)

>> Flickr (https://flickr.com/)

Social media moves so fast that what is popular one day could be gone or passe the next. Stay up to date so that you can be sure you're using the best channels to make your social media strategy successful.

Note what news, stories, photos, and videos are trending the most and what themes are getting the most likes and shares. Once you identify where you customers spend most of their time online, join those channels and then join the conversations. Monitoring and engaging in dialogue with customers and prospects provides the best information of all.

There are many ways you can also set up online monitoring of your business name or keywords. Google Alerts is one of the largest, and you can set up keyword monitoring or even phrases. You choose if you want daily or weekly alterts. Other services are available to help speciically monitor social media mentions, the most common being Hootsuite. Hootsuite has a free option that will let you monitor up to three social profiles. (A social profile is a social media account, like your Twitter account, Facebook profile [or page], Instagram, or YouTube.)

Take advantage of your own social media followers. Ask your virtual friends on LinkedIn, Facebook, and Twitter what's on their minds and for opinions, suggestions, and ideas about topics of interest related to your industry. You're not likely to get enough feedback to have statistical significance for any new idea or recommendation, but you'll gain insights on how some of your customers feel and identify trends you may want to research further.

Photo sites such as Pinterest, Flickr, and Instagram are highly visual, with members' selections of photos, graphics, and other visual art that provide insights into how people are thinking, feeling, and living and how trends, needs, and concerns are evolving. By studying such websites, you, too, can be an anthropologist of sorts, studying your own culture to seek business and marketing needs and opportunities, or even just to update the vocabulary, terms, or *shortcode* (abbreviated terms or acronyms for common phrases, such as LMK for "let me know") you use in your marketing communications.

Blogs

Other outlets you need to monitor are influencer blogs. No matter your industry, there are many voices out there, and you need to identify the ones your customers most listen to. For example, if you're positioning your products for those who value minimalist living, subscribe to the most popular blogs available. Today, one of those is The Minimalists, which is written by two leading subject matter experts with more than 4 million readers. Chances are they have a lot of influence on what products their followers view and purchase.

Bloggers are some of the most powerful influencers, so pay attention to what they say and recommend. After you identify the influencers in your market, be sure to not only subscribe to their blogs but also work to come up with blog or story ideas that support your products and encourage them to write about them. Just like journalists, they're always looking for new ideas, products, and insights to write about so that they can be relevant and gain more followers. These people should be on your lists for sending press releases, news bulletins, story ideas, and so on.

It is important to also pay attention to using links in blogs to help increase SEO optimization. Both internal links that drive to your own website and external links will help.

REMEMBER

When asking for input and information on websites and in virtual web communities, be honest about who you are and why you're asking for advice. If you tell people you're in charge of marketing your product and want to know what they think of your new ad, many people will offer their views freely. If, however, you pretend to be someone outside the company who's just trying to insert business questions into an innocent chat, people will see through you, and the loss of trust will outweigh any potential good you could have gained. Honesty and transparency are the keys to successful research in online communities.

Monitor blogs and social and news sites to read what people are saying about your category, competitors, and maybe even your brand. Take note about what makes them happy or not so happy, and identify appropriate actions to avoid making mistakes.

Following thought leaders to get current with reality

In addition to surveying your customers about their expectations from your category and brand, you can identify opportunities for your business, analyse choices, and determine product development plans by following thought leaders in your category and general business areas.

For example, if you want to see how other businesses spend their advertising budgets, you can find many associations and think tank organizations that provide insights on this every year. Knowing how similar or complementary brands are spending their advertising dollars can give you some insights on what is most likely to pay off and what channels are getting the most attention from consumers that you target as well. Large brands — business-to-business (B2B) and business-to-consumer (B2C) sectors — spend thousands on research to determine the best path to a strong ROI, or return on investment, so pay attention to what they're doing.

TIP

Some sources for learning how both B2B and B2C brands are spending their advertising and marketing resources include

>> Winterberry (www.winterberrygroup.com/)

>> HubSpot (www.hubspot.com/)

>> The Data and Marketing Association (formerly the Direct Marketing Association; https://thedma.org/)

>> Statista (www.statista.com/)

>> eMarketer (www.emarketer.com/)

Whatever decisions you're turning to research to help you make, it helps to plot out the variables so you can see clearly the pros and cons and the opportunities and risks. Table 1-1 is a sample decision grid to help you get started. Plotting out the information you collect and insights you gain can help you visually see any situation more clearly and guide your decisions in the right direction. You can plot out questions for customer campaigns, media buys, product development, partnerships and alliances you seek, and so on.

TABLE 1-1   **Analysing the Information Needs of a Decision**

Decision	Information Needs	Possible Sources	Findings
Choose between banner ads on influencer blogs or websites and e-mail advertisements to purchased lists.	How many actual prospects do the blogs and websites under consideration actually reach?	Sales reps and media kits are initial contact points.	Three leading blogs covering our industry have a large following, but only half of these are among our top prospects. May not be worth it?
	What are the comparable costs per prospect reached through these different methods?	Analyse costs for each method and number of people reached. Divide cost by number of people and compare.	E-mail to purchased lists is one-third the price of banner ads on key blogs.
	Can we find out what the average click-through and response rates are for both approaches?	Contact other advertisers to learn about their ROI and quality of leads generated form sites listed.	ROIs from other advertisers are below expectations for our current budget.
	Which channel is most used by our larger competitors? And what is the average return?	Ask for client references from e-mail list brokers.	Quality of leads from banner ads are not as strong as those we can purchase from target opt-in lists that have been identified as likely to buy within 30, 60, or 90 days.
	What e-mail lists are available that replicate readers of sites with most industry presence?	Review industry averages for e-mail results from sources such as HubSpot.	Extra cost may have higher ROI in long term.
		Review media analysts' sites for ad spends and average return on web banners versus e-mail.	Banner ads are producing lower results than in past years and reach many people we don't need to reach right now. We need outlets that produce leads more than brand awareness, which seems to be the biggest value for the sites we've monitored.
Conclusions?	We need to find websites that cater to more specific, targeted audiences but cost less.	We can do this by identifying influencer blogs with small readership and small fees to maintain awareness among key audiences.	Our current plan should be to buy targeted lists while looking for smaller, less expensive sites to introduce our brands and identify future lists.
		We can find e-mail lists that replicate these readers from various sources.	

List the decisions you need to make and map out your questions. Creative information-gathering is key to determining the best answers. Figure 1-1 depicts a market research process that can be of value.

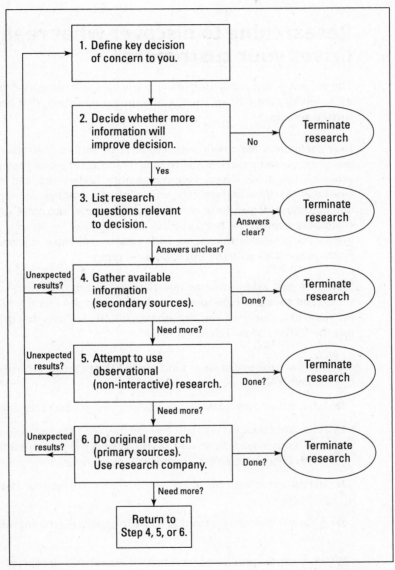

FIGURE 1-1: Follow this market research process to avoid common errors.

A good question is thought-provoking and affects your future actions and successes. If you come upon a really good question, research it carefully. You'll find that the first question breaks down into many more specific ones that, when answered, help you make a good decision.

Researching to discover what really drives your customers

The success of any marketing plan for any business category depends on the ability to identify the ESP, or emotional selling proposition, that best applies to your core customers.

How consumers feel about your products or service, customer service policies, and their overall experience with your brand determines your success and your product's fate. Research can help you identify, understand, and eventually manage consumer reactions and feelings, which influence 90 percent of people's thoughts and behaviour. If you focus on identifying some of the more extreme views that customers express — both positive and negative — about your category and brand, you'll be able to connect with greater emotional relevance and stand out from competitors with the same old messaging.

Instead of just asking routine questions related to customers' satisfaction, wait times, and so on, include some questions to help you identify how they feel. Here are some ideas for questions to help you identify feelings that drive choice beyond just the feelings after a choice is made:

>> What was the emotional or functional fulfilment sought when making a purchase?

>> What is their main goal when purchasing your product category?

>> After doing business with you, how did they feel? You can leave it open for their input or guide them with feelings you want to assess. Maybe include words like *content, excited, creative, neutral, appreciated,* and *valued.*

>> Did you make them feel any differently from when they purchased from a competitor?

>> What was the main reason they chose to explore purchasing from your brand?

>> What was the primary element that influenced their decision to purchase from you versus a competitor?

» What is their decision criteria for your product category?

» What are the primary expectations they have for the brands they are considering?

» What do they like most about your brand?

» What do they like least about your brand?

» How happy have they been with purchases and experiences from others in your category? What generated happiness or lack of?

These and other questions are key to helping you identify the feelings that drive consumers' research process and brand choices, which are critical to engaging in a manner that gets them to yes. When you add questions about feelings to customer satisfaction questions, you can get realistic and actionable insights on how to best communicate and engage emotionally with each of your customer segments.

TIP

As you gather information about feelings and satisfaction ratings, you can draw a graph of all the features of your product, rated from negative through neutral to positive. Most features cluster in the middle of the resulting bell curve, failing to differentiate you from the competition. A few features stick out on the left as notably negative — you must fix those features fast! Other features, ideally, stand out on the right as notably positive. You need to nurture and expand on these features, and don't forget to promote these in all your marketing communications.

Asking questions that get valid results

How you ask questions matters. If you are too vague, you'll get vague answers, which may or may not give you the right guidance. If you simply ask yes-or-no questions, you won't be able to identify the degree of positive or negative thoughts toward that issue and how to compare and prioritize answers.

TIP

The best scale on which to ask customers to evaluate their experience with you and your product is a scale of 1 to 5, with 1 being low and 5 being high. Anything more complicated makes it difficult for consumers to answer, which increases the drop-out rate and makes it more difficult to analyse and identify trends and feelings upon which you can act. For example:

1	2	3	4	5
Very poor	Poor	Average	Good	Very good

You can change the variables to Disagree Strongly, Disagree, Neutral, Agree, and Agree Strongly, and other attributes.

For example, a bank may want customers to rank checking accounts (average), savings accounts (average), speed of service (poor), and friendliness of tellers (very good), along with many other factors to describe the bank in detail.

REMEMBER

Your high-ranking attributes from the survey represent the features you should be promoting to others and talking about in your social media posts and online sites. The low scores can help you identify your failings and set priorities for improving your customer experience. To clarify which ones are worthy of the most attention, you can ask customers to rate the importance of each listed item. Then you can focus your improvement efforts on the more important attributes.

Surveys are cost effective for getting a collective understanding of your strengths and weaknesses from your universe of customers and prospects and your specific customer segments. With all the affordable survey tools available today, such as SurveyMonkey (`www.surveymonkey.com/`) and Constant Contact (`www.constantcontact.com/index.jsp`), you can afford to conduct surveys among your general customers and each of your core segments to better communicate to the specific emotional needs and current place in your product's life cycle.

For example, you may want to set up your surveys among demographic groups within your industry to identify different decision processes, emotional needs, price points, purchasing cycles, and so on. You should also sort out groups based on their relationship with you. These groups may include

>> Lapsed customers

>> Current customers

>> Potential customers with prior contact (often referred to as a warm list)

>> Prospects with no prior contact (often referred to as a cold list)

>> Male versus female shoppers

>> Baby boomers versus millennials

TIP

When you create surveys for customers, you're not only asking them questions about themselves, but you're also sharing information about your brand. Use these tools to communicate key differences in an informative manner. For example, you may want to ask, "Did you know that ABC Brand maintains the highest customer satisfaction rates in the quick print industry?"

The leading question helps you identify how effectively your communication is getting across and lets you share something of value in a way that's more subtle than bragging on LinkedIn, which can get mixed results.

Checking Out Net Promoter Scores and How to Find Yours

Today, one of the most common benchmarks for how a brand is doing is its Net Promoter Score, or NPS. This is primarily a score on how highly you rate for customer referrals, yet it's something many consumers look for when choosing between brands. In short, the NPS is an index that ranges from −100 to 100, which shows the likelihood of customers to recommend a company's products or services to others. It helps marketers determine not just the possibility of referrals but also the satisfaction rates and thus potential loyalty of current customers.

Many tools can help you get a solid read on your NPS. If you use SurveyMonkey, these questions are already crafted and ready to be added to your survey in a way that will get you a valid response. You can also get real-time NPSs on a regular basis through tools such as those offered by Satmetrix (www.satmetrix.com/). Do some research to find the tools that best fit your current digital and customer relationship management (CRM) platforms.

TIP

If you use your own survey platform and want to do your own calculations instead of using a tool from a software company, you can find calculators online to help you. One example of a free service you can use is NPS Calculator (www. npscalculator.com).

To give you some perspective, the average NPS for life insurance companies in 2016 was 31; it was 58 for department/specialty stores and 2 for Internet services (yes, 02). Companies with some of the top scores include Nordstrom at 80, USAA at 77, Ritz-Carlton at 72, and Apple iPhone/iPad at 60, according to Satmetrix, one of the leaders in NPS systems and findings.

REMEMBER

A good benchmark for you is to look up the index for your industry and how your competitors score. Find your NPS and aim to execute marketing strategies that will help you get and stay ahead of your competitors. For consumers doing research on which brands to buy and which to avoid, these scores matter!

Beyond asking questions to determine consumers' likelihood to purchase from you and refer you, your surveys should also ask questions to guide you in developing your product line. For example, if you're in charge of a 2-year-old software product that small businesses use to do their planning and financials, you may want to ask questions that will help you determine the following issues:

>> Should we launch an upgrade or keep selling the current version?

>> Is our current marketing program sufficiently effective, or should we redesign it?

>> Is the product positioned properly, or do we need to change its image?

Asking Really Good Questions on Surveys

A survey is only as good as the insights it generates and your ability to get people to respond. How you write, present, and promote your survey all factor into the results you get. Before you can write a survey that provides insights that will enable you to stand out from the competition and increase customer loyalty, you have to define your goals. Ask yourself the following questions:

>> What do I need to know about my customers to really be able to serve them better?

>> What is missing in my body of knowledge about my customers in terms of who they are, what goals they seek to fulfil with my products, and how my products simplify or improve their lives?

>> What do I need to know about personality traits, emotional drivers, psychological states of mind, and feelings toward my category and brand that apply to my customers in order to prepare more relevant creative and promotional campaigns?

>> How do I plan to use the information I collect about customers and their needs?

>> What am I willing or able to provide customers in exchange for completing my survey?

TIP

You also need to ask yourself what level of statistical significance you're willing to accept and base your actions upon. Typically, you should strive for at least a 95 percent confidence level. The good online survey tools available for you to use for minimal costs include the ability to determine the number of responses needed for a given confidence level. A rule of thumb is that you need 385 responses among a national database of thousands reached to be able to append your results to the greater population.

After you define your learning goals, it's time to start developing your survey. Your questions should be crafted in a way that is clear to understand and easy for respondents to answer quickly. Writing clear questions is essential to get statistically valid results that reflect not only your sample of respondents but also your greater population.

REMEMBER

Here are some guidelines to asking questions that get answered and provide valid results:

>> **Ask only one question at a time.** Avoid questions like, "Do you think customer service and product variety are important?" If your response mechanism is yes or no, you really can't determine whether they are answering yes to customer service or product variety.

>> **Don't ask questions you don't need to know.** Do you really need to know what your customers' income or education level is in order to serve them?

>> **Don't get personal.** If you ask questions that go beyond their public activity or presence, customers will feel uncomfortable and could be concerned about how you will use information about them.

>> **Ask questions about things you can act on.** This way your customers can see clearly how answering this question can impact them in a positive way. For example, asking, "Do you agree that the wait time for us to serve you is too long?" clearly states that you are looking for ways to improve their experience with you.

>> **Mix up the format of your questions.** Instead of asking all multiple-choice or yes-or-no questions, intersperse all types throughout your survey to keep respondents' minds fresh and give you additional insights at the same time.

>> **Always include one open-ended or essay question so you can hear the voice of your customer.**

If you're not sure what to ask your customers or how to word your questions so that you get valid, statistically significant results, no worries. Tools like SurveyMonkey provide prewritten questions on themes most marketers need to explore that market research experts have vetted for unbiased results. You can also use their calculators to determine confidence intervals. One of the best reasons to use a platform like SurveyMonkey is the ability to easily collect responses and analyse them with the click of a button.

TIP

Here's a tip from small business expert Raewyn Sleeman, owner of Nimblwit in Vancouver, Canada: Don't assume that your preferences for staff, processes, and store environment match your customers'. Assuming preferences can slide you into failure. Increase your chances of success by asking customers to complete an anonymous written survey in exchange for a small free gift. The survey could ask them the following:

>> What would you change if this was your business?

>> What would you change with the people?

>> What would you change with the processes of getting service here?

>> What would you change with the store (or online) environment?

After you get feedback, share it with someone that you trust to tell you the truth, who isn't in the business, to get his opinion of the overall changes to make. Finally, know that if you ask customers and then don't make any changes, they will likely think less of your business than before you asked.

Writing ESP Surveys

Well, this is where it gets tricky. It goes without saying that asking the unconscious mind a question and getting a solid result is a difficult thing to do. But a big reason for doing surveys is to uncover the emotions that drive the decision process and ultimately choice and loyalty. Asking questions about how customers feel is a good start.

You may also want to ask a marketing expert with consumer psychology and behaviour marketing expertise for some help asking questions. This person can guide you on how to ask the same question in two or three different ways so you can see how emotionally charged, or conflicted, or confused your customers may be about a topic. One marketer did this when surveying customers about climate change and learned a great deal. For one, what people said about their values did not match up with their intended or likely actions. And interestingly enough, those who highly valued environmental protection as a life goal scored very low on willingness to contribute even $5 a month to help out. The marketer gained huge insight by that contrast. These are the kinds of questions you need to ask to see how customers truly feel versus how they say they will act.

Here's a sample question that can help you gain actionable insights based on feelings, not just past transactions:

>> Of the following, which is most likely to cause you to donate $5 a month to reduce the amount of waste you contribute to landfills?

- Knowing you are helping to preserve your local environment for future generations

- Knowing you will be reducing your personal imprint on the local environment

- Knowing the earth around you will be cleaner and safer for your family's immediate and long-term health

How consumers answer these questions reveals a great deal and helps you identify the values that are most likely to capture their attention and influence their behaviour.

Today's consumers are less interested in receiving "personalized" information from you that just reiterates what they already know, such as what they just bought from you. Ask questions about what type of personalized information would be meaningful to them and add those variables to your customer profiles.

REMEMBER

Consumers are more willing to answer surveys if you make it about them and not just about you.

Preface your survey by indicating that you will use the information to better serve them. If you plan to keep all answers confidential, tell them that, too. Transparency regarding how you plan to use and share their information is critical to completion and building trust with your customers.

Be prepared for feedback about any controversial topics you may bring up. Some marketers once did a survey for a client that was promoting a programme to reduce carbon emissions, and by simply asking respondents whether they believed in climate change, the marketers generated quite a bit of angry mail. However, they took those comments to heart and added them to their research findings as well.

TIP

Don't oversurvey. Use discretion as to how much and how often you ask. Keep surveys to 15 questions or fewer and do only one survey a quarter or less often if you want to get responses.

Paying Wisely for Market Research

With all the marketing technologies available today for monitoring the voice of the customer, you have many options to choose from for gathering information. You can do your own research, tap into existing systems to insert your questions, or hire a research firm to design and execute various tools for you.

TIP

Often, getting a list of prospects to survey is the greatest expense. To help lower this cost, look for opportunities to add questions to a survey being conducted by an industry publication or consulting firm. Some websites make customers answer questions to get access to a full news article. Check in to the costs of surveys like those that reach prospects to which you don't have easy access. Some vendors that offer this option include

>> Darwin's Data (https://darwinsdata.com/)

>> PaidViewpoint (https://paidviewpoint.com/)

>> BzzAgent (www.bzzagent.com/)

>> Viewpoint Forum (www.viewpointforum.com/)

>> Tellwut (www.tellwut.com/)

>> Opinion Outpost (www.opinionoutpost.com/)

>> OneOpinion (www.oneopinion.com/)

>> Panelpolls (www.panelpolls.com/)

Browse the latest lists of survey panels through a Google search, or look at sites like www.surveypolice.com, which ranks polls based on feedback from users, and then collect price points and proposals from several before choosing one to run with.

In most cases, you can purchase survey accounts on a monthly basis or an annual basis. And in some cases, you can use these online tools for free — however, with limited access and data collection.

TIP

Online sources that enable you to design surveys and pay as you go or with a low-cost annual fee include tools like SurveyMonkey (www.surveymonkey.com), Crowdsignal (https://crowdsignal.com), Constant Contact's Listen Up option (www.constantcontact.com), and GutCheck (gutcheckit.com) for one-stop survey shopping. Working online, you can design survey questions, select a sample design, and (using your own database or, increasingly available, a sample arranged by the host site) send out your survey, collect data, and tabulate it. Does it make sense? Are you wiser as a result? Well, not every time. It takes practice and persistence to figure out how to extract useful findings from tables of survey responses, but at least it's less expensive to trial balloon some questions through these sites than through traditional full-service survey research firms.

If your website gets a good amount of visitors a day, put questions on your home page. A question with general appeal (something everyone's invested in or curious about) may actually boost visitors at the same time it generates useful data for your marketing decisions.

TIP

You can also add questions to the channels by which you communicate with your customers. For example:

>> If your customers order via a website, post questions for them there.

>> If they talk to a call centre, script some questions for the call centre staff.

>> If customers receive visits from salespeople or reps, brief the sales force about your questions and how to ask them without pressuring customers or prepare a simple e-mail they can send with some questions to answer.

Discovering Low-Cost and Even Free Ways to Find Out What Matters Most

Knowledge is power. As trite as it may sound, knowledge is still the most powerful source you have to help you make smart decisions about your product and how to appeal to and build relationships with your customers.

As a marketer (and a small business owner), you're never done learning. When you think you know all you need to know about your market and customers, you start to lose your competitive and profitable edge. You need to build and execute learning plans that cover all aspects of your market, your brand, your products, your customers, and the opportunities and threats you face. For example:

>> Who wants what?

>> Which markets are going to grow and be hot, and which aren't?

>> What really drives choice?

>> How do different generations react to different messages, themes, and promises?

>> What functional alternatives exist to our offers, and how do they impact our goals?

It's amazing how many businesses and other entities stagnate by working hard but not working smart to really know how to build their businesses sustainably. The following sections provide a lot of ways — some cheap and others free — to boost your marketing intelligence.

Observe your customers

Consumers are everywhere — online and offline — shopping and observing all the messages and offers around them daily. As a marketer, you need to observe them, too, and with marketing technologies available today, it's getting easier. Offline, you can observe customers at your place of business and watch them browse your products, merchandising displays, pricing, and so on. Online, you can observe their attitudes and feelings and potential behaviour through social listening tools.

Many different programs "observe" what customers are saying, pinning, and posting online and generate reports back as to what attitudes are prevalent among which groups, what people think about your brand, and most importantly what they are saying, and so on. You can find free tools that show the reach of your tweets, the likes and shares of your posts, and what topics trend the most on any channel on any given day.

Some of the technology available that helps you observe customers is social listening tools, which are available at many price points, including free.

TIP

One of the most recommended free listening tools per Brandwatch (www. brandwatch.com/), a site that lists various marketing product reviews, is Mention (https://mention.com/en/), which reports back on the influence of social media posts on more than 100 social sites. With this tool, you can get regular reports about the strength, sentiment, passion, and reach of the posts associated with your brand and score how well you're doing with certain keywords, hashtags, and so on. You'll also find out how many minutes were spent observing your message, how many tweeted or commented on a given post, and whether the sentiment about a given message was positive, neutral, or negative.

If you really want to understand consumers and the themes, issues, beliefs, attitudes, and emotions that drive behaviour in real time, it doesn't get much better than this. Other free listening tools include Hootsuite (https://hootsuite.com/) and TweetReach (https://tweetreach.com/). Of course, you can purchase highly robust systems customized for your specific needs on a SaaS (Software as a Service) basis. Some recommended by *PC Magazine* include Sprout Social (https://sproutsocial.com/), Synthesio (www.synthesio.com/), and Brand24 (https://brand24.com/). Before signing long-term contracts, look for services that offer free trials so you know what you're getting before you commit.

REMEMBER

Whether you're in B2B or B2C, you can learn a great deal about your customers by observing them online and offline. Integrating these efforts and technologies will pay off in the short term as you get new attitudes and intents in real time and the long term as you can cater your persona and messaging around the values that don't change with trends.

Observation is often underrated yet highly valuable. For example, when managers from the Boston Aquarium hired a researcher to develop a survey to determine the most popular attractions, the researcher told them not to bother. Instead, he suggested that they examine the floors for wear and for tracks on wet days. The evidence pointed clearly to which attractions were most popular. That was easy!

TIP

Observe customers at the point of sale and document what they spend the most time browsing, what questions they ask, what statements they make, and so on. Did they seem anxious, at ease, excited, or neutral about your offers if selling in B2B or while browsing your store? In B2B marketing, take time to observe what matters most to your clients' job security. Research by Google and Motista show that when you can tie a sales message and offer to personal value, you're eight times more likely to get a premium price for your product. Find ways to discover what matters most to your clients and link your product/service to those values.

You can find out about customer satisfaction every day by asking for feedback via e-mail after a product ships or by leaving comment cards on sales counters. If you ask for a review directly, you can avoid unwanted and often unwarranted reviews on social channels like Yelp, which do influence attitude and choice, right or wrong.

TIP

When sending out surveys, always ask for e-mail addresses and permission to contact customers with further information to better serve them, promotions, industry news, and so on. With their e-mail address, you can monitor them with your social listening tools and add them to your survey databases.

REMEMBER

Keeping up with customer opinion is a never-ending race, and continuously asking and analysing questions is the only way to stay the course. The best way to succeed is by asking questions directly of your customers.

Do competitive research

Knowing your competitors' offerings and values is just as critical as finding out what your customers need and want. What emotional and tangible values do they promise and deliver, and how do you compare? Beyond knowing how your pricing and customer service differs, you need to know how they position themselves in the market so you can position yourself better. Create a grid like the one in Table 1-2 and refer to it often as you create your own messaging and time your own promotions.

TABLE 1-2

Competitive Research

	You	Competitor A	Competitor B
Slogan			
Promises			
Position			
Special offers			
Industry awards			
Social followers			
Pricing			
Customer ratings			
Product comparisons (strengths, weaknesses)			
Service comparisons			
Other			

Track their sales, promotions, and special offers and time yours accordingly. Keep track of what their customers like and don't like and position your brand as the better alternative. Create and maintain a competitive grid to help you stay on top of your goals and the competitive environment in which you operate.

TIP

Also gather information on your competitors' marketing programmes, especially how they're getting their marketing messages out. Are they advertising with a fast-growing social network you hadn't considered? If you have even a modest budget, consider the options for online research by firms like WhatRunsWhere (www.whatrunswhere.com), AdClarity's media intelligence (www.adclarity.com), Numerator (www.numerator.com/), or Adbeat (www.adbeat.com), all of which can help you benchmark your ads (especially online advertising) against top competitors or role-model marketers (larger companies with the resources to spot new opportunities and trends quicker than you).

Harness the power of one-question surveys

One of the main reasons customers don't complete surveys is because they are too long and no one has more than a minute or two to give you, if even that. What works in a world where people communicate in sound bites for Twitter, LinkedIn, videos, and more is brevity. One of the most effective ways to get answers is thus asking one question at a time. Determine what you need to know most to develop better marketing programmes and service, and ask just that question.

Delivery mechanisms for one-question surveys include e-mails, websites, and your social media assets. If you do one question at a time, you can get away with more surveys. Having a question or a poll on your web page makes your site more interactive and thus engages visitors longer. Just make the questions meaningful to both you and your customers. If they see answering the question as something that will benefit them, they're more likely to respond.

Ask questions that help you understand perceptions and value. For example, if your company focuses on environmental issues and you're trying to reduce plastics in the landfills, ask about the values that lead to purchasing products that are impeding your progress, such as the following:

> Do you think bottled water is healthier than tap water? Yes or No

You can pay news sites to ask your question before giving access to articles on their site.

TIP

You can learn a great deal about markets, consumers, incomes, and so on by studying census data for your marketplaces. Check out Canada's Census Programme at `www12.statcan.gc.ca/census-recensement/index-eng.cfm`.

Establish a trend report

Set up a *trend report,* a document that gives you a quick indication of a change in buying patterns, a new competitive move or threat, and any other changes that your marketing may need to respond to. You can compile one by e-mailing salespeople, distributors, customer service staff, repair staff, or friendly customers once a month, asking them for a quick list of any important trends they see in the market.

TIP

Your trend analysis should also include careful tracking of what bigger competitors in your space are doing because they may be setting marketing or product trends that affect the rest of their industry. Tracking media coverage is easy on Google or other search engines. Also read their press releases on PR Newswire (`www.prnewswire.com`) to see what they have to say about themselves. Track changes on major competitor websites, too, either manually or (if you want to follow several) by using a service such as LXR Marketplace (`www.lxrmarketplace.com`), Watch My Competitor (`www.watchmycompetitor.com`), Competitor Monitor (`www.competitormonitor.com`), Alexa (`www.alexa.com`), or Digimind (`www.digimind.com`). You can also use these services to track competitor mentions in social media and compare them to mentions of your brand. Benchmark your website against competitor stats on HubSpot's Marketing Grader (`website.grader.com`).

TIP

Researchers wanting to do their own competitor monitoring at no cost may use Google Alerts to create customized search criteria for tracking competitor online activity (www.google.com/alerts).

Probe your customer records

Browsing your data files and models is also a good way to stay abreast of your market trends and your customers. Browse your data models and customer profiles to identify trends in demographics, interests, political affiliations, and lifestyle. Trends of interest around which you may build promotions or messaging include

>> Employment level

>> Personal hobbies and interests

>> Credit levels/debt levels

>> Family status

>> Political affiliations

Test your marketing materials

Before you launch anything to the public, you can easily get some feedback very affordably to help you identify any problems ahead of time. Send your e-mail campaign or social media post to a handful of customers and get their feedback. Ask what made them want to read the ad or not read it. What intrigued them about the offer? How relevant was it to them? Fix any issues you identify and get ready to launch with more effectiveness.

With e-mails, you can test the same body copy with different subject lines to see which generates the best open and click-through rates, enabling you to work more efficiently than ever. Testing is a great way to determine what emotions, offers, promotions, and so on really appeal to your mass consumers and your segments.

Interview defectors

Losing customers is not always a bad thing because it gives you an opportunity to discover what you're doing wrong, which is critical if you want to keep getting it right. Following are some ways to find out where you're weak and need to improve:

- » Ask your customers why they're opting out of your e-mails instead of just providing an opt-out button. Ask whether it was the content, customer experience issue, frequency of e-mails, or lack of relevancy.

- » When customers abandon a shopping cart, program your CRM to send an e-mail to find out why. Was it because they lost interest, found a better price, or simply forgot?

- » Stay in touch with lapsed customers and survey to find out whether they defected to a competing brand, had a bad experience, or just lost interest in your product.

When you find out why customers no longer want to engage with you or purchase your products and services, you often rekindle relationships that last for years. Customers like to know they're noticed and appreciated, and when you right a wrong, loyalty actually goes up.

Create custom web analytics

Make sure your web tracking/analytics program tells you more than traffic counts and sources. Attributes to follow include monitoring sales, repeat sales, lead collection, quality of leads (measured by rate of conversion), sign-ups, use of offers (such as you may post on a business site on Facebook, for example), and overall revenue and returns from web-based promotions. These numbers tell the story of your marketing successes and failures online and give you something to learn from as you go.

TIP

Many firms now offer quite sophisticated and powerful research tools for tracking your brand and competitors on the web, especially in social media. It may be worthwhile to look into the costs and benefits of options such as Brandwatch Analytics (www.brandwatch.com) or The Social Studies Group (www.socialstudies group.com), a firm that studies conversations on social networking sites to gain ideas about attitudes and trends.

Riding a Rising Tide with Demographics

Monitoring demographics of your market, such as the ethnic makeup of your market, average age, spending power, and family structure, provides you with good clues as to how your marketing ought to evolve. If your business caters to women, for example, an example of sources and statistics you should know and monitor carefully is this: More women than men are going to college, and the trend is growing over time. Add this to a slower trend toward pay parity, and the suggestion is that women will outpace men as the educated and leading gender at some point in the not-too-distant future. (Source: Forbes.com article on the trends in enrollment for men and women over several decades.)

Whatever your business, pick a growing group you think you may be able to build long-term relationships with, and tailor your offerings and message accordingly. Back out of shrinking categories and regions, and go where the growth is.

REMEMBER

Knowledge is the foundation for success no matter what type of business you operate in. Continuously learning about your customers, market, and competition can often be the difference between success and failure.

Chapter **2**

Creating a Winning Marketing Plan

Rome wasn't built in a day. Flight didn't happen overnight. Apple, IBM, Kraft Foods, and GE didn't become top of their game in just a matter of weeks, either. All had a carefully concerted plan with goals, action items, timelines, and more that would help them launch, scale to mass distribution, establish leadership, and grow as efficiently and profitably as possible.

In the past, it often happened that when people had an idea for a great new product, they built it in their basement and made their fortune by being in the right place at the right time. These stories are not so common now, unless you're a genius at building smartphone or software apps that a bigger company actually wants to buy. But again, those stories are few and far between.

To succeed, no matter what business you're in, you need that same kind of plan, a guiding blueprint that defines your brand, your market position, goals and vision, and customers. This same plan needs to map out how you plan to put a competitive stake in the ground and how you'll generate leads, close sales, and grow to reach your profitability, initial public offering (IPO), or exit plan goals.

This chapter focuses on building a plan or road map to get your business moving in the right direction in today's rapidly changing market climate. As you likely already have a product and customer in mind, the chapter starts with understanding how your product fits in to your current market and competitive landscape, and suggests actions for giving your business the greatest possible chance to succeed.

Gathering the Marketing Plan Components You Need

The surest way to success today is to have a solid plan for building and growing business — one that covers product development, market identification, capitalization goals, growth initiatives, marketing and distribution programmes, budgets, financial projections, and more, depending on your ultimate goals for growth or selling to investors or other firms.

The key elements or considerations in a marketing plan for today's technology-driven marketing world include but aren't limited to the ones in the following sections. These just represent a start for any business.

First, the basics

Just like a builder, you need to start your marketing plan by laying a strong foundation on which to build your branding, sales, customer engagement, and other programmes. Your foundation needs to start with the basics such as defining your product, figuring out how it fills tangible and emotional needs, and determining how it fits in to the current marketplace. You also need to define what you want to accomplish with your business.

REMEMBER

Following are some basic questions to answer to get you started:

>> **Product:** What product are you selling, and what physical, emotional, and functional needs does it fulfil?

- **» Goals:** What are your goals? What do you hope to achieve in terms of revenue, profit, scalability, growth, and expansion? What are your short- and long-term goals for operating capital and profits?

- **» Customers:** Who are your customers? Who are your customers in your core and segment demographics? For example, if your core demographic is middle-aged women, how can you further segment this group to be able to reach those with the highest propensity to purchase your product? And who and what influences your customers?

- **» Market:** What other products can your target consumers buy instead of yours? How do you compare in terms of access, price, quality, reputation, distribution, features, warranties, and other elements that affect choice?

- **» Channels:** Where will you sell your product? Will you sell it online direct to consumers via your own e-commerce store? Will you sell to retailers via intermediaries and distributors? Will you have your own physical location/storefront? Will you sell direct to businesses via a sales team? You need to map out the pros/cons and costs of each so you can see a clear path to scaling distribution that's affordable and profitable, too.

Now, some more complex concepts

After you have defined your goals and your product and how they fill valid consumer and market needs, it's time to start thinking about how you are going to sell your product to earn revenue and fund your business for growth. You need a plan for getting customers to purchase your product in the first place, raising funds from investors to help you scale quickly to capture current marketing opportunities, and deciding how you will build your brand through marketing initiatives that are sustainable and successful.

Some of the questions you need to define follow:

- **» Promotion:** How will you launch your product to spark trial? How will you keep those that try it coming back? By referring others? What special offers and discounts can you execute without hurting profit margins? How often? How can you employ tactics such as guerilla marketing and growth hacking to get to mass distribution quickly?

- **» Financials:** What profit margin do you need to make to break even, expand, and engage in research and development for new editions, ancillary offerings, and expanded product lines? How much of your revenue will you allocate to marketing? Do you need investors? Can you secure enough capital through Kickstarter, or do you need some serious venture capital funding behind you to get you going? How much are you willing to give up?

>> **Marketing:** The biggest mistake marketers can make is to assume that they know all the answers and that they can promote and sell their products with a few social posts, with articles by good bloggers, or by simply opening a cool e-commerce store. Anyone with that attitude toward marketing a product has dummied down the marketing process in a way that can seriously impact her success. And it's not good.

And now some even bigger considerations

REMEMBER

No plan is complete without an end goal in sight. There are many reasons for starting and building a business. These might include building a family business that can sustain generations, growing a business to sell so you can retire early, or building a business that enables you to change the world. Whatever your ambitions, dreams, or goals, map out a plan. Knowing your end goal will help you build a more efficient plan and help you avoid wasting resources and money, doing things that really don't matter "in the end."

Here are some considerations to think about:

>> **Growth:** What funds, resources, and plans do you have to grow your company, and how do you intend to reach your one-, three-, and five-year goals? If you don't have one-, three-, and five-year goals, this would be a good place to start.

>> **Year-over-year objectives:** Set objectives, or line-item goals, that you can measure to determine your business's true progress. For example, "Increase average annual customer value by 5 to 6 percent" and "Shift 25 percent or more of our catalogue customers over to website ordering" or "Achieve 3 to 4 percent of market share in new territories" if you're opening any as part of an expansion strategy.

>> **Exit strategy:** Are you developing a product line or a brand that you hope to eventually sell to a larger company, maybe a competitor, so you can retire or start a new business? Are you hoping to build an enterprise that you can take public or just a successful business you can pass on to your firstborn should she prove interested and worthy?

Addressing the Four Ps

Every marketing plan needs to address the four Ps — *price, product, promotion,* and *place* — because, essentially, they represent the foundation of your business and the assets you have to sell and market your goods. You need to flesh out your product and pricing strategies, place of distribution strategies, and promotions so you can compare your strengths to your competitors', monitor your progress in each of these areas, and see how your efforts get you closer to or further from your goals.

REMEMBER

The purpose of your marketing plan is really to outline the actionable items most likely to push your *product* forward in the market, building out your *places* of distribution as efficiently as possible, *pricing* your products for trial and loyalty, and *promoting* your product and brand using the channels and tactics that best reach and influence your customers and their influencers. These may include print and digital ads, content marketing, engagement, and events, online and offline, to create awareness and sales and to build customer acquisition and retention.

Conducting a SWOT Analysis

Even though the SWOT analysis has been around for years, it isn't and won't ever be old-fashioned or out-of-date. You can't define and improve your position in any market unless you know your

>> Strengths

>> Weaknesses

>> Opportunities

>> Threats

REMEMBER

You need to continuously define these four elements. The world, consumers, and your markets are dynamic, not static, and if you don't continuously monitor your strengths, weaknesses, opportunities, and threats in real time (rather than the past), you'll fall behind, and once you're behind a competitor who adapts regularly to market and customer changes, good luck catching up and ever getting ahead.

TIP

One of the most efficient ways to do a SWOT analysis is to map out your answers and those of your top competitors' at the same time. This way you can more clearly see just how strong those "assumed" strengths compare to others. So open a spreadsheet on your computer, or get out the handy pen and paper, and start mapping out your SWOT. Do this frequently to ensure that you're on top of your own market position, focusing on the right opportunities and the right challenges to overcome, and are aware of what your competition is doing. You need to be only one step ahead of the others in your space to be in a position to dominate market and mind share — two important goals for any marketing plan.

Following are some starting points for what to include in your SWOT analysis:

>> **Strengths:** Identify the strong points of your product(s), brand image, and marketing programme so you know what to build on in your plan. Your strengths are the keys to your future success.

>> **Weaknesses:** Pinpoint the areas in which your product(s), brand image, and marketing programme are relatively weak. For example, perhaps you have several older products that are losing to new competitors or functional alternatives and your plan needs to address how to adapt or cut these products.

>> **Opportunities:** Your situation analysis needs to look for opportunities, such as new growth markets, new communications, or distribution channels for reaching customers, potential partners for collaboration or bundling, and so on.

>> **Threats:** A threat is any external trend or change that can reduce your sales or profits or make it difficult to achieve your growth goals. Common threats include new technologies that create new competitors, large competitors that can outspend you, and economic or demographic shifts that cut into the size or growth rate of your customer base.

Table 2-1 is a hypothetical example of how you can organize a competitive SWOT analysis. You should also take the time to outline each area for your business from a product, branding, market position, sales, capitalization, and growth perspective.

TABLE 2-1   **Sample SWOT Analysis**

	Your Product	Competitor 1	Competitor 2
Strengths	More features	Strong brand awareness	Lowest price
Weaknesses	Newcomer to market, not proven	Mediocre quality	Undercapitalized and may lack funds for product development
Opportunities	Take market share by communicating value of distinct features	Completed IPO so could put more money into developing new features that could compete with ours	Opportunity to take market share due to pricing strategy
	Bundle with complementary brand with established channels in place		

	Your Product	Competitor 1	Competitor 2
Threats	Higher price may prevent newcomers to category from trying	Lower quality can result in consumers switching to new brands like ours and so can the lack of features like we have	Competing mainly on price and that can be countered with ESP marketing tactics
	Low marketing budget		
	Economic slowdown, low consumer confidence levels		

Creating a SWOT analysis that compares you to your competition is a must if you want to keep ahead of the game or be aware at all times of what you need to do to get ahead if you're not there yet. Today's markets move fast, and you need to be prepared to act fast to jump over any hurdles you face and jump on opportunities before they disappear.

Before completing your SWOT grid, collect information about your competitors' promises, product claims, industry awards or rankings, pricing models, advertising messages, persona, and promotions. The more armed you are with information, the better prepared you are to identify your SWOT high points and low points and how they compare to competitors.

Some information worth gathering about your competitors include

>> **Company:** Describe how the market perceives it and its key product.

>> **Key personnel:** Who are the managers, and how many employees do they have in total?

>> **Financial:** How strong is its *cash position* (does it have spending power, or is it struggling to pay its bills)? What were its sales in the last two years?

>> **Sales, distribution, and pricing:** Describe its primary sales channel, discount/pricing structure, and market share estimate.

>> **Product/service analysis:** What are the strengths and weaknesses of its product or service?

>> **Promises and claims:** What promises and claims related to benefit, value, performance, and quality do they make, and how do you compare to these? Can you position yourself according to what they really deliver?

>> **Promotions and offers:** What promotions do they execute that can cut into your sales or tempt your customers to switch to their products? What is the timing and pricing differential of these promotions, and how can you schedule yours to offset any impact?

Armed with this information to add to your competitive SWOT analysis, you'll be ready to succeed more efficiently than you can imagine.

Focusing on Functional Alternatives

Another key analysis you need to do involves understanding how your product compares to functional alternatives — that is, products that aren't really the same as your product but perform some or many of the same functions and are designed for the same basic outcomes. Software platforms and applications compete with functional alternatives quite a bit.

For example, consider digital asset management platforms, content management systems, and marketing resource management systems. In reality, all are designed to do much of the same things and produce the same outcomes — higher efficiencies in creating new versions of content for cross-channel distribution that can be delivered to individuals with personal relevance. But each system is slightly different, which puts it in different software/technology categories and thus makes each system a functional alternative to another.

You need to decide how you support or compete with functional alternatives and then build action items into your marketing plan. Questions to ask yourself include

>> What business category best describes where you are now?

>> What business category best describes where you aspire to be to maximize long-term profitability?

>> Where do you currently fit in your primary category? If you made it on Gartner's Magic Quadrant, would you be considered a leader, challenger, niche player, or visionary?

>> Can you tether your brand in any similar categories to get visibility among those shopping for functional alternatives? So if your product is a content management system, should you also be promoting yourself as a viable option for those shopping for digital asset management systems? In the IT world, technology changes so quickly that there's a good chance your target consumers don't understand the difference themselves.

Understanding Why Collaboration Matters So Much

We are and will continue to live in a sharing society. Businesses that bring people together to share resources, collaborate on getting things done, and help each other with daily living are those that have thrived in recent years. Here are some fairly recent examples:

>> Uber, where drivers with cars helps travellers who need transportation

>> Airbnb, where homeowners share rooms with travellers who don't want the cost of a hotel

>> TaskRabbit, where people with time do errands for those who are stretching to get it all done

Many businesses collaborate with others, even competitors, to create a more robust product, service, or experience for customers whom they both target and service. Co-Society (www.co-society.com), a platform that brings international businesses and executives together to collaborate on new ideas and innovations, put out a report outlining several cases of successful business collaborations that create mutually beneficial outcomes. These include examples of innovations that improve the world, such as when Microsoft and Toyota teamed up to produce better information systems in cars, and marketing programmes, such as when American Express funded a joint promotion with Foursquare to show how mobile technology can benefit consumers and restaurants accepting American Express.

TIP

Look around your marketplace. What common goals do consumers have? What challenges, goals, and aspirations do they share? What other businesses or organizations support your value proposition and align with your vision? And then ask yourself the big question: How can you bring brands and people together to solve a common problem or to achieve a common goal?

Try to build collaborative efforts around your brand's emotional selling proposition (ESP). When you do this, you end up with movement, not just a product and a brand. Companies that are perceived as moving toward a better world are those that are succeeding in this new era of consumerism.

Teaming up on CSR

Your corporate social responsibility (CSR) strategies for giving back, furthering environmental support, promoting charitable and community causes, and so on are a good foundation on which to build your collaborative efforts. Map out what you'll do on your own or with other groups as part of your marketing plan. Schedule your actions, measure them, and communicate them to your customers and stakeholders because knowing what you've done and are doing matters to consumers today. This likely won't change anytime soon.

Here's a good example of how collaborating for causes bigger than profits can pay off. Ecologic Brands, Inc., is a young business dedicated to reducing the environmental harm of disposable bottles by making them out of recycled (and compostable) cardboard pressed into a thin, smooth bottle shape with a thin recycled (and recyclable) plastic liner. The innovative design needed to be tested in market to move from design stage to actual packaging for goods in market. So the company's founder, Julie Corbett, and her team looked for a marketing partner that strongly valued sustainability and had the visibility to introduce the packaging innovation. They were able to forge a partnership with Seventh Generation, Inc., a company that makes plant-based healthy household cleaning products, which featured the distinctive Ecologic packaging for natural laundry detergent. This partnership resulted in helpful sales revenue for Ecologic Brands and valuable visibility and publicity at a critical time in its development.

Building kinship, not just relationships

Marketers need to start building people-to-people not just brand-to-people connections. Brands have typically focused on building relationships with customers based on their past purchases, product preferences, expressed interests, and so on. Yet, as J. Walker Smith pointed out, the new era of consumerism now requires building people-to-people connections, or kinship.

Smith, executive chairman of Kantar Futures, a strategic insight and innovation consultancy service for global brands, and member of the North Carolina Advertising Hall of Fame, emphasizes the importance of building kinship among customers, not just relationships, which people have been conditioned to do for years. Here are some of his insights on what this means and why it matters.

Kinship is about the process of building social currency with others by how we treat them and by our familial connections. True kinship is built on utter transparency and the priority of fostering relationships that matter over building business and finally on purpose. Do you focus on maintaining close ties as you would within a family unit, and are you willing to make sacrifices to build those ties? Establishing kinship in business requires focusing on enhancing and supporting lifestyles, not just completing transactions.

Here are the fundamentals of a kinship economy:

>> Culture, creed, commerce.

>> Booming interest in relationships for which kinship is the gold standard.

>> Social currency is the medium of exchange.

>> The bottom line is how you treat people.

It's a world in which brand marketers must relearn the business they're in — no longer the business of brands but the business of kinship and social currency, or to put it in a word, *connections*.

REMEMBER

Facilitating relationships is what brand marketers need to do as well. People will engage with a brand when it provides something they can share with kith and kin. Such social currency is what people want to spend these days, and only after that are people keen to spend dollars and cents. Brand marketers need to shift their focus to what people want most nowadays, which are stronger relationships with other people, not closer more revealing relationships with brands. People want people connections, and in a marketplace where relationships among people are the highest priority, the gold standard for brand marketers is the highest form of relationships, which of course, is family, which in turn means that kinship is the principle that must animate brands today to engage consumers in a compelling and effective way.

To include kinship strategies in your marketing plan, ask yourself the following questions and create action plans around your answers:

>> What elements does your company culture have in common with the core culture of your most valued customers?

>> What lifestyle values do your consumers embrace and live and that your corporate values support? Are these environmental, social, or charitable?

>> What opportunities exist within your markets and communities for bringing you customers and employees together in a common cause?

>> How can you build your CSR programme around events and causes that you can do jointly with your customers?

>> What customer appreciation or thought leadership events can you host in your community that will bring people together with your customers in ways that provide value and benefits far beyond your products or services?

After you answer these questions, build action items around your answers and add these to your marketing action items and timeline.

REMEMBER

More than 70 percent of consumers say they'll sign up to volunteer alongside a brand's personnel for a cause they believe in. How can you organize events that bring your customers and staff together, not for transactions, but for moving the world in a better direction? When big companies organize their regional staff into teams that interact with their communities to further local causes, they suddenly become "local" businesses led by "friends or people we know" rather than another big corporation.

Expanding Your Target

Every marketing plan outlines who your target audience is, what they look like demographically, and the transaction and lifetime value they represent to your brand. It goes without saying that your primary goal is to reach and influence this group of potential consumers and purchasers to capture their lifetime value.

Yet you also have other critical targets you must communicate to and "sell" to if you want your core customers' business. These targets are the influencers over purchasing and brand choices within your category. Some are direct, others not so much. Some are obvious and others more subtle.

Influencers take on many different personas and attitudes and look very different if you're in B2B or B2C. Influencers are the most influential drivers of purchase choices because they're the most trusted sources to which people turn when making decisions. According to research from Nielsen's Global Trust in Advertising survey, 92 percent of consumers trust completely or somewhat trust recommendations from people they know, the number-one influential source. Second is consumer opinions posted online, which 70 percent completely or somewhat trust. Keep in mind that people don't know these consumers, but they still trust peers over paid advertising, which validates the wisdom of building strong communities to support your brand, online and offline.

Table 2-2 presents examples of influencers that can impact sales and loyalty in various industries.

TABLE 2-2   **Examples of Influencers**

B2B Influencers	B2C Influencers
Industry analysts (Forrester, Gartner, Hoover's)	Peers (family, friends, professional associations)
Media covering innovations, advancements, and business news in your industry	Reviews on sites like Yelp and Amazon
Peer networks such as associations or societies bringing together chief marketing officers (CMOs), chief technology officers (CTOs), sales executives, product developers, graphic designers, architects, and so on	Social media sites such as Pinterest, Instagram, and Facebook
Product review sites such as bloggers that put out a Top 10 Widgets in 2019 report and so on	Bloggers on related topics (fashion, cooking blogs, and forums for consumer reviews, advice, and so on)
General print, radio, and TV news	Online news sites for category, general news outlets
End users who can influence department purchasing agents (radiology technicians influencing biomed purchasers)	End users who can influence selling channels via product, medical, and services requests
Peer reviews including testimonials on a brand's site and on review sites	Consumer reviews and posts on shopping sites

Monitoring and reacting to trends

Studying market trends to determine market influences on sales that are out of your control and how your sales and market share compare year to year and against your competition will help you better see your strengths, weakness, opportunities, and threats. When you do a trends analysis, you should include information about the following:

>> The size of your market — is the buying population growing or shrinking?

>> The transaction value of each sale and the annual value of each customer going up or going down.

>> Functional alternatives that have been gaining in prominence and sales.

>> Economic indicators that could impact sales in your category, such as housing starts, housing sales, unemployment, job growth, and wages.

Take note of all these and other market indicators so you can build your plans according to gains or losses. If the past period's program doubled your market share, seriously consider replicating it, if all the marketing and economic conditions remain constant. If you see a shrinking population that could impact sales out of your control, despite the best-made plans and product quality, adjust your output so you don't end up with inventory you can't sell and thus tie up your capital, which could be better spent elsewhere or put in reserve to protect your financial stability.

On the other hand, if your market share stayed the same or fell and no outside market factors influence this, perhaps you're ready for something new.

Developing the customer experience

Your marketing plan needs to encompass all the elements in the preceding section and how you plan to gain awareness to build sales — the overarching goal of any plan and business. In addition to the marketing campaigns you plan to execute and the sales goals and projections you need to identify, you need to plan out the customer experience.

Customer experience, or CX, campaigns are replacing marketing campaigns because, overall, customers care more about the feelings fulfilment and trust you create than the prices or benefits your offer. In fact, in the marketing department, chief experience officers are replacing chief marketing officers because the experience brings people back for more much more often than the price they paid.

Your customer experience needs to include plans for a meaningful journey on a path that evolves somewhat like the following:

>> Initial contact, sales support, and consultations (if applicable)

>> After-sale decision reaffirmation

>> Customer service protocols — how you respond to missed expectations, product issues, repairs, technical support, troubleshooting needs, and so on

>> Kinship opportunities — building intimacy beyond products through interaction at live events related to products and/or common causes

>> CSR — how you involve and engage your customers in your culture, values, and causes

>> Evangelism — how you enhance the emotional value of your brand relationship in ways that inspire your customers to introduce you to others

>> Communities — how you bring your customers and prospects together to form hives that support your brand and engage all in a joint cause and mission

>> How you adapt each step of the journey for your various segments, global markets, or cultures

TIP

Just like many software programs can help you execute a marketing plan, you can find many software applications for helping you manage and execute a successful customer experience and journey. Just do an Internet search for "customer experience software" and start reviewing the dozens of options that exist at various price points.

Creating a Working Marketing Plan

After you've worked through your goals and identified where you stand in terms of your SWOT analysis, functional alternatives, who your customers and influencers are, and opportunities for building kinships rather than just relationships, it's time to start putting your plan on paper and assigning actions, time tables, responsibilities, and metrics.

Taking the time to think through and write a marketing plan is essential to success for many reasons. It helps you and your entire team to clearly understand your goals, vision, current knowledge, actions you plan to execute, and the budget you have to spend on those actions. Essentially, it organizes your knowledge, defines your priorities, and sets your tasks and schedules and gets everyone on the same page.

A successful marketing plan encompasses all the elements discussed up to now throughout this chapter and assigns actions to associated goals. Here are some of the reasons that justify the time spent in organizing a workable plan:

>> A plan helps you identify the best practices, eliminate the unprofitable ones, and keep everything on schedule and on budget. Many businesses don't have a plan spelled out and just react to opportunities that may or may not pay off. Having a plan helps you work smarter and more efficiently.

>> The planning process helps you think through what needs to be changed to improve your results, and putting things in writing often adds clarity of focus to necessary tasks.

>> Planning helps clarify and control key elements of your marketing plan, such as branding, pricing, content, selling strategies, and more.

Naturally, planning takes time and energy. But its payback is rapid and large. Unplanned marketing rarely, if ever, pays off. Without a plan, you risk making knee-jerk reactions to try to get ahead, and that can be very costly in the long run.

Another big benefit of planning is that it gets you thinking creatively about your marketing programme. As you plan, you find yourself questioning old assumptions and practices and thinking about new and better ways to boost your brand and optimize sales and profits.

TIP

Software programs can simplify and support marketing planning. Most planning tools include templates you can use individually or interactively with a team. Some options to choose from include

» LivePlan (www.liveplan.com) from PaloAlto Software makes it easy for a team to work remotely on the same plan at the same time.

» SecurePlan (www.secureplan.com), also from PaloAlto Software, offers sales and marketing plans as well as general business plans from the same source.

» Enloop's (www.enloop.com) online planning tools are slanted more toward financial plans but still of some use.

» Mplans offers free sample marketing plans and sells the quite sophisticated Sales and Marketing Pro software download (www.mplans.com).

» Usually free, but less sophisticated, are the marketing forms and templates Entrepreneur offers (www.entrepreneur.com/formnet/marketingforms.html).

» G Suite (Google's apps for businesses; https://gsuite.google.com) includes interactive tools that simplify sharing, editing, and creating documents and other resources collectively with multiple authors.

» Smartsheet (www.smartsheet.com), a cloud-based planning platform that carries through to project management by the team. It also offers links for crowdsourcing.

» SCORE (www.score.org; the nonprofit set up to help U.S. small businesses) offers a suite of free templates for marketing strategy and plans.

Mapping Out Your Action Steps

The next step is to start mapping out your action items. Following is a solid way to organize your thoughts and outline your actions so your document becomes a true action plan, not just a good idea put in writing.

Step 1: Complete a situational analysis/summary

The first step is to outline the circumstances or situation that you are facing at the present moment. For example, where does your brand stand today in terms of marketplace and opportunities? What is your current position in your general market, and how are you poised to move ahead, or how are you at risk to fall behind? What are your constraints related to resources, funding, ability to scale, and so on? Explain the current situation as concisely as possible so all team members get an understanding of where you are and where you need to be.

Step 2: Establish your benchmark

When setting your goals, keep in mind what you have achieved, which actions have paid off, and set a starting point, or benchmark, from which you want to build and improve upon. Questions to ponder to help you do this include the following:

» What results did you achieve in the previous period in terms of sales, market share, profits, customer satisfaction, web visibility, or other measures of customer attitude and perception?

» What levels of customer retention, size and frequency of purchase, or other indicators of customer behaviour did you end the period with?

» How capable are you today for delivering on current desires and expectations of customers?

Your benchmark serves as a reality check for where you are and the foundation on which you should build your goals.

Step 3: Define your goals

While you are working on everyday goals for marketing and sales, don't lose sight of your long-term objectives. Learn from the moment to set goals for improvement and additional growth in the short and long term. What are your primary goals for the next period? Clearly, all objectives should lead to more sales, customers, and profits, yet you need actionable and measurable goals to help you get to the top of your game and stay there. What are your goals for market share? Quantify your goals by including sales projections and costs, market share projections, sales to your biggest customers or distributors, costs and returns from any special offers you plan to use, sales projections and commissions by territory, and so on.

Step 4: Take note of lessons learned

A postmortem on the previous period helps identify any mistakes to avoid, insights to take advantage of, or major changes that may present threats or opportunities. Also include lessons learned from competitors or even dissimilar businesses that have had good (or bad) luck with marketing initiatives you may want to try. Include any results from A/B testing of ESPs, campaigns, offers, promotions, channels, events, and so on.

TIP

Review results of third-party testing organizations, such as BounceX (www.bouncex.com), to help you learn from others' mistakes without having to pay the same price.

Step 5: Outline your strategy

Your strategy is the big focus of your plan and the way you'll grow your revenues and profits. Keep the strategy statement to a few sentences so that everyone who reads it gets it at once and can remember what the strategy is. Think like a sports coach: "Where is the opportunity to win, and what resources do we put in the game to score, dominate, and win?"

Your strategy outlines how you'll respond to the information you gathered in Steps 1 through 4 to help you find your strengths, weaknesses, opportunities, and threats to collaborate, influence influencers, and build kinship on top of relationships. For example, if you identify that you're strong at reaching middle-aged women, one point of your strategy may be to reach and convert young adult women to your products and brands so you can nurture the next generation of customers. Your action items (see the next section) will then outline how you'll reach this goal.

Check out Figure 2-1 for an example of how a marketing strategy leads first to specific marketing objectives and then marketing tactics.

Step 6: Commit to action items

You may want to outline the specific actions in your marketing plan and again in a spreadsheet so you can map out timing of execution, due dates for materials needed, roles and responsibilities, and the status of each action item. Here's an example of what this may look like:

FIGURE 2-1:
How objectives
and tactics
flow from your
marketing
strategy.

Sample Strategy
Create a hip new brand of dog treats and sell it to younger, active pet owners.

Sample objectives:
Brand the product to appeal to hip, younger consumers.
Build awareness and interest through the web, advertising, press coverage of events, and word of mouth.
Get at least 10,000 households to try samples of the product.
Build distribution through the web and retail grocery and pet stores.

Sample tactics:
Product: Design a product that makes dogs healthier and more energetic. Brand it to appeal to younger, hip pet owners.
Pricing: Price it slightly above competitors' products to signal that it is a specialty product and to fund an aggressive marketing campaign.
Placement: Make it available both on the web and through pet stores. Expand to grocery stores as soon as volume allows.
Promotion: Create a catchy, hip brand and logo. Use events, social networks, print advertising in magazines with the appropriate demographics, and in-store displays to communicate the product's special image and message.

© *John Wiley & Sons, Inc.*

Task	Description	Actions	Due Date	Owner	Status
Influencer outreach	Identify influencers over purchase and brand choice with voice among key constituents	Identify bloggers, analysts, columnists, speakers, and more	Deliver 5/17	Staff 1	Complete
			Approve 5/19	Staff 2	Approval pending
			Execute 5/24		

Step 7: Build learning plans

If you have a new business or product, or if you're experimenting with a new or risky marketing activity or trying new channels or offers, set up a plan (or pilot) for how to test the waters on a small scale first. You need to determine what positive results you want to see before committing to a higher level. After all, wisdom is knowing what you don't know — and planning how to figure it out.

To learn and ultimately succeed, everything you do must be measurable and testable. Set up tests for every action to determine how it worked against past efforts or to determine the best approach. Just be sure to identify the tests you need to do for the coming year to be as efficient and effective as possible.

You may want to include actions such as the following in a yearly learning plan:

>> Identify new research projects, such as Voice of the Customer programs, that help you identify what matters most, new attitudes, new customer demand expectations, satisfaction rates, and so on.

>> Try out direct marketing campaigns via A/B tests to identify a new champion or validate current champions that will still work in the new year's environment.

>> Test channels for promotions to identify best response and return.

>> Check new distribution channels to see whether you can identify more efficient and less expensive methods or partners.

>> Examine new market segments to identify secondary customer groups you can nurture for future gains.

>> Test lists to see which providers provide the best performing lists and the best overall returns.

>> Compare year-over-year (YOY) response for past and present campaign messaging and offers.

>> Experiment with engagement programs online and offline to see which best build relationships and kinship.

REMEMBER

Don't think of your plan as written in stone. In fact, your plan is just a starting point and is an evolving process. As you implement it throughout the coming year, you'll discover that some things work out the way you planned and others don't. Good marketers revisit their plans and adjust them as they go. The idea is to use a plan to help you be an intelligent, flexible marketer and guide your resources while being ready to change as quickly as markets and customers often do.

TIP

Always look for ways to maximize efficiencies in all you do. If buying advertising space is part of your plan, buy in bulk, or three insertions/placements rather than just one at a time. This way you save money and give a new channel a chance to pay off better, because one ad presented one time in one place likely won't get acted on as much as the same ad presented multiple times to the same people.

Keeping It Real: The Do's and Don'ts of Planning

Marketing programmes can easily get overwhelming, and when this happens, you set yourself up to fail. Keep your activities and goals reasonable, based on what you can do. If you try to do too much, you can waste a lot of resources and miss a lot of opportunities, both of which you want to avoid. The following sections illustrate common ways marketers lose money and some effective strategies for using your resources wisely.

Don't ignore the details

Good marketing plans are built from details such as customer-by-customer, item-by-item, or territory-by-territory sales projections. Generalizing about an entire market is difficult and dangerous. Your sales and cost projections are easier to get right if you break them down into their smallest natural units (such as individual territory sales or customer orders), do estimates for each of these small units, and then add up those estimates to get your totals.

Don't get stuck in the past

REMEMBER

Don't rest on your laurels, and don't "do what you've always done" unless that is paying off and has every chance of continuing to do so. Build on your best-performing elements of past plans and omit those that didn't produce high returns. Be ruthless with any underperforming elements of last year's plan. Also, monitor your plan over the business cycle and adjust it as you go so you can catch problems early and avoid wasting too much time and money on underperforming activities.

Don't try to break norms

If you're trying to offer a product or service that interrupts life as usual for your customer groups, you'll likely be disappointed. Build a product or service and a marketing plan that your customer can realistically support. For example, businesses are seeing a decline in travel budgets for mid-level managers at large and small companies. If you're offering a workshop for this group of professionals that involves expensive travel to a resort town and a good share of play time, your audience likely won't be able to get it approved. *Junkets* (leisure trips disguised as business trips) don't usually get approved in any business culture anymore, even for higher-up executives. So instead of trying to change this reality, change your offering and your expectations to fit your customers' reality, not your own wishful thinking.

Don't engage in unnecessary spending

Always think through spending options, and run the numbers before committing to anything or any salesperson with the "perfect" solution. Just because something is new or you can buy it at a good price doesn't mean you should. Have a plan for what you need, what you can spend, and how you'll measure your ROI for each spend, and stick to it to avoid losing money on losing investments.

TIP

Before committing to an expensive advertising agency with high overhead to cover, do some analysis to determine what outside resources you really need. With all the digital tools available today, can you do some of the ad and collateral design in-house? Also look for freelancers who can help with designing and deploying digital assets.

Do set reasonable boundaries

REMEMBER

Don't make your ambitions greater than the resources you have available to pull them off. If you're currently the tenth-largest competitor, don't write a plan to become the number-one largest by the end of the year. You need to grow at your own pace, not a competitor's, in order not to overextend your financial and human capital resources. To build revenue, you may need to start out in a niche market and then expand as you have the capital to do so. Be careful how much debt you leverage, and always monitor your sales goals and actuals to ensure that you can stay ahead and not get in a deeper hole if you're in one to begin with.

Do break down your plan into simple subplans

If your marketing activities are consistent and clearly of one kind, you can go with a single plan. But if you sell ancillary services, like consulting or repair, to support your core products, you'll need to map out plans for integrating and selling these other services and products as well. They may fit into one sales proposal, or they may be secondary pitches to customers you close.

If you have multiple regions, locations, or e-commerce sites, how does your over-all marketing plan support these areas, and what specific plans do you need to add to address their specific needs and goals?

REMEMBER

If your plan seems too complicated, simply divide and conquer. Then total everything up to get the big picture for your overall projection and budget. For example, if you have 50 products in five different product categories, writing your plan becomes much easier if you come up with 50 sales projections (one for each product) and five separate promotional plans for each category of product.

TIP

Every type of marketing activity in your plan has a natural and appropriate level of breakdown. Find the right level, and your planning will be simpler and easier to do. Following are some methods to help you break down your planning:

» Analyse, plan, and budget sales activities by sales territory and region (or by major customer if you're a business-to-business marketer with a handful of dominant companies as your clients).

» Project revenues and promotions by individual product and by industry (if you sell into more than one).

» Plan your advertising and other promotions by product line or other broad product category because promotions often have a generalized effect on the products within the category. What is your budget for public relations/ publicity, videos, collateral production, ad buys, social media site/page development, lists, promotions, printing/mailing, and so on?

» If you have a single bestselling product that carries your company, consider a separate publicity and customer experience plan for it. You should also plan product-oriented activities on the web, such as blogs and fun videos that go viral, to keep a buzz going about your star product.

Preparing for Economic Influences

When preparing your marketing plan, you need to factor in economic trends and issues of which you have no control. Watch the leading published economic indicators and regularly monitor the numbers. If you notice a decline for more than two months in a row, look closely for any signs of sales slowdowns in your own industry and be prepared to take action.

Monitoring economic influences and cycles can help you avoid a false sense of security. In the 1990s, economic growth was fairly steady. When economic growth suddenly began to slow in December 2007, marketers faced major problems as their markets slowed down. Stay on top of economic trends by cities, and especially for those of the cities in which you do the most business.

The Conference Board (www.conference-board.org), a nonprofit in New York City, compiles an index of leading economic indicators that has successfully predicted the last half dozen recessions. However, it has also predicted five recessions that didn't occur, so if you slavishly cut back every time the economists publish negative forecasts, your marketing plans will be too gun-shy and conservative. You have to take some risk to grow, but if you watch the economic weather closely, you can scale back sooner than most marketers when it becomes obvious that economic growth is slowing.

TIP

When your own sales are weak *and* economic forecasts are poor, cut back aggressively on variable costs like printing, promotions, design of new materials, and so on. You need to ensure that you can always cover your fixed costs, which include your office lease, utilities, and so on.

Budgeting Your Game

A critical component of your marketing plan is clearly your budgeting. You need to come up with line-item expenses — costs for each line of activity you include and plan to execute — and manage your overall expenses accordingly. If you don't budget, you can easily overextend yourself by engaging in those "special opportunities" that arise unexpectedly. Add a few of those together, and you can really impact your bottom line, and not always for the better.

Your playbook should include your pricing estimates and allocations for each step of the way to your goals. Figure 2-2 shows an overview of how to organize your marketing plan line items financially so you can better allocate your resources and see directly whether they align with your priorities and greatest competitive needs. If you evaluate your expenses against projected sales as shown in Figure 2-2, you can estimate your profit or loss from your marketing investments and activities.

Identify an initial cost figure for what you want to do with each component. Total these costs and see whether the end result seems realistic. Is the total cost too big a share of your projected sales? Typically, advertising and marketing spends are about 2 to 3 percent of projected sales. Are your estimates in line with your brand's historical marketing budgets?

REMEMBER

Don't budget more than 10 percent of your revenue toward marketing unless you have good reason to believe (from past experience) that the return on marketing investment will be there. And don't commit to a full year of expensive marketing. A first-quarter plan is more cautious and commits you to only a fourth of a year's spending. Take it one step at a time.

TIP

If your marketing plan covers multiple customer groups, you need to include multiple spreadsheets (such as the one in Figure 2-2), because each group may need a different marketing programme. For example, the company whose wholesale marketing programme you see in Figure 2-2 sells to gift stores — that's the purpose of that programme. But the company also does some business with stationery stores. And even though the same salespeople call on both customer groups, each group has different products and promotions. They buy from different catalogues. They don't use the same kinds of displays. They read different trade magazines.

Consequently, the company has to develop separate marketing programmes for them, allocating any overlapping expenses appropriately (meaning if two-thirds of sales calls are to gift stores, then the sales calls expense for the gift store programme should be two-thirds of the total sales budget).

Overview of Programme to Target Retail Store Buyers	
Programme Components	**Direct Marketing Costs ($)**
Primary influence points:	
– Sales calls	$450,700
– Telemarketing	276,000
– Ads in trade magazines	1,255,000
– New product line development	171,500
	Subtotal: $2,153,200
Secondary influence points:	
– Quantity discounts	$70,000
– Point-of-purchase displays	125,000
– New web page with online catalogue	12,600
– Printed catalogue	52,000
– Publicity	18,700
– Booth at annual trade show	22,250
– Redesign packaging	9,275
	Subtotal: $309,825
Projected Sales from This Programme	$23,250,000
Minus Total Programme Costs	– 2,463,025
Net Sales from This Marketing Programme	**$20,786,975**

FIGURE 2-2: A programme budget, prepared on a spreadsheet.

© *John Wiley & Sons, Inc.*

Managing Your Marketing Programme

The main purpose of the management section of your marketing plan is simply to make sure you have enough human capital and bandwidth to get the work done. This section of your plan summarizes the main activities that you and your marketing team must perform to implement your marketing programme. Use this section of the plan to assign these activities to individuals, justifying the assignments by considering issues such as an individual's capabilities, capacities, and how the company will supervise and manage that individual.

Sometimes the plan's management section gets more sophisticated by addressing management issues, like how to make the sales force more productive or whether decentralizing the marketing function is worthwhile. If you have salespeople or distributors, develop plans for organizing, motivating, tracking, and controlling them. Also, develop a plan for them to use in generating, allocating, and tracking sales leads. Do you need a system like Salesforce (www.salesforce.com) to help them stay on track and optimize productivity?

Start these subsections by describing the current approach and do a strengths/weaknesses analysis of that approach, using input from the salespeople or distributors in question. End by describing any incremental changes or improvements you can think to make.

TIP

Make sure you've run your ideas by the people in question *first* and received their input. Don't surprise your salespeople or distributors with new systems or methods. If you do, they'll probably resist the changes, causing sales to slow down. People execute sales plans well only if they understand and believe in those plans. Getting them involved early with idea generation and strategy development also helps gain their buy-in and implementation.

Projecting Expenses and Revenues

Managing your marketing plan and the execution of such involves establishing processes, boundaries, timelines, and budgets, such as

>> Estimating future sales, in units and dollars, for each product in your plan

>> Justifying these estimates and, if they're hard to justify, creating worst-case versions

>> Drawing a timeline showing when your programme incurs costs and performs program activities

>> Writing a monthly marketing budget that lists all the estimated costs of your programmes for each month of the coming year and breaks down sales by product or territory and by month

TIP

If you're part of a start-up or small business, consider doing all your projections on a *cash basis*. In other words, put the payment for your year's supply of brochures in the month in which the printer wants the money instead of allocating that cost across 12 months.

Also, factor in the wait time for collecting your sales revenues. If collections take 30 days, show money coming in during December from November's sales, and don't count any December sales for this year's plan.

A cash basis may upset accountants, who like to do things on an accrual basis. Cash-based accounting keeps small businesses alive. You want to have a positive cash balance (or at least break even) on the bottom line during every month of your plan.

If your cash-based projection shows a loss some months, adjust your plan to eliminate that loss (or arrange to borrow money to cover the gap). Sometimes a careful cash-flow analysis of a plan leads to changes in underlying strategy. One approach may be to get more customers to pay with credit cards rather than invoices; this can shorten the average collection time and greatly improve your cash flow as well as spending power and profitability. (Flip to Book 4 for more on cash flow and other important bookkeeping and accounting principles.)

Several helpful techniques are available for projecting sales, such as buildup forecasts, indicator forecasts, multiple-scenario forecasts, and time-period forecasts. Choose the most appropriate technique for your business based on the reviews in the following sections. You can use several of the following techniques and average their results.

Buildup forecasts

Buildup forecasts are predictions that go from the specific to the general, or from the bottom up. If you have sales reps, ask them to project the next period's sales for their territories and to justify their projections based on their anticipated changes in the situation. Then combine all the sales force's projections to get an overall figure.

If you have few enough customers that you can project per-customer purchases, build up your forecast this way. You may want to work from reasonable estimates of the amount of sales you can expect from each store carrying your products or from each thousand catalogues mailed. Whatever the basic building blocks of your programme, start with an estimate for each element and then add up these estimates.

Indicator forecasts

Indicator forecasts link your projections to economic indicators that ought to vary with sales. For example, if you're in the construction business, you find that past sales for your industry correlate with *GDP* (gross domestic product, or national output) growth. So you can adjust your sales forecast up or down depending on whether experts expect the economy to grow rapidly or slowly in the next year.

Multiple-scenario forecasts

Multiple-scenario forecasts start with a straight-line forecast in which you assume that your sales will grow by the same percentage next year as they did last year. Then you make up what-if stories and project their impact on your plan to create a variety of alternative projections.

You may try the following scenarios if they're relevant to your situation:

>> What if a competitor introduces a technological breakthrough?

>> What if your company acquires a competitor?

>> What if the government deregulates/regulates your industry?

>> What if a leading competitor fails?

>> What if your company experiences financial problems and has to lay off some of its sales and marketing people?

>> What if your company doubles its ad spending?

For each scenario, think about how customer demand may change. Also consider how your marketing programme would need to change to best suit the situation. Then make an appropriate sales projection. For example, if a competitor introduced a technological breakthrough, you may guess that your sales would fall 25 percent short of your straight-line projection.

WARNING

You really can't be sure which scenario, if any, will come true. So another method involves taking all the options that seem even remotely possible, assigning each a probability of occurring in the next year, multiplying each by its probability, and then averaging them all to get a single number.

Time-period forecasts

To use the *time-period forecast* method, work by week or by month, estimating the size of sales in each time period, and then add these estimates together for the entire year. This approach helps you when your programme (or the market) isn't constant across the entire year. Ski resorts use this method because they get certain types of revenues only at certain times of the year. Marketers who plan to introduce new products during the year or use heavy advertising in one or two *pulses* (concentrated time periods) also use this method because their sales go up significantly during those periods.

Entrepreneurs, small businesses, and any others on a tight cash-flow leash need to use this method because it provides a good idea of what cash will be flowing in by week or by month. An annual sales figure doesn't tell you enough about when the money comes in to know whether you'll be short of cash in specific periods during the year.

Creating Your Controls

The controls section is one of the most important elements of a marketing plan because it allows you and others to track performance. Identify some performance benchmarks and measurable values, often referred to as key performance indicators (KPIs), and state them clearly in your plan. You should set KPIs for your overall marketing programme and actions and for each individual line item or business unit. For example, you can define KPIs for the following:

>> Sales activities

>> Marketing spends and action items

>> Web traffic from search activities

>> Customer service and support for resolving conflicts

>> Customer engagement sales from online and offline chats

>> Distribution channel performance

As you monitor the KPIs and results for various aspects of your business, you'll better be able to see where your resources are needed most, where you can cut back expenses, and where your strong points and weak points are when it comes to profitable operations and ROI.

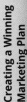

Creating a Winning Marketing Plan

Chapter **3**

Digital Tools and Tactics That Work

Marketing with digital channels today is somewhat like trying to hit a moving target as the tools, tactics, and trends change more quickly than most can imagine. And because nearly all marketing today is connected to a digital channel, platform, analytics tool, or device, the term *digital marketing* is somewhat of an oxymoron.

No matter what business you're in, the role you play, or the size and scope of your market, you need to understand and stay on top of digital marketing tools to succeed on any level.

Although digital technology introduces exciting opportunities to open new markets and engage with customers like never before, it also comes with the following challenges:

>> Digital tools are constantly changing. As soon as marketers master one, another comes up.

>> Because of the ability that digital technology offers for highly personalized communications, customers have grown to expect it, making traditional marketing methods less effective and putting more pressure on marketers to keep up with rapidly changing technological developments that enhance customers' overall experience.

>> Being able to manage the breadth and depth that digital channels offer marketers for communicating to customers any time and any place is another challenge. In the old days of marketing, brand managers just had to worry about developing a clever campaign with a good offer and getting a good media buyer to negotiate ad buys with magazines, newspapers, radio and television stations, and outdoor companies.

Now, marketers have to identify the best opportunities within numerous channel categories for several customer segments and then customize versions of all elements of each campaign to be personalized for every customer segment or persona, adapt the format for every channel they plan to use, and then deploy quickly and frequently. Oh, and then they have to monitor social media dialogue and online review sites and respond quickly to avoid losing consumer interest, their reputation, or sales.

Mind-boggling! But thankfully, manageable. The trick is to map out a detailed plan based on how your customers use and respond to digital channels to guide how you spend your time and resources communicating, placing ads, and creating meaningful experiences online. Otherwise, you can keep yourself busy and not really go anywhere.

After you have a plan in place as to which channels you need to use and how you need to use them, you then need to have a plan for which technology investments make the most sense for your desired reach, outcomes, and budget.

This chapter provides some insights on several digital channels that drive customer engagement and sales and some tips for how you can integrate these into your marketing plan. You also find guidelines on how to efficiently manage and deploy content across multiple channels.

TIP

If you want more in-depth information on the channels discussed here, check out the latest edition of *Social Media Marketing All-in-One For Dummies* by Jan Zimmerman and Deborah Ng (Wiley).

Noting the Digital Channels You Can't Ignore

REMEMBER

To start, Table 3-1 lists current digital channels and tools you need to embrace, manage, and at least begin to master as you build your marketing plan and allocate your time and money. If resources are slim, pick a few to start with and then expand as you're able. Regardless, you need at least a basic understanding of the channels and tools your customers (and competitors) use to execute a sustainable marketing program and competitive business.

TABLE 3-1 ## Digital Channels

Social Channels	Digital Tools
Facebook	Podcasts
Twitter	Videos
LinkedIn	Webinars
Pinterest	Games
Instagram	Content management systems

Because Facebook has more monthly active users (MAUs) than Twitter, Instagram, and others combined, this chapter starts there.

Using Facebook for Engagement That Builds Sales

Facebook is an incredibly important marketing tool. To effectively use Facebook for customer conversations, promotions, and relationship building, you need to build a content marketing plan specific to this channel and an advertising plan.

WARNING

Don't post anything just because you can. Posting without a messaging plan may actually do more harm than good because if it's not meaningful, you'll lose likes, follows, and readership, and each of these is hard to build back.

Following are some guidelines for putting together a content and advertising plan for Facebook; however, this planning guide applies to all other social media channels mentioned in this chapter. Instead of repeating these tips for each channel, use the following as your guide for building a presence and dialogues with your customers on Twitter, Instagram, LinkedIn, and other sites.

Developing a successful Facebook plan

Facebook is where many people document their life story and share their greatest moments. It's also a great place for brands to tell their stories and do so in ways that support the values of their core customers. As you build a plan to tell your story and engage in dialogue with core customers, keep in mind that Facebook is for stories, not sales pitches. Using this channel the way consumers use it will help you achieve greater success and return on the time you spend posting, sharing, liking, and more.

Here are some key elements you need to establish as you work on your Facebook marketing plan:

>> **Define your purpose.** Do you want your Facebook page to be a place where you have meaningful dialogues with your customers? Or a site that promotes your products, provides promotional codes and discount coupons, announces your sales, and the like? Or is your page a place to share stories about your people and business to better humanize your brand? When you answer and prioritize these questions and others like them, you're better poised to make your Facebook efforts pay off.

>> **Set your goals.** Facebook offers many different opportunities and outcomes for businesses in all areas. The trick is to set specific goals and have a plan to help you measure your progress toward achieving them while using your time wisely.

Some goals you can achieve through Facebook include

- Learning what trends, attitudes, and needs are important to your customers at a given time

- Interacting with customers to discover what they like about your products and brand and what else you can be doing

- Attracting more prospects by posting about relevant topics

- Driving customers and prospects to your website where you can better direct them toward a transaction

- Growing your e-mail permission database through Facebook promotions

- Communicating with customers and prospects for whom you don't have an e-mail address
- Building your social presence and prospect base through likes, comments, and shares of your current followers
- Creating a stronger brand image
- Putting together a community, or a hive, around your brand

These same steps apply to other social media pages and channels, so just repeat the steps that apply when building out your brand's digital presence.

The following sections present some tips and examples that will enable you to succeed at reaching many of these goals. But first, note that you can't achieve any of these goals unless you have followers and friends connected to your page. Use all your social channels to invite people to connect with you on Facebook (and others like LinkedIn) and post content that's worth sharing with their friends to build your base. Always include links for your page on your website, e-mails, content elements, and in marketing materials.

Consider doing an e-mail campaign for the sole purpose of getting people to follow you on Facebook and other channels. Let consumers know what they'll gain in terms of insights and interaction if they choose to follow or connect with you.

Determine your metrics

Like any programme, make sure you have a mechanism to measure the impact of your efforts toward your goals so you can see whether you need more resources to keep up with the opportunities created or need to make some changes to have a better impact.

Facebook Insights — a dashboard with metrics and analytics for your page — is available on business pages and provides valuable insights to help you see what your followers liked and didn't like, engagement level per post, which posts got the most likes, and whether you got likes from searches, shares from others, or Facebook advertisements, and more. It's important to pay attention to trends and comments on your page so you can discover what matters most and identify problems before they escalate.

Learn by asking questions

Opportunities to learn valuable and actionable insights on Facebook are many. For example, you can find out what matters most to your followers and what drives behaviour from the dialogue you create, the questions you post, the comments you get back, the posts your customers like or don't like, games your customers play, and by watching what your competitors are doing.

Ask questions. Most people like to comment on Facebook and have their voice heard. Just look at all the "talk" during a political season, surrounding a common cause, or a sports matchup. Posting questions for your followers can provide some great insights from their answers and comments.

For example, if you're a carpet cleaning company, here are some questions you may want to ask:

>> When it comes to cleaning your carpets, what motivates you most:

- Having your house look clean and fresh?
- Getting rid of germs that can affect your health?
- Getting that brand new look back again?

TIP

People often respond if they like you, want to voice their opinion, or if you offer an incentive. Facebook has a poll application (find it at `www.facebook.com/simple.polls`) you can use to create and post and monitor results, making it easy to analyse. Or you can just post a question and see what kind of dialogue it inspires. With Facebook's poll application, you can share your poll by e-mail, which helps increase traffic to your page.

WARNING

If you have a small following, be careful about using the polls app versus just posting questions to spark dialogue. If few people respond to your poll, it can send a signal that you aren't worth following on Facebook.

Make your question or poll open-ended and thought provoking rather than a yes-or-no question. Instead of, "Do you like watching soccer?" ask, "What do you like most about watching women's soccer matches?" Doing so will help you discover your customers' values and motivators.

REMEMBER

You need to monitor your page and control the content instead of letting others control it for you. You don't want customers to go to your Facebook page and see customer complaints to which no one responded. When this happens, newcomers to your site see a good reason not to do business with you and no explanation or resolution that could inspire them to still give you a chance.

Interact and build

Clearly, you can interact with customers in many ways on Facebook; you're really just limited by your time and imagination. Because Coca-Cola has one of the most liked and followed Facebook pages, with more than 107 million likes and followers, its page is a good one from which to gain ideas and inspiration.

For example, when someone posts about Coke, the brand responds. One fan commented on how he liked the little Coke cans but couldn't find them. Coke responded by asking for his zip code (in a personal message, of course) so it could help him find them. On another occasion, a fan asked whether Santa would give him a job. Regardless of whether this was sarcastic or serious, Coke responded with a link to its employment page.

The key to building relationships on Facebook is twofold:

>> Post content worth reading and commenting on.

>> Respond to the good, the bad, the funny, and the serious.

If consumers feel ignored or invisible on your page, you'll lose them.

TIP

If you want shares to help build your reach, the most effective way is to post things that are fun, engaging, humorous, or just really cool. Cool photos, funny videos, and inspirational stories seem to get the most shares.

Keep in mind that the best content isn't always about driving a sale but more about engaging and creating rapport, trust, and communications with your followers. When you achieve these attributes, sales will follow. The best content strategy is to post fun, positive, inspiring, and relatable content that tells a story in which your customers can see themselves.

Creating content that gets response, dialogue, and leads

Creating a story in which readers can easily see themselves is the best way to spark interaction, dialogue, and new leads. But simply posting a well-written status update is not likely going to fill up your inbox with new prospects waiting to be sold something. However, if you post content that invites response and interaction that includes others' thoughts, feedback, and expertise, you will be more likely to start a conversation that could get you the right kinds of leads for your business.

Here are some tips for lead-generating content on Facebook:

>> **Be brief.** Remember, people typically have short attention spans, which seem to be getting shorter all the time with all the distractions and demands on their attention. To up engagement, keep your content short. If you want to provide more information about a topic in a post, provide a link to a full article.

>> **Direct to website.** Directing people to your website for more information on a post you shared is always a good idea, and then be sure to follow up by asking people for their e-mail to get the full story. Offer white papers, links to columns, links to news coverage for your brand, and so on. You can also post about special sales and discounts available on your website.

>> **Invite a response.** Don't just post a point, an opinion, or a fact. Spark dialogue by asking fans what they think. Do they agree? Share your stories and encourage followers to do the same. One comment often inspires another, which makes your page more interesting and gives fans more attention for their own voice, too.

>> **Provide tips.** People like how-to tips and will often follow a site just to get more. If you have something of value that's actionable and helps others, post it. If you can, break up your list of how-to tips into a series to give you content that inspires people to come back for more.

>> **Use hashtags.** Hashtags simply give your post more chances of getting seen, on Facebook and on other channels. Include at least one but not too many, and some research says that two work best.

REMEMBER

Prepare a content plan and stick with it. It's easy to spend all day posting and reading comments on your page and others' pages and accomplish little, if anything, else. To avoid wasting your time and that of your followers and friends, make your content meaningful and actionable.

REMEMBER

Facebook is best used for interacting and building relationships. If you use it too much to promote sales and offers, you risk losing credibility and fans.

Advertising on Facebook

If you're not able to build your base through the tactics in the previous sections, or you want to get to mass quickly, consider advertising on Facebook. You can do this through boosting your post for a nominal fee or by purchasing Page Like or Offer ads. Here's the difference:

>> **Boost post:** You pay a nominal free, maybe $5, to get your post pushed out to people in a demographic you choose. The more you pay, the more people see your post.

>> **Page like ads:** These are ads with a Like button for your page that are sent to audiences of your choice. If they "like" the button, they become followers of your page.

>> **Offer ads:** You can use an Offer function provided by Facebook to post offers on your page. You can pay to have that offer boosted to people not following you to get more exposure for it. If you have a Facebook page, you likely see these in your News Feed quite a bit.

Building Your Twitter Presence

Although Twitter can be frustrating for the long-winded because you have to keep your posts to 280 characters or less, it does add value for building your brand's presence. For one, Twitter helps start conversations with followers and can be used to post links to your more in-depth content on LinkedIn, Facebook, and, of course, your website. (See Chapter 5 in Book 6 for more about building a website.)

A key advantage of Twitter is that it helps you find people with similar interests by suggesting people you can follow. And if you post enough interesting content on a given topic, Twitter encourages others to follow you, too.

You can build your Twitter base by doing the following:

>> Searching a keyword related to your brand and then clicking on People associated with that term. For example, searching "consumer behavior" on Twitter results in dozens upon dozens of people to follow.

>> Including hashtags for your tweets so that people can find your posts.

>> Posting your Twitter handle in your e-mail signature, on your web page, and on handouts for trade shows and live events. Encourage followers on your other social channels to follow you on Twitter as well.

>> Creating an interesting profile page and tweeting regularly about things that are of interest to consumers interested in your product and brand.

>> Tweeting about something more than just your latest offer or white paper. Start conversations on objective themes to attract like-minded people.

>> Linking your Twitter account to your Facebook account so that your tweets show up on Facebook, too.

REMEMBER

Twitter has more than 330 million users and is still growing. It keeps you connected in real time to your customers and maintains your presence in channels that consumers use daily in all industries.

Igniting Your Social Presence on Instagram

Instagram is a photo-centric social network that lets you tell your story through imagery — photos and videos. It's popular among younger audiences and omits a lot of the chatter, good and bad, from other social sites. In 2019, Instagram had around 1 billion users, making it another must-use site for reaching today's consumers.

Because a picture can be "worth a thousand words," Instagram is a great way to communicate quickly about brand events or happenings and to tell your story through the power of images. Most people access it via their smartphone, which limits your reach, but it helps boost your mobile strategy and share your brand stories.

TIP

The best way to be successful on Instagram is to use high-quality photos that are interesting, inspiring, and engaging. You can also upload your Instagram photos to other social sites, including Facebook, Twitter, Flickr, and Foursquare.

Expanding Your Network through LinkedIn

Although many people use LinkedIn to advance their careers and build far-reaching professional networks, LinkedIn also serves a valuable role for businesses. It's different from other social media channels and needs to be treated as such, or it can backfire on you. For one, LinkedIn is *not* for promoting products and attracting leads; it's for promoting your industry expertise, knowledge, insights, and business happenings and for posting your job openings. LinkedIn is widely used by B2B brands to identify decision makers at companies with whom they'd like a relationship and to strike up a meaningful conversation. Many companies in the B2C space use it to promote their workplace culture and attract new employees because it has a popular job centre, which attracts job seekers and employers.

As of this writing, LinkedIn has 645 million members, making it another must channel for businesses, especially B2B. IBM's page is a great example of how businesses can use LinkedIn. It has more than 7 million followers and keeps the content on target and worth reading.

Here's a brief overview of the fundamental elements of a LinkedIn page for businesses:

>> **About Us:** Like personal profiles on LinkedIn, your page starts with a summary of your business. You can state whatever you want to about your company and change it as often as you want to.

>> **Affiliated pages:** You can add affiliated pages to your main page that provide details about your product lines. IBM has 12 showcase pages, which include IBM Watson Health, IBM Watson IoT, and IBM Cloud.

>> **Updates:** Your updates are your posts, articles, links to articles, insights you want to share, and other information that helps define your brand. For a business, these may include inspirational quotes from your CEO, financial results, announcements about live events on other channels, such as Facebook, and insights about your product and development and of your corporate social responsibility.

The following sections explore some of the best features on LinkedIn for businesses and marketers alike.

Groups

A good use of LinkedIn is to create your own group. Find a topic of interest in which you're a thought leader and start a group to share insights and exchange ideas. If you start a group, your role is to set the rules, monitor posts, manage posts, initiate conversations, and keep it going. Every time a new post is made on your group page, all members get an e-mail notification, which helps to keep your topic and expertise on members' minds. A group is tough to keep up with if you're stretched for time, so make sure you have a plan for keeping your group active and inspired.

Here are some tips for getting a group going:

>> **Define the purpose.** Is this group for exchanging ideas about innovations, solutions, trends, breakthroughs, and case studies on a given topic?

>> **Set the rules.** Put your purpose and rules on your site for all to see. If your rules are no job posts or promotions of any kind, follow through. As the manager, you can delete posts and eliminate violators.

>> **Invite members of your network to join, and promote your group on your individual page as well as other social channels.** Keep inviting people to join regularly, because the bigger the group, the greater your network and reach.

>> **Monitor all activity.** If you set your group up to be an open group, you'll likely get a lot of fake accounts and spam posts. If you don't delete these, you may lose the members you value.

>> **Post often.** Post articles, insights, links to white papers, videos, research findings, event coverage, and personnel news. Keep your content business-oriented and leave the promotional, fun posts for other channels like Facebook and Twitter.

Engagement

The best way to get noticed on LinkedIn is to post meaningful articles or updates several times a week if possible. Topics that get engagement include articles you've written, news coverage of your brand, events, trade shows, personnel news, how-to guides, checklists, and links to your blog or new information on your website.

Here are some tips for driving engagement:

>> Include a link to a landing page in your posts; by doing so, you can double your engagement.

>> Post thoughtful questions and encourage others to share their insights.

>> Add an image. LinkedIn claims that images can result in a 98 percent higher comment rate.

>> Link to your videos on YouTube, which will play directly in your LinkedIn feed and could increase your share rate by 75 percent.

>> Respond to comments in a way that encourages more comments and gets more people commenting.

TIP

For every post, LinkedIn provides analytics, such as the number of impressions, clicks, interactions, and percentage of engagement to help you see which topics do best. Like other sites, you can pay to sponsor an update for more money and more exposure.

Promoting Your Brand with Pinterest

With an average monthly active user number of around 291 million, Pinterest can't be ignored, especially by B2C businesses that want their products and creative uses of their products to go viral. Pinterest is widely used as a bookmark of ideas for recipes, home decorating, crafts, holiday décor and goodies, fashion, and do-it-yourself projects.

Per a report from September 2019 posted on www.expandedramblings.com, a site that posts stats about various social channels, 60 percent of Pinterest users are female and roughly 40 percent are male. Roughly 67 percent of all users are millennials. Around 55 percent of online shoppers in the United States claim that Pinterest is their favorite social media platform.

So if you cater to women who like to make, bake, follow fashion trends, and the like, Pinterest just might be for you. If users like your post, they can really increase your exposure by sending it to their e-mail and Facebook contacts or sharing it on other social channels.

TIP

Pinterest is an idea board. You pin what you like, and your pins get communicated via other social channels, giving the creators of those ideas added exposure. The better the picture and the most clever the ideas, the greater the number of pins you'll receive.

You can create boards of images and ideas of interest to you and include images from others on these boards. If people click on these images, they can be directed away from your page so be careful about sending viewers to other pages or sites.

Pinterest can also be a good place to sell your products. You can promote your pin like on other sites and even set up a shopping cart so people can purchase from you without leaving Pinterest. The shopping cart works much like those on Amazon.com and eBay. You're buying from a seller using its platform. If you use Pinterest for business, make sure you set up a business account so you can get analytics about your most popular pins, shares, repins, likes, and demographic information about those visiting your Pinterest account.

Discovering Digital Tools That Drive Brands

Beyond understanding the basics for using popular social media channels, you need to discover how to use popular digital tools for building your brand presence, network, customer base, and, of course, sales. When choosing digital tools and activities, you should focus on those that can best help you build your visibility, grow your social networks, and, most importantly, grow your in-house e-mail list. Building your e-mail list is truly one of the most important outcomes of all digital activities because e-mail drives some of the best return on investment (ROI) you can get from any marketing activity today.

Some of the most visible and affordable digital tools appropriate for any business include podcasts, webinars, videos, and games, which are discussed in the following sections.

Podcasts

Started in 2003, podcasts are huge, and for good reason. For consumers, they play right to their mobile and digital lifestyle. You can listen in the car, at the gym, at the spa, while grocery shopping, while walking, while riding the metro — anywhere you can take your phone or tablet. The most popular platform for podcasts is Apple iTunes. Other platforms include Stitcher, TuneIn, and BlogTalkRadio.

For marketers, podcasts are a great way to achieve goals that include

>> Educating your target consumer groups to provide objective decision assistance while positioning your team as trusted advisors and sources for key information

>> Establishing you and your leadership team as authorities in your space

>> Building your e-mail list and social networks

>> Increasing your search engine optimization (SEO) results

>> Adding value to your website through more valuable content

TIP

Doing a podcast gives you access to key businesspeople who wouldn't otherwise take your call. Instead of calling to sell them something, you're calling to invite them to get exposure. This can help you establish relationships with influencers in your space and get them talking about you and your products. Whenever you interview a guest, encourage him to e-mail his networks to listen to the podcast, introducing you, your content, your podcast, your leadership, and your brand to a network that you otherwise wouldn't have access to.

Before starting a podcast, you need to be sure you're fully committed. It doesn't do any brand any good to spend time and resources to launch a new program and then not stick with it. Podcasts take planning, time, and effort, but, when done right, they can deliver a strong return.

Here are some tips from various podcasters to help you get started:

>> **Target a niche group.** If you start a podcast on a broad topic trying to reach a broad audience, you'll likely be broadly disappointed. You'll be more effective if you specialize with a niche topic to build momentum and get you noticed.

>> **Decide on a format.** Most podcasts are between 20 and 30 minutes. Formats range from interview-type shows to how-to tips, tutorials, and such. Choose a format that you can keep up with and that keeps your listeners listening.

>> **Keep it brief.** Modern society suffers from attention deficit due to all the information overload people experience daily, so treat your podcast accordingly. Get your main message across early on to avoid disconnects, and don't ramble on just to fill the time. Stay focused, meaningful, and on target.

>> **Commit to frequency.** Some successful podcasters claim that they podcast three times a week to get started; however, a good frequency to maintain is once a week.

>> **Build a library.** Before you promote and launch your podcast, record several sessions so you can air content consistently and build your base.

>> **Invest in quality.** Make sure you have a good microphone and deliver good quality without noise clutter that can be distracting and cause people to stop listening.

>> **Link to your digital assets.** Post your podcast archives on your website and link them to your Twitter account and your blog. Make them easily available for people to find and of course share with others.

>> **Promote it everywhere.** Invite people to listen to your podcasts through e-mail campaigns, LinkedIn announcements, Facebook posts, and so on. Post links to your podcasts on bookmark sites, like Reddit, and YouTube channels.

You can use your podcast to grow your e-mail base as well by offering free material to your listeners. Encourage listeners to go to one of your social sites to download a paper, a coupon, and so on in exchange for registering with their e-mail.

TIP If you get enough downloads and listeners, you can even monetize your blog through sponsorships. Some of the top podcasts, like *Entrepreneurs on Fire*, get thousands of dollars a month in sponsorships.

TIP Make your podcast fun, a bit disruptive, and borderline irreverent, and dare to be daring. People like listening to things that have a little surprise element, not just what they expect to hear.

Webinars

Although podcasts work well for B2C and B2B brands, the webinar is a powerful tool mainly for B2B brands that can help with lead generation, relationship building, and cementing a position of authority in any given industry. In many ways, webinars are easier to pull off than podcasts because you don't have to commit to a weekly schedule or produce a series to have ready to go before you launch your program.

The benefits of webinars are many. Here are just a few:

>> **Affordability:** You can use free apps such as Google Hangouts, or you can subscribe to a service like GoToWebinar, Webex, or ReadyTalk. Skype also provides a free service for group voice and video calls and screen sharing.

You can subscribe to services that can handle up to 100 callers for around $50 to $100 a month. Your fees will depend on what features you want and your attendee number limits. Check out some of the webinar platforms to find what works for your budget. Some of the features you may want beyond audio and voice calls and screen sharing include

- Archiving
- Mobile-friendly features
- Multiple rooms
- Ability to edit your recordings
- Integration with social media and Microsoft Outlook
- Ability to change presenters
- Ability to monitor attendees' focus (get signals when they open other screens on their computer during your presentation)

>> **Authority:** When you share knowledge that enhances a customer's life, you become a valued advisor and authority, and quite often, that positioning can take price out of the equation for purchase decisions. Also, when people learn from someone, they tend to trust that person and give him their business.

>> **Awareness:** Even if you get only 20 people to attend your webinar, you'll likely get a lot more visibility than that. If you promote your webinar on your social networks and to your e-mail list, news channels for your industry, and more, you can get literally thousands of impressions for your expertise and position as an authority on the topic on which you're presenting. This is worth it alone because most of this visibility is free.

TIP

As you consider systems to subscribe to, look for a system that will grow with your needs. If you want to do small-group events or weekly webinars with client teams, you can keep your numbers small and use a free system.

Following are some tips for organizing and pulling off a successful webinar or two:

» **Be free.** Consumers are used to getting good content for free these days and are more and more reluctant to pay for it. So even though you may charge for strategic advice or in-depth training courses, you should still create a webinar that has substance. Just don't give away so much that you cannibalize sales of your other programs. This mainly applies to consulting services or agencies that provide strategic advice and sales or marketing training as part of their revenue streams.

» **Be smart.** A webinar should help to tease your bigger offering — be it consulting, training, software services, and so forth. You need to position your webinar as valuable on its own while subtly getting people more interested in your programs that aren't free. You have to give away a little bit of your expertise to whet the appetite for more. Just pay attention to how much you give away that attendees can execute on their own so that you don't end up cutting yourself out of future sales.

» **Be relevant.** Pick a topic that's meaningful, current, and provides realistic actionables for attendees. Purchasers will invest their time if they believe they'll gain something they can put to use toward achieving their business goals.

» **Be professional.** If you use an app and decide to use a webcam and your screen for the webinar, keep it professional. Nothing is quite as distracting as seeing a speaker talking in his bedroom with a messy bed in the background. True story.

» **Be giving.** Provide takeaways that are actually useful. Many presenters offer their slides as a bonus for attending the webinar. Others offer discounts on products, services, or further training programs that aren't free. And others offer white papers or free audits of attendees' marketing material or other items. Many times those free audits turn into great long-term clients, and they can signal a vote of confidence in what you do and your willingness to invest in the process.

» **Be present.** Market your webinar everywhere. Post invitations on all your social media channels. Send notices to trade associations, chambers of commerce, and business alliances. E-mail invitations to prospects, customers, and channel partners. Post on LinkedIn groups as well as your own page. Get it out there that you're an authority and are sharing secrets to success. After you're done, record your session, create a PDF, and send links to anyone who didn't attend. Archive it on your website, too.

A big reason to do webinars is to build your base. You're giving people knowledge for free so make sure you get their e-mail address in return. Require contact information to register for the event and access any archived files.

No-shows to webinars are quite common. That's okay and expected. The attrition rate is fairly high for free events because things come up, and if you haven't paid for it, you're not losing anything. Be sure you get e-mails for all registrants so you can offer the archive link both to those who attended and those who didn't.

Videos

You've likely noticed videos have been taking over photos in your Facebook and LinkedIn feeds and are popping up more frequently in your e-mail boxes, and slide shows on websites are moving over for videos. HubSpot shares some powerful statistics to validate why this happening and why you need to jump on this bandwagon, too. Here are just a few:

>> Videos in e-mail lead to a jump in click-through rates of between 200 and 300 percent.

>> Videos on a landing page can help your conversions increase by 80 percent.

>> Videos combined with a full-page ad can boost engagement by 22 percent.

>> Videos can increase likelihood of purchase by 64 percent among online shoppers.

>> Videos included in a real estate listing can increase inquiries by 403 percent.

>> Videos inspire 50 percent of executives to seek more information about a product.

>> Videos inspire 65 percent of executives to visit a marketer's website and 39 percent to call a vendor.

>> Most importantly, 90 percent of video watchers say that videos help them make purchase decisions, and 92 percent of those viewing them on mobile devices share videos with others.

The point is clear: You need to create videos if you want to engage customers and sell more products. And because YouTube is the second-largest search engine, next to Google — well, enough said.

Another reason you must include video is because most of your competitors are doing it, and that can leave you out in the cold if you're not.

The following sections explore ways to create effective videos for any business as well as specifics for B2C and B2B.

Creating effective videos

The one challenge of using videos is that a lot of videos are competing with each other. In fact, on average, users are exposed to 32.3 videos a month, or roughly 1 a day. So how do you create videos that build your business and use them effectively in your marketing mix? Check out these tips:

>> **Create an emotional reaction that drives people to contact you for further information.** This is where it gets fun. Like all things you do in any medium — print, digital, or mobile — your content needs to have actionable value, and that value can be improving people's circumstances, inspiring them to live a better life, or guiding them to do their job better so they achieve their goals and advance their career.

>> **Regardless of your business genre, keep your video short and to the point.** This isn't your chance to produce a Hollywood blockbuster. It's simply a way to tell your story with a medium that appeals to the senses and makes your brand come to life. Keep your videos around two to three minutes long.

>> **Before you debut your videos publicly, test them.** Ask non-employees and even non-customers to sit through your videos and give you feedback. Good questions to ask include

   ● Did it keep your interest?

   ● What was the main message you took away from this video?

   ● Did it inspire you to inquire more about our product or service? If yes, why? If no, why not?

   ● Was the length appropriate?

   ● Did you think the production quality of this video was in line with other brand videos you've watched?

>> **Like any marketing communications, always include a call to action and a response mechanism.** Stay away from promotions because they'll expire before you're ready to stop using the video. Make it clear how to contact you for more information through e-mail, website, phone numbers, and social channels.

>> **Use professional footage and images.** Your video can be text based, like a slide show, or it can be a true video with all the moving parts. Regardless of the format you choose, use the highest resolution and quality possible. Your reputation is on the line per the quality you project. If you're a high-tech

company and you use low-tech video, that transfers to the perceived quality of the products you develop and sell.

>> **Create a YouTube channel to house all your videos.** You can archive videos on YouTube and on your website. For either option, include a transcript of your video to help you achieve higher SEO results.

Sunny Lendarduzzi, a Canadian who has become a YouTube training sensation, offers a course called "YouTube for Bosses" that can help anyone start and build their online presence on YouTube. This comprehensive course offers everything from how to film and edit videos to how to utilize keywords in your YouTube videos and will get you started or accelerate your current channel. Visit https://sunnylenarduzzi.com/youtube4bosses.

Looking at B2C and B2B considerations

For B2C, you can add a little more fun and focus on life messages, not just brand messages. Coca-Cola does a great job of this. Its YouTube channel has more than 3.2 million subscribers. Its "Happiness Machine" video, which shows a Coke vending machine dispensing "doses of happiness," has more than 10 million views — an inspirational mission and message that helped build the emotional equity of the Coke brand.

Here are some tips for using videos in the B2B world:

>> Create product demo videos to showcase the features that set your products apart.

>> Show how your products compare to competitors' when applicable and how your products fulfil your viewers' needs.

>> Include statements from your company leaders to show their vision and help tell your brand story.

>> Include customers talking about their experience with your product and your team. Video testimonials are powerful because viewers can see the body language, the smiles, and the looks of relief and also hear the excitement in voices that written testimonials don't provide.

Again, consumers like to see brand stories in which they can see themselves. They want to be the proud father or the mom being thanked by her Olympian child as shown in Proctor & Gamble's "Thank You Mom" ad series that makes many moms cry no matter how many times they watch it. They want to be the vacationer on the beach, the newly engaged couple, the happy family, or the thriving executive.

REMEMBER

Find ways to associate your brand with what matters most to your consumers and then get creative and start writing video scripts that tell your story in conjunction with the goals they have for their lives.

Online review sites

Another digital tool you can't ignore are online review sites, like Yelp and Google. Although you don't populate content directly on these sites, you can influence it.

When you have a happy customer, ask him to write a review on Yelp, Google, and other sites you know your customers use. Research by Nielsen shows that more than 70 percent of consumers trust online reviews, even though they don't know the reviewers. If people read a bad review about your business, you could lose their interest right away.

TIP

You need to continuously monitor all review sites to look for comments about your brand. Respond immediately to negative comments and offer a solution. You can turn an angry customer into a happy one if you resolve his concern quickly and appropriately. And you're showing prospects that you're willing to do what it takes to keep customers happy.

Many of the complaints on these sites are petty, but the one-star review from a customer that had to wait five minutes more than expected can take your average down and make you look bad in comparison with competitors.

Monitoring reviews will also help you determine whether you're being sabotaged by competitors posting fake reviews to ruin your reputation. If this is the case, you can report it to the review site and try to get this resolved.

REMEMBER

You can't repair your reputation if you don't know it's damaged. Monitor review sites regularly and always respond. Thank good reviewers for their time and words and offer to work with those who weren't so happy with you. Research shows that when you resolve customer issues, you increase their loyalty to you.

Posting testimonials on your website isn't as credible as a review posted on a third-party site, which you didn't review and approve ahead of time. Take the time to ask customers to do this. If you treat them well, they'll usually find time for you.

Fun and games work, too

Marketing is really all about fun and games — literally and figuratively as gamification is rapidly increasing as a profitable way to engage customers and build relationships. Everyone likes the thrill of trying something different, playing a game to test his chances for success, and getting unexpected surprises.

Games tap into people's most powerful drivers of choice — the neurotransmitters that trigger hormonal rushes that make people feel happy, excited, energized, or fearful and threatened. Those feelings dictate behaviour, and when people get feelings that make them feel confident and powerful, they go back for more. Games do this! And when games are associated with brands, people assign those good feelings accordingly and often go back for more.

In a world that seems to thrive on instant gratification, games can be very rewarding. Games reward behaviour, and that behaviour can be as simple as making a purchase, sharing a post on social media, referring a friend, and so on. Brands win, too, by getting results pretty quickly when they deliver a game that has a reward attached to it. For example, if a consumer completes a behaviour, such as registering for your newsletter, you can send him a game that has a reward attached to it as a token of appreciation. He plays the game and gets a reward, and that makes him happy and willing to engage with you again.

Todd McGee, CEO of CataBoom, an automated game company, points out that giving customers a game to play that enables them to win a reward has a more powerful reaction than just giving them a reward because "winning" releases that dopamine rush. When that happens, it increases positive feelings about the experience and brand exponentially.

You can create games in various formats, such as digital scratch cards, slot machines, trivia, puzzles, and polls. You can even create skill-based games that present a little more challenge but can also increase engagement as consumers keep trying to win.

While the nature and creativity of games played may change over time, human nature never will. People like the thrill of the chase and the chance to win something. And the more you can tap into that for your brand and provide a "winning" experience, the greater your loyalty will be.

TIP

Game platforms come in a variety of options and include SaaS models like that offered by CataBoom. To do games right and within regulations for social media and others venues, you need to work with a game expert. To see examples of how you can create games and use them to engage your customers, visit www. cataboom.com/platform.

Getting customers to come back

Brands using gamification find that customers do indeed come back for more. Games that offer a prize, such as a free product, for winning are becoming regular points of engagement between brands and consumers. If it takes just a few seconds of time to engage and the payoff is to win something worthwhile, people keep going back.

Todd McGee has seen 80 percent of customers who were sent a game from a brand return to that game to keep playing for prizes. This kind of return participation is making games a new type of loyalty programme, especially if games pay off in product prizes or points that can be redeemed for products of choice.

REMEMBER

Rewards aren't always tangible. A good reward can be just knowing you beat your own score or reached a level of play you didn't think you could. It's not always about the end reward but more about how you felt during the experience. Brands that spark dopamine experiences are more likely to spark greater customer satisfaction and loyalty.

Consumers like to win experiences, not just "stuff." Think about offering unique content, special access to VIP services or offers, or a chance to do something people wouldn't normally get a chance to do.

Engaging customers

When customers play your games, they're engaged with your brand even when they're not actively shopping. This kind of increased engagement often leads to more sales and enhanced loyalty. CataBoom has seen 50 percent of targeted consumers engage with brands when games are delivered along with a reward.

Higher engagement pays off in many ways, such as the following:

» Positive experiences that drive positive feelings make people want to engage with the brand in various settings, online and offline.

» Customers tend to tell others about their positive brand experiences by posting online or verbally referring others to a brand.

» When people engage with a brand on multiple levels, they tend to trust it more, and when they trust that brand, they purchase more.

TIP

Games can be used to accrue points to cash in for big prizes or to reward instantly with $1 or $5 off your next purchase. Instead of sending coupons like others do, you can give your customers a more engaging experience through games.

Advertising on the Web

Given the huge amount of time consumers spend online, you can't dismiss the importance of online advertising in addition to social media activity. Here's some perspective: Nielsen reported in 2018 that American adults spend more than 11 hours consuming media each day across various screens and channels, including tablets, smartphones, computers, multimedia devices, video games, radio, DVDs, DVRs, and of course TV. Of a 24-hour day, that is substantial. Think about it. If you add 8 hours for sleep, you're now up to 19 hours a day of time committed, leaving about 5 hours for all else, like eating, dressing, finding your keys, commuting to work, and then, of course, your work activities that don't involve a screen.

Although that number may seem staggering, it's also very telling of the importance of your brand being "seen" on screens. Following are some insights and guidelines for how to do this through advertising.

Search-term marketing

People conduct millions of online searches a day on search engines like Google, Yahoo!, and Bing. Advertising on these sites in any format can clearly get your brand name exposed to a lot of potential prospects.

The challenge is to get your site to show up on the first page of a search listing that likely produces millions of results. To do this, you can bid to purchase the top search terms, but that is usually very expensive. If you're in a general category, like pet supplies, bidding on and getting the best search terms to boost your ranking may be out of reach per your resources, and there's a good chance that others in your space have locked up those best words that currently fall on the first page of results.

For example, if you're in the pet supply business, consumers searching the term "pet supplies" will likely get millions of results. Good luck getting on top of that list and buying those terms.

An alternative is to purchase *long-tail keywords* — that is, long descriptive terms, not just the main universal term. A long-tail keyword search may be "pet supplies Denver, CO," which generates a lot fewer results because it's a narrower search. If you go a bit deeper and search "pet supplies self-grooming Denver, CO," you'll get even fewer results.

Various groups researching search trends have discovered that 60 to 70 percent of page views result from long-tail keywords. If consumers are using long-tail searches so should businesses when it comes to buying search terms, not just because you can capture a lot of views for your URL but also because they're much cheaper.

TIP

For marketers, this signals a big opportunity. Find out what customers like best about your products and determine what you want to be known or found by — your inventory, special services, experiences, or location. Buy those long-tail terms on Google AdWords (see the next section) and see how much more exposure you get.

Google AdWords for ads as text, banners, and more

With Google AdWords, you create a campaign, such as an offer, and then decide whether you want to have it show up as text in search listings, a display ad, such as a banner on the top of the page, a video ad on YouTube, or an app ad, which runs across the entire Google network. You then choose the following:

>> Geographical area, or target searchers in a given area.

>> Radius, or target searchers within a certain radius of your place of business.

>> Which search terms you want to bid on so your ad gets top visibility.

>> Your budget. You pay only for actual clicks so AdWords sends you only as many as your budget allows.

You get continuous access to your results — how many people see your ads, how many clicked through to your website, or how many called you for more information. AdWords also manages ads on YouTube because Google owns it.

TIP

WordStream, an online advertising agency, offers a free AdWords performance grader to help you see whether you're getting good results or wasting your money on your current words. Although it wants you to buy its services as a result of your score, it may be worth checking out at www.wordstream.com.

Here's a brief outline for starting an AdWords campaign:

1. **Set up a free AdWords account.**

   Just go to https://ads.google.com/home/.

2. **Decide on the format you want — search-term ad or text among the listings, display/banner ad, video ad, and so on.**

   AdWords has templates you can use for pretty much any format.

3. **Link your ad to key terms you think people will use in searches.**

   Do this by following a specific search engine's instructions for advertisers and entering your bids for specific search terms in the relevant form. Again, long-tail keywords are less expensive, more available, and work.

4. **Tell the Internet search engine how much you'll pay for a click on your ad.**

   This is your *bid*. For example, we may commit to a bid of 50 cents for a click on the search term "marketing advice." So if someone follows our link from his search to our website, we owe Google 50 cents. If our bid is higher than anyone else's bid, our listing appears before any other commercial listings at the top of the searcher's screen, which increases the probability of that person clicking on our listing.

5. **You track the results.**

   Based on what you learn, you can keep tweaking your ad, the formats you use, your terms, your reach, and so on until you get the results you want and need.

TIP

Take a look at monthly and year-to-year trends in searches on Google by using Google Trends (`www.google.com/trends`). This site can alert you to slow periods (searches for many business-oriented terms fall off sharply in December), allowing you to time your pay-per-click advertising to peak search periods.

Getting the most out of each format

With a text search ad, you pay to have your URL and brief description at the top of the search listing. This consists of a headline, your URL, phone number, a one-line description, your address, and some links to key pages on your website. You may want to have a page go straight to your top seller, or your About Us page. You need to use your words wisely and stick to terms that create emotionally relevant reactions, intrigue, and interest for these to work.

Banner ads (those brightly colored rectangles at the top of popular web pages) are the web's answer to display advertising in a print medium or outdoor advertising on a billboard. They're good for building awareness of your brand, but not much more than that. Whether you place them through an online agency or AdWords, you need to have a good, compelling headline that gives people a reason to click and learn more. It can be a strong call to action or a statement or visual that creates curiosity and intrigue. Have your ad direct people to a landing page about the offer you promoted so you can keep the momentum going toward a conversion. For ideas on banner ad designs, offers, headlines, and creativity that work, just search for "good banner ads" and you'll get plenty of sites with fun examples.

TIP

Like with outdoor billboards, a lot of copy won't get noticed or read. Keep it simple and to the point. It helps to have your URL on your ads in case people don't click through right away so you have at least gained exposure for your web page.

You can place your ad on sites beyond the AdWords platform. Explore online ad agencies and brokers for good rates on good placements, and then monitor your results.

In addition, web ad agencies offer lots of creative options, including interactive ads such as *widgets,* which are banners with an overlay of a pop-up interactive box that usually asks for an e-mail address in exchange for a chance to win some contest or prize. You can also animate a pop-up or regular display ad or include video in it.

Or you can use one of the skyscraper formats to create something that looks like an old-fashioned printed coupon, with the addition of a live form for entering an e-mail address and linking to a landing page where the offer's details are provided and the deal is sealed.

Then there's the *interactive*, a web display ad that invites the viewer to try his hand at something entertaining or useful. For example, a kitchen design company may run an interactive display ad with content aimed at homeowners and remodelers with a call to action, such as "Click here to use our kitchen design software for free." The trick with interactive web ads is to quickly send people to a landing page where they fill in a short registration form, allowing you to capture their information before you give them access to the free tool or toy.

TIP

Like anything with marketing, it's easy to get carried away and not realize how much you're spending on a given initiative. Set a budget before you start purchasing space online and AdWords. If online marketing seems to be working well, maybe spend 10 to 25 percent of your ad budget accordingly, or 1 to 2 percent of your revenues.

REMEMBER

If your web marketing efforts lose money by not delivering enough leads to pay off, move on. Don't spend good money on bad results. Remember, too, that if an ad doesn't work on a small scale, it's not going to work on a big scale. Keep experimenting with formats, messages, and offers until you find a combination that produces results you need.

Using Automated Customization to Work Smarter and Faster

With the advent of all the digital channels and data-driven insights we have today, we face a new set of challenges. One of the biggest challenges is how to manage, produce, and effectively deploy all the content needed to reach target audiences with relevant messages across an expanding array of digital and even traditional channels.

As mentioned earlier, you need to customize content to individuals and personas to gain attention, influence behaviour, and capture sales. But if you market to thousands of customers, sorted into various customer segments, with different needs, different cultures, different locations, and different generational attitudes, you have a lot of repurposing to do for each campaign you execute. Being able to do this quickly and efficiently is often the difference between a brand's success or failure. No small task or amount of pressure here.

Consider this scenario: You want to promote a new product that supplements an existing one. You want to communicate this to each of your target segments and your current customers in all the markets in which you operate. And you want to use e-mail, Facebook, mobile, web banner ads, and printed point of sale (POS) displays at all the retail outlets that sell your products. You need to customize each element for each persona targeted, maybe even each geographic location targeted. Oh, and you want to target Spanish-speaking and English-speaking customers at the same time. On top of all of this, you're offering an introductory price for a limited time only so it's critical that all pieces are in market at the same time for all markets you serve. And you have to get it out in a matter of weeks to take advantage of seasonable buying cycles.

So think about that for a moment. If you're targeting even just four consumer segments in just a handful of different locations, you need a lot of versions for each element you use in your campaign. In many cases, your content customization costs can increase by 300 percent or more according to Perry Kamel, a leader in the content management technology field. If you're paying an agency $50 to $250 or more per piece (varies by type of content) to build out those versions, that adds a lot of time and money to the cost of your campaign and makes your ROI goals all that more elusive. And if you don't meet the ROI goals set by your CEO or board, your job could be on the line. The pressure builds.

Thankfully, marketing technology has evolved to include robust systems that enable mass multi-channel customization, which provides an affordable and quick solution to this scenario. With the right technology and relevant messaging, you can increase your outcomes by 30 to 40 percent, Kamel points out, who has achieved this level of results consistently for clients in various industries. Add that to the savings in production, and now your ROI can be mind-boggling in a good way.

Table 3-2 presents a more detailed comparison to see how time and cost savings can add up.

TABLE 3-2 ## The Time and Cost Savings of Automating Content Versions

Task	Conventional	Automated
Design and assemble templates for segments	12.25 hours @ $110 per hour	0.25 hours
Brief agency, await concepts, review concepts, check art, await edits, and review edits	7 days	1 day with no agency involved
Approve artwork and deliver production-ready art to producers	$1,348	$28

REMEMBER

The point here is simple: A successful marketing plan can and should embrace all channels without worrying about the cost and time to produce and deploy, no matter how big or small your business is. Technology exists to make it actionable and affordable to execute omni-channel campaigns and communications to thousands, even millions, of customers and prospects efficiently.

TIP

Here are some tips for choosing the right platform for your budget and marketing plan:

>> **Look to the clouds.** Cloud-based systems are the most efficient way to store, access, share, and use your digital assets. Your team players, employees in remote offices, agencies, resellers, distributors, channel managers, and so on can then access all assets any time and get items to market quickly. Just be sure to choose proven systems that will meet your security requirements. Cloud systems are most often priced as SaaS models, allowing you to buy monthly subscriptions to use the platform based on your needs and budget.

>> **Use templates.** Creating a new design and/or shape for every content element you need can be cumbersome. Look for a system that has templates that support all content types, online and offline, that you can customize for your channel and production needs that are then automatically resized and reshaped for various channels and screen and production requirements.

>> **Consider multi-format options.** Many campaigns integrate printed and electronic POS material with mobile, social, and digital channels. You'll need these materials to be produced in sync with each other, especially if you're sending display materials to distributors or retail outlets that you want in place while social channels are engaged to drive customers to those locations.

>> **Check content analytics.** Look for a system that can help you track content usage across your enterprise for specific assets and determine outcomes for various elements. This capability can help you eliminate wasteful elements and focus on executing those that drive the most revenue and profitability.

Chapter 4

Using Print in a Digital World

Print is not dead. And it never will be because consumers still react more emotionally to tactile communications. It's just human nature. As the world increasingly turns digital, you may think it's okay to bypass printed direct mail, newspaper ads, and collateral. It isn't.

Studies confirm that print still matters:

» Brand recall for print ads is 75 percent compared to 44 percent for digital. (Canada Post)

» Print actually generates greater comprehension than digital. Many studies show that people read printed articles longer and are more engaged because they're tangible and create a greater sensory experience. They also have fewer distractions, such as moving objects and links on web pages.

A Canada Post/True Impact study alone shows that print takes 21 percent less cognitive effort to process and that recall for a print piece was 70 percent higher than a digital ad.

Although print media options are shrinking due to the advantages of web-based advertising and promotions, it should still be a major part of your marketing programme. When done in conjunction with your digital programmes, it can be very cost effective. Print is a powerful tool as a first introduction to your brand and a mechanism to drive people to digital assets to learn more and engage directly.

Understanding the basics of a print campaign is essential, whether you're a do-it-yourself marketer for your own small business or a marketing manager for a mid-sized or larger organization. This chapter helps you create and design print materials that can build your brand awareness, generate leads, and help drive customers to your advertising with digital programs, such as e-mail, websites, and social channels, and use them together to create better brand engagement with your customers. Print, even in a world where many are addicted to screens, can have a powerful impact on sales and return on investment (ROI).

REMEMBER

When designing anything in print, your purpose is to spark engagement and drive consumers to your point of sale, be it a physical location or online store, and ultimately stimulate a sale. Think ahead to that goal:

>> If your product sells in stores, create signs, packaging, displays, or coupons that echo your print brochures and ads and remind the buyer of that theme.

>> If the sale occurs on a website, make sure the ad sends prospects to a landing page where the offer from the ad is highlighted and it's obvious what to do next.

>> If you make the sale in person, use handouts like catalogues, white papers, fliers, order forms, or brochures that are consistent with the promises and brand positioning in your print ads and online presence, including Facebook, Twitter, and LinkedIn. (See Chapter 3 in Book 6 for more about these digital tools and tactics.)

REMEMBER

Always maintain the same brand persona and value propositions in your print material that you do in your online and point-of-sale materials. Even if you're writing something that's informative or instructional (like a product manual), the professionalism and utility of the communication will make a strong impression about the character of your brand. If you're in healthcare and your material is sloppy and full of mistakes, bad grammar, or confusion, consumers likely won't trust you with their health. Every detail matters.

Creating Printed Marketing Materials

In general terms, print materials need to follow the same rules as digital to capture attention and secure engagement. Brochures, *tear sheets* (one-page, catalogue-style descriptions of products), posters for outdoor advertising, direct-mail letters, catalogues, and even blogs and web pages all share the basic elements of good print advertising: good copy and visuals mixed with eye-catching headlines. They also all require a common look and feel that unites the separate pieces and furthers your brand position and persona. Understanding print and how to use, design, and integrate it into your omni-channel marketing plan is critical to building your brand's visibility, value, customer engagement, sales, and ROI. The following sections cover the essentials of print materials.

Exploring elements of successful print materials

Just like newspapers tell a news story, your print material — collateral, brochures, fliers, and ads — tell your brand story. Print materials you should integrate into your marketing mix include display ads for local and regional publications and fliers and brochures to hand out at networking events, trade shows, and so on.

REMEMBER

Following are some of the necessary parts to help you tell your story at a glance and with detail after you get readers' attention.

>> **Headline:** Your headline, the large print at the top or most visible in your design, must present your emotional selling proposition (ESP). This is one chance to attract customers to your story.

>> **Subhead:** The optional addition to the headline provides more detail, also in large (but not quite as large) print. Copy here usually backs up the headline but in a way that creates more curiosity or clarification.

>> **Copy or body copy:** The main text section tells your brand story and is laid out in a readable manner, much like what printers use in the main text of a book or magazine.

>> **Offer:** If you're placing an ad or building a flier around a sale, make sure your offer is one of the most dominant aspects of your piece, followed by a strong call to action, or CTA. Your offer is the specific product or promotion you're promoting, and your CTA is the mechanism by which you want customers to respond. For example, your offer may be 15 percent off regular prices for a limited time, and your call to action may be to go to your website, e-mail, or call you. Regardless, these elements must stand out and be easy to find.

>> **Visual:** Because 90 percent of people's reaction to marketing materials is driven by their unconscious mind, colours and images you use are critical to your success because they set the tone for your message and brand story before consumers read a single word.

>> **Caption:** Copy attached to the visual explains or discusses that visual. You usually place a caption beneath the visual, but you can put it on any side or even within or on the visual.

>> **Trademark:** A trademark is a unique design that represents the brand or company (like Nike's swoosh). You should always register trademarks and copyright all your materials so no one can infringe on the unique way you tell your brand story. (Flip to Book 2 for more details on intellectual property.)

>> **Logo:** A company's logo often serves as a trademarked version of its name. Often logo designs feature the brand name and include the company's slogan.

>> **Slogan:** A slogan is an optional element consisting of a short phrase evoking the spirit, personality, and ESP of the brand. One classic example is Michelin's "Because so much is riding on your tires." This statement coupled with a visual of a baby on a tire makes you think hard on what matters much more than price. It works. Despite a higher price, Michelin continues to be on the top-sellers list for tires worldwide.

>> **Digital links:** One of print's most valuable roles is to drive people to your website where they discover how your product can improve their lives and can interact directly with members of your team. Also directing them to your social sites like Twitter, Pinterest, and Facebook (see Chapter 3 in Book 6) is important because it helps consumers do the research they most often do before making brand choices. If you give them only a phone number and they don't want to call anyone for risk of being pressured to buy, there's a good chance you just lost a prospect.

Designing print materials that capture attention and sales

Design embodies the holistic feel and layout of your brochure, ad, or other printed marketing materials and is vitally important: It's the first impression people have with your brand's story and values and helps them determine consciously and unconsciously whether your persona reflects their own and whether to engage. Your colours, fonts, layout, images, and other visuals have less than three seconds to signal relevance and intrigue to your reader. Photos reflecting the way your readers see themselves, or want to see themselves, often successfully spark engagement and so does your colour palette.

The following tips and insights apply to all print formats — ads, fliers, and bro-chures. These same design elements apply to much of your digital assets as well.

>> Great advertising has to rise off the page, reach out, and grab readers by appealing to the values and aspirations that drive them. In the cluttered world of modern print-based marketing, this design goal is the only one that really works! If you're designing an ad for a local magazine or newspaper, spend some time looking at the current ads for various businesses and your

competitors to see which ones stand out. Avoid designs like those that don't, and gain inspiration from those that do.

>> Many software programs offer design templates for brochures, fliers, and other print materials that can guide you. Many are inexpensive and easy to use, such as Microsoft Publisher.

>> Regardless of your role — sole proprietor, business owner, or marketing manager — you should always design your ads with the intent to repurpose your design for other channels. You should be able to scale your design to be printed as a flier that you can hand out at trade shows and networking events or as a poster that you can display at community events that you may sponsor, and then you should be able to easily transfer your design to a digital format for a web banner, social media post on LinkedIn or Twitter, pin on Pinterest, and so on. Be sure you use high enough resolutions of all images in your design to be able to scale up, which is critical for print quality.

Working with a professional designer

If you don't have the time, talent, or desire to design ads and other printed materials, you can find many affordable options for hiring freelancers. Just search the Internet for "freelance graphic designers," and you'll get lots of options.

TIP

Another great resource is your local college. You can hire design students at a lot less per hour or project, and they'll often work together with fellow students to offer you even more creative perspectives.

When selecting a designer, review each candidate's portfolio thoroughly. Only hire someone whose body of work matches your sense of style and quality and get recommendations from past or current clients to make sure the person has a reputation of getting the work done on time, on budget, and on goal.

TIP

Before hiring any designer, write up a creative brief. This is the blueprint from which the designer will work to build your brand's image and lay out your offer and message. This creative brief should contain elements from your marketing strategy, such as colours and fonts. You should direct your designer to include the following items:

>> **Colours:** Which colours and colour combinations reflect the emotions and attributes you want associated with your brand and specific message?

>> **Fonts:** Do you want sans serif or a customer design, size, and so forth? Which fonts best appeal most to the generation you're targeting?

>> **Imagery:** What icons and logos should your designer use?

>> **Visuals:** Do you want photos, cutout boxes, charts, and so on? Provide stock photos you've purchased or original photos you own that you want to use.

>> **Layout:** Do you want columns to make your ad look like a news article or body copy that flows like a letter? Which best reflects the mood you want to create and the credibility you need?

Your designer should provide you at least three options for designed pieces, based on your creative brief. After you choose a design, you then need to make sure the design fits the right specifications for how it will be printed.

You also need to ensure the following:

>> All photos are at a high enough resolution to ensure good print quality. Typically photos that are 300 dpi (dots per inch) or higher will work well.

>> Your design needs to be able to scale up or down to easily go from a flier to an ad without losing clarity and quality. Scalability is important because many publications today have print and digital versions, and often purchasing a print ad gets you a place in the online version as well.

>> You have purchased rights to use any photos or images you've included.

>> Your ad or brochure wasn't created in a template from a software program that contains images and other design elements for which you haven't purchased the rights to use.

REMEMBER

Always get a project fee, not an hourly rate. Low hourly rates can cost more than projects done at higher rates if the designer isn't as good or efficient. It's about the end cost to get the end product — concept, design options, edits, and final execution.

Using online sources for design services

If you're just starting out and need a good graphic identity for your brand, you can check out some fun and cost-effective ways to tap some of the best talent available. Sites that can connect you to designers who in turn bid on your project include

>> Freelancer (www.freelancer.com)

>> Crowdsite (www.crowdsite.com)

>> LogoArena (www.logoarena.com)

>> DesignContest (www.designcontest.com)

>> Hatchwise (www.hatchwise.com)

- » Logo Design Guru (www.logodesignguru.com)

- » DesignCrowd (www.designcrowd.com)

- » 99designs (99designs.com)

You can get great prices and work from these freelancers that are heavily vetted and proven to participate in the bidding process. Another route is to set your project up as a contest and purchase the one that wins. For example, 99designs hosted a logo contest for a beer brewer from Waterbury, Vermont. The cost of the contest was less than $300, drastically less than most traditional logo designs.

Doing the design on your own

Anyone with a basic computer and printer can now set up shop and create her own fliers, brochures, business cards, and ad layouts. In fact, Pages and Microsoft Word both include a number of excellent templates that simplify layout and allow you to bang out a new brochure or other printed marketing piece quickly. Any graphic designer you hire will eschew Word and Pages and use the Adobe professional design programs (currently available at a fee of about $50 a month from Adobe Cloud at www.adobe.com/products/creativecloud.html).

If you have experience using these programs, then you may want to design your own print materials (as well as websites and so much more), but if you've never used them, they're not recommended. It takes a while to figure out how to use the programs, make edits efficiently, and create a design worthy of your brand. In the end, your time may be better spent managing your marketing and sales rather than learning how to master a software application and design processes. Do, however, take a look at Adobe Marketing Cloud (www.adobe.com/marketing-cloud.html), which many marketing departments now use to help them manage programmes.

If you're a consultant or own and operate a small business regionally, you can use design software for just about anything, including your logo, business cards, signs, website, and so on. Take a look at the do-it-yourself logo options on sites like www.flamingtext.com, www.logogarden.com, and www.logomaker.com.

TIP

Designers often experiment with numerous layouts for their print ads or other printed materials before selecting one for formal development. Whatever approach you take to becoming a do-it-yourself designer, it's strongly recommended that you experiment with layouts the way pro designers do. The more layouts you look at, the more likely you are to get an out-of-the-box idea that has eye-grabbing power.

Figuring out why fonts matter

Just about every element of advertising, print, e-mail, website, and other marketing material design has been tested, and testing which font best is no exception. Studies show that which font you choose not only increases comprehension, but it affects response to your call to action, making your font one of the most important choices you make regarding your printed marketing materials.

The right font for any job is the one that makes your text easily readable and that harmonizes with the overall design most effectively. For a headline, the font also needs to grab the readers' attention. The body copy doesn't have to grab attention in the same way — in fact, if it does, the copy often loses readability. The following sections help you find the font that will make sure your printed marketing materials improve readability, comprehension, and action.

Choosing a font style

You have an amazing number of choices, because designers have been developing typefaces for as long as printing presses have existed. Your word-processing software will have many of the basic options, including classics like Helvetica, Times New Roman, and Arial.

TIP

Check out Adobe Fonts (https://fonts.adobe.com/) for nice displays of many more options, where you can call up most popular fonts or create lists by style and type.

A clean, sparse design, with a lot of white space on the page and stark contrasts in the artwork, deserves the clean lines of a *sans serif typeface* — meaning one that doesn't have any decorative *serifs* (those little bars or flourishes at the ends of the main lines in a character). The most popular body-copy fonts without serifs are Helvetica, Univers, Optima, Arial, and Avant Garde. Figure 4-1 shows some fonts with and without serifs.

Traditional fonts used for books, newspapers, and similar materials are serif fonts like Century or Times New Roman. The most popular body-copy fonts with serifs include Garamond, Melior, Century, Times New Roman, and Caledonia. Figure 4-2 shows an assortment of typeface choices, in which you can compare the clean lines of the sans serif typefaces with the more decorative designs of the serif typefaces.

Fonts without serifs that are easy to use include Arial, Avenir, Calibri, and Gil Sans. These have a more contemporary clean look and are good for readability and comprehension as well. However, studies show that serif fonts test higher in comprehension and recall tests.

FIGURE 4-1:
Fonts with and
without serifs.

Serifs

Serif

Serifs

Sans serif

Sans Serif	Serif
Helvetica	Century
Univers	Garamond
Optima	Melior
Avant Garde	Times New Roman

FIGURE 4-2:
Popular typefaces
for ads.

REMEMBER

In tests, Helvetica, Times New Roman, and Century generally top the lists as most readable, so start with one of these typefaces for your body copy. Research also shows that people read lowercase letters about 13 percent faster than uppercase letters, so avoid long stretches of copy set in all caps. People also read most easily when letters are dark and contrast strongly with their background. Reverse font, or font that is lighter than the background, such as white font on black, has been shown to lower comprehension by more than 80 percent, so if you use it, use it sparingly to make key points stand out in a design but not for your body copy or main story. Black 12-point Helvetica and Times New Roman on white are among the most readable fonts for a printed marketing piece, even if it seems dull to a sophisticated designer.

As a general rule, use complementary fonts for the headline and body copy. For example, you can use Helvetica for the headline when you use Century for the body, and vice versa. Or you can just use a bolder, larger version of the body copy font for your headline. Work to make the headline grab readers' attention, stand out from the body copy, and ultimately lead vision and curiosity into the body copy's text.

Making size and style choices

All fonts are available in many sizes, most readily from 8 to 72. The main thing to consider is how the size looks in the format you have to work within. Make sure your ad doesn't look too crowded by using larger font, and don't make it so small that it's hard to read. If people's first impression is that your ad or brochure will take energy or time to read, they'll typically opt out. Studies show that size 14 has the greatest readability, but 11 and 12 are common.

TIP

Consumers don't like to have to work to read a message, they tend to read type quite conservatively, and they find traditional designs instinctively appealing. The spacing of characters and lines, the balance and flow of individual characters (with some white space around them or an appropriate illustration to break up the text) — all these familiar design elements please the eye and make reading easy and pleasurable. So when you need to provide emphasis, try to do so in a conservative manner. For example, try simply bolding your body copy before resorting to a new style of type. Too many type styles may reduce your design's readability.

REMEMBER

A good design uses two type families and varies the size of them, mixing in appropriate italics, bold, or reverse type if the overall design benefits from it. Figure 4-3 shows a black-and-white print ad laid out using Garamond and Helvetica, which are traditional, easy-to-read fonts. Some graphic designers avoid them because they like to be less traditional and more creative, but as the figure shows, these two type families lend themselves to clean, attractive, appealing, and (most important) *readable* designs.

Don't just use a new or different type of font because you can. Stick with popular fonts, in popular sizes, except where you have to solve a problem or you want to make a special point.

TIP

Your eye can't distinguish easily between fonts that are only one or two sizes apart, so specify a larger jump than that to distinguish between body copy and subhead or subhead and headline. For example, if your body copy is set in 10-point Times New Roman, you need to set subheads at least two steps up (steps being defined by standard point sizes: 9, 12, 14, 16, 18, 24, 36, and 48, although in-between sizes can also be used).

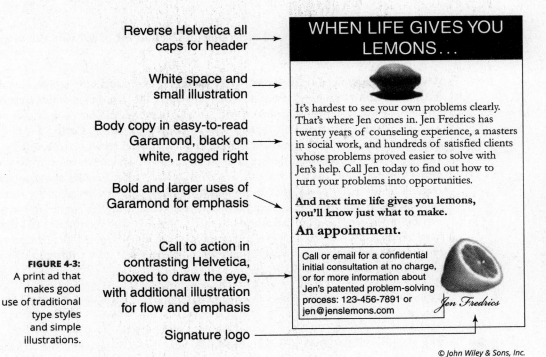

Reverse Helvetica all caps for header →

White space and small illustration →

Body copy in easy-to-read Garamond, black on white, ragged right →

Bold and larger uses of Garamond for emphasis →

Call to action in contrasting Helvetica, boxed to draw the eye, with additional illustration for flow and emphasis →

Signature logo ──────

WHEN LIFE GIVES YOU LEMONS...

It's hardest to see your own problems clearly. That's where Jen comes in. Jen Fredrics has twenty years of counseling experience, a masters in social work, and hundreds of satisfied clients whose problems proved easier to solve with Jen's help. Call Jen today to find out how to turn your problems into opportunities.

And next time life gives you lemons, you'll know just what to make.

An appointment.

Call or email for a confidential initial consultation at no charge, or for more information about Jen's patented problem-solving process: 123-456-7891 or jen@jenslemons.com

Jen Fredrics

© John Wiley & Sons, Inc.

FIGURE 4-3: A print ad that makes good use of traditional type styles and simple illustrations.

Digging into more font details

If you decide to be your own designer, you should familiarize yourself with some of the minutiae you don't know you don't know. These include

>> **Font versus typeface:** A typeface refers to the overall style, and the font, the specific variation of that style. For example, you can use Arial, Arial Narrow, Arial Black, Arial Rounded and then add bold, italics, and so on.

>> **Copyright:** In most cases, a typeface such as Arial is not copyrighted and can be used in your ads and marketing materials. Customized fonts, such as the font created for the classic Coca-Cola logo, are usually copyrighted and require purchasing rights to use.

If you want a wide variety of unique fonts you can use for your materials, you can use sources such as Google Fonts (https://fonts.google.com/).

Using flow for engagement and clarity

How pieces flow and look to readers is critical for securing engagement, without which you have no response. *Flow* is the smooth movement of attention from an entry point, around the page, and to an end point. In marketing, the entry point is almost always the headline, and the end point is either the brand name and logo or a call to action.

Whether in a brochure or a print ad, white space matters. Psychologist Ken Larson did a study at MIT on how font and layout affect people's emotions, which in turn affect their interest and engagement with an ad. He found that how copy flows on a page and the amount of white space affects interest in reading, clarity, and cognitive focus. In a lab setting, readers were given an ad designed for *The New York Times,* one with a poor, busy design and one with a good design where copy flowed more easily around the visuals and left more white space. Results showed that readers of the good design felt more positive emotions while reading the same copy as those with the bad design, and they experienced higher cognitive focus, mental processing, and clarity. Another key finding was that the readers felt that it would take less time to read the good copy, and, in today's world, that is critical because consumers don't have a lot of time to give, nor are they willing to do so, to read your sales message.

As you create your ad, you need to create visual interest while creating the right flow and copy/visual balance.

REMEMBER

In a really well-designed print ad, brochure, website, or blog page, the writing and the selection of font styles are just a part of the bigger-picture design, which ought to draw the viewer through a well-planned flow of reading and viewing experiences. If the flow is inviting, the design appears simple and the copy easy to read, and the likelihood of your ad getting noticed and read significantly increases.

Producing Effective and Efficient Print Collateral

Word-processing or graphics software, a good inkjet or laser printer, and the help of your local photocopy or print shop allow you to design and produce brochures, fliers, and more quite easily and affordably. Print collateral that still provides that tactile connection with a brand and its message includes fliers, brochures, and sales kits where fliers designed in a cohesive order are organized in a printed folder. The following sections provide some tips for making each of these formats effective in today's highly digitized world.

Designing fliers for grounded results

Fliers serve a big purpose for just about every brand. Gone are the days when prospects pore over long brochures to determine interest in your product and brand.

People have been trained to think and read in sound bites and short statements that fit the word count limits of social media. Your print material needs to cater to that new way of processing information. This is the value of producing at-a-glance sheets, which are one-page fliers that present your brand's value when customers have time to only glance at your material.

At-a-glance fliers that work consist of the following elements:

» **Imagery:** A powerful visual that represents the end result of what you sell. Peace of mind about your financial investments? A happy, healthy pet? A software platform that increases efficiency, making staff happier as they perform better? This visual can be a photo around which you wrap text, or it can be a soft undertone creating the desired emotional connection and impression over which you put text with your key messages.

» **Bullet points:** Instead of trying to fit your brand's dissertation onto one page with 10-point font, identify the top three key values you offer, the top solutions to problems you provide, and your competitive distinctions and craft brief but powerful bullet points about each.

» **Brand anchor:** Following the bullet points that show what you offer and how your brand fulfils real and emotional needs, include a summary statement about your brand that anchors your overall value and advantages of functional alternatives and competitors. This may include information about your Net Promoter Score (NPS), industry awards, company growth, and other details that communicate your strength and back up your product promises.

» **Contact information:** Your bullet points and anchor serve as teasers to encourage readers to go online to your website and social pages to learn more and, ultimately, inquire about a product or service. Make sure all your contact points are clear and easy to find. List your LinkedIn, Facebook, and Twitter contact info, not just your e-mail and phone number.

Developing brochures and self-mailers with specific marketing goals

Brochures, especially those that can double as a self-mailer, are still worth the investment because they're still appropriate in some forums, such as trade shows, networking meetings, and customer events.

Many brochure designs foolishly waste money because they don't accomplish any specific marketing goals. Like any marketing efforts — print, digital, or live — you need to ask some key questions about how you'll use a brochure before your put the time, energy, and money into producing one. For example:

>> Who will read the brochure?

>> How will they get the brochure?

>> What should they do after reading the brochure?

Without a specific focus and purpose, your brochure is likely to miss the mark and risk being just another boring marketing piece that could represent any of your competitors and fail to engage prospects in your message and encourage them to reach out for more information. The most common and appropriate purposes for a brochure are to

>> Act as a reference on the product, or technical details of the product, for prospects

>> Support a personal selling effort by lending credibility and helping overcome objections

>> Help prospects identify how you differ from the competition

>> Determine how your product and brand fill a real or emotional need or solve a current problem

>> Generate leads through a direct-mail campaign

TIP

When planning your copy, review your ESP. The headline on your front cover needs to address your ESP, and the key copy points that you focus on need to show how you do just that. Revisit the copy points you chose in your at-a-glance flier (see the preceding section) and add more substance, evidence, examples, and such to each of those points.

You want your copy to be consistent and story the same across all touch points. The difference is how much space you have to back up your claims (use references and authoritative stories to add credence) and how much detail you can go into about your products and services.

Instead of using three bullet points to tell your story, turn those three bullet points into sections and use headlines that describe what's in those paragraphs.

If space allows, consider including some of the following elements:

>> Key competitive distinctions, differences, and advantages

>> Customer satisfaction scores, NPS, and testimonials

>> Customer testimonials or case histories

>> Quotes from staff members illustrating their passion for quality and commitment to serve customers

Drafting an effective layout for your print brochure

An effective print brochure follows this standard layout:

>> The appeal, with its enticing headline and compelling copy and visual, goes on the front of the brochure — or the outside when you fold it for mailing, or the central panel out of three if you fold a sheet twice.

>> The sections covering the main three points of focus go on the inside pages.

>> The fact base, needed for reference use, goes in the copy and illustrations beneath your subheads.

TIP

>> When folded, the back page should leave ample space for mailing insignia and postage information. Be sure to check out current guidelines for mailing requirements at www.usps.com before you print your mailer because regulations and requirements change.

You can produce your brochure in small or large format and be effective either way.

>> For larger brochures, plan your copy and design elements to cover the span of 11-x-17 paper, which when folded in half makes for a four-panel 8.5-x-11 brochure.

>> Smaller formats span an 8.5-x-11 paper size, which folds into three narrow panels about the width of a single newspaper column.

Designing a brochure is relatively easy to do. Just pick your favourite publishing software and get started. Whether you use a Mac or PC, you have many options for designing both small and large format brochures.

WARNING

If you don't know what each part of your brochure does, then you need to redesign it. Otherwise, that brochure becomes a waste of time and money.

Although you can lay out a brochure in many ways, you should choose the format that is most cost effective for you to produce and which format you're most likely to mail. If you don't include a section for mailing insignia on the back, then produce it for the least-expensive mailing costs, which would be a #10 envelope which fits an 8.5-x-11 piece of paper folded in thirds. Larger format brochures that unfold as full 8.5-x-11 pages are a good format as well and can be folded in half for a larger mailer, which does get better response than the smaller mailing pieces; however, the larger the foldout size, the heavier the brochure and the higher the price to mail.

Most copy stores accept e-mailed copies of files and can produce short runs of your brochures (as well as pamphlets, catalogue sheets, and other printed materials) right from your files. However, if you need thousands of copies, you should look into offset printing, which is a more cost-effective option at that quantity. *Offset printing* is how most books, magazines, and newspapers are printed. The printer makes a plate of each page, and the printing press automatically inks the plate, transfers or "offsets" the ink to a rubber blanket, and then transfers that to the page.

You can also do smaller runs (100 or less) right from your own colour printer. Buy matte or glossy brochure paper designed for your brand of printer (HPs work well for this) and simply select the appropriate paper type in the print dialogue box. Today's printers can produce absolutely stunning brochures, but you have to fold these brochures yourself, and the ink cartridges or toners aren't cheap, so print as needed rather than inventory a large number of brochures.

Placing Print Ads That Generate Leads

Print ads are still productive and cost effective, especially for niche or small businesses. The key to successful media purchases for ads of all sizes is twofold:

>> Purchase space in publications that directly reach your prospects with a high propensity to engage or purchase.

>> Have a goal in mind. If you're not Pepsi, Apple, Honda, or another brand with household recognition around the world, advertising to promote your brand's name isn't likely to pay off quickly, if at all. Advertising with a specific call to action is much more likely to generate leads. Successful print ads have a value-add offer, such as a seasonal sale, limited time free gift with purchase, and so on.

You don't have to be a big brand with a big budget to purchase advertising space. You just need to be smart about it. If you live in a big city, you're going to pay big prices to get in your daily newspaper. However, many other affordable options can help you get the awareness and attention you need. The following sections provide just a few ideas to pursue.

REMEMBER

Before you commit to any publication, though, keep the following in mind:

>> **What are the rack rates?** Advertising tends to be priced on a *cost per thousand of readers* reached basis. Rates are calculated by the cost of buying that ad, divided by the number of readers who read the publication, and then multiplied by 1,000, so you generally get as much exposure as you're willing to pay for. Buying ads in small-circulation publications allows you to reach specific niche audiences more effectively and increase your ROI while avoiding the risks associated with larger, more general publications.

>> **Who does it reach?** Does this publication reach decision makers or influencers? Ask sales reps to give you a breakout of the readership demographics so you can determine whether they represent your customer base or not.

>> **How many highly valued prospects does it reach, and what percentage of the total readership do they represent?** If a publication has 10,000 readers and you care about only one-tenth of the readers, you're paying to reach 10 percent and wasting money on the other 90 percent.

>> **What are the costs?** Just like with digital media, you need to determine your cost per reach. Sales reps for each publication other than your local, nonprofit newsletters should be able to give you an idea of the average response current advertisers get so you can determine the potential cost effectiveness.

>> **How much can you negotiate?** Just because a rate is printed in a media kit doesn't mean that is what you have to pay. If you're a first-time customer, ask for an introductory rate so you can test the publication. If you want to place your ad more than once, look at the 3x, 6x, and 12x rates. Also check for rates that include your ad in both the print and digital version of the newspapers.

>> **What are your values?** Beyond the monetary value of each publication you choose, you need to keep in mind the values and causes with which you're associating. As we mention in earlier chapters, aligning with like values and demonstrating support for worthy causes and ideals is critical for building your brand's value and sales. Just because a rate is low doesn't mean it's a good value because associating with the wrong values can do more long-term damage than you can add up.

REMEMBER

Also keep in mind that frequency in print matters. Placing an ad once will likely disappoint because consumers need to see something on average three times before it really sinks into their psyche, and even more than that in most cases to act on it. Choose a publication you can afford to keep purchasing to create continuity and brand awareness. If you can afford a rate only one time, move on to something you can keep up with because in most cases, one ad isn't going to do much for your bottom line.

TIP

In addition to finding a publication you can afford to advertise in regularly, use economical print media, such as brochures, blogs, mailings, and e-mails. (You figure out how to design a brochure earlier in this chapter.) If you operate on too small a scale or budget to afford print advertising, try turning your ad design into a good flier and mailing it. You can send it to 500 names and see what happens. That's a lot less risky and expensive than buying space in a magazine that goes to 200,000 names — some of whom may not care at all about what you're offering. Or you can search for smaller-circulation publications with a more local or specialized readership where the rates may be much cheaper.

Cheap but powerful publications

Following are some ideas for local organizations that produce publications that are not only affordable but also powerful channels for reaching the right customers for your brand and elevating your brand position at the same time. To be most effective, include a line of support for the cause at hand rather than just your sales message.

REMEMBER

Keep the scale of your print advertising (or any advertising for that matter) at such a level that you can afford to run an ad that may produce zero sales. Although zero sales certainly isn't your goal, it's always a possibility, and you want to base your buying decision on that possibility while you're experimenting to find an effective venue for your ads.

Nonprofit clubs and charities

No matter where you live — city, suburb, rural Canada, or resort town — many local organizations communicate regularly to members of your community, and they're often looking for brands such as yours to help underwrite the cost of publishing their newsletters. As a result, they offer inexpensive opportunities to advertise in print and digital newsletters. These are powerful outlets to reach people united in a worthy cause, and when you support their passion, they'll often support you over competitors that choose not to support them via advertisements. Some groups to look into include

>> Rotary, Elk, and Lions clubs.

>> Library districts.

>> Charities such as the Canadian Cancer Society, Muscular Dystrophy Canada, and the Canadian Red Cross. These often have publications they use for fundraising and member communications.

>> Sports clubs, such as youth soccer, ski racing, volleyball, and lacrosse.

>> Homeowners associations. Many homeowners associations produce magazines to keep residents informed and connected. These offer a specific reach and are ideal for local businesses, like carpet cleaners, veterinary practices, restaurants, and spas.

Local theatres

Community theatres are another great resource for inexpensive advertising. Placing your ad in a playbill shows your commitment to the arts.

Professional associations and networking groups

Small and large cities all have local chapters of larger professional organizations and often produce print newsletters or even magazines to communicate regularly to members. Often many options exist within one organization.

>> Chambers of commerce.

>> Business partnership organizations.

>> Local chapters for professional organizations. Every industry typically has a few options in a given community, so do your research to find them. Here are some examples:

  - Canadian Marketing Association

  - Canadian Business & Marketing Association

  - International Association of Business Communicators

  - Association of Canadian Advertisers

Local and small-town newspapers

You can find hundreds of newspapers and weeklies with circulations in the tens of thousands and rates one-fifth to one-tenth the price of big-city newspapers (and even less expensive when compared to major national magazines). Even though you don't reach as many people, you can reach high-quality prospects nonetheless. When browsing which newspapers to buy, ask about circulation trends. Some are losing print readers to their website, so be sure to know what you're really getting from your investment. The challenge is that readership is declining for local papers, and many of them are folding or going to online-only formats.

Ad size

What size ad should you buy? The answer depends in part on the design of your ad. Does the ad have a strong, simple visual or headline that catches the eye, even if it's only a third of a page in size? Or does the ad need to be displayed in a larger format to work well?

TIP

You should also consider goals associated with your ad. If you're promoting an end-of-season sale and want to move inventory fast, you may want a bigger ad to make sure you get a lot of attention to drive big amounts of traffic. If your goal is more to introduce your brand to a new audience and establish a presence or awareness, you can probably achieve this with a series of smaller ads with compelling copy that tells your brand story over time.

Table 4-1 provides some general statistics on what percentage of readers *notice* an ad based on its size, according to a study by Cahners Publishing Co.

TABLE 4-1

Selecting the Right Size Ad

Size of Ad	Percent of Readers Noticing Ad
Fractional (part-of-page) ad	24%
One-page ad	40%
Two-page spread	55%

No surprise here that the bigger the ad, the bigger the impact. But also consider the fact that the percentage of readers noticing your ad doesn't go up in proportion to the increase in size. Doubling the size of your ad gives you something like a quarter more viewers, not twice as many. That's partly why the cost of a full-page ad isn't twice the cost of a half-page ad. For example, a full-page, four-colour ad in *Health* magazine costs 59 percent more than a half-page, four-colour ad. The same ad run at full versus half size probably attracts, at most, about a third more reader notices, meaning your cost per reader exposed to the ad is higher for that full-page ad than for the half-page ad (although your impact on each of those readers may be greater with a larger ad, which is why the cost per reader can be set at a higher level for a larger ad).

Ad impact

After placing your ads, it's time to sit back and wait for the phone to ring. Or not. If only it were that easy. Measuring print isn't as easy as measuring direct response where you can link a sale to individuals in your database and to specific promotions. And asking new leads how they heard about you isn't reliable because many will tell you they heard your ad on the radio. Now what?

In truth, measuring the impact of your ad needs to start long before you place it. Here are some ideas for simple, affordable ways to determine whether your design, message, offer, and publication choices worked:

>> **Ask for feedback.** Although focus groups were a common way to generate feedback in the past, they're not as popular now due to the high cost to facilitate and the lack of reliable feedback due to group think and other issues. You can get some of the same insights for free by simply asking people you know for candid feedback. Ask friends in your industry and outside of it for their first reaction to your ad and how likely they are to act on the offer. Even if they're not in your customer segments, their feedback on readability, emotional value of the headline, and interest in and believability of the body copy is valuable.

>> **Test outlets, messages, offers, and designs.** You can code your ads by the size, day of week, and offers to determine which works best and produces the greatest ROI.

>> **Post on LinkedIn or Facebook.** Before spending a lot of money to go to print, post your ad in its creative form on your social media pages. Gauge likes, shares, and comments to determine how people reacted to the offer and message. No comments or likes? Post again and incentivize people to give you feedback by offering a small token, such as a coffee shop gift card.

>> **E-mail your ad.** This is a cheap and great way to test your offer but also, most important, your headline. Use the headline as your subject line to see how many opens you get for each headline tested. Use the top-performing subject line as your headline for best results in print. You can e-mail your ad to friends, associations, and people that follow you on social media. Doing this also ensures that they see your ad in case they missed it in their daily news feed and enables you to get the feedback you want from high-propensity prospects.

>> **Code each ad you place.** Every ad you place in print should have a specific code to help you identify specific leads generated. Set up your codes to help you determine which publication, ad, call to action, and offer worked best. Consider the following when coding your ads:

- Use a different phone number or e-mail address for each publication purchased.

- Direct readers to a separate landing page for each publication and/or each offer you promote. Give the landing page a URL that will help you identify which outlet and which ad generated the best traffic.

- Use discount codes for each outlet. If you advertised in a local weekly and a local entertainment guide, you may want to code your ads as such to determine which offer and which outlet worked best. For example, in a weekly newspaper ad with a 20 percent offer, ask customers to reference 20OFFWeek when ordering in person or online (maybe differentiate between print and online by adding "print" and "web"). Or in an entertainment guide, use an offer code like 20OFFFUN.

Always use different codes and response mechanisms for different outlets and digital versus print formats to help you identify the best use of your media budget in the future.

REMEMBER

Any experiments you can run as you do your marketing give you useful feedback about what's working and what isn't. Always think of ways to compare different options and see how those options perform when you advertise, giving you useful insight into ad effectiveness.

own site

» Creating a strong website for engaging customers and building relationships

» Using design elements that enhance the stickiness of your website

» Developing a web marketing strategy

» Driving sales with landing pages, PURLs, blogs, and more

» Making money off web traffic

Chapter **5**

Building a Website That Engages and Sells

Not all that long ago, websites were little more than digital brochures that simply served as informational pages about a business, its products, and how to contact it for more information. Now, websites have become dynamic communities where ideas are shared, advice is given, and live engagement takes place. More importantly, consumers have come to expect websites to be a place where they can get comprehensive information about a product and the brand and engage directly with brand representatives to learn more as they research their options and make carefully concerted choices.

In addition to having a website that sets forth your brand story in an engaging way that inspires others to stay tuned and want to be part of your story, you need to ensure that all your digital assets support the tone and persona of your site. This is critical because your website is like the mother ship, or the hub, of all your brand identity. Your digital assets, such as ads on Facebook, Twitter, and other sites you've chosen to appear on, point your customers back to the hub where they can engage with real people, learn about your brand story and products, and choose whether to engage on a journey with your brand or another one.

This chapter outlines some tactics and techniques for building a strong identity on your own site and supporting it with consistency across all your digital assets.

Creating and Managing a Web Identity

REMEMBER

Your *web identity* is the sum of your messaging and persona on your own site and other digital sites, such as blogs, social media sites, search engine listings, and product review sites. Managing and controlling this identity should be a top priority for your marketing team. You shouldn't take it lightly because the values, persona, credibility, and trustworthiness you project affects consumers' interest in doing business with you.

Part of managing this identity involves managing the company you keep. Just like people often judge you by the friends you associate with in the real world, they will also judge your brand by the sites on which your logo, messaging, and promotions appear. If you don't want to be seen as a brand that supports unhealthy living, don't advertise on a site that promotes eating unhealthy diets. Just the appearance on a site implies indirectly that your values are the same. Again, don't take this lightly unless you want to take on the daunting task of reputation management.

When building a website, you need to start with the realization that a website is no longer a nicely designed information centre but rather a portal for all your web activity and a tool that establishes your brand identity and image. For example: Your main home page creates the first impression many will have of your brand. Your site will also have many other entry points, or landing pages, for visitors coming through specific activities, such as social media pages, search engines, online contests you set up, specific offers, links directly to a form to register for an event or download a paper, and many more.

Each of these landing pages is critical and must maintain the same persona, projected values, and identity as your home page. They must also easily direct visitors back to your main site and overall menu.

The following sections take a closer look at what you can do to establish and manage your web identity.

Understanding what consumers expect

Just like perception is everything, "expectations" are everything when it comes to marketing. When shopping, most people have expectations about a product price, quality, features, benefits, and so on while looking at options for purchase. Consumers expect to find certain elements that meet those expectations when browsing on a brand's website during the purchasing process. Expectations are not just limited to product features and prices but also for information about the brand, its leadership, and values. The latter is especially true for B2B purchases. Some examples of the information consumers seek to fulfil or deny their expectations include

>> **Product detail:** Product detail is anything from features and functions to specifications and pricing. This information is important because shoppers are likely comparing the details of your product to others they are considering so sometimes the more detail you provide, the greater the chance of closing the deal.

>> **Leadership:** Many purchasers, especially in B2B, want to know about the leadership of a business. If they're buying an IT application that they'll need to live with for a few years, they want to know how stable and experienced your leaders are to determine your staying power. They may even want to know who some of your backers and investors are for added assurance that you have the ability to fund your growth and their account.

>> **Testimonials:** Consumers want to know what others are saying about their experience with your products and your overall persona. Even though most people don't put bad reviews on their website and those present are always positive, it still helps to see what others say so you can form your own expectations.

>> **Corporate social responsibility (CSR):** Consumers care what brands are doing to give back to communities and move the world toward a better place. They want to support movements such as those offered by TOMS and Patagonia, not just shareholder goals. Many turn to websites to see what a brand is doing, and what they find about CSR values, initiatives, and results often determines the brands they choose.

>> **Engagement:** Gone are the days when customers were willing to sit on hold to ask a question about a product or a return policy. Consumers now go to websites and expect to be invited to chat with a knowledgeable customer service representative in real time and really quickly. Online engagement and chat are becoming more and more critical for websites, especially e-commerce sites.

>> **Policies, FAQs, and terms:** Consumers want easy access to your return policy, shipping methods, shipping costs, customer service processes, sizing guides, and so on. Being able to find these easily simplifies their research process. If they can't find this information on your site, they'll go to another site and likely find it there.

>> **Communities:** People want to engage with others with like values and compare ideas, products, insights, and more. Look at all the chat communities for car owners, computer experts, programmers, and home chefs. Making your site engaging beyond live information about your products is another key strategy for keeping people on your site and getting them to come back — two fundamental goals of web marketing for any business.

>> **Efficiency:** For e-commerce sites, people expect to be able to find what they want quickly and check out as simply as possible. Again, the longer it takes to check out, the more likely they are to leave.

REMEMBER

Having all the information consumers seek on your website in an easy-to-find format is critical to making your web investment pay off and to capturing sales. The quicker people find what they want, the longer they'll stay on your site and the greater chance you have of closing the sale. "Stickiness," or how long a person "sticks" on your site before bouncing off to another, is a key metric for the success of your website and something you can easily measure with web analytics.

Standardizing your web identity

When building your web identity, you need to be clear and consistent, and all you do needs to reinforce the emotional selling proposition (ESP) and value proposition that define your brand and core values. A top goal should be to have your brand recognized and reinforced *everywhere* that you're present, on and off the web.

TIP

As simple as it seems, the URLs you use are important. Besides your company name, which is a given, find URLs that define what you do and purchase them for your website as well. For example, if your business is a pet boarding facility called Five Star Lodging for Pets, not only get the URL for that name but also consider purchasing a URL that will come up on the search engines, such as `www.petlodging.com`, `www.luxuryhotelfordogs.com`, and `www.safeboardingforpets.com` — kind of like hashtags come up for tweets or pages with common terms.

TIP

Your URLs should be consistent with your other social site names and tags, such as your blog, Facebook page, Twitter page, Instagram account, and LinkedIn account (see Chapter 3 in Book 6 fore more about these platforms). Using your brand name as often as possible helps reinforce your presence, but in some cases it doesn't work for a handle or is too close to another account's name. In this case, you can add a simple defining word, such as *best, leading, info,* or *blog,* to help connect the account or page to your brand. Per the earlier example, a good name for a blog or Facebook page may be FiveStarLodgingBlogforPets.com.

Take the time to register all possible URLs that relate to your brand before someone else does and then tries to sell them to you for thousands. If you're a consultant, register your personal name and your brand name. If part of your name reflects your region, such as Intermountain, register the short versions and the long version.

REMEMBER

For example, Intermountain Healthcare, which owns hospitals and clinics in a tri-state area in the United States, owns the domains of www.intermountain healthcare.org and www.ihc.org. It also owns the .com, .org, and even .biz versions of that name. Purchasing all potential URLs drives more people to your site as they search for you and helps them find you faster and easier, while also protecting your identity. If you own the .com version and someone else owns the .biz version of your URL, you can easily get caught up in a case of mistaken identity, and you just don't know what kind of business you may get mistaken for. Paying that minimal price for a domain name is worth all the hassles of repairing issues associated with confused identities or losing customers to another site or to the frustration of not being able to find your brand quickly.

REMEMBER

Also, make sure your domain name doesn't violate someone's trademark. Check web addresses against a database of trademarks (in Canada, you can do this search for free by going to www.ic.gc.ca/app/opic-cipo/trdmrks/srch/home), or ask a lawyer to do a more detailed analysis if you think you may run into an issue. The trademarked domain name you want may be available, meaning you can register it at a site like www.register.com because nobody else has yet, but if you begin using it, the owner of the trademark may sue you. See Chapter 4 in Book 2 for details on trademarks.

After you register your website, take steps to protect your new domain name. Purchase options such as multi-year registration and protection against lapsing due to late payment. Again, people are out there just waiting for a site to expire so they can quickly purchase it and sell it back to you for thousands. Consider purchasing private domain registration, in which your host doesn't give out your personal details as the owner of the site.

TIP

If an obvious misspelling for your site exists, register that, too. The alternate names can be set up as simple redirects, and they'll keep a competitor from owning a domain that may receive some of the traffic you generate.

Creating an Engaging Website

This is where it gets fun . . . and complicated. Fun because you have a blank story board in front of you and many tools at your fingertips for painting and telling your brand story in ways that make your customers want to be a part of it. Complicated because at the time of this writing, well over 1 billion websites are on the Internet. This means that there's a lot of competition to get people to go to your website and stay on it!

For perspective, if consumers search for "furniture stores in Ontario," today they'd get about 145 million results to browse. If you're one of those sites and you're lucky enough to get them to open your page, you have the added challenge of keeping them there. This is where the design and messaging of your home page needs to be more than just a pretty picture.

The first impression you create for visitors coming to your site is influenced by the colour, fonts, and layout of your page. If you want people to feel excited and energized by your brands and products, you need energetic colours that stimulate happy, fun moods to dominate your colour palette. You also need to have fonts that reflect their persona or sense of self. You can choose fun fonts like Chalkboard that create a playful, whimsical feeling, or traditional fonts like Times New Roman that reflect a tone of academics, knowledge, or news. Both have an impact on the browser's immediate snap judgment about the relevance of a given site. (See Chapter 4 in Book 6 for more about fonts.)

After you've assured the unconscious mind that your site reflects their persona with your initial colours and style, you need to immediately engage your visitors and enable them to find what they're looking for quickly so they stay on your site. You can do this effectively in many ways. But before you get into design elements, you need to have a few goals in mind when designing your site, which are explored in the following sections.

Watching your KPIs

Clearly, your first goal to creating a web page is to drive traffic. But there's more to measure than traffic. You need to know what people are doing once they get to your site and how long they stay there. Without this information, you really don't know how your investment is paying off, and you can't monitor the activity and interests of your customers when it comes specifically to their experience with your messaging, branding, and sales experience on your own page.

The following sections present a few key performance indicator (KPI) goals from the experts on web analytics and marketing.

Bounce rate

The bounce rate is the percentage of visitors who are directed to a page on your site and don't go past the first page they land on. Your goal is to get them to dig deeper to engage them with your message and move them toward a sale. Or two.

On average, according to various reports from many different analysts, bounce rates range from 20 to 90 percent of visitors, meaning that this percentage of people leave after viewing just one page. And with this huge range, it covers just about everyone.

The lowest rates tend to be for e-commerce and retail sites and the highest for websites that share news and information. A good bounce rate goal is pretty much any number under 50 percent.

TIP

Google Analytics shows the following bounce rates for a few specific types of sites. Use these benchmarks as a starting point for your own website and check your own Google Analytics reports to see whether you're above or below average. Google Analytics provides information on all the following for your website to help you monitor daily how well your site is working for you. It's easy to sign up at www.google.com/analytics.

Type of Website	Average Bounce Rate
Content websites	40–60%
Lead generation	30–50%
Blogs	70–98%
Retail	20–40%
Service sites	10–30%
Landing pages	70–90%

TIP

Here are some ways to keep your bounce rates low:

>> Give visitors a reason to stay, such as a promotional offer they don't want to miss.

>> Present something inspirational and relevant, such as a video on a topic that can help them solve a problem or feel better about the world.

>> Don't offer links to go elsewhere. Don't tell them to check out a partner's page, an industry report, or link to a coupon somewhere else because they're not likely to come back to your site.

>> Implement better design, content flow, and access to desirable information.

Average session duration

It goes without saying that the longer people stay on your website, the stronger your chance is of converting them to customers. Average session durations vary across the board, but what matters most is monitoring your own session duration. This is defined by the duration of each visitor, which you can track with Google Analytics, which divides the average length of each user's session by the number of sessions. It's not the same as *time on page*, which gives you the amount of time each user spent and an average for all users on each page of your site.

Your goal is to, again, give people a reason to come back to your site and stay longer. If your average session duration and time on page numbers decrease, it's time to think about changing your site so users get a new experience when they come back and doing some things differently to make it more engaging.

Following are some ways to do this:

>> Include a brief and emotionally relevant video on your home page to create a mood for your visitors and introduce them to the value you offer.

>> Try a slide show to showcase who you are or products you represent. Despite the advent of home page videos, slide shows are still widely used and can be just as effective if the images and messages are powerful and relevant.

>> Plant a live webcam in your office so visitors can see your place of work live and "feel" like they just walked into your real-world office. People can get a view of your lobby or main work station. If you have something more interesting, like employees installing a new kitchen or landscaping a public playground, you're likely to really achieve more time on page and a great average session duration.

Pages per session

If you have a good site that's meaningful to your audience and provides them with the information or products they seek, they'll view more pages on your site. It's that simple. To see how you're doing, you can review your page view counts and unique page views. Page view counts tally in more than one view of the same page by an individual, and unique views count only one view per individual so you don't get skewed data if one person continues to go back to the same page during a given session, giving you the impression that that information or product is more popular than it actually is.

Again, averages bounce all over the place, but if you can achieve two pages per session and around two minutes per session, you're doing well.

Making content king on your website

So if you're not an e-commerce site with lots of product pages for people to view as they shop, how do you get people to view more pages when they come to visit so you can engage them longer and increase your chance of converting them to a sale or other desired transaction? You've heard it before: *Improve your content.*

To achieve your web "stickiness" goals of more time onsite and more time per session, you need to keep your content focused on what matters most to consumers at the time they choose to go to your web page. Here's a little exercise to help you:

1. **List the top reasons people come to your website directly, not organically.**

   For example:

   - To get information about your product

   - To check out your prices

   - To read about your return policies

   - To look for sales

   - To assess your leadership

   - To find your product or systems, results, and capabilities to see whether they meet needs

   - To compare your products or systems, results, capabilities, features, and so on to competitors'

2. **List the top content themes or topics they most often seek.**

   Some of these might include the following:

   - **Product comparisons:** Be brave. Show how your product's features and prices compare to others. This level of transparency builds trust and most often takes price out of the equation.

   - **Purchasing guides:** These are popular with both B2B and B2C customers because no one wants to experience decision regret. Purchasing guides can include how not to overbuy technology, insurance, or too much house for your income.

   - **How-to guides:** Even if you offer a service, customers tend to bond better with brands that show them how to do it themselves. They often realize that they're not an expert or don't have the time, so they call you to come do it for them.

- **White papers on marketing, selling, and technology topics:** These don't have to be long, just meaningful and actionable.

- **Research findings:** Everyone loves research and learning what other people are thinking. Nielson makes many reports available to its website, as does HubSpot, which also creates infographics you can use in your own presentations. This is a great strategy because all who use its infographics help it strengthen its position as a leading marketing analytics CRM authority.

If you don't know the answers to complete this exercise, you just found a new question or two to ask in your customer surveys (check out Chapter 1 in Book 6) and on your web surveys (continue on to the next section for more).

Driving traffic with content

To use content to increase your website's time on page and engagement value and level, you need to think like a publisher, not an advertiser. No one reads the same news over and over again, and the same rule applies to reading website content.

Keep content newsworthy to attract and engage visitors and keep it in line with your sales goals to make sure you're not providing a free news site but one that will pay off for you as well. Craft stories, reports, insights, and guides that are meaningful and subtly drive people back to you to help them achieve related goals.

TIP

Today's most exciting web content is often published in social media first and then linked into the main website from Twitter, YouTube, and so forth.

REMEMBER

The useful or interesting content you add to your site to boost visits isn't the same as that call to action that drives sales. Keep the call to action and the compelling sales copy top level and nest supportive content below it in the navigation hierarchy so as not to set up obstacles to quick sales or opt-ins.

What if you do everything you can to build traffic but your website continues to be ignored? Then you may want to hire a search engine optimization (SEO) consultant or agency. Most of these firms (such as Wpromote; see www.wpromote.com/ for details) work for a fairly reasonable fee.

Web surveys

A great way to engage customers when they land on your website is to ask them to take a one-question survey to help you better understand what matters most to them. A lot of people like to take the survey so they can see how their peers voted or answered as well. Ask questions that spark curiosity and help visitors validate their own challenges and needs. If you're a B2B site selling marketing services, you may want to ask something like the following:

>> What is your number-one marketing challenge?

>> Does your CEO trust you and your marketing team?

>> What do you believe is your most powerful marketing tool for the coming year?

Many marketers are curious to see how their peers answer those questions. If you do this to increase your engagement and stickiness, here are a few suggestions:

>> Make respondents give you their e-mail address to see other's responses and vote/answer the question.

>> Upon answering, automatically offer to direct visitors to your archived questions so they can see answers to other questions, again increasing engagement and time on site.

>> As applicable, have the answers to your questions direct visitors to more content on the topic on your site. If you asked the question about marketing tools, direct viewers to a free download for a white paper on the marketing tools/services you provide.

Critical components of content

In addition to populating your website with pages about your products, promotions, customer testimonials, leaders, and competitive advantages, some basic content has become important for consumers as they research and choose brands from whom they want to purchase. These include

>> **Compatible or complementary products:** This is especially important if you're a technology company. Purchasers may want to know what companies you've aligned with so they can assess compatibility and application program interface (API) with other programs they may have purchased.

>> **Your news:** Create a page to house all your business news. Include press releases and articles for which your leaders were interviewed or in which your people or brand were mentioned.

>> **Your blog:** People want to experience your thought leadership, and that is really what a blog is. Make it easy for people to read what your experts are saying by making your blog easy to find. Update it often to keep your messages current and your voice strong in your industry.

>> **Your videos:** If you have product demo or customer testimonial video, or videos of your leaders communicating about your brand, host them in one library on your site as well as throughout your site. Make them easy to find and share with others.

>> **Resources:** Do you have white papers you've used to get people to come to your website in the first place, research studies, customer survey results, Net Promoter Score (NPS) reports, and other information that would be of value to consumers' decision process? Even though you may have links to these materials throughout your site, house them in a library or separate page for easy access. Before enabling downloads, always ask for e-mail addresses so you can build your permission-based e-mail lists.

>> **Your jobs:** Be sure to build a page about your jobs that reflects your persona and enables you to attract people who are a good fit for your culture. Make this a mini-page that communicates about your values, experience, passion, and team. This is a critical component of your site because it influences your company's growth and competencies. Treat it accordingly.

REMEMBER

Your content is either static or dynamic.

>> Static content is content that you don't change much, like your leadership profiles, contract information, mission statement/values, and so on.

>> Dynamic content refers to the content you change often to change the experience prospects and customers have when visiting your site. This can include your promotions, web contests, new white papers offered, limited time information, news stories, product features and highlights, customer and partnership highlights, and so on. These can change weekly or bi-monthly or whatever works best for the frequency at which customers come back to your site or what your resources dictate you can do.

Integrating Key Design Elements

Unless you live under a rock, you've likely noticed that the design trends for websites change as often as, if not more than, politicians change their positions — which is a lot.

A few years ago, the trend was to make your page look like a digital version of *USA Today* — headlines with teaser statements everywhere in hopes of driving you deeper. Then, they went to a more boxy design with a large masthead for promotions, sales buttons, and other teasers or value statements, followed by a navigation bar, and then maybe a video and more boxes with links to product pages and so on.

And now the trend is to have a very simplistic visual presentation. Often, a single image, a slide show, or a video starts upon opening and takes up most of your screen, leaving you to have to search or keep rolling your mouse for navigation or click to enter buttons to appear. Maybe next year, they'll be back to the boxy approach. Regardless, some key design strategies will never change with the trends because they follow how the human unconscious mind processes information. And remember, human nature never changes. For web browsing, that process is referred to as the *golden triangle*. The following sections discuss this as well as how to develop your web persona and go from concept to actual website.

Using the golden triangle

Google researched how people view search results and found that most people start on the left side of the masthead or top of the page, browse right, and then read the top three items and choose one. That kind of validates search engine optimization (SEO) and search engine marketing (SEM) expenditures. Other studies from other groups like MarketingSherpa show that people do the same on web pages. They start at the left, shoot over to the upper-right corner, and then browse down the left side of the page. So what, you say? It's actually a big what.

You need your core messages, calls to action, and most valuable leads to get people to dig deeper on your page in this triangle. If your call to action buttons, free offers, and such are in that big vast space outside of the triangle, you likely won't fulfil visitors' needs to find something relevant immediately before they switch to another site. That's where you can lose a lot of gold in terms of engagement that leads to sales.

REMEMBER

Skip the design trend changes for how a website should look and design it around how consumers look at sites.

Per the golden triangle, that top inch of your page, or masthead, is really critical because that is where the eyes stop and browse first. This is where you get to hammer home a consistent, memorable, clear brand identity on the web, tease a current promotion, broadcast new news, and so on. You'll note that news sites often use the top inch (after highly paid advertisements these days) for breaking news and that their content then follows the flow of the golden triangle.

Web designers and users generally accept that the top inch or two of every web page is branding space for whoever controls that page. You want to use that top inch or two to present your brand name plus a short tag line, logo, and special promotional links and messages. Be careful, though, because this space can easily get cluttered with multiple logos, messages, and promotions.

TIP

To ensure that you're taking full advantage of this top inch or so, select type, colours, and a visual logo that tie into your overall branding. Change out your icons, news, or teasers/promotions so that they're fresh and capture attention of repeat visitors. You can do a quick audit of your web brand identity right now by looking at the top inch of every page you control. Is it as consistent and as strong as it can be?

Developing your web persona

Designing your website is as personal as how you dress every day. It's a reflection of who you are, your persona, your energy, your values, and your way of positioning yourself to be part of a hive of like people and attract them to your space, personally or professionally. So instead of letting someone tell you what your site should look like, start profiling the persona or type of people you want to attract. Following is an exercise to get you started.

>> What's your brand's personality? Spunky, traditional, reserved, outgoing, daring, rebellious, or trendsetter?

>> Describe or list characters, celebrities, or people you know who embody that personality.

>> What do these people wear every day? To a formal event? Would they show up at a black-tie event in a tux with red high-top sneakers? Would they get married in a black dress?

>> What are the aspirations, goals, and status levels your characters or persona seek?

>> What books do they read? What television shows do they watch? Or what Instagram and Twitter pages do they follow?

>> How can you include actual customers in your web strategy to help appeal to new customers?

>> Can you create a movement around your persona? What values and causes move them? Can you engage them with design and with a joint cause?

Now take a step back and start thinking of creative elements that reflect this persona. How can you use some of these to appeal to your customers? How can you do this quickly with graphics, words, headlines, and invitations to join a common cause so that your customers immediately know, consciously and unconsciously, that they've found a website that's like them, part of their tribe, their hive, and a place where they belong?

Repeat this exercise to help you direct your logo design and print presence as well.

TIP

Wildfang is a good example of this very strategy. Its mantra is to be a wild feminist, and its clothing reflects the feminist style. It includes customers and causes and pretty much invites you to be part of its tribe the minute you visit. Check it out at www.wildfang.com.

Going from design concepts to an actual website

After you have some ideas, sketch out a story board for the images and elements you want to project in your home page and how you can adapt those into themes that transcend all pages. Then start designing, either by yourself or with a designer who can do it quickly for you. If you prefer the DIY route, tons of options provide templates you can use outright or modify to fit your style and needs. Check out tools available from GoDaddy, WordPress, eHost, Wix.com, Squarespace, and many more.

TIP

Before signing up for a "freemium" account, which always seems to get you paying for something somehow, ask around to see what platforms and tools others like and have had an easy time using, deploying, and updating. You can waste numerous hours on programs that don't work as easily or seamlessly as promised.

When you find a good template to use, you need to start adding your own photos and content. If you use your own photos, make sure the resolution is good as well as the artistry so you look professional, not haphazard. You can buy images fairly inexpensively from many sources, especially if you need them only for your website because you can purchase low resolutions at lower costs. Check out stock photography sources such as Getty Images (www.gettyimages.ca/?language=en-GB), iStock (www.istockphoto.com/ca), or Shutterstock (www.shutterstock.com). Also look for useful images on Flickr (https://flickr.com/), where photographers set up pages to share their work. If you like an image, contact the photographer directly. You may be able to use it for a modest price or even for free. The body of work there is growing rapidly.

TIP

Here are some ideas for improving your overall web experiences:

>> **Use streaming video and animation to engage.** You can use these for showing a speaker in action, demonstrating a new product or providing services, and supporting the consumer online.

>> **Keep the navigation clear and simple.** Make sure your site is easy to navigate and that your menu is easy to find and follow. Drop-down menus make it clear and easy to find what you're looking for.

>> **Take time choosing an Internet service provider (ISP).** As you're using your website to help build your business, look for a system that meets your current needs and can grow as you grow. It's not always so simple to switch down the road. If you used a template from an ISP to build a site, you'll lose that template and need to build your site again if you change to another one. Be sure to pay attention to what features are standard and which are extra, and whether shopping carts are included. Many basic website templates do *not* include a shopping cart, so make sure you choose one that offers this if you need one or think you may down the road.

REMEMBER

>> **Use responsive website design.** Because consumers browse websites on many different devices — smartphones, tablets, and desktop and laptop screens — you need to make sure your website automatically adjusts to each. Today, most website builders have responsive website design (RWD) capabilities, which serves all devices with the same code that adjusts for screen size so you don't really need to worry about this. It's a good idea to check your site on all your devices once in a while to make sure no glitches occur.

>> **Change up your content.** Because websites are relationship-building and informational tools, you need to change the experience and the content to keep them interesting. For e-commerce sites, you wouldn't have the very same promotion or product highlight on your home page every single day, either. If customers come to the very same site all the time, they'll lose interest as they've "been there, done that."

>> **Offer a clear and simple method for getting through your site and completing your call to action.** The fewer clicks it takes your customers to find what they're looking for, the better chance you have of selling. Instead of just listing "ladies sweaters," make your site searchable by size, colour, and occasion. This helps people find what they want faster and without having to sift through dozens of photos, which can lead to boredom, frustration, and a bounce off your page.

>> **Ask visitors to opt in right away.** One of your top goals should be to encourage visitors to complete a form with their contact information so you can add them to your database and nurture relationships based on their interest that drove them to your site in the first place. It can be an offer to qualify for a consumer discount, an upgrade, an informative B2B newsletter, registration for your frequent buyer programme, and so on.

>> **Get personal.** Every time you go to Amazon, the home page is filled with suggested products that reflect your past purchases and browsing sessions. Thankfully, technology for all things on the Internet is developing so quickly that the ability to do this is getting more affordable to the point that small businesses can do it, too. Personalization platforms enable you to track the source of all visitors, monitor their behaviour and intent, and create personalized web experiences for them based on past behaviour. You can also personalize your web page for segments and fill these pages with product recommendations based on what a specific group of customers tend to browse and buy.

>> **Test.** Many web content management systems have A/B testing capabilities so you can continuously test what messages, offers, layouts, templates, and so on get people to go deeper into your site or complete your call to action. Never stop learning if you want to get ahead and stay ahead.

TIP

There are many personalization platforms and web content management systems to consider for delivering highly relevant content, conducting personalization, creating landing pages, integrating blogs, monitoring visitor behaviour and intent, and more. Search for personalized webmail platforms and web content management systems, and compare prices so you can find a system you can afford. Personalization platforms are typically subscription-based or SaaS-based models and can vary from $59 to $250 or more a month, depending on the number of websites you manage and other variables.

Driving Traffic via SEM and SEO

SEM is *search engine marketing* and encompasses all things that you do to make your page more visible on organic search lists. SEO is *search engine optimization*, a subset of SEM, and is what you do to maximize the number of visitors to your site by making sure it's one of the top listed sites on all searches. HubSpot defines the different tactics as follows:

>> SEM involves tactics like paid search or pay-per-click advertising.

>> SEO includes tactics on and off your web page.

- On-page tactics include keyword placement throughout your site, blog posts, social sharing options within your content to get more shares, and so on.

- Things you do off your page may include forging links with other websites that support and complement your own site — for example, linking your site with a partner's site so you get more hits from search engines. Social bookmarking, such as sites like Reddit and StumbleUpon, are great ways to get higher search rankings as your page comes up in many different places.

Here are some guidelines or suggestions to consider for SEO and SEM. If you question the value of doing SEM, just remember, there are more than 1 billion websites out there, some say even closer to 1 trillion. So good luck getting found randomly.

>> **Make sure you have a strong presence on the web and then manage that presence.** Your web presence encompasses your sites or accounts that bear your name and drive people to your URL. Channels that help build your presence include YouTube, Facebook, LinkedIn, Flickr, your blog, and other accounts that help your name come up more often and higher in the search rankings. (See Chapter 3 in Book 6 for more about these social media channels.)

>> **Provide a site map.** The fewer links a search engine has to navigate to find content relevant to a specific search, the higher it'll rate your site. A well-designed site map cuts the search engine's journey down to just two links. A large website needs a separate page for its site map, whereas simpler pages can place the map on a navigation bar that's visible from every page. On your map page or navigation bar, list all pages by title or topic and provide a direct link to each one.

>> **Communicate directly with your customers to build traffic.** Search engines look at traffic when ranking pages, so anything you do through direct communication with your customers to build traffic can help. Offer free informational or entertaining content people will want to visit and download. Consider making your website a resource for customers and noncustomers alike so as to maximize the amount of interaction with visitors. Free webinars and white papers can help boost your presence.

>> **Build links to related sites to improve your ranking.** Put a tab or button on your home page that's labeled Links, or if you want to pump up its appeal, label it The Best Links, Recommended Links, Our Pick of Links, or something like that. To find sites to link to, do your own searches and see what sites appear in the top ten listings. Then visit each of them and see whether you can find appropriate places and ways to link to them from your site (and vice versa, if possible). A company that distributes products for you or a professional association in your industry is a natural to link to your site. Build such links and the higher-ranked sites tend to draw yours up toward them. But make sure you have useful content to justify those links! Very brief reviews of the linked-to sites may increase the value of your links page and thus build usage and traffic.

>> **Build a family of sites and social networking site pages around your hub website.** Doing so may capture traffic out on the rim of your web presence and direct it toward your hub. Include single-purpose, single-topic satellite pages and optimize the META tags for these pages so they rank higher than your main site in searches specific to their topics.

>> **Advertise steadily enough to amplify search engine traffic.** Traffic increases rank on most search engines, so a promotion that drives traffic to your website gets amplified by follow-on traffic that comes from search engine visibility, which in turn creates more visibility.

TIP

If you're a sole proprietor, such as a business consultant, accountant, computer expert, or other professional, you don't really need to invest in web technology for sites designed to attract masses of consumers. Although you still want to build traffic, your greater need is to focus on a smaller audience of people who likely need your services due to their proximity of location or direct needs for your service. In many cases, these people know you from another setting. In this case, keep giving them reasons to go to your site. E-mail them links to information, reports, coupons, news about your business, your speaking schedule if you do public speaking, and so on. To drive more people to your site so you can build your prospect base, use keywords effectively and bid on Google search terms that are highly specific to your area of business or niche.

TIP

If you're a niche marketer on the web, you may find it more effective to emphasize your own expertise as the spokesperson for your brand. Blog in your own name and post a short video seminar or how-to demonstration on YouTube. In addition, look for ways to build visibility in professional online venues, perhaps by offering content to newsletters and signing up to be listed with professional associations and then linking those sites to your hub website. The more you build your voice in the industry as a thought leader or expert in a specific skill area, the more you can build your site's traffic and the more attractive you become to others whom you may want to link your site to for mutual credibility and traffic building.

Creating Landing Pages, Blogs, and More

As mentioned earlier, websites have many entry points besides the home page. Creating secondary entry points, also known as *landing pages,* is a common and wise tactic to get people to your site at the highest point of relevance and to enable you to track the effectiveness of an email, mobile, social, or print campaign. Google Analytics easily identifies the entry page for your visitors, so this is a solid and inexpensive way to test your campaigns. Landing pages are secondary pages to your main site and include direct links to and the same navigation as your other pages, just as all secondary pages do.

Some reasons you may want to do a landing page include

>> Testing a new campaign to see how many people respond to a new message or offer

>> Driving people to a page to register for a free gift, a white paper, or a discount code to use when purchasing products on your main page

>> Getting people to take a survey as an objective way of initiating communications with you

>> Launching a new product or service and wanting this to be the focal point of your communications for a given time period

>> Creating a specialized website that will attract a different demographic or customer group

>> Supporting a specific campaign and maintaining the momentum of that specific message or offer while it's in play

Following are some guidelines for how to use landing pages effectively as part of your overall marketing programme and web strategy and how to build your position of authority with a blog.

Using landing pages effectively

If you advertise on the web, you should consider a separate landing page for each ad campaign — and not just ad, but a full campaign. If you have a series of three to five ads in a campaign promoting the same product or service, call to action, or messaging, all those ads should include a link to one landing page that supports the corresponding strategy and goals. This will help keep the momentum of your campaign message and call to action and help you measure results better.

Following are some traditional ways to use landing pages:

>> A *transactional* landing page (also called a *lead capture page*) finishes the job the ad started by persuading visitors to complete some kind of transaction, such as making a purchase or signing up for a membership or special offer. Special trial offers are often effective on transactional landing pages. Write a transactional landing page like you would any good ad or catalogue copy by keeping the copy short and to the point to keep people on site. Because many people landing on this page won't complete the call to action you offer, include another way to engage so you can at least capture their information for your database and future communications, such as a free report or a coupon for their first purchase, which they can use then or later.

>> A *reference* landing page is designed to fill the visitor's informational needs by providing useful content, such as links, reviews, and professional listings. Marketers for associations and nonprofits tend to use reference landing pages more than for-profit marketers do, but this type of page can be helpful in a wide range of ad campaigns. If you build a reference landing page that has rich enough content to attract a steady flow of thousands of visitors a month, you can sell advertising on it and turn it into a revenue stream.

>> *PURLs* are personalized URLs that include the name of the recipient in the URL name — for example, www.johndoe.ABCInsurancerate.com, or www.bestinsurancerates/johndoe.com. This tactic plays a role in creating a personalized experience for customers and prospects and can help to increase the impact of a personalized website. You can use PURLs as links in digital campaigns utilizing e-mail or mobile and print. In fact, PURLs initially were highly used in print direct mail and, when tested against non-PURL landing pages, have shown a substantial impact on results. Most realistically, PURLs aren't likely to increase your response rate because they're not as unique or unusual as when they first were introduced. However, they do create a direct sense of recognition and personalization, both of which can help you get a new relationship with a customer off to a good start.

If you have a complex business and product offering, you may want to create landing pages for each specific category you offer. IBM is a good example. It has landing pages that are actually complex websites on its different product categories and within its categories. It offers cognitive products, such as Watson, which is a supercomputer that combines artificial intelligence and deep analytics that can then guide digital conversations with consumers.

TIP

Regardless of the type of landing page you employ, be sure to track visitor traffic and conversion rate. Getting a lot of people to your website who don't do anything but browse isn't going to build your business and generate sustainable sales and profitability. Track your *conversion rate*, which is simply the percentage of visitors who fulfil your call to action or other desired goal, like signing up for your e-mail list, accepting your special offer, registering for your newsletter or discount code, or making a purchase. Ultimately, you want to optimize this ratio. Experiment with ads that attract people who are easy to convert; also experiment with the copy, layout, and offer on your landing page. The more you experiment, the more you discover about how to convert visitors at a good rate.

Using blogs to build brands, not bog them down

Blogs serve many purposes for businesses of all types. Some use them as landing pages to get you to the main website in hopes of getting you to go deeper and engage in a sales transaction. Others use them to build their voice and credibility in their space. And others use them as sources of income by getting a lot of followers whom advertisers want to reach.

Blogs can build your position of authority in your space, attract partners and customers, and have a lot of other positive results. But if you don't commit resources to blogging frequently and effectively, it can really bog you down. It's like newsletters used to be. A lot of people could get the first one out but couldn't seem to execute a second. Don't let that be the case with your blogs.

Regardless of your purpose, blogs are an important element in your web strategy and overall marketing programme. According to research reported by HubSpot, businesses that use blogs as part of their web strategy receive 67 percent more leads than those that don't.

Simply put, a *blog* is really just a column that you host that gives you a voice in your industry and social and personal circles. In business, blogs can help you secure a position of authority as the leader or visionary in your field. They can also instill a sense of trust as people tend to believe others who are top experts in a field in which they seek products, services, information, or help.

TIP

The trick to making blogs successful is to write simple, relevant, and actionable articles and post them frequently enough that you stay top of mind as a leading resource for your business category.

Your blogs can be hubs for written articles, visual storytelling, or photo essays and stories. Blogs that use images and even videos tend to do better than those that don't. In fact, video blogging — that is, using videos instead of written content — is popular to the point that a new term has been coined, *vlogging.* Creating a YouTube channel for your vlogs is a great way to increase views, which in turn enables you to better monetize it.

TIP

Most website building platforms include a blog as part of their website template and hosting plan. You can also use other services to host your blog. Just make sure you can measure the traffic, time on page, and other elements and how the blog leads to your main website.

REMEMBER

Your website is often the first impression people have with your brand and needs to be everything they expect to get them to engage. Do some research to find out what consumers in your space want when browsing brand and product websites, and follow through. Make your website about their needs first, and engage them through personal relevance to guide them deeper into your site toward conversion to a sale or other desired behaviour.

If you were going to a job interview for your dream job, you wouldn't skimp on the details. You'd be prepared to talk about the business, how you can contribute, and your qualifications for contributing, and you'd make sure your appearance was spot on for the details and professional for the purpose. Do the same with your website. In a sense, it's a one-way interview with your prospects and customers. When you add online engagement or chat to your website, it becomes a dialogue. Be prepared to be relevant and interesting in either case.

Monetizing Your Web Traffic

If you can successfully execute strategies outlined in this chapter to drive traffic, and lots of it, you can start to monetize your website through paid advertising. The best way to get advertisers for your site is, of course, to build a site worth advertising on because of the interesting content, experience, or community that you've built. The next best way is to align with an affiliate network, which is an intermediary for ads just like you may have intermediaries for your product distribution.

REMEMBER

The trick to getting any of the following monetization methods to pay off is simple: Have good content that's worth visiting your site to get. The best content is not only emotionally relevant, but it's also actionable. Most people don't have time to read websites just because they're there; people read articles and content when it provides a direct value that they need at the time. Quite often, that great content answers a how-to question for personal or professional goals.

You can expect some various payment plans from affiliate networks. The most common include pay per impression and pay per click, which we explore further in the following sections. (You find out how to use these for your own advertising needs in Chapter 3 of Book 6.)

Pay per impression

This payment method accrues income by the number of times the ad is displayed on your site. Every time a unique visitor views your ad, that is considered an *impression.* At the time of this writing, the average payments are about $2.80 per 1,000 displays for display ads on your site, $5.00 per 1,000 displays for ads within e-mails, and about $3.00 per 1,000 displays for ads aligned with videos.

You can place your own ads on sites you think are relevant to your business or see what ads are going for on popular sites at www.buysellads.com. At the time of this writing, the cost per thousand impressions ranged from $0.25 to $8.00.

Pay per click

With this method, you get paid every time someone clicks on the ad on your site. Amounts actually paid out can be higher than paying for each 1,000 displays as described in the preceding section. The range varies greatly, so do some homework before deciding which method works best for you.

As companies in the web marketing space come and go quickly due to the increasing presence of groups like Google, it's best to do you own search and explore worthy options that come up.

REMEMBER

The best affiliate network is one that focuses on the same genre of business, product, category, or customer needs that you do. If you're offering a nutritional product and want to attract ads about nutritional products that supplement yours, look for affiliates that have a presence in this same space.

Google AdSense (www.google.com/adsense/start/) is another option worth looking into for getting ads on your website. Essentially, Google AdSense places sponsored ads on websites it determines to be relevant to the advertiser through a series of algorithms. You apply for inclusion in the AdSense program and get a code you can very easily add to the HTML code of your site.

Index

IPO (initial public offering), 100, 466
ISP (Internet service provider), 562
iStock, 561
iTunes, 508

J

job ads, writing, 364–365
job autonomy, avoiding burnout with, 407–408
job descriptions, 357–361
  flexibility, 360
  job title, 361
  model, 358–359, 360–361
  salary range, 361
  soft skills, 360
  tasks and qualifications, 359–360
job fairs, 368
job rating checklist, 424
job-sharing, 402–403
Johnson & Johnson Credo, 178
joint copyright, 139
journals
  defined, 267
  entries in, 270
Journals account, 267
judicial sale, 86
junkets, 485

K

Kamel, Perry, 522
karoshi. *See* burnout, avoiding
key performance indicator (KPI), 493, 552–554
  average session duration, 554
  bounce rate, 553
  pages per session, 554
key success factor (KSF). *See* critical success factors (CSFs)
keywords, 116–117, 518
kinship, building, 474–476

L

land, as non-current asset, 325
Land account, 278
landing pages, on websites, 565–567
landlord's agent, 53
Larson, Ken, 536
last-chance warning, 434
Launch Academy, 22
lawyers, 26–27, 68–69
  advice about compensation, 392
  employee disciplinary action, 431–433
layoffs, 437–438
layouts, print ad, 539–540
lead capture page, 566
leading questions, 376
leaseback of equipment, 99
Leasehold Improvements account, 279, 325–326
leases
  equipment, 84–85
  with option to purchase, 84
  terms of, 41
Legal and Accounting account, 287
legal strength, 153, 157
Lendarduzzi, Sunny, 514
liabilities, 327–328
  current, 281–282, 327
  defined, 265
  long-term, 282–283
  non-current, 328
  overview, 281
licensed insolvency trustee, 87
lifestyle, customer, 206–207
likelihood of confusion, 156–160
LinkedIn, 443, 545
  developing marketing plan with, 504–506
    engagement, 506
    groups, 505–506
  videos, 512

About the Authors

John Buchaca, an intellectual property law attorney, is a former software engineer and occasional inventor, and has worked with Henri Charmasson for many years. Before becoming a lawyer, he worked in ocean acoustics analysis and modeling and computer programming. His undergraduate degree is in applied mathematics. He lives in San Diego, California where he is a partner at Charmasson, Buchaca & Leach, LLP, an IP law firm.

Henri Charmasson is an attorney with a decades-long career in the field of intellectual property (IP) law. He has been a naming adviser to major corporations. Henri is also an inventor with his name on numerous U.S. patents and an entrepreneur who sits on the board of several small business corporations. In his early engineering career, Henri designed computer hardware. Henri has authored several articles and delivered lectures on patent, copyright, trademark and trade secret topics, and written an authoritative treatise about the art of naming companies and branding new products. Born, raised, and educated in sunny Provence, France, he's found in California the ideal place to exert his enterprising spirit.

Andrew Dagys is a Chartered Professional Accountant and risk management expert. As a best-selling author, he has written and co-authored more than a dozen books, mostly about investing, personal finance, business, and technology. Andrew has contributed columns to major Canadian publications. He is a frequently quoted author in many of Canada's daily news publications, including *The Globe and Mail, the National Post,* and *the Toronto Star.* He has appeared on several national news broadcasts to offer his insights on various current events and topics. Andrew considers writing books, and collaborating with talented publishing partners, to be one of life's most truly amazing experiences.

Lita Epstein earned her MBA from Emory University's Goizueta Business School. She designs and teaches online courses on topics such as accounting, payroll, and starting your own business. She's written more than 40 books, including *Stock Charts For Dummies, Reading Financial Reports For Dummies,* and *Trading For Dummies.* Lita was the content director for a financial services website, MostChoice.com, and managed the website Investing for Women. Lita has been a daily newspaper reporter, magazine editor, and fundraiser for the international activities of former president Jimmy Carter through The Carter Center.

Margaret Kerr and **JoAnn Kurtz** are lawyers, and they are also both entrepreneurs — and they have the bumps, bruises, and scars to prove it. Occasionally, they find a minute of free time here and there, which is how they came to be the authors of, among other books, *Buying, Owning and Selling a Home in Canada* (now in its second edition); *Canadian Tort Law in a Nutshell* (with Laurence Olivo, also in its second edition); *Legal Research: Step by Step* (with Arlene Blatt, another one in its second edition!); *Make It Legal: What Every Canadian Entrepreneur*

Needs to Know About the Law; and *Facing a Death in the Family*. They're also the authors of another excellent *For Dummies* book that's to die for — *Wills and Estate Planning For Canadians For Dummies*.

Cécile Laurin (Ottawa, Ontario) is a Professor of Accounting at Algonquin College of Applied Arts and Technology in Ottawa. She also taught part-time at the University of Ottawa. Her career began in public accounting, performing audits with the firm now known as KPMG. She then became the chief financial officer of three engineering firms, and the international law firm Gowling Lafleur Henderson LLP, now Gowling WLG. She obtained a Bachelor of Administration and a Bachelor of Commerce (Honours) from the University of Ottawa, and is a member of Professional Accountants of Ontario and Chartered Professional Accountants of Canada. She is the co-author of *Bookkeeping For Canadians For Dummies* and has written several learning tools for professors and students in accounting. Cécile has also developed several distance-learning courses offered through Algonquin College.

Jeanette Maw McMurtry held positions at DDB Worldwide and Ketchum, American Express, Intermountain Health Care, and a few high-tech start-ups before she became a CMO for a direct marketing agency in Denver, Colorado, where she became entrenched in database marketing and personalization. She then started her own consulting firm and emerged as a leading authority on psychology-based marketing. Jeanette is a frequent speaker at global marketing events, a columnist for marketing magazines, and has been featured as a subject matter expert by CNBC, Forbes.com, and others. She is the author of *Big Business Marketing for Small Business Budgets* (McGraw-Hill).

Harold "Max" Messmer is chairman and CEO of Robert Half International Inc., the world's largest specialized staffing firm. He is one of the foremost experts on human resources and employment issues. His entire business is built on the promise that the success of any company is based on the extent to which attracting and keeping outstanding talent is top priority.

Steven D. Peterson, PhD, is coauthor, along with Paul Tiffany, of *Business Plans For Dummies,* which was nominated as one of the best business books of the year by *The Financial Times.* He is founder and CEO of Strategic Play, a management training company specializing in software tools designed to enhance business strategy, business planning, and general management skills. He created the Protean Strategist, a business simulation that reproduces a dynamic business environment where participant teams run companies and compete against each other in a fast-changing marketplace. He holds advanced degrees in mathematics and physics and received his doctorate from Cornell University. For more information, visit www.strategicplay.com.

Paul Tiffany, PhD, is a professor of management at the Haas Business School, UC Berkeley, and has previously served as an Adjunct Professor at the Wharton School, University of Pennsylvania. He is a management consultant to numerous firms and agencies all over the world focusing on the art and science of business strategy, planning, and management concepts.

John A. Tracy (Boulder, Colorado) is Professor of Accounting, Emeritus, at the University of Colorado in Boulder. Before his 35-year tenure at Boulder, he was on the business faculty for four years at the University of California in Berkeley. Early in his career he was a staff accountant with Ernst & Young. John is the author of several books on accounting and finance, including *The Fast Forward MBA in Finance, How to Read a Financial Report,* and *Small Business Financial Management Kit For Dummies* with his son, Tage Tracy. John received his BSC degree from Creighton University. He earned his MBA and PhD degrees at the University of Wisconsin in Madison. He is a CPA (inactive) in Colorado.

Nada Wagner, MBA, is one of the principals of Next Wave Marketing and held positions such as Director of Centre of Entrepreneurship and Corporate Development with Centennial College, Toronto; General Manager of Canadian Business Resource Centre, Toronto; General Manager of a manufacturing firm in East York; Controller of the Canadian subsidiary of a German-based multinational manufacturer. Nada has a Master of Business Administration degree from Richard Ivey School of Business, University of Western Ontario, and studied adult education with St. Francis Xavier University, Antigonish, Nova Scotia.

Publisher's Acknowledgments

Senior Acquisitions Editor: Tracy Boggier

Compilation Editor: Georgette Beatty

Editorial Project Manager: Christina N. Guthrie

Technical Editor: Jane Stoller

Proofreader: Debbye Butler

Production Editor: Siddique Shaik

Cover Photos: © lalcreative/Shutterstock; Canadian flag © alexsl / iStockphoto

Take dummies with you everywhere you go!

Whether you are excited about e-books, want more from the web, must have your mobile apps, or are swept up in social media, dummies makes everything easier.

Find us online!

Leverage the power

Dummies is the global leader in the reference category and one of the most trusted and highly regarded brands in the world. No longer just focused on books, customers now have access to the dummies content they need in the format they want. Together we'll craft a solution that engages your customers, stands out from the competition, and helps you meet your goals.

Advertising & Sponsorships

Connect with an engaged audience on a powerful multimedia site, and position your message alongside expert how-to content. Dummies.com is a one-stop shop for free, online information and know-how curated by a team of experts.

- Targeted ads
- Video
- Email Marketing
- Microsites
- Sweepstakes sponsorship

20 MILLION PAGE VIEWS EVERY SINGLE MONTH

15 MILLION UNIQUE VISITORS PER MONTH

43% OF ALL VISITORS ACCESS THE SITE VIA THEIR MOBILE DEVICES

700,000 NEWSLETTER SUBSCRIPTIONS TO THE INBOXES OF

300,000 UNIQUE INDIVIDUALS EVERY WEEK

# of dummies

Custom Publishing

Reach a global audience in any language by creating a solution that will differentiate you from competitors, amplify your message, and encourage customers to make a buying decision.

- Apps
- Books
- eBooks
- Video
- Audio
- Webinars

Brand Licensing & Content

Leverage the strength of the world's most popular reference brand to reach new audiences and channels of distribution.

For more information, visit dummies.com/biz

PERSONAL ENRICHMENT

9781119187790
USA $26.00
CAN $31.99
UK £19.99

9781119179030
USA $21.99
CAN $25.99
UK £16.99

9781119293354
USA $24.99
CAN $29.99
UK £17.99

9781119293347
USA $22.99
CAN $27.99
UK £16.99

9781119310068
USA $22.99
CAN $27.99
UK £16.99

9781119235606
USA $24.99
CAN $29.99
UK £17.99

9781119251163
USA $24.99
CAN $29.99
UK £17.99

9781119235491
USA $26.99
CAN $31.99
UK £19.99

9781119279952
USA $24.99
CAN $29.99
UK £17.99

9781119283133
USA $24.99
CAN $29.99
UK £17.99

9781119287117
USA $24.99
CAN $29.99
UK £16.99

9781119130246
USA $22.99
CAN $27.99
UK £16.99

PROFESSIONAL DEVELOPMENT

9781119311041
USA $24.99
CAN $29.99
UK £17.99

9781119255796
USA $39.99
CAN $47.99
UK £27.99

9781119293439
USA $26.99
CAN $31.99
UK £19.99

9781119281467
USA $26.99
CAN $31.99
UK £19.99

9781119280651
USA $29.99
CAN $35.99
UK £21.99

9781119251132
USA $24.99
CAN $29.99
UK £17.99

9781119310563
USA $34.00
CAN $41.99
UK £24.99

9781119181705
USA $29.99
CAN $35.99
UK £21.99

9781119263593
USA $26.99
CAN $31.99
UK £19.99

9781119257769
USA $29.99
CAN $35.99
UK £21.99

9781119293477
USA $26.99
CAN $31.99
UK £19.99

9781119265313
USA $24.99
CAN $29.99
UK £17.99

9781119239314
USA $29.99
CAN $35.99
UK £21.99

9781119293323
USA $29.99
CAN $35.99
UK £21.99

dummies.com

dummies
A Wiley Brand

Learning Made Easy

ACADEMIC

9781119293576
USA $19.99
CAN $23.99
UK £15.99

9781119293637
USA $19.99
CAN $23.99
UK £15.99

9781119293491
USA $19.99
CAN $23.99
UK £15.99

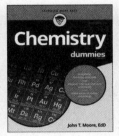

9781119293460
USA $19.99
CAN $23.99
UK £15.99

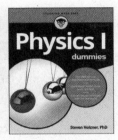

9781119293590
USA $19.99
CAN $23.99
UK £15.99

9781119215844
USA $26.99
CAN $31.99
UK £19.99

9781119293378
USA $22.99
CAN $27.99
UK £16.99

9781119293521
USA $19.99
CAN $23.99
UK £15.99

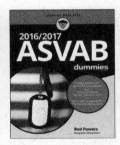

9781119239178
USA $18.99
CAN $22.99
UK £14.99

9781119263883
USA $26.99
CAN $31.99
UK £19.99

Available Everywhere Books Are Sold

dummies.com

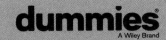

dummies®
A Wiley Brand

Small books for big imaginations

9781119177173
USA $9.99
CAN $9.99
UK £8.99

9781119177272
USA $9.99
CAN $9.99
UK £8.99

9781119177241
USA $9.99
CAN $9.99
UK £8.99

9781119177210
USA $9.99
CAN $9.99
UK £8.99

9781119262657
USA $9.99
CAN $9.99
UK £6.99

9781119291336
USA $9.99
CAN $9.99
UK £6.99

9781119233527
USA $9.99
CAN $9.99
UK £6.99

9781119291220
USA $9.99
CAN $9.99
UK £6.99

9781119177302
USA $9.99
CAN $9.99
UK £8.99

Unleash Their Creativity

dummies.com